M000026112

Callaloo or Tossed Salad?

Callaloo or Tossed Salad?

EAST INDIANS AND THE CULTURAL POLITICS OF IDENTITY IN TRINIDAD

Viranjini Munasinghe

Cornell University Press

Ithaca and London

THIS BOOK HAS BEEN PUBLISHED WITH THE AID OF A GRANT FROM
THE HULL MEMORIAL PUBLICATION FUND OF CORNELL UNIVERSITY .

Copyright © 2001 by Cornell University

All rights reserved. Except for brief quotations in a review, this
book, or parts thereof, must not be reproduced in any form without
permission in writing from the publisher. For information, address
Cornell University Press, Sage House, 512 East State Street, Ithaca,
New York 14850.

First published 2001 by Cornell University Press
First printing, Cornell Paperbacks, 2001

Printed in the United States of America

LIBRARY OF CONGRESS CATALOGING-IN-PUBLICATION DATA
Munasinghe, Viranjini.
    Callaloo or tossed salad? : East Indians and the cultural politics
of identity in Trinidad / Viranjini Munasinghe.
        p. cm.
    Includes bibliographical references and index.
    ISBN 0–8014–3704–0 (cloth : alk. paper) — ISBN 0–8014–8619–X (pbk.
: alk. paper)
        1. East Indians—Trinidad and Tobago—Ethnic identity.   2. Trinidad
and Tobago—Ethnic relations—Political aspects.   3. East
Indians—Trinidad and Tobago—Politics and government.   4. Trinidad and
Tobago—Politics and government.   I. Title.
    F2122 .M86 2001
    305.891'4072983—dc21   2001002378

Cornell University Press strives to use environmentally responsible
suppliers and materials to the fullest extent possible in the publishing
of its books. Such materials include vegetable-based, low-VOC inks,
and acid-free papers that are recycled, totally chlorine-free, or partly
composed of nonwood fibers. Books that bear the logo of the FSC
(Forest Stewardship Council) use paper taken from forests that have
been inspected and certified as meeting the highest standards for
environmental and social responsibility. For further information, visit
our website at www.cornellpress.cornell.edu.

Cloth printing   10 9 8 7 6 5 4 3 2 1

Paperback printing   10 9 8 7 6 5 4 3 2 1

For my Father and Mother
P. C. and Indrani Munasinghe
With love and gratitude

Contents

Preface

I first encountered the Indian presence in the Caribbean when the West Indian cricket team visited my native Colombo. Unaware then of the colonial history shared by the West Indies and Sri Lanka, as a child I remember puzzling over the "Indian" names and faces of Alvin Kalicharran and Rohan Kanhai. The twists and turns that ultimately brought me to study the Indian diaspora in Trinidad capture poignantly the paradoxes of "naming" and the politics of identity, interwoven as they are with those fraught relations between empires and colonies. When I was a child growing up in Sri Lanka, the neighboring Indian people were the significant "other" that fascinated me. Ultimately traveling to the United States to pursue graduate studies in anthropology and believing in the fundamental tenet of the discipline that one needs to immerse oneself in a radically different conceptual world, I found it only natural to focus on India.

It was in the United States that I learned about the Indians in Trinidad and elsewhere in the Caribbean. The thought of Indians who had lived for more than a century in this part of the New World immediately piqued my interest. But when I went to Trinidad first in 1986 and then in October 1989–October 90 to learn about the "other," the "Indian," in a geographical, cultural, and social setting that was totally unfamiliar to me, I soon realized the disjunction between my own categories of "Indianness" and those of Trinidadians. Many Trinidadians claiming Indian ancestry tended to include me as "one of them." I would explain to them that I spoke a different language (Sinhala), that I was a Buddhist, and that Sri Lanka and India are independent nation-states. Yet these criteria seemed to matter little to them. They acknowledged some differences between us: my hair was darker, much darker, than that of East Indians, they claimed, and of course I spoke differently from them. But the fact remained that despite the separation I had drawn between Indians and myself, for these Indo-Trinidadians I was part of that imaginary homeland they claimed as those of Indian descent in Trinidad. Paradoxically, I had come to embody my own definition of the "other."

The thrust of this personal narrative is to underscore a cardinal argument of this book—that names or categories have very little to do with objective facts of lineage. The largely arbitrary selection of some factors over others to signal a particular category does not mean that these selected criteria are natural indices of difference. The significance of this statement carries immense political import for a nation-state such as Trinidad and Tobago, which is understood by locals and foreigners alike to be extremely heterogeneous. Just seven miles from the coast of Venezuela, the two-island republic of Trinidad and Tobago lies at the southernmost tip of the Caribbean archipelago and stands out in many ways from the rest of the region. Unlike neighbors to the north, Trinidad does not depend primarily on agriculture and tourism but is the most industrialized nation in the Caribbean, largely because of its oil and natural gas reserves. Its population of approximately 1.2 million (in 1990) boasts a 98 percent literacy rate and enjoys one of the highest standards of living of any developing country.[1] In 1990 the per capita income of Trinidad and Tobago was US$3,190, much higher than that of Jamaica (US$1,180) or Guyana (US$300), for example (World Bank 1992:9). Their understanding of themselves as modern and cosmopolitan is a source of pride for many Trinidadians.

Trinidad and Tobago is populated by people who claim descent from a number of mixed origins—European, African, East Indian, Amerindian, Portuguese, Chinese, Lebanese, and Syrian among others.[2] But the ways in which Trinidadians draw distinctions among themselves are fundamentally shaped by the dichotomy they see between those of African descent and those of Indian descent. One cannot assume the claimed differences between "Indo-Trinidadians" and "Afro-Trinidadians" as natural facts merely

1. Throughout this book I have deliberately retained the statistics of the 1989–90 period since this was when the fieldwork was conducted. Where relevant, I have noted significant changes that have occurred since.

2. The ethnic composition of the two islands comprising the nation-state of Trinidad and Tobago is significantly different. People claiming African descent largely populate Tobago. Since this book is primarily about Trinidadians claiming East Indian descent, I focus my analysis on Trinidad. Of a total population of 1,213,733 in 1990, the ethnic composition of Trinidad and Tobago according to the 1990 census was the following: African descent, 39.6 percent; East Indian descent, 40.3 percent; White, 0.6 percent; Chinese, 0.4 percent; Mixed, 18.4 percent; Other, 0.2 percent; and Not Stated, 0.4 percent (Central Statistical Office 1997 and 1998).

because they are presented as such in popular discourse in today's Trinidad. The concept of difference, after all, registers in human consciousness only when significance is imputed to what are essentially arbitrary factors. I lay the empirical and theoretical foundation for this idea by illustrating how the distinction between Afro-Trinidadian and Indo-Trinidadian in the form of "ex-slave" and "indentured coolie" labor—a dichotomy heavily invested with the vagaries of a colonial political economy built on exploitative labor schemes—emerged even before the two groups encountered each other. This book is primarily about how this dichotomy originated and the significance it took on in the political life of the island. The story is not a Manichean one. It is rather an exploration of the difficulties people face in coming to terms politically and culturally with the legacies they inherit from a colonial past as they attempt to forge a national identity in the post-colonial era.

The terms *Indian, East Indian, Indo-Caribbean*, and *Indo-Trinidadian* refer to those claiming Indian ancestry in different parts of the New World, but they carry different connotations. In Trinidad *East Indian* and *Indo-Trinidadian* signify to the politically conscious varying degrees of marginality vis-à-vis Trinidadian national identity. Although *East Indian* is the more common term, it signifies a greater degree of marginality than the term *Indo-Trinidadian*, which is most evident in political and academic arenas. *Afro-Trinidadian* encompasses all non-Whites who situate themselves within the color spectrum spanning Black to White. In short, they are those who visibly display African ancestry. The term *Afro-Trinidadian* too is rarely used by common people and is largely restricted to academia and politics. The more popular term for those of African descent is *Creole*. In contrast to *East Indian, Creole*—when used as a noun and not as an adjective as in *Creole White* to mean "local White," or when used without a qualifier as in *French Creole*—signifies native status par excellence in Trinidad. The term *Negro* is also prevalent in common discourse but is never used by local academics or the politically conscious, who prefer *Black, African*, or *Afro-Trinidadian*. The term *Colored* refers to those with mixed African and European ancestry. There are also terms signifying finer gradations of color, such as *Brown, Red*, or *Black Black*, which encapsulate characteristics beyond skin color such as quality of hair, facial features, and comportment. The only term to designate East Indian mixture is *Dougla*,[3] which signifies East Indian and African ancestry. But it operates differently from the category *Colored* because it is used not so much to categorize a group of people as to demarcate individuals.

3. Many Trinidadians understand Dougla to be the Hindi word for bastard. The word is probably a derivative of the Hindi word Doglā meaning "not of pure blood or breed, mean-blooded, cross-bred, hybrid, mongrel" (Platts 1965:534).

To write this book I had little choice but to use these very emic categories. My use of ethnic terminologies in contrast to most Trinidadians' usage is premised on the understanding that these terms signify *projected* differences as opposed to *natural* ones. By combining a Barthian view of ethnicity that posits the existence of ethnic groups insofar as they are claimed to exist by the "natives" themselves with Richard Handler's (1985) call for a "destructive analysis" of ethnicity (elaborated in the next chapter), I try to avoid reification of native explanations of emic categories as natural by, first, problematizing the very genesis and reproduction of emic distinctions about ancestral groups in this book. Second, persuaded by the Barthian subjective position on ethnicity, I treat such emic distinctions as very real to the subjects themselves. To accede that ethnic distinctions are real in terms of the material, social, and symbolic consequences they bear on people's lives does not imply, however, that *real* means inscribed in nature. The ontological distinction I maintain between real and natural allows me to take seriously the claims of Trinidadians about differences that characterize their population without reinscribing analytically their explanations for such differences. Third, I attempt to maintain some dissonance between my own use of terminology and Trinidadians' by primarily but not exclusively using the terms *Indo-Trinidadian* and *Afro-Trinidadian* to refer to the projected dichotomy between those Trinidadians claiming Indian descent and African descent when adopting the voice of the analyst.[4] Since these are not yet common terms in lay discourse in Trinidad, they afford me the necessary critical distance to write this book. Yet even this strategy has its limitations. These terms are hardly free from emic definitions or the forces of history. The distinction between the two is indelibly stamped by a colonial history that positioned the Indian and African, or East Indian and Creole, in dichotomous terms. Because of this history, even when politically conscious Trinidadians today use *Afro-Trinidadian* and *Indo-Trinidadian*, they tend to treat them as natural categories. Despite these difficulties, I adopt *Afro-Trinidadian* and *Indo-Trinidadian* as the analyst's categories, for want of a better solution, and I provide a rationale for those few deviations from this strategy.

Much of this book is about the profound implications of naming. Meanings and nuances conveyed by specific categories of identification are subject not only to change over time but also to contestation. Indo-Trinidadians struggle to reconcile the traditional dichotomy between the terms *Trinidadian* and

4. In some cases I retain historically appropriate terminology, for both practical and analytic purposes. Thus I use *East Indian* as opposed to *Indo-Trinidadian* precisely to connote the marginality this term embodies when appropriate. Similarly, I use *Creole* and not *Afro-Trinidadian* because *Creole* captures the relevant nuances having to do with class and ethnic distinctions for the particular historical moments under discussion.

East Indian so that their group too can benefit from the privileges accorded to native status. Indo-Trinidadian efforts at national redefinition powerfully illustrate that names invested with the burdens of history also hold promises of defining the future.

I find it impossible to identify any particular moment in my life when people began to contribute in their myriad ways to this first book. A book after all is more than the culmination of an intellectual project. I dedicate this book to my parents because without them it simply would not be. My brother, Lalith, and sister, Hiranthi, have always been there for me in their own idiosyncratic ways, and for this I am grateful. I'm forever indebted to my husband, David Ethridge, who not only created the maps for this book but also made count-less sacrifices for me without ever making it seem so. Through the years he has been my gentlest critic and a pillar of strength. To my little daughter, Is-mini, thank you. Your carefree, happy disposition has kept me sane and cen-tered, always reminding me, even in life's trying moments, that life can still be delightful.

A number of friends, some directly and others indirectly, contributed to the making of this book. Thank you to Mandakini Arora, Lanfranco Blanchetti, Ramez Elias, Robert Goddard, Lynne Hester, Jennifer Krier, Barry Maxwell, Natalie Melas, Charles Rutheiser, Raphael Sebastien, Jim Sidbury, Rachel Weil, Brackette F. Williams, and Sunn Shelley Wong. Two dear friends in particular I cannot thank enough: Bobby Mohammed for his kindness, sense of humor, and captivating philosophical ruminations on life, all of which contributed to this book; and Carla Freeman, who not only painstakingly read and commented on many versions of this work but simply has always been there for me.

To Professor Michel-Rolph Trouillot, who introduced me to the Caribbean and who later became my adviser, I owe a great deal. His enthusiasm and ex-citement for intellectual inquiry proved infectious. Even after graduate school his guidance, criticism, and encouragement continue to sustain me. I am grate-ful to Professor Sidney Mintz, who taught me many important lessons about an-thropology, history, and the Caribbean as a graduate student at Johns Hopkins University and who went beyond the call of duty to comment on parts of this book. I also thank Professor Kathryn Verdery, who pushed me to think more clearly on issues concerning ethnicity and nationalism. I benefited enormously from the teaching and guidance of two exceptional scholars during my early graduate training at Duke University, Professor Carol Smith and Professor Richard Fox. This book gained as well from the detailed comments of my good friend Drexell Woodson. I am particularly thankful to Nigel Bolland and Daniel Segal for their close reading of the manuscript and their extensive comments.

One's ideas hardly develop in a vacuum. The works of two people in particular have greatly shaped my own thinking. Brackette F. Williams's 1989 article "A Class Act" has been foundational in my conceptualization of the relation between ethnicity and nationalism; and Daniel Segal's work on colonial race categories in Trinidad has been central to the arguments I develop in this book and elsewhere.

I thank Professor Jim Peacock and Professor Ruel Tyson and the staff of the Institute for the Arts and Humanities at the University of North Carolina—Chapel Hill, where I undertook the initial revisions for this book supported by a Rockefeller Postdoctoral Fellowship. I also thank the Society for the Humanities at Cornell University, which funded a summer field trip to Trinidad in 1998. I am grateful as well to the Hull Memorial Publication Fund of Cornell University for the generous subvention.

Much of the revision for this book was undertaken at Cornell University. I benefited greatly from the supportive and intellectually stimulating environment provided by my colleagues. I wish particularly to thank Ted Bestor, John Borneman, Jane Fajans, Davyyd Greenwood, David Holmberg, Kath March, Gary Okihiro, Steven Sangren, Meredith Small, Terence Turner, and Andrew Willford. I am also very grateful to the students I had the pleasure of working with. It was only later when I turned to revising the book that I realized the extent to which my conversations with them both inside and outside the classroom had influenced my thinking on issues of nationalism, race, and ethnicity.

I owe much to Peter Agree and Fran Benson of Cornell University Press for their enthusiasm and support for this project and for the patience and efficiency with which they guided me through the various stages of publication—thank you. My warm thanks to Teresa Jesionowski, senior manuscript editor, for her patience, to Kim Vivier for her fine copyediting, and Do Mi Stauber for her expert indexing. I'm grateful to Mr. Isaiah James Boodhoo for permission to use his beautiful painting.

Finally, I turn to the people in Trinidad, many of whom went out of their way to welcome me and help me understand their points of view. I thank the faculty of the University of the West Indies at St. Augustine for facilitating my research. Among them I would like to mention especially Dr. Bridget Brereton, Dr. Kusha Haraksingh, Dr. John La Guerre, Dr. Walton Look Lai, Dr. Kenneth Ramchand, Dr. Kelvin Ramnath, Dr. Rhoda Reddock, Dr. Selwyn Ryan, and Dr. Kelvin Singh. The library staff at the university was immensely helpful, especially at the West India Collection. Ousman Mohammed at the National Archives in St. Vincent Street went out of his way to help me locate documents. I'm also thankful to all the cultural and religious activists who shared their thoughts and concerns with me.

I am deeply indebted to the people of Cambio. The graciousness with which they made my husband and me feel comfortable in our new setting put us at ease. They shared their thoughts and included us in their more intimate circles: inviting my husband to join the village soccer team and gently chastising me for not knowing how to cook roti were just two of the immeasurable ways they made us feel welcome. To this day my husband and I remain overwhelmed by the generosity and hospitality of three families in Trinidad: the Mohammeds, the de Montrichards, and the Caders. They are largely responsible for making our visits to Trinidad immensely pleasurable, and they extended to us the ultimate courtesy of making us feel at home in their homes. In conclusion, I remember fondly and sadly Hamid Ram John and Faizal Mohammed, who have now passed away. To all these people I extend my sincere thanks and appreciation.

VIRANJINI MUNASINGHE

Ithaca, New York

Callaloo or Tossed Salad?

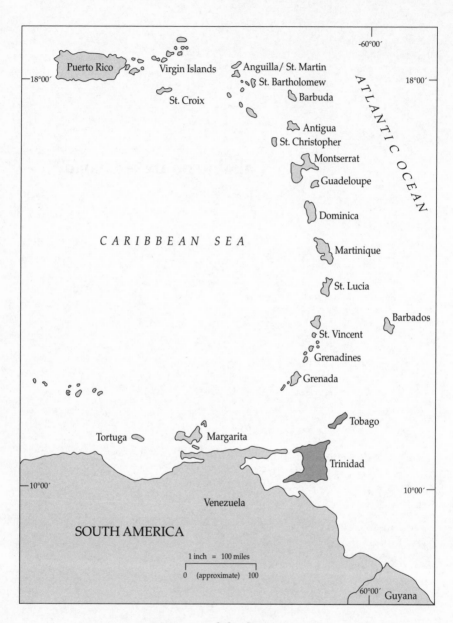

Map 1 Trinidad and its vicinity

[1]

Introduction

In this our country and the whole Caribbean
We all got to stand up and speak against discrimination
Trinidad was first ruled by the Caribs and Arawaks
Then ruled by the Spanish, White man and now the Blacks
But the Indians have never yet been ah ruler
Because talk is that they don't want ah Indian Prime Minister
But we must change this situation, after Williams, Georgie and Robbie
In the next General Election
I say, put in the Indian man

—Social commentary performed in song by Mukesh Babooram
    and Sita Sahodra in *Equality* 1990, 7

Themes

The sentiment that the time has come to consider seriously the possibility of Indo-Trinidadian rule, since all other ancestral groups have had their turn, speaks to the dynamics of racial politics in post-colonial societies that have been historically configured as excessively heterogeneous or plural. State power is conceived as a prize or privilege that only a single ancestral group can enjoy at any given historical period. Claims to state power, in turn, are intrinsically linked to the realm of culture. Because of the almost total annihilation of the indigenous population during the early colonial period, the various ancestral groups comprising Trinidad and Tobago's population who trace their origins to the Old World were burdened with a certain historical task: to create legitimate grounds for claiming native status that did not hinge on autochthonous ties to the land itself. Contribution to and suffering on behalf of

[1]

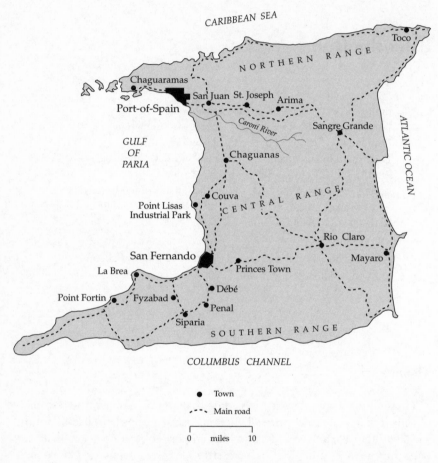

Map 2 Trinidad

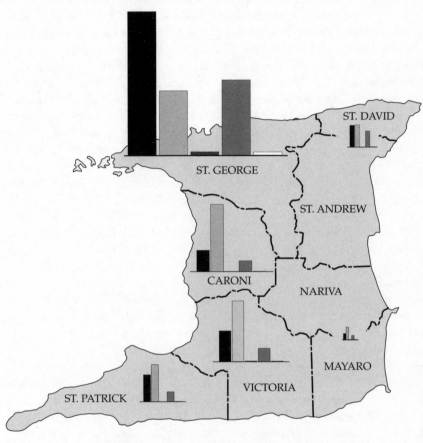

	African	Indian	White	Mixed	Other	Not Stated	Total
St. George	228,367	102,147	5,500	119,659	4,808	2,997	463,478
St. David/St. Andrew	21,137	21,593	72	15,566	313	156	58,837
Caroni	35,861	113,827	260	18,073	387	423	168,831
Nariva/Mayaro	8,965	18,264	57	6,176	81	63	33,606
Victoria	62,146	130,662	1,094	28,813	920	577	224,212
St. Patrick	47,551	65,614	107	17,251	293	298	131,114

Map 3 Distribution of ethnic groups in Trinidad, 1990. Source: Central Statistical Office, *Annual Statistical Digest, 1996* (Trinidad and Tobago, 1998).

the nation were pivotal ideological criteria for establishing which group, leading up to and since independence (in 1962), possessed the legitimacy to define the symbolic (cultural) coordinates of the emergent nation.

This book attempts to unravel the "politics of cultural struggle" (B. F. Williams 1991) between two historically subordinate ancestral groups—those claiming African and Indian descent in Trinidad—in their efforts to position themselves positively vis-à-vis the nation during and after the colonial period. The book is also an exploration of the limits to and possibilities of historical consciousness. Why are certain thoughts "unthinkable" and not others in particular historical moments? In 1989–90, when I conducted my research, many Trinidadians, including Indo-Trinidadians, expressed the opinion that an "East Indian" as prime minister of Trinidad and Tobago was unthinkable. Yet the very fact that the unthinkable had entered discursive consciousness indicated that it posed a real political possibility. Thus the efforts of Indo-Trinidadians to redefine the symbolics of the nation were integrally linked to the creation of an appropriate ideological climate in which they could realize the unthinkable—acquisition of state power. The "cultural work" Indo-Trinidadian leaders were engaged in during the late 1980s and early 1990s suggested to me a rather radical strategy. Unlike earlier East Indian protests that were largely confined to sectional concerns, the contemporary strategy moved boldly to the national arena itself, contesting the very ideological and structural place historically assigned East Indians within Trinidadian society.[1] Through their cultural and political activity these leaders challenged the implicit claim that East Indian ethnic identity was necessarily antithetical to Trinidadian national identity and sought to introduce what they believed to be East Indian elements alongside hegemonic Afro-Caribbean elements within the symbolic space of the nation. In short, they aimed to become a legitimate part of the nation by redefining the term *Trinidadian* and not *East Indian*. In this effort they targeted issues formerly perceived as privileged and incontestable: Afro-Trinidadian control of the state and cultural representation of the nation.

In November 1995 the unthinkable happened. An Indo-Trinidadian–dominated coalition (the United National Congress, or UNC) came into power, and Basdeo Panday became the nation's first "East Indian" prime minister.[2]

1. Here I deliberately use the term *East Indian* to signify the marginality attributed to those Trinidadians claiming Indian ancestry, particularly in the representation of them as bearers of a discrete culture that was antithetical to European and New World cultures. When I use this term instead of *Indo-Trinidadian*, it is to emphasize and reference this marginality.

2. The UNC came into office by a slim margin, a two-seat majority owed to a tenuous coalition with the minority party, the National Alliance for Reconstruction. It is estimated that 80 percent of East Indian voters but less than 60 percent of non–East Indian voters participated in

This dramatic turn of events surprised everyone, including myself and even those observers who had predicted the eventual political ascent of East Indians. It had happened much earlier than anticipated. A schoolteacher who claimed Indian ancestry told me that Patrick Manning, the leader of the defeated People's National Movement (PNM), was so surprised that "he couldn't think straight for the next couple of days." On the night of the election even Panday, I was told, could not believe his party had won certain constituencies. Whereas most Trinidadians claiming Indian ancestry were elated at the results of the election, Afro-Trinidadians, according to Selwyn Ryan, were "stunned, tearful and traumatized" (1996:335), with calypsonian Cro Cro lamenting: "November 7th, I see Black Man Cry; Look blood still running from Black People Eye" ("They Look for Dat" in Ryan 1996:335). Nevertheless, the transition proceeded smoothly, and the prevailing mood was one of "give the man a chance."[3] Although the UNC victory might suggest that the cultural work of Indo-Trinidadian leaders and activists had paid off, electoral victory does not necessarily signify the symbolic arrival of Indo-Trinidadians as legitimate nationals. Therefore, I hesitate to draw a causal link between the two moments. Instead, this book attempts to understand the various dimensions informing the Indo-Trinidadian cultural intervention to change the symbolics of the nation.

The events of 1995 provide a point of entry into a larger story concerning the politics of cultural struggle in nation-states that have been indelibly stamped by the colonial experience. I believe the arguments presented here have implications for conceptualizing that articulation between "ethnics" and the nation-state beyond the particularities of the Trinidadian case and more generally the Caribbean. Unraveling the intricacies of Indo-Trinidadian strategies for national redefinition led me to confront two paradoxes. First, given the prevailing nationalist ideology of Trinidad and Tobago as a multicultural, cosmopolitan nation, why is it that certain ancestral groups continue to insist they are symbolically marginalized? Since this question is applicable to most nations claiming multiculturalism as *the* national principle, this may seem a mundane if not trivial point. I argue otherwise. Nations that claim a multiculturalist ideology on the basis of cultural/racial difference as a cardinal principle more often than not mask homogenizing narratives, narratives that some contemporary academic writings on nations have safely relegated to eighteenth- and nineteenth-century models of nationhood in their cele-

the elections (*New York Times*, January 1, 1996). See Ryan 1996:chap. 14 for a detailed analysis of the elections.

3. Bridget Brereton, personal communication 1998.

bration of "hybridity" in this age of late-capitalism. Revisiting the racial hierarchies that were established during the colonial period in Trinidad, I illustrate how the semantics and material configurations of race laid the ideological foundation for two potential national narratives, one of homogenization through racial and cultural mixture (signified in the concept Creole) and one of the continuation of ancestral diversities (Segal 1994). Both these narratives revolve around notions of purity, but each narrative privileges some purities over others. I argue that it is through the dialectical interplay of these two nationalist narratives that we can understand how some purities, like that projected to East Indians in Trinidad, are positioned at a considerable symbolic disadvantage vis-à-vis the nation. Only through such a reading of the national ideology of Trinidad can we understand why some groups persist in claiming symbolic marginalization in a multicultural nation that allegedly includes all its citizenry as formal equivalents. By interrogating the very claim of symbolic formal equivalency, we can gain insight into how principles of symbolic exclusion continue to operate, however obliquely, in other multicultural nation-states to privilege some groups over others.

The second paradox had to do with the Indo-Trinidadian leaders' strategy itself. Since the concept Creole had historically been pivotal in pronouncing native status in Trinidad and by extension the West Indies as well, why, I wondered, did many Indo-Trinidadians display such fierce resistance to inclusion within this category even as they continued to insist that they were legitimate Trinidad and Tobago nationals? Again, this observation on my part was hardly novel. All Trinidadians and scholars of Trinidad know that East Indian and Creole are constituted as mutually exclusive categories in Trinidad. Therefore, the Indo-Trinidadian strategy to redefine the nation in plural terms so that "Trinidadian" included not just Creole but Creole and East Indian seemed self-evident, hardly needing explanation. Yet the intriguing question for me remained why it was unimaginable for these Indo-Trinidadians to think of themselves as Creoles. To resolve this quandary, I turn once again to the colonial period, in particular to the emergent race discourses that dichotomized the Africans and the Indians for reasons that had ultimately everything to do with the labor needs of a political economy centered on monocrop plantation agriculture.

The argument that colonial structures continue to inform the politics of cultural struggle in contemporary Trinidad may be disturbing to some. In our haste to uncover "agency" and "subaltern" voices that run counter to hegemonic structures, we sometimes tend to dismiss the articulation between hegemonic structures and alternative/resistant schemes. This is not to say that Trinidadians were categorically unable to articulate alternative visions or enact practices that went against the grain of dominant structures. Indeed, the abundant literature on acts of resistance and the creative cultural syncretisms that emerged in the New World during and after slavery illustrates precisely the resilience and creative genius of Caribbean peoples. Likewise, ample evidence in this book points to human agency—for example, the political posturing of Indo-Trinidadians during the colonial period and the radical strategy they pursued in more recent years, the anticolonial movement spearheaded by the Creole middle-class intelligentsia, and the creative cultural disposition of both Afro-Trinidadians and Indo-Trinidadians to forge novel and vibrant cultures in the New World within oppressive systems bent on denying their very humanity. Yet these same instances that celebrate the human capacity for creativity and resilience also demonstrate the limits to human agency. Why do certain visions become imaginable and not others? It is this inquiry that led me to the rather disconcerting realization that it is largely *within* that articulation of colonial hegemonic structures with human agency that we can make sense of the story I hope to tell.

The village ethnography (especially in Chapter 6) also underscores this point. Despite the rhetoric of Indo-Trinidadian villagers in Cambio which consistently attempted to draw a distinction between themselves and Creoles—usually on the basis of claimed moral and cultural superiority to Creoles—I found that in practice these same villagers exhibited behaviors that could appropriately be labeled Creole. By this I do not mean, as most conventional analyses imply, that they were adopting Afro-Creole[4] patterns; instead, I suggest that Indo-Trinidadians also possess or express that creative disposition to entertain multiplicity without necessarily a sense of contradiction, a characteristic normally ascribed to Afro-Creoles as typically creolized behavior. Again, the puzzle was to understand the seeming inability of the wider society, the subjects themselves, and even some scholars of the region to recognize and acknowledge this dimension of East Indian creolized behavior. For an explanation I turn to the structural dichotomy between East Indian and Creole, an offshoot of the colonial race hierarchy, as well as local and foreign academic discourses on creolization (as formalized in the Creole society thesis) that minimized East Indian elements in their theoretical conceptualizations of creolization. By conflating the analytical concept creolization with the ideologically defined empirical category (or the emic category) Creole—signifying Afro-Creole persons—even those architects of the anti-

---

4. Since *Creole* can also signify other ancestral groups, I use the prefix *Afro* to refer specifically to those Creoles claiming African descent.

[7]

colonial struggle (Creole middle-class intelligentsia) ironically reinscribed, at least partially, the very structures they sought to undermine.

The argument I present here, that Indo-Trinidadians too may be considered creolized without the suggestion that they are assimilating into Afro-Creole cultural patterns, goes against orthodox thinking on the matter. Indo-Trinidadians' creative capacity to forge novel cultural forms in the New World by piecing together diverse elements tends to be eclipsed in popular and academic representations of Indo-Trinidadians as bearers of a particularistic Indian culture or assimilators into wider Euro- and Afro-Creole patterns. To make my point I return to the social commentary in the epigraph. The fact that activists of the Indo-Trinidadian cause chose a musical genre explicitly associated with Afro-Creoles—calypso—to convey an East Indian viewpoint is not without irony. But, I suspect, to these "calypsonians" this creative synthesis hardly warrants explanation and as such is testimony to the very existential basis of Indo-Trinidadian identity, which is to be "East Indian" in an irrevocably Trinidadian fashion.

Terminology

A book that proposes to describe and analyze ethnic relations in a Caribbean country needs to be clear about its terminology. Specifically, I want to justify why I have opted to subsume what in many if not most contexts are articulated at the local level as "race relations" under the theoretical rubric of ethnicity. I do this partly for practical purposes, to avoid arbitrary oscillation between the two discourses of race and ethnicity as if they were interchangeable. But the implications of clarification go beyond the mere practicalities of deciding what language to use in a discussion of social heterogeneity and call on the analyst to advance our thinking about the meanings and implications of the use of one terminology over the other—in this case ethnicity as the overarching theoretical framework, encompassing both race and ethnicity without implying that race is reducible to ethnicity.

Following recent academic trends, studies concerned with social heterogeneity in the Caribbean have been increasingly framed within the discourse of ethnicity rather than that of race. Indeed, this book too is an attempt to understand the relationship between an "ethnic group," the East Indians, and "the nation" of Trinidad. This terminological move from race to ethnicity has troubled some theorists of race who rightly argue that to euphemize race with ethnicity, especially in the North American context, is to minimize "the historic political and economic inequalities that underlie racial classification"

(Sanjek 1994:8).[5] From this perspective ethnicity is understood to be a "positive" group identity, one that is primarily internally generated and expressive of cultural identification, in contrast to race, which is linked to external processes of exclusion (Banton in Sanjek 1994). The copious voluntarism attributed to "ethnic agents" in Fredrik Barth's (1969) classic study, *Ethnic Groups and Boundaries,* and models generated from the North American context, where the term *ethnic* has been traditionally reserved to signify the diverse European origins of the privileged groups, were in part responsible for eclipsing the power dimension and the projection of ethnicity as a positive identity used by subjects to forward their own interests. Increasingly, however, theorists working in other world areas have pointed to the structural inequalities that generate ethnic identifications.[6] In short, not all historical subjects have equal say in fixing identities for themselves. In this sense it is imperative that anthropological analyses of ethnicity move beyond the "native viewpoint." As Brackette F. Williams says:

> Anthropological analysis of identity formation processes within a population that shares a political unit require the recognition that not all individuals have equal power to fix the coordinates of self-other identity formation. Nor are individuals equally empowered to opt out of the labeling process, to become the invisible against which others' visibility is measured. The illusion that self and other ascriptions among groups are made on equal terms fades when we ask whether those who identify themselves with a particular ethnic identity could also successfully claim *no* ethnic identification. If their group became the dom-

---

5. A similar point was made in the early 1970s by Vincent, who called for an analytical separation between minorities and ethnic groups because "the widely ramifying use of ethnics for peoples of all groups in the United States leads too easily to an assumption that opportunities to be won from accommodation politics are open to all, when this is demonstrably not the case" (1974:378). In the same vein R. T. Smith argues that although struggles accompanying structures of inequality are often expressed through images of "primordial identity" and invented traditions, "to afford those images an undue salience by using the term ethnicity distracts attention from the continuing power of racism, and trivializes more complex processes of nationalism" (1995:187). See also Wolf 1994.

6. The many excellent and rigorous analyses which go beyond ethnicity as a tool for agents to maximize their own interests and which rightly situate ethnicity within processes of macro socio-structural inequalities (with emphasis varying from history to political economy to cultural logics) are too numerous to note here. I mention only a few that cover a broad geographical area and also some of the earlier works that anticipated this trend: Hechter 1975, Patterson 1975, Brass 1976, Coulon and Morin 1979, Ragin 1979, Enloe 1981, Fox et al. 1981, Okamura 1981, Comaroff 1987, Fox 1990, Norton 1984, Dominguez 1977, Handler 1988, Kapferer 1988, Wallerstein 1991, B. F. Williams 1991, Verdery 1994, Malkki 1995, Kelly 1995, Khan 1995, Yelvington 1995, Daniel 1996, Lowe 1996, Lavie and Swedenberg 1996, Tambiah 1996, Gupta and Ferguson 1997, and Maurer 1997.

inant power group in the political unit such a claim might be possible. (1989:420; emphasis added)

Ethnic groups are seen as an outcome of nation-building projects that seek to create homogeneity out of heterogeneity.[7] Through a selective process of cultural appropriation dominant members of society (the privileged "race" and "class") determine the ruling cultural ensemble of civil society in their efforts to create a metonymic relation between their group and the nation. This process in turn devalues or denies the link between the selected appropriations (now elevated to national symbols) and the contributions of marginalized others to the nation's patrimony (B. F. Williams 1989). These marginalized others, or ethnics if you will, now rendered visible in contrast to the invisible ethnics who come to metonymize the nation, lie at a considerable pragmatic and ideological disadvantage vis-à-vis the ideologically defined nation. From this perspective, then, ethnicity, like race, is indelibly linked to external processes of exclusion in certain contexts like the one described in this book. This is not to trivialize the concerns expressed by Roger Sanjek and others but rather to emphasize the extent to which meanings attached to "objective" analytic categories are inflected by specific contexts. Accordingly, the theoretical framework I propose for ethnicity in the next chapter encompasses both internally generated (that is, subjective) and externally imposed mechanisms of boundary maintenance within polities labeled nation-states. This particular conceptualization of ethnicity can theoretically speak to the dynamics shaping local expressions of race relations without minimizing the operations of power inequalities.

There is another sense in which "race relations" can be characterized as "ethnic relations." Categories are historical products or abstractions created to order the empirical world. Although the terms *ethnicity* and *race* operate to classify human difference, for academics and laity alike the globally familiar referents for race and ethnicity are rooted in ideas about biology and culture, respectively.

From its earliest formulations in both popular and academic conceptions, ethnicity necessarily implied cultural differences but not always biological ones. In anthropology the debate between Moerman and Naroll in the 1960s firmly established subjective criteria, that is, natives' definitions of themselves, as opposed to the existence of objective cultural ones, as the defining element for ethnicity (Moerman 1965, 1968; Naroll 1964, 1968). This reasoning dovetailed with the constructionist view of culture that undermined

---

7. On ethnicity as an outcome of the interpenetration of race, class, and culture in nation-states, see B. F. Williams 1989.

the notion of cultural groups as fixed, discrete, and bounded units.[8] The subjective dimension of ethnicity was emphasized in Barth's (1969) seminal analysis of ethnic groups as a form of social organization rather than mere culture-bearing units. By shifting the unit of analysis from the internal constitution of discrete groups to the ethnic boundary, he gave primary emphasis "to the fact that ethnic groups are categories of ascription and identification by the actors themselves, and thus have the characteristic of organizing interaction between people" (Barth 1969:10). The primacy attributed to internally generated definitions forced a reconceptualization of the relation between culture and ethnicity: "Although ethnic categories take cultural differences into account, we can assume no simple one-to-one relationship between ethnic units and cultural similarities and differences. The features that are taken into account are not the sum of 'objective' differences, but only those which the actors themselves regard as significant" (Barth 1969:14).

It is this insight of Barth's that has been elevated to verity in current academic understandings of ethnicity despite quarrels with other aspects of his model. If we subscribe to this view, as I do (with the qualification that not all groups have the power to label themselves and others, thereby situating ethnicity in the context of unequal power relations, a concern somewhat peripheral to Barth), then theoretically speaking at least, one can make the claim that an "ethnic situation" exists if the actors themselves deem it so. Unlike with race, we see a convergence of academic and lay understandings regarding the ontological status of ethnicity—because they both rest at the level of a claim or belief. But the convergence is only minimal. It does not imply that academic analyses should merely replicate lay discourses, which often express their ethnic identifications in the language of primordialism. A more appropriate stance would be the kind of "destructive analysis" suggested by Richard Handler (1985). Handler warns of the possible pitfalls of sharing "ethnographic authority" with subjects in the study of ethnicity and nationalism precisely because of a convergence in lay and academic presuppositions based on a Western theory of cultural difference:

> The culture theory of nationalist ideologues and ethnic leaders neatly matches that of mainstream anthropology, which envisions (and authoritatively depicts) a world of discrete, neatly bounded cultures. Given such deep-seated agreements between scientist and native, outsider and insider, observer and object, students of nationalism and ethnicity must take special care to ensure that their

8. Not all academics have followed this trend. The literature that treats ethnicity as a primordial identity attests to this fact. See, for example, A. Smith 1986. The constructionist view of culture gained much interdisciplinary currency with the publication of *The Invention of Tradition* (1983), edited by Eric Hobsbawm and Terence Ranger.

respect for their subjects' world view does not degenerate into a romantic desire to preserve inviolate the other's subjectivity. (1985:171)

One of the strategies Handler suggests for a "destructive analysis" of ethnicity is to avoid the terminology used by one's subjects to refer to themselves
even if such a stance may seem heretical (1985:178) and contradictory to the
Barthian position elaborated earlier. Yet Handler's is a rhetorical strategy to
avoid academic reifications of native explanations of their ethnicity. The
Barthian view that posits the existence of ethnic groups insofar as it is
claimed to exist by the natives themselves does not necessarily preclude a
"destructive" analysis of ethnicity. To subscribe to the idea that ethnicity exists at the level of a claim or belief does not necessarily imply complicity on
the part of the analyst with the native viewpoint. Although the anthropologist
and the native can agree on the existence of a subject for analysis, that is, the
ethnicity claimed by a particular group, the anthropologist's object of analysis
can diverge considerably from native explanations. After all, Handler's object
of study is the ethnicity *claimed* by Quebecois in Canada. In short, a constructionist position on ethnicity that resists "buying into native ideology" can
work in conjunction with a subjective definition of ethnicity.

How then can we justify, theoretically, the encapsulation of "race relations"
within the framework of ethnicity? "Races" are categorical identifications
that hierarchically position human populations on the basis of purported biological ancestry. Selected physical or behavioral traits, when rooted in biology, are given an innate ontological status: natural and immutable. The biologization of such traits constitutes the indelible marker of race, the relevance
of which is ultimately determined by a given context. Biologization makes of
a social construction a system based on the transmission of traits by birth; it is
the necessary mechanism for the creation of race. Phenotype, often perceived to be the crucial determinant of race, is only an offshoot of the process
of biologization—one of the many social constructions of race. This is why
people who are phenotypically "White" can continue to be labeled "Black."
As we shall see, it is also the biologization of behavior that excluded the
Trinidadian Portuguese, who claimed European ancestry, from the White
category, on the basis of their alleged "unclean" economic behavior, that is,
their colonial identification as "dirty shopkeepers."

A necessary element in popular understandings of race is biologization, the
idea that humans can be separated into discrete groupings based on objective
biological criteria. Academic understandings of the term, however, deny the
existence of such objective biological criteria as a basis for race but concur
that as a socially constructed system of beliefs regarding human difference,
race has very real consequences. Theoretical formulations of race then locate

its ontology at the level of belief, which is culturally and socially constituted—a formulation that resonates with academic/theoretical definitions of ethnicity. Theoretically speaking, one could claim that race and ethnicity have the same ontological status, that is, they exist at the level of a claim or belief regarding human difference as opposed to objective criteria. Since ethnicity more so than race speaks to the socially constituted nature of identifications, it can stand as the overarching framework within which race relations are situated. Therefore, I choose to encompass race within the rubric of ethnicity.

Yet at a lesser level of abstraction race and ethnicity do not share the same ontology. One is contingent on notions of biological difference, the other on notions of cultural difference. This is an important distinction because it points to different principles of subordination as they unfold in specific contexts. Thus to claim that ethnicity, like race, operates as an exclusionary mechanism, as I did earlier, does not imply that the two terms are commensurable. Indeed, following Sanjek (1994) and Joan Vincent (1974), I argue that the two terms should be kept analytically separate: although both are idioms that operate globally, their specific meanings are nearly always determined by historically situated contexts. Put simply, we must take seriously the point that who and what the terms *ethnic* and *race* designate in the United States are not the same in Trinidad or elsewhere, despite resonance among the various contextually determined discourses.

The colonial encounter in Trinidad generated a discourse on race specific to Trinidad, and Trinidadians continue to use the vocabulary of race to express the perceived heterogeneity of their society. Here groups are demarcated on the basis of phylogeny (the evolution of a genetically related group as distinguished from the development of the individual), color (the continuum between Black and White), and ancestral origin (Europeans, Africans, and East Indians).[9] The allocation of these terms for the respective groups is uneven, however. Afro-Trinidadians are designated by all three terms: a phylogenic term, *Negro*; a color term, *Black*; and an ancestral term, *African*. White Trinidadians are designated by two terms: a color term, *White*; and an ancestral term, *European*. East Indians are designated only by an ancestral term, *East Indian* (Segal 1993). In Trinidad color and ancestral origin are the selected characteristics for biologization. The relevance of these traits for race demarcation varies according to groups and contexts. Thus in the case of the Portuguese the biologization of their behavior assumes greater significance than their ancestral origin.

These three criteria—phylogeny, color, and ancestral origin—also enable

9. I draw substantially on Segal's (1993) semantic analysis of Trinidad's racial categories.

contemporary Trinidadians who claim different racial ancestries to appeal to a common unifying element, despite the pervasive heterogeneities that characterize their respective groups.[10] It is this feature of "race" that enables people to use continuously the terms *East Indian*, *White*, *Negro*, *Chinese*, or *Portuguese* as if they represent homogeneous entities, even though the picture is highly complicated in reality. The homogeneity imputed to the people under such rubrics is betrayed not only by socioeconomic distinctions that obtain within them but, more important, by the diluted status of the blocks themselves, as evidenced by the notion that to be Trinidadian is to be "mixed," an issue explored in Chapter 4.

The term *race* is vividly present in intellectual, political, and everyday discourse in Trinidad. The term *ethnic*, however, is largely limited to the intellectual (and sometimes political) arena and has not penetrated common discourse. The term *ethnicity* is explicitly used in Trinidad in academic and political formulations, but in common usage ethnicity is only implied when members of a group define *the* ethnic, which is always *their* ethnic. Hence an idiom of ethnicity paralleling that of race does not exist in Trinidad, but an ethnic situation does. Discourses on race relations among intellectuals, politicians, and other opinion makers often use the term *ethnicity* interchangeably with *race* in order to differentiate among groups. Consider, for example, the title of a book edited in 1993 by Ralph Premdas, an academic at the University of the West Indies, Trinidad: *The Enigma of Ethnicity: An Analysis of Race in the Caribbean and the World.* Examples such as this are common in scholarly, political, and to a lesser degree, lay accounts.[11] In part, this conflation is due to a change in the constituent groups that have become the subject of race relations. In today's Trinidad, relations between Afro-Trinidadians and Indo-Trinidadians are the focus of national debate. The relations between Whites and Blacks, the prominent subject of debate during independence and the "Black Power" struggles (1970s), have receded to the periphery.

The established idiom for capturing the relations between Blacks and Whites in Trinidad, and for the Caribbean generally, has consistently been

10. This tendency of Caribbean people to classify their world through pure categories that connote discrete ancestries even if the objects of classification are highly "impure" is wonderfully illustrated by Lee Drummond for the case of Guyana: "The people of the Pomeroon insist on an ideology of pure types, which are constructed out of the only available material—processes of interethnic mixture" (1980:365).

11. It is important to note that the tendency of Trinidadians to conflate race and ethnicity is not a result of confusion but signals instead a complex and changing articulation of social, political, cultural, and economic forces structuring the transition from a colonial to a post-colonial state. See Munasinghe 1997.

race. With respect to Indo-Trinidadians, that is no longer so. Whenever Indo-Trinidadians are the subject of discussion, the terminology of ethnicity tends to supplant that of race, partly because of the different referential bases for race and ethnicity. The primary referent for race, as I argued earlier, is the biologization of selected traits. For ethnicity, in contrast, the primary referent is culture, the biologization of which can vary. That is, cultural traits can also be perceived as immutable—or they can be regarded as adaptable in varying degree. Even within the idiom of race the only demarcator for East Indians is their ancestral place of origin, which has to do directly with culture difference, not race. They are not classified by or assigned terms that imply biology directly, such as phylogenic or color terms. The propensity of East Indians to be identified primarily on the basis of cultural difference is largely an outcome of colonial discourses that projected the East Indian as a culturally saturated being. The tendency to label East Indians in ethnic terms is partly based on the *cultural* demarcation of their "race." Since the globally familiar definition of ethnicity rests on the concept of cultural difference, the criterion that defines East Indians as a "race" in Trinidad—ancestral origin—also facilitates their identification as an ethnic group.

In contrast, the significant markers for differentiating between Blacks and Whites are not cultural. Historically, the Black-White polarity grew out of both physical and cultural constructions. Over time, however, the two groups were seen to share a culture.[12] Again, colonial discourses that projected Africans as a people who were culturally naked allowed for the social recognition of cultural exchange between Whites and Blacks in which Blacks could become "respectable" by adopting White cultural norms and practices. Even though Blacks could become culturally "almost White," for the most part social constructions of biology continued to divide them. Hence race (in this instance the projected difference of biologized phenotypical traits) provides the idiom for capturing Black-White relations. In contrast, in Creole–East Indian relations the area of significant dissonance is thought to be cultural. Accordingly, ethnicity, with its emphasis on cultural aspects, serves to characterize these relations. Phenotypical differences between Creoles and East Indians matter, but in this instance the larger perceived difference is cultural.

The propensity to interchange race and ethnicity in academic and political discourses that focus on relations between Indo-Trinidadians and Afro-Trinidadians stems partly from this difference in significant markers, one

12. Hence the voluminous literature on Creole societies in the Caribbean that addresses the nature of this cultural exchange.

based on phenotype, the other on culture. The terminology of race tends to dominate in society-wide discourse because it can handle both Afro-Trinidadians and Indo-Trinidadians.

From a strictly theoretical perspective, local tendencies to subsume ethnicity under race in certain contexts can be in part justified by the cultural stability or inertia imputed to East Indians. If, as I stated earlier, the primary referent for race is the biologization of selected traits, then the very image of the culturally saturated East Indian attests to a biologization of East Indian cultural traits, which are viewed as immutable, ingrained in nature. In contexts in which East Indian cultural traits are depicted as immutable, East Indian ethnicity is therefore transformed into a racial identity.

Even though at the popular level race discourse predominates, the tendency to associate Blacks with race and East Indians with ethnicity is significant. Elsewhere (Munasinghe 1997), extending Daniel Segal's (1993) analysis and drawing on broader European orientalist and race discourses of the eighteenth and nineteenth centuries, I locate this tendency as a function of these discourses, which subjected Africans and East Indians to different principles of subordination pivoting around the "culturally naked" African and the "culturally saturated" Indian. These divergent principles in turn operated to situate the respective groups differentially vis-à-vis the emergent nation during the post-colonial period, hence my insistence on the analytical separation of these two terms even when for heuristic and practical purposes we may find it useful to subsume one term within the other. It may be disconcerting to some that I have chosen to frame this study as one about ethnicity, given the fact that local articulations of social heterogeneity are primarily expressed through the idiom of race. The strategy is deliberate. Persuaded by Handler's argument for a destructive analysis as opposed to a dialogic one for ethnographic studies of ethnicity and nationalism, which calls for a certain terminological dissonance between lay and academic designations, the constructionist approach to ethnicity provides the necessary analytical tools to critically engage local narratives that are for the most part racialized. It is my intention that such a critical distance will allow me to contribute, in the spirit suggested by Handler (1985:18), "to a dialogue that respects natives by challenging rather than romanticizing them."

[2]

Ethnicity and Nation

A baffling characteristic of ethnicity is that at the same time as ethnic sentiments and movements are rapidly gaining ground in the international arena, the claim that ethnicity does not exist in any objective sense is increasingly accepted in the academic community. How can something thought not to exist have such profound consequences in the real world?

On Abstracting Historical Categories

Categories are historical products. Not only do they delineate a particular social reality, but they are themselves shaped by this reality. Yet the act of categorizing may itself reify the category: the true dialectical relation between social reality and the category is then replaced by a one-way relation. In this way the category is removed from the flux of daily living practices; it becomes an abstraction from ongoing social reality, which it serves to explain by naming. But the matrices of social practice are constantly changing; those concrete aspects that categories are supposed to describe change, too. Soon the fit between category and social reality begins to diminish. Thus the scramble to theorize an invariant definition of ethnicity that holds true for all places (and for all time, according to the primordialists) is largely futile. Many of the debates among theorists regarding the ontological basis of the category result from a confusion of the assumptions underlying lay, political, and academic uses of the term. Following Brackette F. Williams (1989), I argue that ethnicity functions in three modes of abstraction, in three specific (though overlapping) discursive arenas:[1] the lay, the political, and the academic.

Ethnicity in Lay Discourse

Ethnicity is not only an analytic concept but also a lay term, at times used and lived in practice by common people and, as such, a concept always in the making. Lay people are largely unconcerned with theory—in terms of formulating abstractions capable of speaking to situations beyond their specific contexts—but aim instead at describing specific social situations in which categories of ascription, including ethnicity, are applied in daily life. Lay usage of the term *ethnic* is always embedded in a particular context with a given ideological frame of reference. In common discourse ethnicity (or any of the glosses that imply it) is believed to mean ascriptive identity, defined by cultural or biological features arising out of a common past. Here, then, abstract ethnicity becomes what it means to be ethnic or, more precisely, what it means to be of such-and-such an ethnic group at a particular time and in a particular place.

In lay discourse the category *ethnicity* is never defined in abstract terms but only implied because it is based on judgments and actions that are always historically situated. It is defined implicitly in terms of content and situation or, more precisely, in terms of historically situated content. Common people rarely use the word *ethnicity*. Rather, they continuously define and redefine "*the* ethnic," which is always *their* ethnic—what they as an ethnic group are or are not in contrast to others. An Indo-Trinidadian can easily list a number

---

1. I use the term *discourse* (as opposed to *language*) because it suggests a complexity beyond the expression of ideas and feelings through vocal sounds or written symbols. From a Foucauldian perspective to say there is a discourse on a particular subject is to emphasize the historical context and the field of force relations (power relations) that have objectified this subject as deserving of knowledge. Discourses are neither uniform nor stable and consist of a "multiplicity of discursive elements that come into play in various strategies" (Foucault 1980:100); therefore silences, as much as what is being said, constitute an integral aspect of discourses. More specifically, discourse also implies that an identical utterance may have varied effects depending on who is speaking, his/her position of power, and the institutional context in which he/she happens to be situated, hence the potential for the reutilization of identical formulas for contrary objectives. Also, no longer does the simplistic division between dominant and dominated discourses suffice. The concept discourse highlights the true complexity and flux behind "what is being said." As Verdery (1991:9) observes, "Discourse acquires its own properties and autonomies beyond the utterances that bear it." Relating it to her own case, she continues, "It is obvious that Romanian intellectuals' capacity to act was limited by their participating in discursive fields, in which no one effectively controlled what was said: as people's words entered into a discursive field, they were instantly available for reinterpretation, to be seized and turned against their speakers."

of traits binding him/her to other Indo-Trinidadians: the emotive tie to India, the territory of origin; the common history of indenture, dietary habits, and rules; kinship patterns; forms of music and dance; and stereotypes defining the natural psychological makeup of "the Indian," to name a few. What he or she defines is not ethnicity but what ethnicity means in this case. In the lay arena questions of cultural authenticity become irrelevant for the subject precisely because authenticity is taken for granted. For example, the fact that *chutney* music is a locally specific Trinidadian form does not deter many Indo-Trinidadians from claiming (and believing) that it is an authentic Indian tradition only recently rejuvenated in Trinidad.[2] The fact that ethnicity is seen as a natural disposition of all peoples even though it is not experienced in the same way in any two places is irrelevant to most people because the defining feature of ethnicity within this discursive field is context-specific and grounded in everyday practice.

Ethnicity in Academic Discourse

Salient aspects of ethnicity in lay usage are problematic in academic usage. The academic community has constructed a supposedly objective category, which is applied to historically situated lay concepts and actions. But these abstract definitions do not always work. Indeed, primordial and even situational/instrumentalist accounts essentialize ethnicity by imputing to the concept some invariant feature, supposedly typical of all historical contexts: cultural sentiment in the first case; economic and political factors in the second.[3] As Carter Bentley (1987:25) notes, "Despite apparent disagreements on fun-

---

2. *Chutney* is a genre of music associated with Indo-Trinidadians that became popularized and commercialized in the 1980s. Epitomizing a hybrid Indo-Caribbean cultural form, chutney music draws from Indian folk traditions, devotional songs, film music, calypso, soca, and rap (Ramnarine 1996). Like the condiment, chutney songs are said to be hot and spicy: fast-paced in terms of beat and often accompanied by sexually suggestive dancing usually (but not always) by females, much to the dismay of many conservative Hindus. See Ramnarine 1996 and Myers 1998:chap. 17.

3. Primordialists view ethnicity as a sentiment rooted in objective cultural traits, "the assumed givens of social existence . . . blood, speech, custom and so on" (Geertz 1973:259; see also Shils 1957 and Isaacs 1974). Situationalists view ethnicity as a social construct about difference, which is motivated by economic and political factors. Geertz is widely recognized as a primordialist, but it is important to note his qualified use of the term "*assumed* givens of social existence" since, as he says, "culture is inevitably involved in such matters" (1973:259). Barth's (1969) seminal work on ethnic groups epitomizes the situationalist model. See Weber 1978 for a situationalist analysis of ethnicity that attempts to account for the affective tie. See Bentley 1987 for a summary of the two schools of thought.

damentals, instrumentalist and primordialist models both seek an objective grounding for subjective identity claims." Not surprisingly, social analyses of the ethnic process lay bare the cultural inauthenticities of real life. This in turn prompts academics to ask how to explain the prevalence of ethnic sentiments if indeed traditions are, as we well know, invented.

More problematic still are comparative analyses that show ethnicity to mean different things in different places. The diversity of ethnic expressions lays the ax to a fundamental premise of the lay concept of ethnicity: that it is a "natural" disposition of humanity. If so, why is it that the Chinese in Guyana appear unconcerned about their ethnic origins in comparison with those in Jamaica (Patterson 1975; Shaw 1985)? Or why is the manifestation of East Indian ethnicity so different in Guyana from that in Fiji? "In Guyana, Hinduism flourishes with the full panoply of public temples and ceremonies. . . . In contrast, Fiji Hinduism is a private, familial, almost an unobtrusive activity" (Jayawardena 1980:434).

Further, as ethnic phenomena gain momentum in international politics, the category itself becomes automatically empowered with an explanatory potential beyond its capabilities. The explosion of ethnic sentiment in the contemporary world lends academic credence to the more abstract and theoretical use of the category in two ways. First, the explosion itself serves to validate the ontological basis for ethnicity as an abstract category, that is, it reinforces the impression that ethnicity must exist, since it is able to manifest itself so powerfully. Second, the academic term becomes empowered with an explanatory capacity precisely because it incorporates a greater degree of abstraction. A high level of abstraction carries the category beyond its variant lay usages and endows it with some extracontextual value. Thus a concept constructed on the basis of events in a specific era is later used to comprehend perhaps only vaguely similar events, even though the particulars of the new case may outweigh any similarities. Theoretical abstractions, so vital for conceptualizing social phenomena, need not be ahistorical and must be refined continuously with respect to history.

When scholars appropriate ethnicity as an analytical category, the concrete features it seemed to define so easily become slippery. As Anthony Smith (1986:6) says, "Ethnic communities, so easily recognizable from a distance, seem to dissolve before our eyes the closer we come and the more we attempt to pin them down." The problem with scholarly appropriation of the term is that many academics still believe ethnicity to connote a "thing," even at this more abstract and analytical level. But ethnicity is a thing only in its lay form, as it emanates from a particular context, that is, in its subject-dependent definition, in which members of an ethnic group are (or think they are) able to define concretely the basis for their felt commonality.

More objectively, ethnicity seems palpable and concrete only from a distance. What scholars perceive as ethnic from afar is in reality a combination of ongoing social processes that evoke in the scholar the image of the ethnic. Ethnicity as such is neither a thing nor even a number of things. It has to be conceptualized not as an essence but as a changing series of processes. These processes evoke an image of the ethnic precisely because, in any given context, they have been assimilated by lay ethnics into their definition of ethnicity before scholars enter the scene.

As B. F. Williams states: "Like race and class, however, ethnicity, along with the systems of classification associated with each of them in different places, has been, and continues to be, the product of combined scientific, lay, and political classification. As a result, contemporary efforts to understand what these concepts label, and what place these labels mark in the identity-formation process, must identify the assumptions underlying the linkages among their lay, political, and scientific meanings" (1989:402). Beyond identifying the underlying assumptions, however, we must trace the ways these diverse meanings have sustained one another. The aim is not to abstain from confusing the different meanings but to analyze the implications of a confusion of meanings that has already left scholars behind.

Ethnicity in Political Discourse

Ethnic situations at the ground level do not inevitably lead to politicization of the ethnic issue. But if and when ethnicity becomes politicized, political terminology is the primary field in which lay and academic meanings of the concept confront each other.[4] The process of constructing an explicit, well-articulated discourse on any particular ethnic situation compels fashioners of such a construction to pick effective symbols and emotive issues out of lay conceptualizations and to appropriate models and language from academic abstractions in order to build a coherent and legitimate case. For example, in Trinidad, to proclaim their desire for cultural and racial distinctiveness, Indo-Trinidadian leaders draw on Indo-Trinidadian sentiments

---

4. It is possible for lay concepts of ethnicity to be uncontaminated by either academic or political meanings of the term. In contrast, academic concepts of ethnicity rely on such lay meanings as sources of raw material for their own "truer" and more abstract conceptions. Where only lay and academic usages of the term obtain, the confusion of meanings between them can be said to be minimal if academic interpretations are not fed back into the community—as is often the case when foreign (usually Western) scholars come to study non-Western societies and publish their findings in erudite Western journals whose audience is limited to the scholarly community. But when ethnicity becomes politicized, the political usage of the term *ethnicity* usually entails the fine art of juggling lay and academic concepts and meanings.

against what they perceive to be a forced cultural and biological integration. They often do so by counterpoising the image of a tossed salad to that of a *callaloo,* a popular local dish in the Caribbean in which a number of distinct ingredients are boiled down to a homogeneous mush. The callaloo is a clear analogy to the melting-pot model of assimilation; the imagery of the tossed salad, in which each piece of lettuce and cucumber retains its "true" identity despite being mixed with "other" ingredients, draws on the plural society model of the coexistence of different (and sometimes incompatible) cultural institutions (M. G. Smith 1965). For reasons discussed later, Indo-Trinidadians are quick to opt for a tossed salad analogy of Trinidadian culture over that of a callaloo. The arena of political discourse, where local academics, politicians, ethnic brokers, and other "practitioners of knowledge" are actively engaged, provides a point of mediation for lay and academic conceptualizations.

When ethnicity becomes a political issue, a series of endless translations of the "ethnic experience" among the lay, political, and academic domains takes place. It is through the speeches of local politicians that ethnic subjects learn that their plight is akin to that of some other group in yet another remote corner of the world. From their leaders they hear of the resource-competition model of ethnicity, and they may become convinced that their historical trajectory is predetermined by the very nature of the plural society in which they live. Subsequently, sectional politics on the basis of ethnicity is usually thought to be a necessary and efficacious form of political activity to ensure the group a piece of the national pie. Thus an important part of the dialectics among the three domains may involve the introduction of academic concepts into the lay arena through political rhetoric. This process essentially collectivizes the individual experiences into an "ethnic situation" and serves to construct a group image on the purported basis of a common origin and a common fate.

In the arena of political discourse a primary task of local practitioners of knowledge is to translate academic jargon into ground-level practices and beliefs that will resonate with the masses. To be effective, ethnic rhetoric must appeal to three specific audiences: the international spectators, for legitimacy; the state representing the national community, for concessions; and most important, the ethnic masses, for political leverage. In order to balance these forces, a selection process in the construction of an articulate ethnic ideology unfolds.

First, only specific cultural features of the ethnic community, those that have mass appeal and are not potentially divisive, are targeted as concerns in the national arena. In the Indo-Trinidadian case divisive issues such as caste are rarely mentioned, but the propagation of Hindi is championed. Second, the chosen symbols of identity tend to be emotionally charged to facilitate mobilization. For example, many Indo-Trinidadians were appalled when a figure approximating the image of their revered Hindu goddess mother Lakshmi was paraded "shamefully" by a band playing during carnival. They took it as a blatant insult to their religion, and Indo-Trinidadian leaders have since used this incident to highlight the insensitivity of the rest of the society toward their cultural sentiments. Third, and most important, the targeted features should ideally be ambiguous enough to facilitate "double talk."

Double talk is necessary to translate what are by national and international standards "illegitimate" ethnic sentiments into legitimate terminology for use in the national political field. Invariably, double talk disguises sentiments that border on racism. In Trinidad, as everywhere, what leaders do not say is often as important as what they do say. For example, when Indo-Trinidadian politicians refer repeatedly to the enormous contribution their brethren have made to the growth of their nation because of a work ethic of perseverance, thrift, and sacrifice thought to be imbued in the Indian psyche, what they are really saying goes beyond a positive assessment of their contribution. Mention of the "Indian work ethic" also invokes the silent but more potent image of the lazy, indulgent "Negro" who is looking only for immediate gratification and knows only how to take handouts. The Indo-Trinidadians' sense of injustice is aggravated not just because of what they are explicitly told—that they deserve a more equitable share of the national pie—but because of what the silence implies: that they, the more deserving and possibly the more capable, have an inferior status in this nation in contrast to those others, who are less deserving. To succeed in double talk, a leader usually needs to be finely tuned to the common person's world view. As we see in Chapter 9, this familiarity is crucial for bridging the gap between ethnic elites and laity and between political rhetoric and lay conceptualizations of the ethnic situation.

The terms *ethnicity* and *ethnic* are continuously deployed, and quite explicitly, in political rhetoric. On the one hand, such terms are sufficiently abstract in that arena to permit the interpretation of a specific ethnic situation as an instance of larger, worldwide phenomena. On the other hand and contrary to its effect in the academic arena, ethnicity in political discourse is sufficiently grounded in a particular ethnic situation to maintain its integrity as a historical category. This is in part because of the way political discourse operates. Political discourse is premised on a "bottom-up" approach (as opposed to a "top-down" academic analysis) in which the degree of abstraction is ultimately limited by the facts on the ground.

Ethnicity as Process and Paradox: The Image of the Ethnic and the Reality of Ethnicities

The elusive quality of ethnicity is a poignant indicator of its true nature. Because we recognize the ethnic with ease, we assume that all ethnic situations are reducible to a set number of common elements. Yet attempts to fix on some common element have remained largely futile, and any conceptualization of ethnicity must account for this inherent tension. Ethnicity embraces both universal and particular elements: universal, because all specific ethnic situations are made public and significant through the academic and political discourses on ethnicity and the international discourse on the nation, making all ethnic situations look increasingly familiar; and particular, because each ethnic situation combines a multitude of varying forces unique to its own historical position.

If, following Benedict Anderson (1991), we comprehend the nation as an "imagined community" in the political sense, it would be apt to describe an ethnic group as an imagined cultural community. Even though the concept of culture is pivotal for ethnicity, this criterion alone is insufficient to distinguish an ethnic community from any other group based on cultural criteria. An ethnic group acquires its significance only because it is an imagined cultural community with an organic relationship to another imagined community—the nation.[5] As we see later, any current discourse on ethnicity necessarily assumes as a silent (and sometimes not so silent) referent the historical contingencies and concomitant ideologies that led to the emergence and consolidation of modern European nation-states in the late eighteenth century. For the moment let us turn to the specific nature of ethnicity that makes generalization so difficult.

An ethnic situation is constituted by a series of discrete but related processes that are operative in different mixes. I do not claim to exhaust all the possible forces here or all their possible combinations; since ethnic situations are always in the making, history invariably will have more to unfold. These components of the ethnic situation include (1) the belief in the existence of an ethnic group (in lay terms) defined by the group itself and/or by those outside; (2) the dominant rhetoric of the group (including its stereo-

---

5. In his attempt to distinguish ethnic groups from other types of collectivities, Geertz (1973) makes the interesting point that only ethnic groups actually threaten the nation because only such units are potential candidates for nationhood: "Civil discontent finds its natural outlet in the seizing, legally or illegally, of the state apparatus. Primordial discontent strives more deeply and is satisfied less easily. If severe enough, it wants not just Sukarno's or Nehru's or Moulay Hasan's head, it wants Indonesia's or India's or Morocco's" (261).

types); (3) a story of origin that associates the ethnic group with a particular territory and with its members' common historical trajectory; (4) a cluster of norms, values, and practices that supposedly have arisen from the group's common history and that the group can relate to on an experiential basis in a fairly unreflexive manner; (5) a cluster of publicly acknowledged cultural demarcators in the form of norms, values, and practices that have been constructed as specific to this group;[6] (6) various interests and motivations behind identity formations; and (7) the existence and role of institutions and agents promoting, defending, or managing these interests and motivations (such as ethnic brokers).

Seeing the ethnic situation as multiple and overlapping mixes circumvents the need to pinpoint some one defining element of ethnicity. Unlike some situationalist accounts, this model enables one to argue that an ethnic group can exist, though it may not have an institutional basis[7] or be cohesive enough to project a group image, as long as a sense of identity is expressed through other means. The expression of group identity can also vary in strength. For example, depending on the context, a group may have a weak institutional basis but a strong sense of belonging, engendered by the belief in a shared history. In contrast, what may look like a rather heterogeneous collection of people may be brought together and an identity created through a solid institutional basis. This process is usually the hallmark of situational accounts of ethnicity.[8] Since this model also enables one to be sensitive to the various expressions of ethnic identity found throughout the world without having to reduce them to one type, the analyst's task is to decipher the different modes in which ethnicity is expressed in any single instance. The uniqueness of each situation derives from the different combinations of varying elements, which can themselves vary in strength.

Although the elements of the ethnic situation just identified refer to forces within the group, they always presuppose the existence of the "other"—usually, the wider society or groups within it. Each of the elements gains significance and meaning only in reference to that other.[9] In short, the model posits that in the concrete, there are only specific ethnic situations, which are always context dependent. What, then, evokes the image of the ethnic in each

6. Components 4 and 5 are derived from a distinction Bastide (1978) makes between the private and public realms of culture. They may overlap somewhat in some situations, but they are not the same.

7. Institutions in this context refer to mediums of socialization such as ethnic organizations, schools, churches, and newspapers.

8. See, for example, McDonald 1986 on Celtic ethnicity.

9. Accordingly, this model takes the boundary as opposed to culture content as the unit of analysis for ethnicity, as first formulated by Leach (1954) and later popularized by Barth (1969).

of these varying ethnic situations? Or, more precisely, what justifies labeling "ethnic" certain similar but not wholly analogous human practices? I argue here that the image of the ethnic obtained from different ethnic situations can be attributed to three interrelated factors: the labeling of previously undistinguished historical processes, an operation that objectifies these events into a coherent whole; the subject-dependent nature of ethnicity in the last instance; and the significance ethnicity acquires from being part of a larger discourse on the nation.

Objectification of Ethnicity

The ontological and epistemological implications of naming what are usually messy and fortuitous conjunctures in time, or as Anderson (1991:4) puts it, the "complex 'crossing[s]' of discrete historical forces," are well illustrated by Eric Hobsbawm. In his introduction to *The Age of Revolution, 1789–1848* (*1962*), Hobsbawm lists a series of words, such as *industry, factory, middle class, working class, liberal, conservative, nationality, strike,* and *ideology,* which gained their modern meanings during this tumultuous period: "To imagine the modern world without these words (i.e., without the things and concepts for which they provide names) is to measure the profundity of the revolution which broke out between 1789 and 1848 and forms the greatest transformation in human history since the remote times when men invented agriculture and metallurgy, writing, the city and the state" (17). Later Hobsbawm observes: "The French Revolution was not made or led by a formed party or movement in the modern sense, nor by men attempting to carry out a systematic programme. It hardly even threw up 'leaders' of the kind to which twentieth-century revolutions have accustomed us, until the post-revolutionary period of Napoleon" (1962:80). Referring to this passage, Anderson concludes that "once it [the French Revolution] had occurred, it entered the accumulating memory of print. The overwhelming and bewildering concatenation of events experienced by its makers and its victims became a 'thing'—and with its own name: The French Revolution. Like a vast shapeless rock worn to a rounded boulder by countless drops of water, the experience was shaped by millions of printed words into a 'concept' on the printed page, and, in due course, into a model" (1991:80).

It is the act of labeling previously undistinguished phenomena that imputes meanings to those phenomena and attributes to them a coherence and integrity after the event. Similar processes and events that may take place in a different historical context after the birth of the concept (in its modern form) can never be perceived in the same light. The fact that these processes have been objectified and have entered a discursive field endows them with a

[26]

new ontological status of constituting "things," which then become capable of happening, of doing things, of being acted on, or very simply of just existing. Our capacity to recognize the ethnic (in its modern form) is derived from the type of memorializing referred to by Anderson. It can be either in the form of print or in the more nebulous form of a "universal consciousness"—where concepts such as religion and kinship may reside.[10] In short, the term *ethnic* has become a part of everyday parlance.

My intention here is not to illustrate the historical contingencies that gave birth to the modern concept ethnicity or to argue that practices corresponding to those we now label ethnic did not exist before the modern birth of this concept. Tracing the term *ethnic* back to its Greek root (*ethnos*) and French root (*ethnie*), which emphasize the cultural rather than the biological aspect, A. Smith (1986:32) claims that ethnic communities—defined as "named human populations with shared ancestry myths, histories and cultures, having an association with a specific territory and a sense of solidarity"—have existed "from the early third millennium BC until today." Yet the real issue lies in the epistemological premises that enabled Smith to make this very assertion. Once a phenomenon has been labeled and given meaning, it is possible to discover similar situations outside the immediate context that prompted the labeling in the first place. Thus irrespective of the historical subjects' consciousness of belonging to an ethnic community, the present discourse on ethnicity is what provided Smith with the distinct language and analytical tools to draw parallels between premodern and modern "*ethnie.*"

The academic, political, and international discourses on ethnicity, on the nation, and on the status of subnational groups within nations have played a central role in the labeling process. They have provided a distinct language for people to label experiences that were previously nameless. Labeling and objectifying lived experience within a whole new international discourse impute new meanings to the processes so labeled because they are deployed and made operational at a higher plane of abstraction. These local processes, even though operating in diverse geographical locations, begin to resemble one another or appear familiar precisely because they are garbed in now familiar discourses.

10. As Anderson (1991:5) does with nationalism, I have deliberately equated the ontological status of ethnicity with that of religion and kinship rather than with a specific ideology, such as Marxism, which has a historical point of origin. Although I argue that the meaning of ethnicity gained significance in the modern era, it is also possible to interpret premodern types of tribal behavior as akin to what we call ethnic behavior today—the crucial fact here being that we can identify premodern forms only after ethnicity has become objectified in its modern form. In contrast, it would be futile to search for Marxist movements in an age before Marx.

Ethnicity and the Subject

Ever since Edmund Leach, in his path-breaking work on the Kachins of northern Burma (1954), emphasized the subjective dimension of identification, which bore no necessary correlation to "objective" cultural criteria, academic discourse on ethnicity has tended to assume the subject-dependent nature of ethnicity. It is with respect to assigning causes for subjective ethnic identity claims that theorists fundamentally disagree (Bentley 1987). The primordialists point to the affective tie whereas situationalists/instrumentalists argue that economic and political interests constitute the motivating factor.

Ethnic identity is expressed both explicitly and implicitly. The problem with assuming the subject as a necessary condition for ethnicity is that the analyst can easily extrapolate from this assumption an unlimited (undue) degree of consciousness and volition on the part of that subject.[11] Yet in most instances ethnic practices and norms embodied in daily rhythms of life are enacted unconsciously; an observer may label certain practices ethnic independent of the subjects' awareness. For instance, an Indo-Trinidadian may perceive an overt cultural form such as a Lakshmi *puja* (Hindu ritual conducted by a pundit devoted to the goddess of light and prosperity, Lakshmi) as an integral marker of identity, but an outside observer might find the habitual Indo-Trinidadian practice of eating roti (unleavened bread) for breakfast and dinner and rice for lunch (which goes largely unnoticed by subjects as constituting an ethnic practice) a more revealing symbol of identity. The question then is, How can ethnicity simultaneously be both subject-dependent and subject-independent?

Most theorists agree that there has to be some level of subjective self-ascription among a people for an ethnic identity to exist. If we ignore this principle, we fall into the fallacy of correlating social groups with distinct cultural traits based purely on observers' criteria.[12] Basically, one cannot study ethnicity in a context where an ethnic situation does not obtain. This may seem obvious. Yet it is obvious only because it assumes so much: namely, a confusion of lay and academic meanings of the term *ethnicity*.

When a scholar enters a specific field situation to study ethnicity, it is only because the ethnic situation there is already named; it has entered the realm of discursive consciousness before the scholar's appearance. Ethnicity at this level necessarily assumes the subject. This does not mean that all ethnic practices and beliefs are subject-dependent, however. As I argued earlier,

11. A criticism often directed at Barth's model.

12. This issue was hotly debated during the 1960s by anthropologists (see Moerman 1965, 1968; and Naroll 1964, 1968). See also Barth's critique of Naroll in his introduction to *Ethnic Groups and Boundaries* (1969).

[28]

much of what passes for ethnic behavior (at least for the analyst) is habitual and preconscious—"pre-ethnic," if you will. But these types of unreflexive practices can be recognized as constituting ethnic practices only because other ethnic practices exist in the lay (and political) discursive arenas, which are consciously recognized as ethnic. A scholar can label "ethnic" the more subtle and habitual practices of a people, and endow them with significance, only because the people themselves have already formulated and articulated their ethnic situation. In this sense, ethnicity is subject-dependent in the last instance.

It is important for several reasons to specify the exact nature of the relation between ethnicity and historical subjects. First, the relationship between ethnicity and the subject is constituted by lay, political, and academic meanings of the terms, meanings that feed on one other and reify the term until everything significant about ethnicity becomes that which is conscious. Ethnicity acquires academic significance after a particular group of people or their self-proclaimed representatives begin to express their situation using a widely recognized lexicon marked with academic and political meanings of the term. It seems certain that much "consciousness raising" is an indirect consequence of the permeation of the local field by academic and political meanings, making significant that which before had been practiced and lived, but namelessly. Thus since people are actively naming certain practices, beliefs, and interests ethnic, the subject-dependent nature of ethnicity appears obvious.

This brings me to my second point. Although theorists are correct in assuming the necessity of indigenous (subjective) ascriptive categories for ethnicity, they tend to ignore the more subtle and habitual realms of ethnicity. Once we agree on the reasons why ethnicity appears so obviously subject-dependent, we can explore that realm which is largely unconscious to the actors. Indeed, the job of the analyst is to tie ethnicity as it appears in discursive consciousness to ethnicity as it resides in practical consciousness, and to explore those aspects of ethnicity that never reach the discursive level. This can open up, in turn, a different means for dealing with the emotive aspect of ethnicity without having to deny its interest-oriented, highly conscious, and manipulable side.

Ethnicity and the Post-Colonial Nation

The common features displayed by various ethnic movements are not a consequence of unfolding ethnic essences but a result of specific historical contingencies, namely, the formation of nation-states and their attendant ideologies in eighteenth-century Europe. There is nothing inevitable or primordial about the formation of ethnic groups. To argue, as A. Smith (1986) does, that culturally homogeneous groups (*ethnies*) existed in the premodern era and that modern nations originated on the basis of these premodern *ethnies*, is to bypass the emergence of an entirely new discursive and material universe within which ethnic group formation is taking place. In her elaboration of the dynamics behind the interstate system, Katherine Verdery (1983:8) suggests that the formation of nation-states in Europe "changed the rules of the game for all subsequent players, setting up imperatives that may have run counter to local development in other societies." Given the fact that nations constitute the overall system of social stratification within which ethnic groups live and function, the rules of the game changed not only for subsequent nations but also for ethnic groups caught within the spatial ambits of emerging nations.

The "pirating" (Anderson 1991) and application of old models to new contexts, and the imposition of European institutions on the colonized world, opened up new avenues for conceiving the nation and the place of ethnic or subnational groups within it. Post-colonial nations, however, did not merely replicate European models. Rather, cardinal precepts informing European models, such as the doctrine of self-determination, the principle of cultural homogeneity, and ideologies of egalitarianism as expressed in the concept "legal/political citizen," were fused with the social, political, and ideological currents specific to the emergent nations. Colonial institutions, and the premium they imposed on post-colonial states, set both limits and challenges to imagination and its realization. History, in short, set the stage for the style in which not only the national community but also its respective ethnic communities could be imagined.

In my discussion of nationalism I build my analysis around the theme of cultural homogeneity for two reasons. First, though few theorists would disagree that the principle of nationalism during the modern era was the pursuit of cultural homogeneity, which dovetailed with the practical drive toward achieving cultural integration and standardization,[13] in the so-called postmodern age some theorists, such as Arjun Appadurai (1996) and Homi Bhaba (1990), argue that the pursuit of homogeneity has been replaced by the celebration of "difference," or cultural heterogeneity, a transition, they claim, that augurs the demise of the nation-state. Areas such as the Caribbean, which have been traditionally represented as excessively heterogeneous, are now celebrated by scholars as displaying a "radical heterogeneity," an aesthetic symptomatic of the new age. Traditional concepts such as

13. I'm grateful to Drexell Woodson for emphasizing the integral connection between the claim to cultural homogeneity and the practical efforts toward standardization characterizing nation-building projects.

Creole, which have been used by both local and foreign scholars of the Caribbean to describe these societies, have been appended to such newer concepts as "cultural hybridity" and are claimed to have global relevance beyond the regional context.[14] The national narratives of the Caribbean, which have long emphasized the cultural diversity of these plural societies, have reified such academic deployments. I hope to illustrate, however, that national narratives of heterogeneity, far from disrupting the logic of the nation-state, have served instead to reinforce its exclusionary principles. This leads to my second reason for foregrounding the principle of homogeneity.

The precise relationship between ethnic groups and nation-states becomes apparent in the articulation of the principle of homogeneity. It is in the pursuit of this putative homogeneity that the dominant race and class come to establish a metonymic relation to the nation (B. F. Williams 1989), relegating "other" groups as peripheral to the national symbolic core. These others, now marked as ethnics, are positioned at a considerable material and ideological disadvantage vis-à-vis the nation-state in that although they possess the right to make claims on the state (as political citizens), their right to control the state is severely hampered by their ideological representation as outsiders. Thus nation-building projects in Trinidad and elsewhere in the Caribbean are not free from the imperatives set by modular European nationalisms. Yet the peculiar way these societies strive to straddle simultaneously principles of homogeneity and heterogeneity also signals that such nationalisms are not wholly derivative of European models.

European Nationalisms in the Age of Empire

The conflation of territorial states with cultural nationalism beginning in the late eighteenth century not only augured a new political order for Europe and subsequently the world but also provoked an obsession with illicit blendings, evidenced by the proliferation of discourses concerning racial hybridity.[15] The accounting of deviance from the White norm, racial hybridity para-

14. See, for example, Hannerz's use of *Creole*: "It used to be that there were only some handful of historically recognized creole cultures, mostly in the plantation areas of the New World, but now we sense that 'creole cultures' may be turning into more of a generic term, of wider applicability" (1996:66). Puri (1999:13) points to the problematic deployment of the concept cultural hybridity by "otherwise unlikely discursive partners—liberal multiculturalism, corporate capital, and sections of the academic Left"—in that they all partake in "the displacement of the politics of hybridity by the poetics of hybridity."

15. I use the term *hybridity* here to refer to its conventional meaning denoting "race mixture." The concepts race or mixture have little to do with hybridity's later application to the colonial setting by cultural critics such as Bhabha (1994), for whom hybridity signifies a moment

doxically signified the desire of the White for the non-White and threatened the claim for permanent difference between the races. During the nineteenth century, the age of empire and nation-building, the obsession with hybridity can be interpreted as an effort toward maintaining the purity of the privileged White races in the face of rampant mixing with the colonial Other. The marking of colonial spaces such as the Caribbean as acutely hybrid aided the colonial project first by displacing the problem of impurity outside the metropolis itself, thereby preserving, however tenuously, the purity claimed by "historic" nations (those nations supposedly embodying a history that is both unique and universal), and second by legitimizing rights of nations to remain empires, since the impurity ascribed to the colonies attested to their non-nation status.[16]

Few theorists of nationalism would disagree with Eugene Kamenka's contention that "the concept of nation and nation-state as the ideal, natural . . . form of international political organization, as the focus of men's loyalties and as the indispensable framework for all social, cultural and economic activities became widespread only at a specific historical period" (1973:6). For Kamenka it was the French Revolution of 1789 that inaugurated a new political order for Europe with its doctrine of national self-determination. This doctrine became the necessary condition for entry into nation status, and aspiring nations in turn had to fulfill certain criteria to justify their claims for self-determination. With the demise of the ancien regime, "the people" replaced absolute monarchs as the source of sovereignty, and subjects were transformed into citizens. The sovereignty previously embodied in the physical persona of the king, a single unit, now transferred to "the people," meant that "the people" had to be molded into a unity, defined and delimited. In short, the historical task for nation builders propelled into the era of Universal History[17] was to define the "self" in the doctrine of self-determination against other structurally similar but qualitatively different selves that now com-

---

of challenge to authoritative colonial discourse. See Young 1995 for a provocative and interesting analysis of European nineteenth-century preoccupation with the question of racial hybridity and his argument that connects colonialism and English national identity with contemporary discourses of cultural hybridity and multiculturalism.

16. It is worth noting how the celebration of hybridity in the form of creolization in the Caribbean reproduces the very colonial discourses that served to subordinate the region ideologically in the first place.

17. For Kamenka (1973) the development of nationalism makes history universal by bringing together the histories of Asia, Africa, and the Pacific with that of Europe. This resonates with Plamenatz's (1973) view of nationalism as setting global standards for progress. On the intimate connection between the nation and Enlightenment/Universal History, see Duara, who attempts to "decouple the deep, tenacious and . . . repressive connection between history and the nation" (1996:4).

posed the legitimate units of the standardized international political order. Some incipient nations, such as Germany and Italy before unification, theorists of nationalism still claim, found the task easier than others because they were "culturally equipped," that is, sufficiently culturally homogeneous, and needed only a "political roof" for the principle of nationalism to be realized (Plamenatz 1973; Gellner 1991). If indeed the principle of nationalism dictated that the cultural and political units be congruent (Gellner 1991), then any claim for an independent state was contingent on the capacity to produce a culturally homogeneous subject of the nation. Social and cultural heterogeneity posed a problem within this scheme. Accordingly, areas of the world such as eastern Europe, Africa, Asia, and parts of the Americas such as the Caribbean that allegedly displayed too much heterogeneity were relegated to the status of "nonhistoric" nations, which were fated to be continuously undermined by "primordial loyalties," in contrast to the "historic" nations of western Europe.[18]

Yet critical historical studies that seek to interrogate rather than reproduce nationalist histories suggest that the divide between "Western" and "Eastern" nationalisms or "liberal" and "illiberal" nationalisms has little to do with the empirical fact of heterogeneity itself and more to do with the capacity of nation builders, as myth makers, successfully to transform heterogeneity into homogeneity. Thus B. F. Williams states:

> The ideologies we call nationalism and the subordinated subnational identities we call ethnicity result from the various plans and programs for the construction of myths of homogeneity out of the realities of heterogeneity that characterize all nation building. The starting point for the definition of purity is not, therefore, some objective point at which "real" purity, or for that matter, authentic culture, exists, but rather the classificatory moment of purification and the range of issues that motivate its invention. (1989:429)

The impulse to create homogeneity out of heterogeneity or purity out of impurity characterizes all nationalisms and nation-building projects.[19] Indeed, the two contrastive models that emerged in Europe, the French revolution-

18. Such a demarcation was crucial for European states engaged in imperial expansion. As Duara, commenting on Queen Victoria's dual status as queen (of England) and empress (of India) observes, "This dualism, this right to maintain empire while being a nation, was centrally dependent on the ability to demonstrate that the colonies continued to remain non-nations" (1996:23).

19. It is important to qualify this statement by acknowledging that the drive toward homogenization is invariably premised on the demarcation of some populations as absolutely Other. I'm grateful to Stefan Senders for emphasizing this point.

[33]

ary democratic model rooted in the Enlightenment tradition and the German classical liberal (ethnocultural) model based on the romantic movement (Brubaker 1992), both point to or assume such pristine moments, even if in radically different ways.

Ethnocultural criteria were secondary to the French conception of nation rooted in the idea of citizen. As Hobsbawm comments, "If 'the nation' had anything in common from the popular-revolutionary point of view, it was not in any fundamental sense, ethnicity, language and the like" (1991:20). At least in theory any person could become French if he or she was willing to acquire the French language and the other liberties, laws, and common characteristics of the free people of France. Despite this apparent inclusivity, heterogeneity created problems, and Hobsbawm admits, "There is little doubt that for most Jacobins a Frenchman who did not speak French was suspect, and that in practice the ethno-linguistic criterion of nationality was often accepted" (1991:21).[20] Though French purity was not explicitly grounded in notions of shared blood or other ethnocultural criteria, the fact remains that the revolution produced a normative model of the French citizen into which "others" could assimilate.[21] As the bearers of Universal History and as the first people to give expression to the universal desire for liberty—the doctrine of self-determination—the French had transformed the historical particular to the Universal. Thus in theory at least, Frenchness was accessible to all, but in the final instance it was the "French" revolutionary criteria of citizenship that defined the Universal. From this perspective one could claim that the French model epitomized the homogenizing impulse of nationalism in its effort to subject the whole world to its universal principles, as demonstrated in the Napoleonic era, when French military expansion was legitimated on the grounds of defending and disseminating the principle of liberty.

In contrast, German nationalism, spearheaded by a literary middle class, defined the nation in cultural terms centering on the conception of the "volk" developed by Herder and the German romanticists. Since German nationalist sentiment developed before territorial and political unification of the "nation" in 1879, the nation was not conceived in political terms or tied to the abstract idea of citizenship. Instead, the prepolitical nation was con-

20. The anxieties around demarcating the cultural contours of Frenchness at the turn of the twentieth century are well illustrated in Stoler's (1997) analysis of *métissage* in French Indochina. The proliferation of colonial discourses around those people who threatened imperial divides speaks to the "tensions of empire" (Cooper and Stoler 1997) embodying both inclusionary impulses and exclusionary practices informing liberal policy.

21. This said, given the fact that it was the Third Estate (the bourgeoisie as universal class) that metonymized the French citizen of the Revolution (Turner n.d.), it is worth pondering the inclusionary ethos often attributed to the revolutionary democratic model of nationalism.

ceived as an organic, cultural, linguistic, and racial community (Brubaker 1992). In contrast to the French variant, Hans Kohn writes, German nationalism "lent itself more easily to the embroideries of imagination and the excitations of emotion. Its roots seemed to reach into the dark soil of primitive times and to have grown through thousands of hidden channels of unconscious development, not in the bright light of rational political ends, but in the mysterious womb of the people, deemed to be so much nearer to the forces of nature" (1994:165). If French nationalism epitomized the principle of homogeneity in the breadth of its colonizing efforts, in the German case the discourse of purity is so rigid that the nation's "primordial" boundaries cannot permit even the possibility of assimilation. As a consequence, even today citizenship rights in Germany are restricted for non-German immigrants "but remarkably expansive toward ethnic Germans from Eastern Europe and the Soviet Union" (Brubaker 1992).[22] In summary, the relation posited between purity/homogeneity and impurity/heterogeneity in the French and German nationalist narratives is contrastive in their identification of a classificatory moment of purification. The French narrative is all about the flattening of impurity or heterogeneity into purity or homogeneity embodied in the ideal of the French citizen. In contrast, the German narrative posits a rigid boundary between purity and impurity, the native and the foreigner. Thus critical historical studies of European nation-building projects clearly destabilize the cultural homogeneity imputed to the old states of Europe and suggest that the "problem" of heterogeneity is not exclusive to post-colonial states.

Yet academic disclosures of impurities that belie European national myths of homogeneity can hardly unshackle the new states, in their efforts to become legitimate nation-states, from the historical imperative already set for them by Europe's claim to a Universal History. Academic disclosures notwithstanding, the fact remains that historic nations were deemed such precisely because they were, for the most part, successful in their *claims* to homogeneity.[23] How, then, do new states caught in spaces that have been

22. See also Senders in press.
23. If one were to situate "situationalism," Verdery (1994) says, an interesting pattern emerges in which the most influential examples of situationalism come from the "Third World" rather than the "First." Verdery concludes that situationalism in the form of people exercising flexible identities is constrained "wherever the process of modern nation-state formation has the greatest longevity and has proceeded the furthest; wherever long-standing nationalist movements have effectively inculcated the sentiment of a single kind of belonging" (37). In short, the homogenizing projects of Europe have produced "self-consistent" national subjects that have less flexible identities than in Africa, Asia, or the Middle East. It is also important to note the exceptions in Europe, however. The disintegration of the Habsburg empire in the nineteenth cen-

marked as acutely hybrid (such as the Caribbean generally and Trinidad in particular), yet faced with the historical task of establishing and maintaining purity in their pursuit of nationhood, attempt to reconcile their paradoxical position? The historical task for nation builders in the post-colonial world is deeply contradictory. On the one hand, they have little option but to emulate the standards of progress set by Europe which demand that they "re-equip" the nation culturally to meet the requirements of progress; on the other hand, such a revamping of culture undermines the very distinctiveness of their cultural identities, which constitute their own forms of "national genius" (Plamenatz 1973; Chatterjee 1993a). This contradiction is further sharpened in the New World. The paradox posed is the following: if the national genius of Creole societies lies in "illicit blendings" (Bernabe, Chamoiseau, and Confiant 1989 in Balutanski and Sourieau 1998), or creolization, how do such societies give expression to their unique genius while simultaneously striving for the universal nationalist imperative of homogenization? I first address the possibilities for carving out an autonomous space for post-colonial nationalisms that are not wholly derivative of western European models (Chatterjee 1993a, 1993b) before turning to this paradox.

Situating the Caribbean between the "Modular" and the "Derivative"

Partha Chatterjee takes exception to Anderson's (1991) contention in *Imagined Communities* that nationalisms in western Europe, the Americas, and Russia supplied the "modular" forms for subsequent nationalisms: "History, it would seem, has decreed that we in the post-colonial world shall only be perpetual consumers of modernity . . . even our imagination must remain forever colonized" (1993b:5). According to Chatterjee, the nationalist imagination in Asia and Africa posits not an identity with but difference from the received modular forms, and a domain of sovereignty is carved out by nationalists long before the colonial contest for political power—thus the story of anticolonial nationalisms begins before the formal battle for control over the state. For Chatterjee anticolonial nationalisms establish a sovereign space

> by dividing the world of social institutions and practices into two domains—the material and the spiritual. The material is the domain of the "outside," of the

___

tury can be interpreted as a failed attempt at homogenization due to various historical contingencies—one of which, according to Segal (1989), was the absence of colonies.

economy, of state craft, of science and technology, a domain where the West had proved its superiority and the East had succumbed. In this domain, then, Western superiority had to be acknowledged and these accomplishments carefully studied and replicated. The spiritual, on the other hand, is an "inner" domain bearing the "essential" marks of cultural identity. (Chatterjee 1993b:6)

Yet Chatterjee anchors the spiritual domain in Bengali language, literature, drama, and art, arguing that despite the influence of modern European literature, aesthetic conventions, and critical discourse, this domain allowed an escape from Western dictates through artists' efforts to develop aesthetic forms that were modern but recognizably Indian (1993b:7–9); this poses an empirical and a theoretical quandary for understanding Caribbean nationalisms. Chatterjee's spiritual domain presupposes native or indigenous peoples and cultural forms prior to Western colonial contact that can serve as spiritual reservoirs for subsequent anticolonial nationalisms. Such an option was not available to Caribbean nationalists. Owing to the early annihilation of the native Carib and Arawak populations, there was no native element to appeal to; nearly all Caribbean people trace their ancestries to the Old World. If a sovereign space was imperative for escaping the dictates of Western modernity, the Caribbean was poorly situated indeed. The Caribbean was created by Western imperial projects that centered on the use of bonded labor for monocrop plantation production of commodities destined for metropolitan markets. The industrial aspect of sugar production, which combined field and factory and heavy machinery, subjected Caribbean people to modern industrial rhythms even before they emerged in Europe. The mostly violent transplantation of people from different continents to satiate metropolitan desires for sugar and other stimulants meant that whole new forms of social organization had to be created. As a result, as Sidney Mintz observes of the Caribbean people:

> Their development was an instance of a precocious modernity, an unanticipated (indeed unnoticed) modernity—unnoticed especially, perhaps because it was happening in the colonies before it happened in the metropolises, and happening to people most of whom were forcibly stolen from the worlds outside the West. No one imagined that such people would become "modern"—since there was no such thing; no one recognized that the raw, outpost societies into which people were thrust might become the first of their kind. (1994:298)

The Caribbean thus repeatedly transgresses neat sociological dichotomies between primitive and modern, Western and non-Western, center and periphery,[24] and in this case the divide between modular and anticolonial nationalisms. Although Anderson emphasizes the New World origins of nationalism, his "Creole Pioneers" of the Americas are primarily restricted to Central and South America, the Iberian part of the New World (Anderson 1991:chap. 4). Too Western and modern to follow in the trajectory of Chatterjee's anticolonial nationalisms, and too northern European in its metropolitan influence to stake a claim, like Anderson's "Creole Pioneers," as "pace setters," the Caribbean, in particular the non-Hispanic Caribbean, yet again subverts neat typologies. To attempt to uncover an uncontaminated discourse of nationalism in such a space is, I believe, a largely futile exercise given the Caribbean's intimate and prolonged relationship with Europe.[25] Though I find Chatterjee's argument compelling, as B. F. Williams states, "to know . . . simply that [the colonialist nationalist project] does not break out of rationalist discourse provides no significant understanding of the consequences of this derivative status for conceptualizations of these new political units in a world where the nation-state is the reigning political unit" (1993:170). The task, then, is to explore how historical particularities of the region, in dialogue with western European models, may have resulted in novel and creative ways of imagining a national community and the place of ethnic groups within it.

Nationalism and Ethnicity in the Caribbean

Ethnic groups and nations are both imagined communities, but their sources of signification are different. Ethnic groups are imagined against the backdrop of the nation whereas nations are formed in relation to state power. Both nation formation and the emergence of subnational identities we call ethnicity involve a process of triangulation characterized by a continuous back-and-forth movement among three points: state power, the nation, and the ethnic group.

But this process of triangulation is itself a movement in time. The ideological and material foundations on which national and ethnic communities are conceived are laid long before their actual moment of formulation. Here, again, history becomes relevant for understanding why a certain nation and

24. On the Caribbean region's nonconformity to divisions of Western academia, see Trouillot 1992. Robotham (1998), discussing the effects of transnationalism in the Caribbean, argues that the period of globalization proper (beginning in 1989) led to an extension rather than a rupture of established patterns of relationship because of the Caribbean's long and intrinsic connection to capitalism and Europe.

25. Indeed, even Chatterjee concludes that although nationalist thought in India was formulated against the West, it remained imprisoned within the rationalist discourse of European Enlightenment philosophies (Chatterjee 1993a; B. F. Williams 1993).

its respective ethnic groups are imagined in a particular way. Only a historical analysis can reveal the points of encounter between the structuring of that unit, which would later constitute the nation, and the structuring of other units, which in turn may be transformed into ethnic groups. The structuring of these units is always mediated through state power.

In colonial societies such as Trinidad where cultural heterogeneity has been objectified as social reality, the positioning of different groups in relation to the colonial state significantly determined the styles in which the post-colonial nations and ethnic groups could be imagined. During the colonial period in Trinidad (1498–1962) the relation between the state and the nation was hardly a complementary one. But as Michel-Rolph Trouillot (1990:26) reminds us, the nation is not always a cultural construct backed by political power: "the nation is not a political fiction; it is a fiction *in politics.*" By removing the element of political legitimacy as a necessary condition for realizing the nation, Trouillot maintains the relation between the nation and the state (as formulated by Anderson 1991) without, however, conceding an essential congruence between the two. Accordingly, he argues that "nation-building can operate within the state, against the state, or in the name of the state" (Trouillot 1990:25).

The role of the state is crucial in understanding the place assigned ethnic groups in societies understood to be heterogeneous. Again, to quote Trouillot, "the nation is the culture and history of a class-divided civil society, as they relate to issues of state power. It is that part of the historically derived cultural repertoire that is translated in political terms" (1990:25). The Caribbean scenario, with its projected cultural heterogeneity, further complicates the relation among culture, history, and the state: "While some observers are now discovering the correlation between cultural identity and claims on the state, those of us who work in the Caribbean have long discovered that this correlation is not a simple one. . . . The nation is not necessarily a cultural construct backed by political power. Rather, it is a cultural construct that offers some claim to homogeneity in relation to political power" (Trouillot 1990:25).

In societies deemed polyethnic, such as Trinidad, the critical question for different ethnic groups becomes which group's perceived cultural repertoire should provide the rudimentary basis for this claim to homogeneity. In the context of the transition to independence this question becomes critical because ultimately it determines who has the legitimate right to inherit the state.

Nation building in societies marked as polyethnic necessarily calls on those nation builders to "manage" their diversity in their race to nationhood. It is important at this theoretical juncture to note that the cultural diversity or heterogeneity attributed to polyethnic societies is a consequence of objectifying processes that render heterogeneity a real social fact. In part this has to do with the very colonial discourses that demarcated colonies as nonhistoric nations on the basis of such cultural heterogeneity. As we shall see, colonized subjects internalized these very discourses and came to perceive their societies as plural. In Trinidad the narrative of diversity gains added significance because historical memory dictates against any claim to a primordial identity for the national subject, that is, the majority in the Caribbean know as historical fact that their ancestors derived from the Old World. Nationalisms in the New World have little option but to incorporate ancestral diversity as a master narrative in their definitions of national identity. In Trinidad the emergence of a national identity that simultaneously straddles the two poles of heterogeneity and homogeneity pointed to a novel way of imagining the national community and its ethnic groups that contrasted with European modular forms, but like the latter, Trinidadian discourses of nativeness were forged on the basis of exclusionary principles.

In reconciling the social fact of ancestral diversity (heterogeneity) with the nationalist imperative of homogeneity, we encounter two nationalist narratives in Trinidad: one of a cosmopolitan plural society and the other of creolization (signifying racial and cultural mixture). Examining a variety of texts catering to tourists, foreign investors, and foreign scholars and depicting a positive vision of the Trinidad nation, Segal (1994) argues that the projected cosmopolitanism of Trinidadian society—the image of a "United Nations in miniature"—suggests a nationalist narrative that emphasizes the continuity of ancestral diversities into the present. The plurality or heterogeneity embodied by the various immigrant groups at the moment of arrival in Trinidad is said to continue into the present. According to Segal, the Trinidadian nationalist narrative celebrates "not the creation of unity from heterogeneity—not the capacity to invent a new identity out of many old identities[26]—but the coexistence of diverse ancestral kinds in 'harmony'" (1994:226). Interestingly, we find this nationalist narrative reproduced in both academic and lay discourses, in the model of the plural society in the first case and in the metaphor of the tossed salad in the second.

I propose here, however, that the Trinidadian nationalist narrative of the continuity of pure ancestral types exists in dialectical tension with another equally visible Trinidadian (or Caribbean) nationalist narrative, one that pivots around the notion of mixture as symbolized by local persons' understand-

---

26. On the creation of new composite identities through racial mixture, see B. F. Williams's analysis of "Englishness" (1991:24). See also Stutzman's (1981) analysis of the symbol of El Mestizaje in the nationalist narrative of Ecuador.

ings of their identities and societies as Creole.[27] The term *Creole* in popular Caribbean usage "refers to a local product which is the result of a mixture or blending of various ingredients that originated in the Old World" (Bolland 1992:50) and which has taken root locally. Like the cosmopolitan narrative, the Creole narrative has its counterparts in both academic and lay discourses, in the model of the Creole society thesis and in the metaphor of the callaloo, respectively. In subsequent chapters (4, 7, and 9) these nationalist narratives are more fully developed. But for the moment suffice it to say that Trinidadian national identity embodies a tension between the two polarities of purity and mixture. As Aisha Khan observes,

> Trinidad, though a self-proclaimed "callaloo" society, cannot unequivocally or uniformly embrace an ideology of a "mixed" national identity, given the concern over potential cultural oblivion that competing ethnic groups allegedly risk. In Trinidad it is the concern over the assumed intrinsic relationship between racial/ethnic assimilation (mixing) and acculturation . . . that makes for a "callaloo" society that remains unamalgamated; it is synchronously "mixed" and distinctive. (1993:189)

It is within this tension that the precise relationship between "the real producers" of the nation and "ethnics" unravels. Therefore, a dialectical reading between the polarities of mixture and purity is necessary to understand how certain groups that are deemed pure, such as the East Indians, have been symbolically positioned outside the imagined national community. Such a dialectical reading complicates the very notion of purity, forcing one to recognize that not all purities represented in the cosmopolitan narrative of Trinidad are accorded the symbolic privilege of nativeness (that is, they are not formal equivalents), and it sharply brings into focus the unequal relations structuring the dynamics between those groups labeled ethnics and those labeled natives.

B. F. Williams's (1991:chap. 1) use of Antonio Gramsci's formulation of a transformist hegemony nicely elucidates this asymmetrical relationship:

> Where the national process aimed at homogenizing heterogeneity is fashioned around assimilating elements of that heterogeneity through appropriations that devalue them . . . it establishes what Gramsci referred to as a transformist hegemony. Under these conditions, those groupings associated with objects, acts, and ideas treated in this manner are placed at both a pragmatic and an ideological disadvantage. If they continue to insist on the root identity of their

---

27. Elsewhere Segal (1993) analyzes Trinidadian narratives of mixture, but in this instance the reference is specifically to "persons" as opposed to the "nation."

selves . . . they are not "true" members of the ideologically defined nation. . . . If, on the other hand, such groups do not insist on identifying the roots of the appropriated elements but instead aim to reduce their marginalization by adopting elements whose roots are ideologically attributed to other groups . . . they may . . . stand accused of riding to the pinnacle of civilization on the coattails of its real producers. (1991:30)

In a transformist hegemony the dominant groups control the production of the legitimate interpretations for the selected cultural appropriations. Williams continues, "The limits of public debate on all issues are established around a set of criteria and a mode of interpreting those criteria that aim to render illegitimate attempts on the part of marginalized others to expand the criteria or to insist on a different mode or even range of interpretations" (1991:31). The following chapters trace the establishment of such a transformist hegemony in Trinidad and Indo-Trinidadian efforts to expand the limits of public debate on national identity.

[3]

Foretelling Ethnicity: East Indians between Ex-Slaves and Planters

The material and ideological coordinates for structuring ethnic relations between Afro-Trinidadians and Indo-Trinidadians emerged from the colonial historical context even before East Indians[1] began arriving in Trinidad in 1845. To be sure, their economic and institutional status as indentured laborers and as latecomers into a society already creolized operated to isolate East Indians from the rest of the society. Yet these material conditions in and of themselves do not necessarily signify "outside" status. A certain idiom for ideologically situating the East Indians' position in relation to the larger society was already in place before East Indians set foot in Trinidad. Under the influence of economic and political factors a colonial discourse around the "African" (ex-slave) and the "Indian" (anticipated bonded laborer) established a specific ideological frame to situate members belonging to these categories vis-à-vis the nation. Once this frame was in place, unfolding material conditions—labor practices, places of abode, and social and cultural habits and behaviors—were interpreted and signified through it, and the frame in turn reified the material conditions themselves as if they embodied these ide-

---

1. In Chapters 3 and 4 I use the terms *Indian* and *East Indian* (and only sometimes *Indo-Trinidadian*), largely to avoid terminological anachronisms. To refer to those Indians who came to Trinidad primarily as sojourners (in terms of initial intent at least) between 1845 and 1917 as *Indo-Trinidadians* would be a misnomer. Here the analyst's categories need to resonate with historically appropriate ones in order to capture these terms' specific nuances. It is also important to retain the term *East Indian* because the marginality it connotes is central to the ensuing discussions. In addition, I use the term *Black* to signify those of African ancestry and *Creole* to signify both those of African and Mixed (Colored) origins, again for reasons of historical consistency.

ological states. The seeds that would germinate as mistrust and antagonism between Blacks and East Indians predated the arrival of indentures. Though the initial causes of this friction were economic, they soon took on cultural meaning.

Pre-Emancipation Trinidad

In the early nineteenth century the supply of labor became the principal problem for Britain's West Indian planters. Although British abolition of the slave trade in 1807 and the Emancipation Act of 1833 had repercussions throughout the Caribbean, each society experienced these events in ways limited to its own history, as well as to its current position within the region and the empire. Compared with other British colonies such as Barbados, Jamaica, St. Christopher, and Nevis, Trinidad—like British Guiana (Guyana)—was a late participant in sugar production. Its resources barely tapped, Trinidad had yet to reach a boom period.

The history of modern Trinidad dates from 1783. Under Spain from 1498 to 1783, Trinidad was largely neglected, relegated to the status of a "colonial slum" (Millette 1985:1). Spanish colonial policy, unlike that of the British and French elsewhere, failed to encourage or harness private efforts for colonial exploitation.[2] The Spanish colonial impulse was motivated in part by the quest for gold and other precious metals; having none, Trinidad was of minor importance. The Spaniards used Trinidad to raise provisions such as cassava, corn, tobacco, sugar, and cattle, much as they did with the larger islands of the greater Antilles (Dunn 1972:15).

The island's neglect was also due to the crown's role in the colonial enterprise. Spain's colonies existed first and foremost for the benefit of the crown. In fear of granting too much autonomy to the colonials, the crown ruled out any possibility of developing its colonies using private Spanish enterprise or foreign capital. Although it lacked the capital to develop the island, the crown also hindered any other development attempts. Hence Trinidad remained economically unexploited for nearly three centuries. A turning point came in

2. Spain's attitude toward Trinidad was governed not only by the particular interests of the Spanish crown but by wider metropolitan rivalries as well. From 1492 to the early seventeenth century the Spaniards were the only Europeans occupying lands in the Americas. After the Anglo-Spanish War (1585–1604) Britain, France, and Holland made their decisive entry into the Caribbean, catching Spain at its weakest moment. These new contenders, especially England and France, aimed at a different kind of colonization based on plantation production and commerce (Dunn 1972:16).

1783, when a *cédula* of population was negotiated by Roume de St. Laurent,[3] opening Trinidad to French migrants from the French islands, Grenada in particular.[4]

Three of the five provisions of the *cédula* would affect Trinidad's subsequent settlement.[5] First, every White settler was entitled to thirty acres of land, and fifteen more for each of his slaves. By tying land to labor, the clause motivated White migrants to bring as many slaves as they could afford. A second provision gave free Blacks and Coloreds fifteen acres of land each, more if they brought slaves. A third provision gave legal sanction to non-White planters as a property-owning class (Millette 1985:16, 17). These last two provisions were especially significant because they allowed the emergence of a large, settled Colored community in the island. James Millette observes: "The central theme of the *cedula* was . . . the introduction of large numbers of new settlers into the Island. As such it laid the basis for the creation of a society entirely different from that which had existed before. The immediate result of the new policy was a dramatic increase in the Island's population and development" (1985:15).

The impact of the *cédula* on the island was substantial. Before 1783 plantation agriculture was almost nonexistent in Trinidad and manufactured goods were barely obtainable. Hardship and disease were common; politically and socially, "government" hardly existed. In 1783 the commerce of the colony depended entirely on the visit of a 150-ton Dutch vessel two or three times a year; the population was a meager 2,813 (Millette 1985:7).

The 1783 *cédula* increased the population of Trinidad dramatically and changed its composition (Table 1). In 1777 Trinidad, with a land area of 1,864 square miles, had only 3,432 inhabitants (Newson 1976:184); Barbados, with a much smaller land area, boasted a population of 82,516 as early as 1768 (Ragatz 1971:30). After 1783 Trinidad's population increased to 18,918 (in

3. The 1783 *cédula* was a result of the 1761 "Family Compact" between Spain and France, which had established a special relationship between the two powers (Millette 1985:3).

4. After the Seven Years' War between France and Britain, Grenada was ceded to Britain. As a result the French, who were Catholics, became increasingly discriminated against, and with the *cédula* of 1783 many fled to Trinidad (Millette 1985:9).

5. The five clauses regulating immigration were (1) foreigners wishing to immigrate must be Roman Catholics and subjects of nations having friendly relations with Spain; (2) an oath of fidelity to Spain must be taken; (3) every White settler was entitled to roughly thirty acres for each member of his family and half as much for each of his slaves; (4) Blacks and Coloreds, being free men and proprietors, received half the proportion allotted to Whites, the allotment to be increased if they brought slaves with them; and (5) after five years' residence all settlers and their dependents undertaking to remain permanently in the island assumed the rights and privileges of Spanish citizens and could be admitted to civil and military offices according to their talents and circumstances (Millette 1985:16).

Table 1 Population of Trinidad, 1782 and 1789

	1782	*1789*
Amerindians	2,082	2,200
Slaves	310	10,100
Free Coloreds	295	4,467
Whites	126	2,151
Total	2,813	18,918

Source: Millette 1985:7, 15

1789); among the Whites, the French outnumbered the Spaniards by a ratio of twenty to one (Millette 1985:25). The English component was negligible.[6] Though Spain nominally ruled, it was mainly the French who governed the island after 1783. Both Spain and England were apprehensive of French hegemony, especially in the heyday of the French Revolution. The outbreak of revolution in St. Domingue (1791) and the triumph of the Jacobins in France (1793) introduced an element of instability into the West Indies, particularly Trinidad. Republican inclinations toward liberty and fraternity, which the Free Colored population of Trinidad was thought to harbor, threatened the legitimacy of colonialism, at least theoretically. Spain, in no position to control effectively tendencies it deemed subversive, offered little resistance when the British took over Trinidad in 1796 (Millette 1985:22–31).

As the architects of the *cédula* had hoped, the French immigrants brought with them not only slave labor but also much-needed capital to exploit Trinidad's abundant resources. The island's first sugar mill was established in 1787, and production increased rapidly. In 1796, for example, "159 sugar plantations produced 7,800 hogsheads of sugar.[7] One hundred and thirty coffee estates yielded 330,000 pounds of coffee; 103 cotton estates accounted for 224,000 pounds of cotton" (Millette 1985:19). Nevertheless, only one-twentieth the potential acreage had been brought under cultivation. Although sugar would dominate the economy by 1810, in 1796 uncertainty regarding Trinidad's future as a slave colony held back plantation agriculture based on slave labor. In the initial years of British rule the issue of how the island should be exploited and settled was vigorously contested between abolitionists, who supported a system of colonization based on free labor, and British capitalists, who desired large, slave-based plantations producing export crops. Colonists and investors anxious to profit from unusually high

6. One of the requisites of the *cédula* was that migrants had to be Catholic. French immigrants outnumbered the English, who were mostly Protestant.

7. According to Trollope (1985:141), writing in 1859, a hogshead equaled one ton.

Table 2 Land Use in Trinidad by Crop, 1808, 1824, and
1832 (in acres)

Crop	1808	1824	1832
Cane	13,976	22,425	27,724
Cocoa	—	9,369	10,380
Coffee	—	1,903	1,200
Cotton	1,740	669	146
Provisions	7,897	5,997	16,004
Negro grounds	—	10,010	—
Pasture	9,260	11,974	10,694
Total	32,873	62,347	66,148

Source: Higman 1984:701

sugar prices rushed to Trinidad just after the British capture. After 1802, however, the British government's willingness to consider the abolitionists' option of settlement by free laborers impeded the growth of the slave population. According to Bridget Brereton (1981:46), "the rate of growth [of the slave population] dropped considerably, with an increase of only 1,150 in 1802–11; there was the same number of sugar estates in 1834 as there had been in 1801." Yet the land under sugar cultivation almost doubled from 1808 to 1832, in contrast with the amount dedicated to coffee and cotton (crops associated with smallholders), which decreased (Table 2). We can assume, then, that "sugar barons" were expanding their enterprises even during this period of contraction.[8]

Trinidad's late entry into the larger Caribbean picture as a major sugar-producing colony helps explain the contradictions that appeared after emancipation. Crop diversity and production unit size indicate that the landholding classes were not a homogeneous group in pre-emancipation Trinidad. Although sugar production had dominated since 1800, agricultural production was always diverse (Table 2) with cocoa, coffee, and cotton assuming significance at different historical moments.[9] But it was sugar that dominated the

8. I'm grateful to Nigel Bolland for this observation.

9. Cocoa, cultivated by Amerindian laborers on Spanish-owned plantations, had been Trinidad's major industry in the late seventeenth century. After a disastrous fungus epidemic in 1725, cocoa production declined, but it was revived in 1756 when a hardier variety was introduced (Brereton 1981:3). During the late 1700s Spanish settlers continued to cultivate cocoa in the valleys of the northern range. Cocoa was not dependent on slave labor in the same way as sugar. For example, in 1815 cocoa used only 3.6 percent of the total slave population whereas sugar employed 59.7 percent. Cocoa was typically a smallholders' crop, cultivated largely by Free Coloreds and Blacks. Between 1803 and 1834 its production soared from approximately 150,000 pounds to 3 million pounds (Higman 1984:59). Cotton and coffee also figured prominently in Trinidad's economy in the late eighteenth century. During the 1780s cotton was the

economy in the years leading up to emancipation. In 1832 sugar and its by-products accounted for more than 90 percent of the total value of exports, with cocoa contributing a modest 6.2 percent and coffee a mere 2 percent (Higman 1984:59).

Though the substantial Free Colored population and the French Creoles constituted a prominent landholding class during this period, their interests did not necessarily match those of the sugar barons. Trinidad had one of the largest communities of Free Coloreds in the Caribbean. In 1825 they numbered 14,983, or 35.4 percent of a total population of 42,250 (Campbell 1992:58). The Free Coloreds of Trinidad, who under the 1783 *cédula* had near civil equality with Whites, were among the most privileged in the Caribbean, especially with respect to landownership (Campbell 1992). This group benefited enormously from the distribution of free land between 1783 and 1812,[10] which consolidated their status as a significant landowning class, especially in North and South Naparima.[11]

The size of landholdings did not necessarily translate into wealth. The wealth of a planter ultimately depended on the amount of slave labor he commanded as well as the productive capacity of his land. Apart from a few Colored proprietors such as Louis Philip, who owned large plantations and many slaves, most of the Colored landowners were not prominent slave owners. Land was both cheaper and easier to obtain than slaves but was of little use without them. In fact, as Henry Fuller, a White sugar planter, reported to the assistant commissioners of compensation in 1834, planters bought estates merely to obtain the slaves, who were then transported to other estates. William H. Burnley, an American-born sugar baron and successful merchant,

---

favorite crop of French settlers, and in 1788 it accounted for 70 percent of the value of Trinidad's exports; by 1796 103 cotton estates were producing 224,000 pounds of cotton (Brereton 1981:17). The French planters also cultivated coffee, producing 330,000 pounds on 130 estates in 1796 (Brereton 1981:17). The output of coffee and especially cotton declined between 1800 and 1834, however, as the production of cocoa and subsistence crops increased dramatically between 1824 and 1832 (Higman 1984:59).

10. Under Chacon, the last Spanish governor of Trinidad (1783–97), 26 Free Colored persons received roughly 1,726 carreaux (1 carreau = 3.2 acres) between 1783 and 1797, which amounted to 4.1 percent of the total land distributed (see also Campbell 1992). After the British takeover in 1797 the land distribution scheme was interrupted; it resumed, under Governors Hislop and Monro, in 1805 and continued until 1812.

11. In 1813 Campbell (1992:108) estimates that there were at least thirty-eight Free Colored planters in the Naparimas with a total of 862 slaves, or approximately 35.1 percent of the estates and 30.1 percent of the slaves in the region. Of the thirty-eight plantations, seventeen were sugar estates, three were coffee estates, one combined coffee and provision cultivation, another combined coffee, cocoa, and provisions, and ten were provision estates. Campbell does not account for the remaining six estates.

Table 3 Slaveholdings by Whites and Free Coloreds Having Five Slaves or More,
by Crops, 1824

Owners	Sugar	Cocoa	Coffee	Cotton	Total No. of Slaves
Coloreds	45	21	23	32	2,202
Whites	206	82	32	7	13,013

Source: Campbell 1976:29

and a leading spokesman for the planter class and the need for immigrant labor, told the commissioners that he had recently purchased Union Valley estate for the sole purpose of obtaining its slaves for work in another estate, leaving to ruin the cultivation, land, and machinery of Union Valley (Campbell 1976:28). Slave labor, in short, was the necessary catalyst to translate landownership into wealth.

White planters were clearly the most significant slave owners, and they dominated sugar, the preeminent capital-intensive, large-scale export crop (Table 3).[12] From the figures in Table 3, we can tentatively conclude that although Free Coloreds constituted a prominent landowning class, their estates and business transactions did not command the same size or volume as those of White planters. Thus Free Coloreds did not represent elite sugar interests. The nature of their small-scale enterprises earned them the contempt of White planters and administrators, who considered their enterprises inefficient. Such an attitude was in some ways predictable; the Englishmen of this period thought the only worthwhile economic activity was the cultivation of sugar, which generated enormous profits. Characterizing the different "mentalities" of the Colored and English proprietors, Carl C. Campbell appropriately remarks:

> Quick money, high profits were the only rationale for a life of exile in the tropics. Ironically to get the quick high profits of sugar cultivation Englishmen were willing to wait until they had accumulated some capital, by fair or foul means. . . . Planting coffee, cocoa, or cotton or breeding cattle on small sized farms was a way of life fit for free coloured creoles, resident in their native environment with no real hope of social mobility. These activities were not the business of English entrepreneurs. (1976:39)

12. As Campbell notes, however, the Colored population's slaveholdings greatly exceeded the 2,202 quoted in Table 3 because that figure does not reflect the number of slaves in units of less than five. In 1813 plantations that engaged fewer than five slaves accounted for one-third of the total plantations in the island; they concentrated on coffee, provisions, cocoa, and cotton, crops favored by Free Coloreds.

In the decades leading up to emancipation sugar production became closely allied to British capitalist and planter interests. As early as 1809 the British enterprises became large-scale and relatively heavily capitalized, supplanting all others, even those of the French Creoles, in the domain of sugar. For example, in that same year English planters produced 12.92 million pounds on 92 estates, while French planters produced 11.94 million pounds on 143 estates (Brereton 1981:47). Accordingly, sugar became increasingly identified with English Creoles, English merchants, and members of large metropole-based firms operating their estates through local agents. This group, and its representative planter class, was intent on economic development based on slave labor; the abolition of slavery in 1834 was for them premature. Lacking sufficient capital to mechanize sugar production, the planters needed some other continuous and dependable supply of labor power. Whereas planters in older British sugar colonies were beginning to feel the limitations of slave labor, those in Trinidad were just beginning to experience its advantages.

Labor Conditions, 1838–1845: Reactions to Emancipation

Emancipation caught various Caribbean planter groups in different postures and attitudes on the road to riches. For the large sugar planters emancipation augmented their problems concerning labor. Lacking sufficient capital, these planters were dependent on a reliable supply of labor to maintain their labor-intensive production units.[13] The end of slavery and apprenticeship in 1838[14] threatened the aspirations of Trinidad's planter class for attaining the heights of production and profit found earlier in Barbados and Jamaica. Accustomed to bonded labor, the planters could hardly envision the viability of sugar production without slaves.

Complete emancipation in 1838 called for a redefinition of labor relations throughout the British Caribbean.[15] Planters were now faced with the

13. Hereafter I use the term *planters* or *plantocracy* specifically to denote the dominant faction comprising mainly sugar planters of English origin. On the state of capital and labor during the 1830s, see Green 1976 and Munasinghe 1994:chap. 3.

14. The Emancipation Act of 1833 stipulated a period of six years of apprenticeship (later reduced to four) in which the ex-slaves remained bound to plantations in order to "ease" the transition, for planters and ex-slaves alike, to freedom.

15. There is a rich literature addressing from different viewpoints the alleged labor problem in the post-emancipation Caribbean. I note here only some key texts: E. Williams 1961, 1984; Drescher 1977; Engerman 1986, 1992; Hall 1978; Green 1976; Bolland 1981, 1984; Marshall 1991; McGlynn and Drescher 1992; Mintz 1979, 1992; and Trouillot 1984, 1989, and 1996.

problem of inducing free individuals to labor steadily, continuously, and cheaply on their former estates. Depending on the idiosyncrasies prevailing in each of the colonies, planters resorted to various strategies. Some adopted a long-term approach, seeking to sever their dependency on labor through technological improvements, but the majority avoided committing capital (Green 1976). Most preferred to curb the economic alternatives available to laborers and to increase the supply of labor through immigration. As Mintz (1979:215) writes, "Thus the reduction of economic alternatives available to the already existing labour supply, on the one hand, and the mechanical increase of that supply on the other, formed the two jaws of Caribbean plantation discipline, once slavery and apprenticeship had ended."

In Trinidad, post-emancipation developments were significantly shaped by the struggle between the planters, who "wanted to make freedom merely a nominal change in status," and the ex-slaves, who "wanted to win a real economic independence of the planter and his operations" (Brereton 1981:76). Trinidad's planters, like those in Guyana and to some extent Jamaica, ultimately used both "jaws" of discipline, that is, the reduction of economic alternatives and the mechanical increase of the labor supply through indenture.

Convinced that freedom meant their impending doom, planters in Trinidad explored the alternative of immigrant labor even before emancipation. Post-emancipation characterization of the labor force as "unreliable, inadequate, extensively mobile, lazy, free-spending and expensive" resonated with pre-emancipation fears.[16] Planters such as Burnley actively generated a specific discourse on the alleged labor situation in Trinidad to support their case for immigration, and the negative portrayal of ex-slaves was a pivotal focus within this discourse. Making a case for immigrants meant derogating the existing population. In time, many of the negative characterizations of the ex-slaves as well as planter caricatures of the anticipated immigrants became imputations of inherent characters and were used by these same groups to undermine each other. Thus the "Negro" carried the same prejudices and

---

16. Pre-emancipation planter fears of the undesirability of free labor were clearly expressed by Burnley and others when they mobilized in defense of slavery. White slave owners led by Burnley organized a committee to investigate the character of the Negro in 1825 with the sole purpose of " 'proving' how vicious and unreliable was free black labour. All the witnesses—and no coloured witnesses were called—testified that the negro slaves were dishonest, immoral, improvident, and of limited mental capacity. The master needed a strong hand to control his childish but potentially savage slaves. It was impossible to cultivate the estates by free black labour. The slaves were better off than free blacks; and slavery was in the interest of the blacks. One could not, it was said, 'infuse European feelings and ideas into African races'" (Campbell 1992:253).

contempt as the White man for the "coolie," as did the "coolie" for the "Negro."

In short, planters targeted the ex-slaves as the cause of their problem and emphasized contract immigrant labor as the only possible solution. Therefore, when East Indian indentured laborers began arriving in 1845, they were already labeled the "big sugar planters' solution."

Foretelling Ethnicity

Metropolitan and local authorities believed that the only worthwhile economic activity in the colonies was the efficient production of sugar. Planters representing big sugar interests were thus in a privileged position to determine the fate of the colony, and those who favored immigration had the authority and voice to create a particular representation of Trinidad, which became privileged as indisputable social and historical fact even before the East Indians came.[17] The interests that motivated this skewed vision were somehow omitted from the narrative. Indenture was primarily a sugar-oriented project and therefore was not equally appealing to all planters.[18] Accordingly, I focus on the discourse created by big sugar interests—largely, English Creoles and metropole-based firms operating their estates through local agents.

The complaints of the plantocracy were well articulated by William H. Burnley, Robert Bushe (a proprietor of sugar estates and attorney for other

17. Kale (1998) makes the persuasive argument that historians' reliance on primary sources (official documents) invariably reproduce planter and other colonial elite discourses as historical facts: "The conventions and standards of evidence that govern historians' constructions of arguments and narratives have contributed to enhancing the authority and value of these official sources. These methodological biases have also contributed to naturalizing the labor shortage that allegedly threatened British Caribbean sugar industries and the economies and societies that allegedly depended on them" (7).

18. Even though as slave owners they had interest in the retention of slavery, the Free Colored planter elites did not openly side with White planters in their defense of slavery. During the 1820s elite Free Coloreds were waging their own battle to win greater civil liberties and did not want to jeopardize their relations with the British government by joining with the White planters to resist amelioration (see Campbell 1992). In fact, many Free Coloreds who were later active in the Legislative Reform Committee (one of the earliest middle-class political organizations, formed in the 1850s) openly opposed Indian immigration and called for reforms that were antithetical to sugar interests. The reformers argued that immigration was an unjustified subsidy to the sugar industry and depressed the wages of free workers (Brereton 1981:143). See Look Lai 1993:chap. 6 for a discussion of Colored and Black elites' resistance to indenture.

estates), and R. H. Church (manager of two estates in Trinidad until 1841), who presented their case to the Select Committee of 1842.[19] Burnley was the proprietor of several estates, and Church was the manager of two estates whose combined acreage came to 668. The evidence they presented to the Stanley Committee regarding the labor problem and its appropriate solution augured the formalization of institutional and discursive mechanisms through which East Indian bonded immigrant labor was directly counterpoised to African free labor.

The problem these planters faced after apprenticeship ended was not absolute labor scarcity. What they lacked was a consistent, compliant, and reliable supply of labor.

Chairman: Has the supply of labour in Trinidad diminished considerably since the commencement of freedom?

Mr. Burnley: The supply of labour has diminished considerably amongst the original labourers on the estates; but very nearly, probably, to the exact amount, the deficiency has been supplied and filled up by immigration.[20] (Stanley Committee 1842:53)

Indeed, between 1840 and 1842 an estimated eight thousand West Africans (liberated from slave ships bound for the New World and then relocated to Sierra Leone and the island of St. Helena) were brought to Trinidad (Stanley Committee 1842:68).[21] Immigration from other West Indian islands and Africa readjusted the post-emancipation imbalance in the labor supply created by those slaves who refused to work on plantations as wage laborers

19. A commission of inquiry appointed in 1842 under the chairmanship of Lord Stanley "to inquire into the state of the different West India colonies, in reference to the existing relations between employers and labourers, the rate of wages, the supply of labour, the system and expense of cultivation, and the general state of their rural and agricultural economy" (Great Britain, Parliamentary Papers, Select Committee on West India Colonies, 1842 [479], XIII). Hereafter this document is referred to as the Stanley Committee 1842.

20. Immigrants from the eastern Caribbean had been flooding into Trinidad because of the relatively high wages and abundance of land. This practice was actively encouraged by the planters even though authorities of other islands objected, and in November 1838 the planters introduced a resolution that rewarded recruiting agents with a bounty for every immigrant they introduced. Between 1839 and 1849 approximately 10,278 West Indians came to Trinidad (Brereton 1981:96). See also Look Lai 1993:13–18.

21. The estimate of eight thousand immigrants for 1840–42 appears high. Brereton's data in contrast show that for 1841–61 only 3,383 immigrants came from Sierra Leone and another 3,198 came from St. Helena (1981:98). Look Lai (1993:15) cites 8,854 immigrants from Africa for 1834–67.

and who found employment elsewhere.[22] If the number of laborers had been sustained by this influx of immigrants, why were the planters claiming that it was impossible to maintain cultivation at pre-emancipation levels? The issue was, in part, one of control rather than sheer supply and demand. According to Bushe, pre-emancipation production levels could not be maintained after emancipation because now laborers worked only nine hours a day, four times a week, during crop time, as opposed to the sixteen to eighteen hours of labor slaves had provided six days a week. Thus on Bushe's calculations the labor supplied by a slave amounted to almost three times that of a free laborer.

The new migrants were not bound by contract to a particular planter. By law (the Stephen Code of 1838), any contract made outside Trinidad became inoperative the moment the individual entered the island (Look Lai 1993:53). This was indeed a pleasant welcome for those immigrants from Sierra Leone and the neighboring smaller islands because once they arrived in Trinidad, the labor demand made it possible for them to negotiate better terms of employment. In want of legal leverage, planters were therefore compelled at first to offer high wages and field assignments based on task work in order to lure these new immigrants. Planters' testimony that relatively high wages prevailed in Trinidad is corroborated by other evidence (Brereton 1981:78; Look Lai 1993:7–8). The daily wage for field labor in Trinidad in the 1840s remained around 50 cents, in comparison with 48 cents in British Guiana, 42 cents in Jamaica, 30 cents in Barbados, and 12 cents in Montserrat, the lowest daily wage (Look Lai 1993:7–8).

In order to drive down wages, planters insisted on contracts, which suggests that what they desired was not a labor market determined by supply and demand but rather a bound labor force. The former slaves, now aware of the privileges associated with their newly acquired status, apparently refused to sign labor contracts. The fact that many ex-slaves entered into written agreements when they purchased land suggests that ex-slaves were not averse to contracts in general but only to those they perceived as inherently unfair, particularly those that bound them to work for much lower wages than the highest prevailing rates. The frustration that these practices caused the planter class is neatly captured in the following exchange:

Chairman: Do the labourers generally object to enter into written agreements?
Mr. Burnley: They invariably object. . . . On the part of the proprietors, we are

22. Despite the absence of concrete data, the general opinion of the surveyor general around 1841 was that, of the approximately twenty thousand efficient working slaves at the time of emancipation, one-third may have retired from estate labor but that this loss was compensated by the influx of eight to ten thousand immigrants (Stanley Committee 1842:74).

most anxious that they should enter into contracts, because we are satisfied that there can be no steady or profitable cultivation until they are established; but I do not think there has been any attempt made by the Government to induce the labourers to enter into contracts; on the contrary, I think the practice that has been pursued by the colonial authorities has rather deterred the labourers from so doing.[23] (Stanley Committee 1842:43)

Burnley's plea to the colonial authorities to make contracts compulsory is clearly an attempt to swing judicial privileges to the side of the plantocracy. Although his interest is purely economic, he cleverly appeals to the humanitarian spirit of this era and provides an additional moral rationalization. Essentially, the legitimizing ground for exploitation had shifted. This meant a shift in vocabulary as well as in ideology per se. Burnley is pushed to argue that compulsory contracts would be advantageous to the prospective laborers in the long run:

Viscount Howick: Should you not apprehend that if contracts were allowed to be entered into out of the island, they would be frequently entered into with labourers quite ignorant of the rate of wages?
Mr. Burnley: I think that probable. . . . But, under the present system, if it is intended to be for the benefit of the labourers, the public officers either go too far or they do not go far enough. In the first instance, a contract entered into, whatever may be the nature of it, whether good or bad, is vitiated and rendered null and void. If this is done solely for the benefit of the negroes, why, after annulling the contract, which may be a good one, should not the same care and attention be paid so that the next contract the negro makes is a fair . . . one? But no attention is paid to that. . . . What is the consequence? The vessel is always surrounded by a number of negro crimps, every one of whom is paid 20s. a head for engaging labourers for the service of individual parties; no written contract is then entered into; it is merely a verbal one; and I am satisfied that under those circumstances the ignorant immigrants who arrive in the island make a variety of engagements which in the result are infinitely more disadvantageous to them than if they were allowed to make contracts out of the island, which might subsequently be examined, and rejected or confirmed by a board in the colony. (Stanley Committee 1842:61).

Burnley is quite aware that the planters will be unable to persuade the laborers in Trinidad to enter into contracts paying wages that are lower than

23. Burnley is referring here to the Stephen Code, which annulled existing contracts as soon as migrants arrived in Trinidad.

the existing rates. Contrary to what he is saying, it is exactly the ignorance of the immigrants that he is counting on. It is they, unaware of the wage rate in Trinidad, who can be manipulated into entering these written agreements. The British representatives, in turn, appear to be quite aware of this manipulation.

> *Mr. Stuart*: Is it not better to let him [the immigrant], upon his arrival in the island, make an agreement than to let him enter upon terms previously to his arrival, when he is perfectly ignorant of the state of affairs in the country? (Stanley Committee 1842:62)

In response, Burnley argues that the present system is disadvantageous to the workers and that contracts will ensure the protection of vulnerable immigrants by holding the plantation owner responsible for their welfare.

After this exchange the committee and Burnley explore other means by which the planter class might regain control over labor power. Alternatives suggested by both sides, such as a system of monitoring labor mobility, the implementation of rents, and limiting access to land, conform to what Trouillot has labeled "preventive tactics" in his discussion of Dominica:

> The measures taken to contain the existing estate labor force were of two kinds: those of a quasi-totalitarian nature, aimed at maintaining by force as many laborers as possible on the plantation, along the model perfected during Apprenticeship itself; and those that tried to contain that labor supply by reducing the economic options available to the former slaves. The latter measures were geared at limiting the laborers' access to (or gains from) productive resources, especially land. (1988:104)[24]

In addition to these preventive tactics, planters discussed "co-optative tactics" such as raising import taxes (on products largely consumed by the masses) and "defensive tactics" (Trouillot 1988:104), namely, the supplementation of the labor supply through immigration.

---

24. Trouillot justifies the term *preventive* for the case of Dominica on the basis that these measures were intended to prevent the spread of the peasant labor process on and off the estates. In the case of Trinidad, however, evidence for a burgeoning peasantry during this time is somewhat scarce and planter characterizations point to the contrary, that is, a retardation of provision ground cultivation. Nevertheless, Trouillot's framework is still applicable if we understand the struggle over the containment of the peasant labor process as an instance of the larger struggle over the control over labor power. See also Bolland 1981 and 1984. Of course, planter strategies to control the labor of slaves and ex-slaves were always in anticipation of or reaction to the resistance of these subordinate groups (see Mintz 1978, 1979).

The significance of these measures comes to light against the background of the alleged lifestyle of the majority of the population, the emancipated slaves and unbound immigrants. In essence, the planters were compelled to portray a lifestyle that supported their grievances and legitimized their solution to the labor problem, immigration by contract. They also could not appear too distanced from the humanitarian concerns then gaining currency in Britain and so sought refuge in a moral discourse.[25] They claimed that the injection of a new labor force would create competition among labor and would ultimately benefit the existing labor force by improving their "moral character." To legitimate this assertion they had first to prove moral degeneration, an especially challenging task since recent reports from the stipendiary magistrates unanimously attested to the general improvement in the disposition of the peasantry with freedom (Great Britain, Parliamentary Papers, Papers Relative to the West Indies, 1841–42 [379], XXIX, 55–59).[26] Representing the larger planters, Burnley rose to the challenge, tirelessly attempting to sway opinion, first by undermining the authority of contrary witnesses and second by carefully selecting his own evidence.

Chairman: What is your opinion as to the moral improvement of the rising generation . . . ?

Mr. Burnley: I am of opinion that the rising generation, instead of getting better and improving, are deteriorating in their morals every day. I observe that in the report of the Colonial Land and Emigration Commissioners . . . (upon Trinidad evidence), they have taken up a contrary opinion. It is from my own inquiries and observation in the island that I judge. I am, therefore, glad to have an opportunity of stating to the Committee my reasons for forming a different opinion. It appears that they have relied entirely upon the opinions given by the clergymen, and paid little or no attention to that of the planters. Now I am certainly of opinion that the opinions of the clergymen are not exclusively to be relied upon, for it is a very invidious task for any gentleman to speak unfavourably of his flock. On questioning them . . . I found . . . they could give no reason for their opinion, except that marriages were much more

25. In 1838 the London Merchants' Association argued for immigration from India by claiming it would help abolish slavery throughout the world: "The promoting and encouraging of free emigration to the British West India colonies, would tend materially to the successful working of the free labour system; and would in time render Great Britain independent of foreign slave countries for all tropical productions, and ultimately be the means of putting down the slave trade, and abolishing slavery throughout the world" (in Kale 1998:54).

26. See also Kale's analyses of Governor Light's refutation of such planter representations in the case of British Guiana (1998:chap. 3) and the arguments put forward by antislavery groups in Britain, which also sought to undermine negative portrayals of the newly freed population (1998:chap. 4). Sewell (1968:108) arrives at similar conclusions for the case of Trinidad.

frequent . . . and that the attendance at church was much more regular . . .
both of which I know to be perfectly correct. But I do not think mere attendance at church, and an increased number of marriage ceremonies, constitute
a sufficient test by which you are to judge of the civilization and moral improvement of the labouring population. In looking at their evidence, when they
were questioned more particularly, the Committee will observe that it is not so
favourable as in general terms they express their opinions. (Stanley Committee
1842:57)

In his testimony Burnley repeatedly sought to correlate moral degeneracy with excessive mobility and the decline of provision ground cultivation.
The planters' desire for a settled, docile, secure, and bonded labor force
depended on portraying members of the existing labor force as extensively
mobile and independent, working when they needed money, not keeping to
any contracts, and leaving whenever they felt they could find better conditions:

Mr. Stuart: But you can form no idea of the amount of annual immigration
which is necessary to produce that result [competition among laborers that will
drive wages down]?
Mr. Burnley: I should be very much afraid of giving any positive opinion on a
subject which depends so much upon a variety of other circumstances. If Government will make such regulations as will be necessary, a smaller amount will
answer; but if the additional population when introduced, are to be allowed, as
they are at the present moment, to wander about throughout the island, without question or control, it will take a greater number; but with proper regulations and restrictions, a smaller number will suffice. (Stanley Committee
1842:70)

In contrast to Burnley's depiction, the ex-slaves appear very anxious to become settled, because they were known to pay exorbitant sums for small al-
lotments of land. All the stipendiary magistrates' reports attest to the phenomenal increase in the number of freeholders and the rise of hamlets and
villages. Accordingly, when Lord Stanley suggested that a better way to encourage "settled habits" might be to give ex-slaves security and interest in the
soil by making land more accessible in the form of leases, Burnley responded
feebly by arguing that Negroes were too ignorant to understand the intricacies pertaining to leases and that their generally distrustful nature would prevent them from signing any document that would legalize such transactions
(Stanley Committee 1842:71–72).

The glaring inconsistency of arguing both for the implementation of labor contracts for "ignorant immigrants" on the one hand and for the futility of lease contracts for "ignorant Negroes" on the other was not an issue for Burnley. *Ignorance* conveyed quite specific images of each group. The immigrants' ignorance boiled down to their vulnerability as cultural aliens. The ignorance of the Negro, in contrast, alluded to an imputed mental deficiency. Such representations prefigured future descriptions and debates concerning the "shrewd" yet "vulnerable" East Indian and the "Western-oriented" yet "childlike" Creole.

On numerous occasions planters used their alleged knowledge of the "negro mentality" to derail any economic alternatives that proved beneficial to the laborers. Douglas Hall (1978) provides a fitting example. In colonies such as St. Lucia, St. Vincent, and Grenada better labor relations were said to prevail because of the system of sharecropping. When such an alternative was suggested for Jamaica, Mr. McCook, an attorney, replied: "The negroes of this country are too independent to wait for remuneration of their labour by any interest in the proceeds of the soil, and their minds are by no means yet settled down. So long as they have the waste lands to cultivate, they will only work for the estates when they please" (Hall 1978:22–23). Similarly, when sharecropping was suggested to Burnley as an alternative for Trinidad, he immediately rejected it on the grounds that planters' interests would be compromised because the laborers would want to cut their own cane and not the planters' during the most profitable portion of the season. More interesting, however, is his McCook type of explanation:

> *Mr. Burnley:* The experiment was tried by one gentleman, with the best intentions, and in a persevering way. The land was taken by a company of Americans, the best working people we have in the island, but it was found that they were enticed away to work at daily wages by the adjoining estates. They alleged, "We cannot work for you, because we have got our own canes and our own crop to attend to." That was met by the reply, "You can weed your own canes to-morrow; here are a few dollars, this is a little job, do come and do it." There was a distant profit in perspective, and an offer of cash in hand, and the result was that they neglected their canes so much that they did not ripen in time. (Stanley Committee 1842:49)

Once again, the planters' alleged authority on the natural disposition of the Negroes was used to curtail the realization of those practices that ex-slaves found truly liberating. This type of maneuvering, so typical during the postemancipation period, is particularly revealing as an example of the hindrances that served to prevent the realization of what Mintz (1992:253) has called the "slaves' vision of the meaning of freedom." According to Hall, "it was the McCooks of the post-emancipation period whose attitudes led to the exodus from the plantations" (1978:23).

In Trinidad, as in many other colonies, the behavior of ex-slaves was troublesome not only to planters but also to others who had less selfish motives, such as the abolitionists and the missionaries. Their fear of the ex-slaves' possible lapse back into "their natural state" provided an ideal point of attack for those desiring bonded labor. Variations on Thomas Carlyle's depiction of the ex-slave gorging himself idly on ripe pumpkins (Mintz 1992:246) were frequently repeated in Trinidad. Burnley and his ilk blamed the prevalent high wage rates for this purported "idle and immoral" behavior, but Mintz is careful to remind us that the disappointments of freedom must be constantly assessed against the fact that "all of the work that freed people did, they had to do within systems that only grudgingly took account of the fact of freedom" (1992:249).

High wages, planters argued, not only encouraged mobility but also inhibited hard work. Economic power allowed Trinidadian wage laborers to enjoy a greater degree of mobility and independence than those in other colonies. According to Burnley, the laborers had to accomplish only two tasks (roughly one day's labor) per week in order to maintain the standard of living they endured during slavery.

Viscount Howick: The labourer lives in much more comfort than he did during slavery, does he not?

Mr. Burnley: There can be no comparison. The labourer is in a better state as to comfort, and luxuries of every description, than in any other part of the world, or than ever existed in any part of the world; for it can only arise from such an artificial state of things, as had been produced by emancipation.

Viscount Howick: By how many hours' labour in the week do you conceive that a labourer can now obtain the same command of the necessaries and comforts of life which he possessed as a slave?

Mr. Burnley: I should suppose one day a week. . . .

Mr. Howard: Is there a great desire on the part of the negroes to obtain foreign luxuries?

Mr. Burnley: A very great desire, indeed; I do not know any race of people who possess it more.

Mr. Hawes: What is the average day of labour that the labourers now give?

Mr. Burnley: I do not think myself, upon the average of the whole number residing upon the estates, that it can be more than three or four tasks a week, which cannot be calculated at more than two days of labour. (Stanley Committee 1842:49)

Though one can disagree with Burnley's explanation that laborers worked just enough to assuage their natural thirst for luxuries, it is possible that laborers exercised their option not to work regularly. Thus in contrast to the pattern observed in other islands during the immediate post-emancipation period, in Trinidad high wages seem to have discouraged provision ground cultivation,[27] and the laboring classes purchased imported essentials as well as luxuries from the Spanish Main (Munasinghe 1994:chap. 3). The huge increase in colonial revenue from import duties seems to support this hypothesis. Between 1832 and 1840, import duties increased from £4,096 to £11,443 (Stanley Committee 1842:78). Even though taxes probably accounted for a substantial portion of this revenue, Burnley claims that trade with the mainland increased tremendously in those crops previously cultivated by the slaves:

> But the fact is, that the island cultivation of provisions, such as the negroes carried on formerly, is reduced to such an insufficient amount, that the trade with the Spanish Main, in those articles, has doubled or trebled in consequence of the demand, so that the island is now fed by plantains, poultry, pigs, and other provisions brought from the Spanish continent, to a great degree. (Stanley Committee 1842:70)

Burnley's testimony is confirmed by the harbor master, Rowley Hill Stewart, who is directly responsible for checking the cargo from Spanish launches:

> *Committee*: Has the trade with the Spanish Main increased at all since 1834?
> *Mr. Stewart*: So far as appears by my books, the trade has generally increased since that period.
> *Committee*: You think the amount of the trade is increasing generally; but has there been any great variation in any particular branch of it?
> *Mr. Stewart*: In one branch, that of imported vegetables and provisions, the increase has been great within the last few years, and particularly so from the end of 1838 until the present period [1841]. For instance the quantity of plantains imported in 1825 . . . amounted only to 159,700; in 1835 it increased to 2,026,700; and in 1840 to [approximately 4,100,000]. Hogs during the same period have increased from 1095 to 4,913. Fowls from 86 dozens to 860 dozens. Turkeys from 87 to 1,081 pair. The import of dried peas, goats, eggs and other

27. Provision grounds decreased from 16,004 acres in 1832 to 6,313 in 1841 (Great Britain, Parliamentary Papers, Papers Relative to the West Indies, 1841–42 [379], 94).

minor articles, have all increased in about the same proportion; and the number of horned cattle which was only 734 in 1835 amounted in 1840 to 4,320. . . .
Committee: To what do you ascribe this immense increase of imported provisions?
Mr. Stewart: Partly to the increase in population, but chiefly to the circumstance of the cultivation of provisions being latterly less attended to by the labouring population, *who, from the high wages given, find it easier to buy than to raise them.* Port of Spain, which was formerly supplied from estates in the island, is now in a great degree fed by imported provisions; and I know as a fact that the town of San Fernando which formerly received its supplies of vegetables and provisions from the neighbouring districts, is now not only furnished from abroad, *but the labourers from the estates in the interior come into town to supply themselves.* (Great Britain, Parliamentary Papers, Papers Relative to the West Indies, Minutes of Evidence taken by the Sub-Committee of the Agricultural and Immigration Society, 1841–42 (379) XXIX:101; emphasis added)

This apparently incongruous practice on the part of the Trinidadian labor force vis-à-vis the rest of the region needs to be seriously considered even if it defies our dominant assumption regarding the freed people's commitment to land and cultivation. High wages gave the laboring population of Trinidad the choice, not readily available in other colonies, of working or not within systems that still circumscribed their freedoms.

To regain control over labor, the planters had either to decrease wages, directly or indirectly, so that the laborers would be forced to work longer hours to maintain previous standards of living, or add a new labor supply to force wages down. In the process of convincing the British government that immigration was indeed the most obvious solution, the planters created a particular discourse. From their perspective, factors such as the mobility of the laboring population, the decrease in the cultivation of provisions, and the increase in the revenue on import duties were integral building blocks of such a discourse. Consequently, all these alleged ills were blamed by Burnley on the "artificially high wage rates." To have argued otherwise for any one component would have undermined the overall logic of the case they were building. For example, the alleged aversion to cultivation and the incessant desire of the ex-slaves for luxury goods not only supported the planters' claim regarding the ex-slaves' excessive mobility and the over-high wage rates but also constituted a moral statement that they thought would appeal to the Select Committee.

The propositions contained in the Select Committee papers reveal the germination of several strategies to be employed later in combating the newly acquired independence of the former slaves. Trinidad, still governed by planter and metropolitan interests, was not prepared to emancipate the majority of its oppressed. As Raphael Sebastien argues, what Trinidad lacked was the emergence of an industrial reserve army, "the creation of [which] . . . is an objective aspect of the dynamic of capitalist expansion" (1978:210). The function of this reserve army essentially is to minimize wages and thus to facilitate capital accumulation:

> The importance of the industrial reserve army to the capitalist is the role it plays in weighing the scale of supply and demand for labor in favor of capital. It is the mechanism whereby capital implements and maintains its minimum wage schedule; the industrial reserve army is what nails the deal between capital and labor in favor of the capitalist. If one did not exist, then he would have to invent it. This was precisely the path resorted to by capital after emancipation. (Sebastien 1978:213)

The planters' interests finally triumphed on July 25, 1842, when a House of Commons committee on the West Indian colonies arrived at the resolution that "one obvious and most desirable mode of endeavoring to compensate for this diminished supply of labor, is to promote the immigration of a fresh laboring population, to such an extent as to create competition for employment" (E. Williams 1982:93, 94).[28] Alternative sources of labor came from North America, the Portuguese islands of Azores and Madeira, and China; liberated Africans from foreign slave ships also contributed to this supply (Ching 1985:207; E. Williams 1982:97; Look Lai 1993). Yet none of these experiments proved to be a success; the immigrants abandoned agriculture and joined the service sector at the first opportunity. The planters' wishes were ultimately fulfilled only with the arrival of indentured labor from India. With this victory the big sugar planters set the tone for future relations between Afro-Trinidadians and Indo-Trinidadians.

The position the East Indians were destined to occupy was inherently antagonistic to that of the Black laboring population.[29] Indeed, it was stated explicitly that the role of the new immigrants was to induce labor competition. The mechanical increase of the labor supply through East Indian indenture crushed the hopes of the ex-slaves and ended the modest privileges they had enjoyed at the end of apprenticeship; agricultural wages, for example, dropped to 30 cents during 1846 alone. The discourses created by sugar in-

28. As Parliament itself was full of members who owned estates in the West Indies, the committee's decision to support the planters is hardly surprising.
29. See Brereton 1974.

terests, in turn, set the ideological frame for structural antagonisms between the two ethnic groups even before their initial contact.

The planters' grounds for legitimizing contract labor rested on a character assault on "the Negro." Those very traits of "Negro mentality," selected by planters such as Burnley, served to forge a stereotype of the Negro or of Creoles in Trinidad as free-spending, luxury loving, and improvident, in contrast to the industrious, diligent, self-sacrificing East Indian. Even more powerful were the planters' assertions regarding Negro aversions to cultivation. The testimony offered by the planters constituted not so much objective assessments of the labor situation in Trinidad as powerful ideological statements, creating a climate of hostility for the two major groups assigned to the bottom rungs of the social, political, and economic hierarchy of colonial Trinidad. Thus when East Indians entered Trinidad, a discourse deriding the moral, mental, and physical attributes of the Negro was already in place for Indians to learn, and later to use, for their own ends.

Of all the alternatives presented to the British government, the entry of Indian indentured laborers into Trinidad in 1845 was clearly the most detrimental to the independent Black labor force. Little was done by the Colonial Office to improve the condition of the emancipated slaves. Although the colonial authorities and some foreign commentators noted the general "improvement" in the "character" of the Negro with emancipation, others more sympathetic to the ex-slaves' predicament feared the deleterious consequences of their neglect by society. Yet these anxieties rested on stereotypes fostered by the planters: "The important matter of immigration is beginning to be settled. The solution seems to have been found, on condition that no account is taken of the former slaves and their descendants, who, left to themselves, without the paternal solicitude of their former masters, are relapsing into barbarism" (Jules Duval, 1859, in E. Williams 1982:95).

The coming of migrants affected the ex-slave population more adversely than their mere abandonment. It not only deflated wages but also diminished job opportunities for Black laborers. The subsequent expansion in sugar production also served to dislodge members of the former labor force from the land they squatted on. Hence the Black labor force came to see the Indians as "scab" labor who had significantly reduced the Blacks' bargaining power with the planters.

The financing of the indenture system was another major point of contention. Two-thirds of the costs were borne by an export duty on commodities such as cocoa, which did not depend on indentured labor. The remaining third was financed by taxpayers in the form of public revenue. This measure was justified on the grounds that Indian immigration benefited the whole community, not just the planters (Brereton 1985:22). Yet the rest of the community did not see these benefits, and this caused unremitting bitter protest from Colored and Black leaders (Brereton 1979; Look Lai 1993), who argued that "the black worker was in fact subsidizing an influx of laborers who were being deliberately brought in to depress wages thereby forcing the African to accept the artificially low wage rate or migrate to other places" (Samaroo 1985:79). According to Brinsley Samaroo, the Black population vented its frustration not so much on the creators of the scheme "but on the visible symbol—the East Indians. The result was a festering antagonism which manifested itself in bitter mutual condemnation between blacks and East Indians" (Samaroo 1985:79). Walton Look Lai (1993) also notes the complicity of Black and Colored leaders in the production of negative caricatures of East Indians.

Though the plight of the indentured laborers resembled that of the Black masses under slavery, at least in terms of the harshness of the system and its dehumanizing effects, it kindled little sympathy among the Creoles (Blacks and Coloreds). The fact that these "heathen coolies" voluntarily chose to engage in work that slaves had performed under coercion only served to foster the contempt of the Creole masses for the East Indians. The Indian was considered a different being by Whites and Creoles alike—a being satisfied with living conditions that other humans found deplorable. Kelvin Singh (1985:36) writes: "The fact that they [East Indians] entered the society as unskilled laborers, bound to the plantations during their indentureship, caused them to be regarded as semi-slaves, people nearest the condition that Negroes had recently emerged from and heartily despised. This contempt was reinforced by the picture often painted by planters and officials of Indians being contented with their working and living conditions." The Protector of Immigrants argued against introducing immigrants from Tenerife on the following basis: "It must be remembered they are very different to the East Indian, who is generally accustomed to greater heat in his own country, where he is only too pleased to work all day (not the seven or eight hours he works here) for eight to ten cents a day . . . the East Indian requires little of the former [i.e., clothes], and . . . [is] known to do a hard day's work on a pound of cold boiled rice. Could the Tenerife people live like this? Again I think not" (in Singh 1985:36). This stereotype of the Indian as an inferior human being who would accept conditions of life that other races would reject prompted the *Mirror* to observe in July 1901 "that agricultural labor in Trinidad was not attractive to those people who have got beyond the stage of civilization that is satisfied with a loin cloth and a pot of rice" (in Singh 1985:36).

The bonded status of the new immigrants fostered an image of the East Indian as both docile and industrious. Their cultural alienness made them more vulnerable to the dictates of the planters. Here at last was a compliant, hardworking labor force bound by contract and with little recourse to flight. As Kusha Haraksingh comments:

> As immigrant workers, the Indians belonged to a category of labor which is generally easier to control than local labor, for it is less secure, less confident of itself and in instances of confrontation easily finds itself facing the weight, if not the wrath, of other social groups. . . . The less pronounced the [cultural] similarity [between the immigrants and the host population] the more effective is the physical uprooting itself as a weapon in the arsenal of control. In the case of immigrant Indians in the Caribbean, the degree of similarity was minimal. (1985:156)

Thus East Indian dispositions that were largely determined by the institutional basis of indenture rapidly became translated into innate "Indian characteristics" of docility and subservience.

Many of the stereotypes of Creoles and East Indians that were propagated primarily by the plantocracy in the immediate aftermath of slavery were selectively internalized and used later by both Creoles and East Indians for their own purposes. For example, the voluntary aspect of indenture served as a marker of East Indian inferiority during the early period of indenture, but today Indo-Trinidadians use this same characteristic, differently labeled, as an indication of their superiority to the Black race. Many Indo-Trinidadians take pride in reminding themselves and others that they, unlike their Black brethren, came to the island not in shackles but as free men and women. The contemporary Indo-Trinidadian effort to redefine the nation and national culture invariably involves a reinterpretation of historical events. Discourse by its nature carries the potential for the reutilization of identical formulas for contrary objectives (Foucault 1980). As we shall see, the events described here and the planters' discourse in particular have figured prominently in the struggle between Afro-Trinidadians and Indo-Trinidadians to claim the nation-state of Trinidad.[30]

---

30. In his comparative study of Guyana and Trinidad, Malcolm Cross (1972, 1996) argues that the more intense struggle for scarce economic resources in Guyana during the colonial period caused relations between Creoles and East Indians to be more "confrontational" there than in Trinidad.

[4]

Situating Ethnicity: East Indians against the Nation

Migration and Indenture

On May 30, 1845, the *Fatel Rozack* arrived in Trinidad with the first Indian immigrants: 225 men, women, and children. Except for a brief period between 1848 and 1852 when emigration was suspended,[1] labor continued to be supplied by India until indenture was abolished in 1917.[2] Approximately 143,939 East Indians came to Trinidad during the indenture years (Ching 1985:217), with the number of male recruits consistently outpacing that of females.[3]

For the British colonial authorities India was a suitable source of labor. India's population was vast, the majority accustomed to agricultural labor

1. Some (de Verteuil 1989:6 and Ramesar 1994:13) argue that financial constraints in Trinidad led to the suspension of emigration during this period whereas others (Kirpalani et al. 1945:33) claim that the government of India suspended emigration owing to excessive mortality rates incurred during the voyage and the period of acclimatization.

2. Despite continuous opposition to indenture by certain groups in the colonies, the system was ultimately abolished because of Indian nationalists' agitation. See Look Lai 1993:chap. 6, Ramesar 1994:chap. 5, and Kale 1998:chap. 7.

3. The recruitment of females posed a persistent problem for the instigators of indenture. The required proportion of females was a highly contested issue among planters, the Colonial Office, and the government of India and varied through the years. As Reddock notes, "These changes reflected the difficulties and contradictions in recruiting *more* women at the same time as recruiting 'the right kind of women'" (1994:29). For a gendered analysis of indenture, see Reddock 1994 and 1986 and Niranjana 1997.

under tropical conditions, and because the country was under British control there was no need for negotiations with foreign authorities. The motivations of colonial authorities and West Indian planters for introducing immigrant labor are clear. Let us now turn to the immigrants and to factors that prompted those brave individuals to cross the "black waters" (*kala pani*) and seek their fortunes elsewhere.[4]

Conditions were indeed grim for the majority of the population in nine-teenth-century India. Most people were landless and at the mercy of land-lords and moneylenders (de Verteuil 1989). Famine and disease posed a con-stant threat to life and livelihood, and for many there was little or no opportunity to improve their general condition.[5] This dismal situation was ex-acerbated by the encroachment of the British East India Company and its strategy of playing off one petty ruler against another. By 1856 the company had extended its rule over most of India and brought insecurity to both the landless masses and the traditional Indian aristocracy. For example, between 1852 and 1857 more than twenty thousand estates were confiscated on grounds of improper title (de Verteuil 1989:3–4). When some Indians finally rebelled against the incursions of the company (as in the famous Indian mutiny of 1857), the British government had an excuse to seize control of all India in 1858. The mutiny was harshly suppressed, and many fled the dire punishments that ensued: execution, imprisonment, and confiscation of property. Others left India for personal reasons. Widows wishing to avoid the curtailment of their freedom by Hindu prescription, petty criminals escaping punishment, and most significant, low-caste Indians who wanted to break away from the rigid caste system also looked to distant lands in search of a better life. As Madhavi Kale notes, "Represented both as victims and as ra-tional maximizers of opportunity throughout the history of indentured emi-gration, Indian indentured emigrants probably included fair shares of both" (1998:136).

When Indian immigration to British Guiana began in 1838 at the initiative of John Gladstone, an absentee proprietor and the father of William Glad-stone, it took the form of a privately conducted enterprise. Public opinion in England, however, propelled by antislavery proponents, forced the imperial government to suspend what many believed to be a "new system of slavery"

4. For more comprehensive analyses of indenture, see Kale 1998, Ramesar 1994, Look Lai 1993, Tinker 1974, Weller 1968, and Mangru 1993. Most of these studies also include British Guiana.

5. On the factors that drove many Indians to destitution during this period, see Vertovec 1992:6–13, Look Lai 1993:chap. 2, Kale 1998:chap. 6, and Ramesar 1994:1–3.

that same year.[6] Numerous humanitarian societies protested to the Colonial Office against the actions of Gladstone and others like him. These protests not only highlighted the plight of the Coolies but also emphasized the detrimental consequences of Coolie migration for the newly emancipated slaves. A petition forwarded by the citizens of Glasgow characterized Coolie migration "as being not only a virtual revival of the Slave Traffic, but the infliction of deep injury on the negroes; in as much as it declaredly proceeds on the principle, that those still more wretched Hindoos will underbid them in the competition for labor. Is this, my Lord, their remuneration for their toils and sufferings, that so soon as they are emancipated from slavery they are delivered over to starvation by being denied an opportunity of working for their bread?" (in Erickson 1934:132–33).

The emigration of indentured Indians was suspended for six years before the newly elected conservative government in Britain and the new colonial secretary, Lord Stanley, renewed it in 1844. Britain had begun to reorient its protectionist policy regarding West Indian sugar toward free trade, which was expected to cause severe economic dislocation in the West Indian colonies.[7] The Colonial Office hoped to offset some of the ill effects by providing the planters with an adequate and cheap supply of labor, hence the decision to revive Indian emigration. Although many Indians fell prey to the unscrupulous tactics of *arkhatiyas* (recruiters), most willingly indentured themselves: with continued employment uncertain even at 6 cents a day for the average laborer in India, the offered wage of 25 cents per day in Trinidad seemed like a fortune (de Verteuil 1989). After 1870 the possibility of acquiring land in lieu of return passage was an added incentive for migration. The handsome annual remittances sent by some Indian emigrants to India (de Verteuil 1989:5) and the testimony of "returnees" (who often went back to the West Indies either by reindenturing themselves or by paying for their passage) may also have played a role in winning recruits.

The vast majority of Indians who settled in Trinidad came from the densely populated central plain of the Ganges—the United Provinces, Oudh, Bihar, and Orissa. Since they embarked from Calcutta, they came to be known as *Kalkatiyas* (Jha 1985:1). They were by no means a homogeneous

6. Erickson (1934:132) argues that it was opposition to the principle of Coolie emigration rather than the disclosure of abuses to the Coolies that caused the practice to be suspended in 1838, because excessive mortality rates among Coolies did not occur until the following year. See Kale 1998:chap. 1 on the Gladstone experiment.

7. The Sugar Duties Act of 1846, which ended the preferential treatment for West India sugar in the British market, meant that West Indian planters had to face the consequences of free trade (Look Lai 1993:10).

group, however: there were religious differences among Hindus, Muslims and Christians;[8] there were caste distinctions; and there were linguistic distinctions[9] and regional differences. Some South Indians, 9,133 in all, also arrived in Trinidad as indentured laborers (de Verteuil 1989:206). They embarked from Madras and henceforth came to be known as *Madrasis,* despite distinctions of language, caste, and point of origin. The Madrasis were thought to be troublesome and less industrious than the Kalkatiyas, and as a result the planters discouraged any further recruitment from the south (Look Lai 1993:110).

Although popular opinion in Trinidad claims that most immigrants belonged to the lower castes, the academic community continues to debate this issue. Between 1876 and 1885 the Hindu immigrants had the following caste derivations: Brahmin and other high castes, 18 percent; artisan castes, 8.5 percent; agricultural castes, 32 percent; and low castes, 41 percent (Wood 1968:144–45). Although such figures tend to substantiate the hypothesis that the majority of immigrants were low-caste members fleeing the grip of the upper castes (Ching 1985:209; Jha 1985:10; de Verteuil 1989:5), historians such as Brereton caution against the accuracy of such records. Brereton (1985) argues that since high castes were far outnumbered by low castes in India, the caste composition of arrivals in Trinidad broadly reflected the Indian situation. Brereton also questions the reliability of the sources that recorded castes. Numerous errors were made because of the ignorance of the registrar and also because immigrants sometimes misreported their castes so they could start afresh in their new place of residence. Recruiters, under the advice of their superiors, actively sought persons belonging to the agricultural castes because they believed them to be better suited to the demands of plantation labor. Many immigrants, even Brahmins, claimed agricultural caste status in the hope of increasing their chances of being selected.

Departing from conventional academic thinking that emphasizes the cultural commonalities of the original Indian migrants, Steven Vertovec (1992) is among the few scholars who argue that they were a heterogeneous group. Their cultural practices and beliefs varied considerably, not only among provinces but also within the districts and villages of their origin. It is in

8. According to Jha (1985:5), there is substantial evidence that some Christians also came to Trinidad, especially from the Malabar coast.

9. The majority of Indians spoke Hindi and its dialects of Uttar Pradesh (Awadhi [Eastern U.P.], Vrajbhasha [Western U.P.]), and Bihar [Bhojpuri]. Jha writes, however, "It is true that Magahi of Patna, Gaya and North Hazaribagh districts of Bihar, Maithili of North Bihar, Bengali of Bengal, Oriya of Orissa, Assamese of Assam, the tribal languages of the Mundas and Oraons of Chota-Nagpur, Tamil of Madras, Telugu of Andhra Pradesh, Malayalam of Kerala and a few other Indian languages were also brought to Trinidad" (1985:14).

Trinidad that the "the diverse population of Indians . . . eventually came to form a mutually agreed-upon life, system of social relationships and set of cultural institutions" (Vertovec 1992:92).

Heterogeneity collapses into homogeneity not only when the host population "objectively" categorizes an immigrant population as a specific type of people but also when an immigrant population consciously builds itself a solidary identity. Structural positioning where conscious manipulation is minimal can also contribute to homogenization. In the East Indian case two such structural positions helped provide a foundation for homogeneity even before the migrants set foot in Trinidad. First, according to Hindu prescription, the mere fact of crossing the ocean meant permanent defilement for the Hindu. Accordingly, from the moment the voyage commenced, the Brahmin symbolically shared the same status as the low-caste Chamar. Second, the long and arduous voyage built close bonds between those who had shared the trials of the journey and became symbolized in the tie of *Jahaji Bhai*, "Brotherhood of the Boat" (de Verteuil 1989:14).[10] This relationship commanded a strong emotional attachment and proved to be resilient long after the immigrants had settled in Trinidad.

The importance of these structural factors lies not in the "erasure of ordinality" (Segal 1989) but rather in how they minimized the significance of traditionally constituted differences, an inadvertent consequence of the commonalities of shared experience, which understandably bore much more relevance to the immigrants' contemporary situation. This point illustrates the truism that within processes of identity formation, what constitute relevant criteria of selection are always context dependent. Thus although the solidarity established during the voyage may have been preeminent at the time of early indenture, those distinctions that had been played down but not wholly erased came to be reconstituted with significant modification as time progressed.[11] Despite the claim of most Indo-Trinidadians and scholars that caste no longer has any significance for Indo-Trinidadians, in contemporary Trinidad the distinction between Brahmin (the highest priestly caste) and Chamar (which designates all Untouchables in Trinidad) is quite pervasive.[12]

10. The length of the voyage varied, three months being about average (de Verteuil 1989:13).

11. After the East Indians settled in villages in Trinidad, the new professional distribution took roughly the following form: "The '*kumhar*' (potter) took to pottery, '*nau*' (barber) to his traditional work, '*teli*' (oil-processor) to his own, some '*Brahmans*' to teaching and priesthood, '*bania*' (grocer) to grocery, and '*ahir*' or '*goala*' to cattle rearing as well as milk-selling"(Jha 1985:10).

12. Vertovec notes the persistence of this same distinction between the Brahmin and the Chamar castes. He also makes the important point that caste in Trinidad, having been dislocated from its systemic role of integrating the layers of identities, economic and religious bases,

In the village I studied, many people situated themselves in one of these two categories.[13] Nevertheless, the historical legacy of indenture provides a narrative of origin that emphasizes commonalities rather than differences.

The terms under which indenture was resumed in 1844 were substantially different from those implemented in 1838. The new system was controlled by the state instead of private individuals. In order to ensure the success of the scheme, the state attempted to regulate every step of the indenture process, from the time the laborer was recruited in India until he or she was returned to India (Erickson 1934:135; Look Lai 1993:chap. 3). An elaborate system of regulations was devised to protect the laborer from abuses and to ensure maximum returns for the investing planters. Measures to protect Indian immigrants, undertaken primarily to appease humanitarians in England and Indian government officials, were a part of a larger effort to legitimate this new system of labor importation. Yet as many scholars point out, such regulations existed only in theory. In practice, the planters had ample opportunity to manipulate the system to their advantage: not only did they command the backing of the local state apparatus in the last instance but they also had knowledge of—and real access to—the legal system. As we see later, the most severe abuses of human freedom occurred within this legal framework.

The immigration ordinance of 1854 set the main parameters for the system of indenture.[14] The immigrants signed contracts in India that bound them to certain terms for the period of indenture. On arrival in Trinidad the Indians were assigned to a plantation, where they had to work for three years. Then they had the option of choosing their employer for the following two years to complete the total of five years of mandatory industrial residence, the prerequisite for becoming legally "free." To qualify for the free return passage to India, the immigrants had to reside in the colony for a total of ten years. After completion of the industrial residence they were again free to choose their occupation and employer for the remaining five years. The law regarding return passage was revised in 1895 and 1898 so that immigrants who arrived in the island after 1895 had to pay a proportion of their return passage (Brereton 1985:23).[15]

---

and essential power relations that underpinned each local caste complex in India, lost its operational value but survived as an aspect of prejudice (1992:95, 100).

13. Two other caste distinctions that prevailed in the village were the Kshatriya, or warrior caste (a high caste), and Ahir, or cattle rearers (a low caste).

14. The legal aspects of indenture continued to be modified until 1862, when five-year contracts were finally introduced (Look Lai 1993:57).

15. In 1895 men were required to pay 25 percent and women 16 2/3 percent of the return passage. In 1898 these rates were doubled (Brereton 1985:23).

The ordinance stipulated a basic minimum wage of 25 cents per day or per task. A task was supposed to be the amount of work an able-bodied man could reasonably be expected to perform in a seven-hour period. In Trinidad planters preferred to pay on the basis of task work because such a system allowed for greater manipulation through extending the duration of the task, a common practice especially during crop time.[16]

Brereton describes the wretched physical conditions in which the Indians lived: "They inhabited barrack ranges, similar to those of slavery days. Each range contained several rooms which measured 10' by 10' × 12' to accommodate a married couple and all their children, or two to four single adults. The partitions between the rooms never reached the roof and there was absolutely no privacy or quiet for the occupants. Cooking was done on the front steps. Latrines were not general on the estates until the twentieth century and the water supply was usually poor" (1985:25). Although by law each plantation was required to have a hospital and fortnightly visits from a doctor, the health of the indentured laborers was generally poor. Malaria and parasite-caused diseases such as hookworm, anemia, and ground itch were endemic to the estates. Of course, conditions varied from estate to estate, but as "bonded" laborers, East Indians were subject to living conditions under which the ex-slaves—now having the option—refused to labor.

Legal Differentiation and Spatial Isolation

The legal status of East Indians established their alienation from the wider society at the very inception of indenture. Because their contracts stipulated that after the period of industrial residence they could return to India, the host society and the Indians themselves believed their presence in Trinidad was only temporary. Singh comments: "The Indians did not first view themselves, nor were they viewed by those who imported them or by other groups in the society, as permanent members of the society, but only as temporary migrants, related to the society in a segmental way, that is, as a part of the plantation economy. Relations with the rest of the society outside the plantation were not a part of the original conception behind Indian immigration" (1985:33). On arrival in Trinidad the East Indians were banished almost immediately to the sugar estates concentrated in the flatland or rolling hills of the western side of the island, later known as the sugar belt. Their confine-

16. On the struggle over the control of labor during indenture, see Haraksingh 1981 and 1985. See also Trotman's 1986 analysis of crime for the period 1838–1900, which links patterns of criminal activity to the structural organization of plantation society.

ment to secluded rural areas minimized any chances of interaction with the wider society and subjected the newcomers to an unusual degree of social and spatial isolation.

Under the guise of curtailing vagrancy, the laws of the 1854 ordinance regulating indentured labor attempted to minimize East Indian mobility. During the initial stage of indenture (1845–54), when the system was still in an experimental phase, the requirement for industrial residence was set at five years and was served by means of short-term verbal monthly or yearly written contracts with the planters (Erickson 1934:136). In 1846, however, when the imperial government launched its policy of free trade and the colonies plunged into economic depression, the planters refused to renew labor engagements with the indentured laborers at the old wage rates. Consequently, many East Indians were reduced to "wandering vagrants" (Erickson 1934:140) in search of employment.

Financial collapse and the problem of vagrancy caused the indenture system to be temporarily halted between 1848 and 1850. To prevent vagrancy, planters attempted to persuade the imperial government to accept a labor code, drafted by Major Fagan, the Protector of Immigrants (or "Coolie Magistrate"),[17] which would have given them greater control over the actions of the laborers. In its effort to protect the rights of the migrants, the government opted for a more moderate scheme based on incentive rather than compulsion. According to Erickson, the new scheme, introduced by Earl Grey, the colonial secretary, "endeavored to check vagrancy by making it profitable for the employer to re-engage his old coolies and for the coolie to remain continuously with the same planter" (1934:141). Despite Erickson's claim that the law offered incentives to both Coolies and planters, his own evidence suggests that real incentive was provided only to the planters, who received a monetary reward of 20 shillings for rehiring an old Coolie and 40 shillings for hiring a Coolie formerly employed elsewhere. The "incentive" to the laborers was in fact a threat: they were subject to fines unless employed under "official contracts." "The coolie was fined 5s. monthly for the period he was not under contract, and 1s. a week was deducted from his wages for unnecessary absence from work [and] in addition, only labor under contract counted toward fulfillment of the industrial residence" (Erickson 1934:141). According to Erickson, the severe economic depression, the unwillingness of the planters, and the "irresponsible" nature of Coolies contributed to the failure of this "noble" plan.

By 1850 economic conditions had improved somewhat in British Guiana

---

17. Interestingly, Major Fagan also won repute for his zealous defense of Indian laborers during his tenure (1845–48) and was eventually dismissed by Governor Harris in 1848. See Look Lai 1993:158–63.

and Trinidad, and these colonies were once again in the market for "Coolies." When immigration was renewed in 1850, the accompanying regulations were far more stringent than those in operation before 1848: "The coolies . . . were deprived of certain important rights which the imperial government had previously regarded as indispensable to the status of a free man" (Erickson 1934:145). Likewise, Look Lai observes a shift "from an extreme liberal commitment to the humanitarian protectionism of the abolitionist lobbies and to the ideal of free labor, to a gradual recognition of the necessity for some form of paternalistic control over the labor force, as a concession to economic pragmatism and to the pressure-group demands of the plantocracy" (1993:52). Under the new law one-year contracts were extended to a period of three years and eligibility for return passage was set at ten as opposed to five years of industrial residence, binding the East Indians even more tightly to the plantations.

Other legal aspects of the indenture system also minimized East Indian contact with groups outside the plantation. For example, indentured laborers were prohibited from leaving the plantations unless they carried an official pass from the plantation authorities. Laborers caught without a pass were subject to imprisonment. The law required even "free" Indians, who had completed their term of industrial residence, to carry their certificate of residence at all times. If any such free Indian was unable to produce his or her papers when challenged by the authorities, he or she was subject to incarceration (Brereton 1979:178, 1985:24; Singh 1985:33).

Although in theory avenues existed within the legal system for indentured immigrants to lodge complaints against their employers, especially through the Protector of Immigrants, ignorance of the law prevented laborers from pursuing such avenues. Brereton comments, "It is doubtful whether most Indians really understood the Immigration Ordinances. They could not pay for legal aid, and usually did not know how to defend themselves. The courts were heavily weighted in favour of the employers and magistrates often awarded excessive sentences [to the Indians]" (1985:24). In contrast, the planters took ample advantage of the legal system to control their supply of labor. Between 1898 and 1905, for example, 11,149 indentured Indians—almost 15 percent of the total indentured population—were prosecuted for absence, desertion, vagrancy, or idleness (Brereton 1985:24).

Haraksingh has appropriately characterized the indentured laborer's situation as a "context of control" in which legal, spatial, and economic factors conjoined to hold the laborer captive in the workplace:

First of all, in the case of indentured workers there was a legal framework; they were obliged to work or in default to face penal sanctions. Then, for all workers

[75]

whether free or indentured, there was a spatial ambit; the planters, through their influence in the colonial legislature, were able to champion and secure policies which confined the workers either to or in the vicinity of the estates. The promotion of indebtedness among the workers kept them imprisoned in economic terms, and consequently under compulsion to perform at the work place. (1985:155)

The legal status of the East Indians functioned to set them apart from the wider community both spatially and socially. The need to carry a pass or certificate of industrial residence invited ridicule from those who had only recently been released from slavery. In 1873 it was reported that Africans frequently taunted East Indians with the phrase, "Slave, where is your free paper?" (Samaroo 1975:42). As Brereton remarks, "To the African, indentureship was no different from slavery, and he was proud that he was free to do what he liked and go where he wanted. Indians on the estates performed the low prestige jobs like weeding, digging, and transporting cane, which Africans chose to avoid. So the indenture status itself contributed to the unfavourable image of the 'coolie.' Africans, once at the bottom of the social scale, now had an easily recognisable class to which they could feel superior" (1985:30).

Occupational Segregation

During indenture, occupational segregation was endemic to the East Indians' status as sugar laborers. Because of constraints imposed on occupational choices, this pattern continued even after the immigrants had fulfilled their terms of indenture. In the second half of the nineteenth century legal and spatial differentiation of the East Indian was consolidated by occupational segregation. Between 1868 and 1880 "time-expired" immigrants were offered ten (later five) acres of crown land in lieu of return passage. The land offered was in the vicinity of the plantations to ensure a ready supply of labor for the planters.[18] Accordingly, even "free Indians" still remained tied to the sugar industry.[19]

18. Reddock points out that since land was made available primarily to East Indian males, East Indian women were once more dependent on men, losing some of the freedoms they may have had previously as indentured laborers when they were economic agents in their own right (1994:33).

19. Look Lai argues that East Indians began to acquire land even before the 1868 change in policy (1993:223).

Around the same period (1866–70) Governor A. H. Gordon, in an effort to reduce squatting by Blacks and Spanish-speaking peons,[20] began to make areas of crown land available for purchase to persons of limited means (Brereton 1979; Ching 1985:220; Singh 1985:34). As a result, substantial segments of the Black population that had remained in the sugar areas withdrew to the rapidly developing cocoa areas spreading from the foothills of the Northern Range to the central area and to the Montserrat Hills and eastward from Arima to Sangre Grande.

Cocoa was ideal for smallholder production because it could be combined with food crops until the trees matured; unlike sugar, its production did not involve an industrial phase. At the end of the nineteenth century cocoa thrived and by the early twentieth century generated greater revenue than sugar. This movement of the Black population toward cocoa and the consolidation of the East Indians in sugar meant that even in the agricultural realm an ethnic division of labor was rapidly emerging.[21]

Other attractive alternatives to the regimented labor demands of the sugar plantations were also opening up for the Black population. As Trinidad's economy gradually expanded in the nineteenth century, the concomitant increase in the circulation of money and growing communication between the towns and countryside created secondary occupations in the towns. These occupations afforded a degree of respectability that work in the cane fields denied, even though wages were not much higher (Singh 1985:34). Most Blacks who moved to the towns became shop and store clerks, artisans, domestics, and hucksters. The more educated Blacks joined the teaching service and lower rungs of the civil service and constabulary. The 1891 census showed that of a total population of 85,852, exclusive of East Indians, 37,854 were engaged in "industrial" occupations, 16,445 in "domestic" occupations, and 4,337 in "commercial" occupations; 2,709 persons were officials and professionals. Thus two-thirds of the non-Indian population was engaged in nonagricultural pursuits by 1891, including a majority of the Black laboring population (Singh 1985:34). While Blacks gravitated toward what they perceived as higher-status occupations, the East Indians were relegated to occupations that carried the lowest status—those associated with the agricultural sector, especially sugar.

20. Peons were immigrants from Venezuela of mixed Spanish/African and Amerindian descent who came to Trinidad throughout the nineteenth century and engaged in primarily small-scale cultivation, especially of cocoa.

21. East Indians were primarily tied to the sugar industry, but some, both free and indentured, were also engaged in cocoa cultivation (Look Lai 1993:109).

Social and Ideological Representations of Indians as Outsiders

Scholars differ about the place occupied by East Indians in Trinidad's colonial social structure. Singh (1985) argues that East Indians initially occupied the lowest rung of the social ladder, suggesting that this group was clearly included in the colonial social structure. Yet this inclusion was nominal, a mere acknowledgment of their physical presence in the island. Given the host of factors—legal, spatial, and occupational—that conspired to exclude this segment of the population from the national unit, others such as Lloyd Braithwaite (1975) argue that East Indians remained outside the social system.[22]

The idea that East Indians were outsiders to Trinidadian society was pervasive during the second half of the nineteenth century, particularly among the non-Indian population. For example, an expatriate schoolmaster, J. H. Collens, who wrote *A Guide to Trinidad* in the 1880s, almost forty years after the introduction of East Indians, referred to them as the "foreign element" and contrasted them to the "natives," by which, of course, he meant the Black population. Ironically, as Ivar Oxaal (1968:38) notes, many of these "natives" had arrived in Trinidad only a generation or two before the Indians and some of them were still in the process of migrating from other West Indian islands, particularly Barbados. Even Blacks who had migrated to Trinidad after the East Indians were perceived as natives simply because of their West Indian origins. Segal (1989:113) argues that the idiom of race and color inscribed two very different principles of subordination for the two ethnic groups vis-à-vis European colonizers, propagating "(1) an image of 'Africans' as persons lacking an ancestral 'civilization,' who, through 'mixing' . . . acquired 'respectability' [and] could become partially 'white' and inchoately 'West Indian'; and (2) an image of 'Asian Indians' as persons so possessed of an inferior, ancestral 'civilization' that they necessarily remained 'East (and not West) Indians,' regardless of their social entanglements in Trinidad" (1989:76).

Even though the notion of East Indians as "outsiders" was amply fostered by concrete policies and practices that minimized their interaction with the wider society, evidence suggests that this popular ideological representation of East Indians as outsiders was as much the result of a particular objectifica-

22. The outsider status of East Indians is powerfully conveyed by Braithwaite in his seminal 1953 study, *Social Stratification in Trinidad and Tobago*. In his diagram depicting social stratification in Trinidad, Indians are located outside the pyramid incorporating the White, Colored, and Black populations even though East Indians constituted 35.09 percent of the total population and had been resident in the colony for well over a century at that time.

tion of social relations that existed between East Indians and the wider society as an accurate representation of social reality itself. Annette Ching concludes: "The physical and social distinctiveness of the East Indians at that time [late nineteenth century] should not be taken to mean that they were outside the social and economic structure of the island. Stereotyped images of peoples were generated within these structures" (1985:219).

To conclude, as many analyses do, that East Indians were outsiders merely because of their represented image not only conflates representations of social reality with reality itself but also precludes the possibility of discovering how such representations are generated in the first place. More important, such conclusions are only half-truths: they may highlight the self-evident aspects of social action, but they tend to overlook the more subtle, habitual aspects that might suggest the contrary. For example, scholars of the indenture period generally feel that the attitudes and behavioral patterns of East Indians themselves contributed to their image as outsiders. East Indians, believing their situation in Trinidad to be only temporary, displayed little enthusiasm to integrate with the wider community.[23] This was certainly true for some, especially the 33,294 immigrants (22.4 percent of the total) who eventually opted to return to India (Ching 1985:217). Still, the majority of Indians gradually abandoned the hope of one day returning to India. For many it was not a conscious decision, and only practical circumstances precluded any possibility of return (Laurence 1985:95). Yet others, who chose to reindenture themselves or even to return to the West Indies after they had repatriated to India, showed a commitment to Trinidad as their home.

In an article commemorating Indian Arrival Day, Indo-Trinidadian historian Haraksingh made the poignant observation that "Indians had begun to think of Trinidad as their home long before general opinion in [the] country had awakened to that as a possibility" (*Sunday Guardian*, May 27, 1990:35). He came to this conclusion through a sensitive examination of East Indians' activities and what they signified in terms of commitment to Trinidad:

> This urge to contribute on equal terms, if more vocal now and therefore more noticeable, has always been present. It was there in the decision of some Indians to trade in their rights to a return passage and to remain in Trinidad. This was tantamount to letting down one's bucket, or even voting with one's feet. Apparently, the concept of a space which can be called home was decisive, for

23. To be fair, it should be noted that these same scholars hasten to add that the conditions imposed by the colonial government to confine the East Indians to the latifundial environment of the sugar belt, together with the Black population's hostile attitude toward them, left the East Indians little alternative but to remain exclusive.

in explaining their decision to stay, surviving Indian immigrants typically say that they had no one in India; that their family was here. This is really a reference to natural and ascriptive family and reveals a definition of homeland as a place where one's family resided.

This particular concept was accorded little credence by those who set the tone of society, and was probably a reflection of their own lack of commitment to any definite space, a legacy of absenteeism, metropolitan education, money in external banks, and familial, social and commercial contracts that rendered territorial boundaries meaningless.

In this context, it was a matter of irony that it was the Indians who had to establish over and over again that their commitment to this space was genuine.

The urge was there too in efforts to redesign the landscape. . . . The trees which were planted around emergent homesteads, including religious vegetation, constituted a statement about belonging; so too did the temples and mosques which began to dot the landscape. (*Sunday Guardian,* May 27, 1990, 2, 35)

By the turn of the twentieth century East Indians had established themselves firmly as permanent settlers in Trinidad,[24] yet they continued to be defined as outsiders because of the principles that dictated their terms of entry into colonial society. Apart from material circumstances, powerful ideological forces functioned to confine this group to its assigned place.

East Indians were essentially latecomers to Trinidadian colonial society, which by the mid-nineteenth century was thoroughly creolized and had a highly elaborate system, based on race and color, for structuring the social relations among people of different ancestries. Nineteenth-century Trinidad in certain respects conformed to the classic three-tier social structure of Caribbean societies in general: Africans and their locally born descendants, the majority population, formed the base; people of mixed descent comprised a middle tier; and elites primarily of European descent (British, French, and Spanish) were at the apex (Brereton 1993).[25] This structure was significantly altered with the arrival of Indians. According to Brereton, "though their economic and 'class' position . . . would have categorized them [Indians] with the third tier, the differences between them and the descendants of ex-slaves were too great. In Trinidad as in Guyana and Surinam, Indians constituted a fourth distinct tier in the social structure" (1993:36).

24. For a detailed account, see Brereton 1979:chap. 9, Laurence 1985, and Ramesar 1994:chaps. 4 and 6.

25. In the same discussion Brereton is careful to point out how Trinidad was also an exception to this model.

Those very distinctions—material, social structural, and cultural factors— that relegated Indians to a fourth tier operated to situate them symbolically outside the core of Trinidadian society. Although both East Indians and Blacks were automatically relegated to a subordinate status vis-à-vis Whites in the colonial racial hierarchy, the principles of subordination differed for the two groups. This difference in turn shaped notions of who could and could not be considered "native."

According to Segal, the historical facts of conquest, slavery, and indenture were understood by Trinidadians as having brought to pre-independence Trinidad three distinct "races": Europeans, Africans, and East Indians.[26] As their respective denominations indicate, these races were identified in terms of an ancestral territory. The Europeans and Africans were also labeled with opposing color terms, *White* and *Black*. A similar conventional color term for East Indians did not exist. Africans or Blacks were designated by a third term as well, the phylogenic term *Negro*. Other, less numerous groups such as the Portuguese, the Chinese, and the Syrians were also distinguished in pre-independence Trinidad. Thus race was signified through terms referring to ancestral lands, color, and phylogeny.

Since the groups entering Trinidad were considered pure races, they were distinguishable not only by their place of origin "but by their point of entry in the colonial order" (Segal 1989:85):

> In Trinidad, every "race" had a distinct *beginning* in the colonial order, since every "race" had been isolated and pure before entering into colonial relations. Thus, to *be* "white" was to *have been* a "master"; to *be* "black" was to *have been* a "slave"; and to be "East Indian" was to *have been* a "coolie laborer." . . .
>
> In sum, the idiom of "race" memorialized particular pasts, and connected those pasts to contemporary social relations. (Segal 1989:86; emphasis in original)

The articulation of class position with the significations of race becomes evident in the distinction between Portuguese and White. In Trinidad and Guyana the term *White* was used contrastively, not only with *Black* but also with *Portuguese*. It was not dark pigmentation that rendered the Portuguese non-White but their relatively impure economic behavior. In pre-independence Trinidad the Portuguese were "identified as dirty shopkeepers" (Braithwaite 1975:44). Ryan describes them as being "in the petty trades—retail

---

26. My discussion of the role of the idiom of race in structuring social relations in pre-independence Trinidad is based primarily on Segal (1993, 1989). These historical events also include the almost total annihilation of the native population.

stores, groceries, rum shops, itinerant huckstering—which did not rate inclusion among those associated with 'whiteness'" (1974:19). Segal concludes that the "contrast between 'Whites' and 'Portuguese' inscribed a distinction of the colonial political economy" (1993:83). He is careful to point out, however, that the idiom of race was not a mere copy of the colonial political-economic order nor did it determine completely a person's class position. Rather, racial categories embodied references to both class position and the significations of race.

This inherent capacity of the idiom of race (as it operates in Trinidad) to memorialize each group's specific past lends insight into how, in contemporary Trinidad, people claiming specific "racial ancestries" are able to appeal to a common unifying element despite the pervasive heterogeneities that characterize their respective groups. It is this feature of race that enables people to use continuously the terms *East Indian, White, Negro, Chinese,* and *Portuguese* as if they actually represent monolithic blocks of ancestral kinds. More significant, this memorialization of ancestral pasts constitutes the ideological cornerstone for the Trinidadian nationalist narrative of a cosmopolitan, multicultural society alluded to in Chapter 2. The currently pervasive Trinidadian nationalist narrative of a "United Nations in miniature" (described by Segal 1994) moored in the nineteenth-century idiom of race posits the continuity of ancestral diversities into the present. In this way the plurality or heterogeneity embodied by the various immigrant groups at the moment of arrival in Trinidad is said to prevail even today. In this narrative the various "purities" embodied by the original ancestral types reproduce themselves as discrete elements, preserving purity at the level of each and every group. Illustrating the complex interpenetration of the lay, political, and academic discursive levels, this popular nationalist narrative in the lay imagination finds its counterparts in the academic arena as the "plural society" model and in the political arena as the "multicultural society" projected in the "tossed salad" metaphor of the nation.

Yet the colonial idiom of race also prefigures another, seemingly contrary, nationalist narrative that pivots around the notion of mixture or impurity. In his semantic analysis of the racial order of colonial Trinidad Segal (1993, 1989) argues that this order was built on the premise that pure races came to Trinidad and the subsequent mixing of these pure races was a feature peculiar to Trinidad (and by extension the West Indies). This point is enhanced by Daniel J. Crowley's observation of Trinidad: "[Here] a number of individuals know of six or more racial and national strains in their ancestry, and there is at least one authenticated case of a man of Portuguese-Carib and Doogla (Negro-Indian) parents who married a girl of Martinique Colored Venezuelan mestizo and Chinese Creole origins. Such people are proud of their mixed origins, and boast that they are 'a real mix-up,' or 'a West Indian callallu'" (1957:819–20). This notion, that to be West Indian was to be variously mixed, and that pure races were those that belonged outside Trinidad, constituted a major ideological axiom through which East Indians came to be defined outside the nation of Trinidad. As we see shortly, it was not the fact that this putatively pure East Indian race did not mix with other pure or mixed races but rather that this mixing was erased rather than memorialized. Consequently, East Indians always remained not only a pure race but by logical extension, external to Trinidad as well.

According to Segal, mixing, which defined nativeness, was represented in the color spectrum defined by the endpoint values of Black and White. All persons with some European and African ancestry were considered Colored, and in this way both a pragmatic and an ideological connection were established between the two groups, a connection thought to be particular to Trinidad and the West Indies. Color or shade, however, was not reducible to a person's pigmentation alone; the texture of hair, skin tone, and facial features all contributed to the determination of a person's position within the color spectrum (Braithwaite 1975).[27] Even though blackness was devalued in the color spectrum, the fact that the category Black constituted a crucial axis in this pervasive system of social classification indicated a recognition of the Black or Colored person's place within Trinidad. In contrast, East Indians were excluded from the color spectrum or any analogous system of genealogical accounting of racial ancestry that would have disclosed their connections with other groups—an astounding fact when one considers that East Indians constituted one-third of the total population in 1870 and that by 1900 they numbered 85,615 persons (Laurence 1985:112).

The connectedness of White and Black and the exclusion of East Indian was also revealed in the use of *Creole*, a word broadly meaning "local" or "West Indian." The word was used as a noun (in reference to persons) and as an adjective to denote persons born or things generated locally, such as food, dress, language, and culture (Segal 1993:87).[28]

27. A person's "color" was not fixed but shifted with contexts and especially with regard to who was doing the observing. See Segal 1989:106–9. Harry Hoetink's (1967) classic concept of the "somatic norm image" is particularly suggestive (in his emphasis of socialization and cultured convention) for understanding the variations we see within the Caribbean—namely, the difference between the Iberian and northwest European–dominated areas—in how people are perceived "racially."

28. In Haiti, I am told, the shoots of banana or plantain are called "creoles" (Drexell Woodson, personal communication 2000).

For a person to be "a Creole," it was necessary, though not sufficient, that he be either "coloured" or one of the "racial" constituents of the "coloured" population—that is, either "black or white."[29] The term was applied to all "blacks" and "coloureds," but only to a segment of the "whites," distinguishing "local whites" from "expatriates" on assignment in Trinidad. It was within this set of "Creoles," extending continuously from "local whites" to "blacks," that persons were distinguished by "colour" or "shade." (Segal 1993:87–88)

If to be Trinidadian (and West Indian) one had to be "mixed up," this in turn meant that one was also Creole. The importance of being considered mixed up is especially telling in the distinction drawn between local Whites and expatriate Whites. The term *local White* specifically referred to the French Creoles but was used in general to refer to the island's plantocracy, irrespective of nationality.[30] Hence British, Scottish, Irish, and even persons of Spanish ancestry were included in this category. Yet despite this inclusivity, the term *French Creole* retained the connotations of the French/British distinction, which characterized the French as "volatile, imaginative, fun-loving, artistic, and generous by contrast with the more decorous, phlegmatic, dowdy English" (Lowenthal 1972:88 in Segal 1993:90). The term *local White* also meant "Trinidad White" or "so-called White," which indicated the belief that despite his or her apparent whiteness, he or she had at least some non-White ancestors. This supposition signifies yet another connection between Whites and Blacks on the social and pragmatic basis of miscibility, which permitted all such persons to belong and be native to Trinidad. By all these standards East Indians were considered foreign.

Whereas the shared localness of the Black, White, and Colored populations was inscribed within the idiom of color, other social representations denied East Indians access to becoming local. It was argued earlier that the objectification of social action facilitated the representation of East Indian relations to others in Trinidad as a negation of relations. Such an objectification was evident in the designation of the offspring of unions between East Indians and Europeans. They too, like the offspring between Europeans and Africans, were considered mixed, and a similar system of fractional and genealogical accounting was used to describe such persons: "He half white, half Indian," or "his father white, his mother Indian" (Segal 1993:93). Segal notes that

29. Segal is careful to point out in a footnote that as an adjective in front of *Indian, Creole* was sometimes used to distinguish locally born Indians from immigrants. Also, in a pragmatic sense, the term was occasionally applied to "non-creoles" to indicate their integration into local society (Segal 1989:92, 1993:111).
30. See Brereton 1979:chap. 3, 1985:116–22.

beyond this racial accounting, we find, in marked contrast to the elaborated distinctions of "color," no other lexical items for persons of "East Indian" and "European" ancestry. There was, then, no "kind" which included all persons of "East Indians" and "European" descent regardless of the "degree" of "mixing,"[31] and similarly, no idiom in which "East Indians" and "Europeans" were the endpoint values of a single, continuous variable: "East Indians" were never placed on a "color" scale with "whites." (1989:115)

This lexical absence did not mean, however, that mixing between East Indians and Europeans was nonexistent. In fact, a number of sources indicate to the contrary. What this lexical absence signified was that mixing, when it concerned the European and the East Indian, was erased rather than memorialized. Since there was no term to keep track of such persons, they were subsequently absorbed into one of the many color or race categories on pragmatic and contingent bases.

A lexical term does exist, however, for the offspring of unions between East Indians and Blacks. This term, *Dougla* (locally understood to mean "bastard" in Hindi), operated differently from that of Colored. It was, and still is, rarely used to designate a collectivity and referred primarily to an individual, who was once again absorbed into the Black or East Indian category, where that bit of Indian or Black blood in him/her became occasionally relevant in specific contexts.[32] Thus once again the mixing, this time between East Indian and Black, was ultimately erased, albeit not completely.

Segal formulates an intriguing theory about why East Indians were represented as "unmixables." He bases it on the different principles of subordination for Blacks and East Indians, grounded in notions of the African as a culturally naked being and the East Indian as a culturally saturated being (though in an inferior culture).[33] In essence, blackness meant an absence, a void capable of being filled. It was this absence that enabled Blacks to be-

31. As proof, Segal (1989:115) correctly points out that no such term can be found in any of the authoritative works on "East Indians," such as Niehoff and Niehoff 1960 and 1967, Klass 1961, and Schwartz 1967, among others.

32. In the late 1980s and early 1990s the term *Dougla* (sometimes spelled *Doogla*) became politically charged when radical East Indian groups accused the National Alliance for Reconstruction of attempting to "Douglarize" the nation by encouraging miscegenation between Afro-Trinidadian males and Indo-Trinidadian females. This charge emerged out of the proposed (but ultimately failed) NAR scheme to institute national service, which the radical groups interpreted as an insidious plot by the government to culturally and biologically assimilate (annihilate?) the East Indians.

33. See Munasinghe 1997, where I elaborate on Segal's (1989, 1993) argument by linking the images of Africans and East Indians to the broader nineteenth-century orientalist discourses on race.

come respectable by adopting White behavioral patterns. Respectability did not remove a dark person's physiognomy but only covered it, and as a result respectability had to be continuously established.[34] Blackness could be "lightened up" because it symbolized an absence, a blank slate on which to inscribe civilization (Segal 1989:111–12). Thus the Black person, because devoid of culture, was inferior but could become respectable by adopting "White" cultural patterns.

In contrast, East Indians were deemed inferior not because they lacked a culture but because they possessed an inferior culture. According to Segal, the presence of this inferior culture

> made the relationship between "East Indians" and "whites" a matter of "either/or": from the perspective of the colonial order, a person was *either*, say, a Hindu *or* a Christian. If the "African" could be partially *evolué*, to borrow a term from the French colonial order, it was because he had nothing of his own. Possessed of languages, religions, and customs which were regarded as inferior cases of what "Europeans" possessed, the immigrants from India and their descendants could not similarly be partially "European." (1993:95)

These images of inferiority, Segal argues, conditioned the possibilities of miscibility. For miscibility to be possible, one of the subordinate terms had to be culturally naked. Thus Africans were capable of being mixed with Europeans but East Indians were not. Mixing between East Indians and Blacks is accorded recognition, since one of the constituents is culturally void (Black), but it lacks a system of elaborate accountability because the mixing of two inferior types is deemed insignificant. Segal notes:

> As a result, immigrants from South Asia and their descendants were neither a part of a locally created "white-Indian" continuum, nor a part of a locally created "black-Indian" continuum. In the constituted absence of local connections, "East Indians" never became "creoles," and had no place on the color scale of the creole continuum. They were emphatically "East" and not "West Indians." In sum, in Trinidad's colonial order, the "East Indian" was situated across a hierarchical disjunction from "Europeans" which, in contextual consequence, constituted a disjunction between "East Indian" and "Creole." (1989:124–25)

Even today East Indians are not designated by the term *Creole*.

---

34. On "respectability," see Segal 1989:109–13. See Wilson 1969 and 1973 for a suggestive gendered interpretation of "respectability" that has relevance for the Caribbean as a whole.

Although Segal's analysis of Creole as mixture is clearly in reference to persons, here I want to extend his analysis by placing mixture or Creoleness at the center of a second nationalist narrative. Given the tendency of nationalist narratives to draw on and revolve around definitions of the "national subject" or the "true native," such an extension I believe is justified. Creole, within this scheme, constituted a nationalist myth about creating impurity or mixture out of purity, out of which emerged a Trinidadian "purity." Yet this Trinidadian purity could admit only certain ancestral groups/purities and not others. That the purities of discrete ancestral groups represented in the cosmopolitan narrative of Trinidadian society are not formal equivalents is powerfully illustrated by the fact that the cosmopolitan narrative on its own cannot explain why certain ancestral groups remain symbolically positioned outside the national core if indeed the dominant narrative is one of a multicultural society. Contemporary Indo-Trinidadian leaders' insistence on supplanting the callaloo model of society with that of the tossed salad suggests that the identification of the particular *unit* within which purities or mixtures are embodied, whether at the level of the individual or the nation, has considerable symbolic import in determining which purities are considered nationally legitimate. In addition, the fact that the Creole narrative of mixture, which became politicized during the period leading up to independence (Chapter 7), also has its counterparts in both academic and lay arenas—in the model of the Creole society thesis and in the national metaphor of the callaloo, respectively—provides further evidence of the extension of the trope of the mixed individual as native to the level of a national narrative.

This narrative, that somehow to be Trinidadian is also to be mixed up, is as prevalent as the narrative of ancestral purities. Paradoxical as it may seem, these two nationalist narratives are not mutually exclusive. On the one hand, Trinidadians easily acknowledge their mixed status. Even Whites, who one might assume have a vested interest in claims to purity, readily admit the illicit blendings that have tainted their genealogies. When I was in Trinidad in 1998, a French Creole in his early fifties from a "respectable" upper-class family recounted to me with amusement his Portuguese, English, Scottish, and East Indian pedigree and concluded that the term *French Creole* is a designation for "so-called Whites," "so called" because in fact they are all mixed! In a similar vein consider Merle Hodge's definition of a Trinidadian: "Perhaps the epitome of a Trinidadian is the child ... with a dark skin and crinkly plaits ... decidedly Chinese eyes ... named Maharaj" (in Khan 1993:183). On the other hand, Trinidadians continuously dissect or calibrate different proportions of mixture by resorting to the original ancestral categories, thereby insisting on defining persons or behavior on the basis of pure types.[35] As Khan observes of Hodge's definition of the Trinidadian child, "every attribute in this composite is disaggregated and identified" (1993:183). Segal (1993:85) too emphasizes this tendency toward genealogical and fractional accounting. As with the term *Dougla*, the fact that all the examples cited above of racial calibration include an East Indian component may seem to run counter to the argument presented—the denial of East Indian mixing. It is not that Trinidadians in their day-to-day interactions are unable to recognize East Indian mixing; rather, at the symbolic level mixing between East Indians and others is either downplayed or erased in the overall system of racial classification.

Insistence on racial accounting on the basis of pure ancestral types subverts the coherence and integrity implied by fusion. That is, when a Trinidadian accounts for a person's racial makeup by saying "he half White and half Black," mixture is acknowledged, but the insistence on accounting on the basis of original pure types denies that complete fusion has created a new type. In this way purity is preserved in the last instance but it is not at the level of each and every group, as implied in the cosmopolitan narrative. Rather, *individuals* belonging primarily to the Black and White ancestral groupings embody discrete proportions of original ancestral purities, evidencing the mixed status of the ancestral blocs themselves—hence their inclusion within the color spectrum. The fact that they embody mixture establishes unequivocally their native status. East Indians, in contrast, never having mixed (in terms of symbolic recognition), are excluded in this second narrative, which pivots around the concept Creole. Thus excluded, they embody as individuals a purity that is a composite whole, testimony to the purity of the ancestral group itself—hence their exclusion from the color spectrum.

The Trinidadian nationalist narrative that emerges out of the dialectical interplay between the two narratives inscribed in the colonial idiom of race distinguishes between two types of purity that are differentially positioned in relation to national identity: the purity of ancestral types that never passed through the cauldron of mixture, and the purities that constitute parts of a mixture. The latter type never represents a whole in and of itself; it is the purity that is created through the calibration of mixed instances. In contrast, the purity supposedly embodied by ethnic groups who never mixed, such as the East Indians, constitutes wholes, and it is this type of purity that the Trinidadian nationalist narrative defines itself against, thus positioning such groups

35. For an excellent analysis of how Guyanese people insist on defining processes of interethnic mixture through an ideology of pure types—namely, ethnic stereotypes—see Drummond 1980.

at a considerable ideological disadvantage with respect to claiming native status in the New World.

The positioning of "native groups"—all those acknowledged in the color spectrum—and East Indians vis-à-vis the colonial state indicates the particular configuring of relations between state and nation and between nation and ethnic group. Clearly, the formulation of the national unit was taking place against the nation during the colonial period. Nevertheless, state articulation of the national unit acknowledged some groups as native while excluding others. These others—East Indians—were then directly counterposed to the nation. In short, while the nation was configured against the state, East Indians as an ethnic group were configured against the nation. Such was the nature of relations in the process of triangulation encompassing the nation, the state, and the ethnic group in colonial Trinidad.

East Indian Upward Mobility

During the last quarter of the nineteenth century the acquisition of land and education constituted the primary means of mobility for East Indians. Yet it is a testimony of Trinidad's ethnic situation that this mobility, which continues today, did not fulfill its potential to integrate East Indians into Creole society. Rather, the very circumstances governing East Indians' mobility served to enhance their alienness. Many achieved success through landownership and education, but this prosperity acquired the peculiar veneer of an East Indian style of success.

Land and Mobility

The disposition of crown lands was a major issue in nineteenth-century Trinidad. At the turn of the century the crown possessed more than a million acres of land, and much of the alienated land was undercultivated. Anticipating a labor shortage for the estates with emancipation, an 1836 dispatch from the secretary of state for the colonies ruled that crown lands should be made inaccessible to the masses. Accordingly, at the end of apprenticeship the smallest parcel of land that could be bought was set at 340 acres and later increased to 680 acres (one square mile). Unable to raise the purchase price, many ex-slaves resorted to squatting. Others, more prosperous, chose to purchase modest plots at exorbitant prices from the planters and formed communities of freeholders primarily on the outskirts of estates (Brereton 1981:89).

In 1869, however, thirty-one years after emancipation, Governor Gordon made smaller amounts of crown land available to persons of modest incomes. According to Brereton's figures, between 1875 and 1900 approximately 122,193 acres were sold, mostly to smallholders who were Creoles, peons, Africans, and British West Indian immigrants, as well as East Indians (1981:90). Most of this land was brought under cocoa cultivation, an exclusively local enclave shared by large planters and peasant producers. In 1887 the *San Fernando Gazette* opined that the bulk of the acreage under new cocoa production was in the hands of Black peasantry, and the 1889 report of the Central Agricultural Board of Trinidad observed that "cocoa production was giving uneducated black men simple, but prosperous lives; with patient industry and no capital they were able to send their sons to college" (in Singh 1985:34).

Between 1869 and 1880 some free Indians accepted the opportunity to exchange their return passage for ten and later five acres of land. This exchange of land for commutation was primarily designed to alleviate the colony's financial liability for repatriation and to retain seasoned plantation laborers. In 1873 353 grants were made, and three new villages were founded in the first two years. In 1872 the population of such settlements was estimated at 1,346 (Laurence 1985:97). These villagers produced rice, maize, peas, and ground provisions, and some ventured into cocoa production, coconut cultivation, and cattle rearing.[36]

Because of the inferior quality of land offered in lieu of return passage, however, most free Indians preferred to purchase their own plots. Between 1870 and 1880 2,614 East Indians accepted land as payment of commutation, and 356 East Indians bought crown land. Only 26 of the 749 commutation payments offered in the next four years were converted into land, however, the recipients opting for cash remunerations instead, while the number of crown land purchasers increased from 47 in 1881 to 134 in 1884 (Laurence 1985:105). The sale of crown land to East Indians grew steadily, and some even pooled their resources and purchased whole estates, as in 1872 when five immigrants raised £18,000 to buy the 260-acre Corial Estate. Between 1885 and 1912 89,222 acres were granted or sold to East Indians, and by the 1890s they had formed numerous free Indian villages.[37]

At the same time, East Indians became increasingly involved in cane cultivation, farming their own lands or renting plots to other farmers. Some also grew cane on estate lands under contract, with the rent being deducted from the estate factory's payments for the cane. A few decades earlier planters

36. On the commutation system and its gradual demise, see Laurence 1985.
37. On the development of two such free villages, see Richardson 1975.

such as Burnley had vehemently opposed sharecropping and enumerated arguments to rationalize why this system would never work in Trinidad. Changes in the economic and political climates, however, compelled the planter class to embrace this scheme in the 1890s when the dynamics of sugar production called for a separation of cultivation from manufacture.

Thus as Eric Williams notes eloquently:

> By a curious irony, the sugar planter who, in the seventeenth and eighteenth centuries, refused to grant land to the white indentured servant, who, after emancipation, tried to prevent the purchase of land by the former slave, found himself obliged in the nineteenth century to grant land to the indentured immigrant in order to reduce the expense of immigrant labour. Indian immigration, designed to compete with the Negro landowners, ended in the establishment of a class of Indian landowners. (1982:120)

For Williams the East Indian contribution was an offshoot of larger schemes, based on "a simple question of finance" and designed by men in power (1982:119).

The sale of lands alleviated the planters' plight in the short term, but it was the East Indians who gained in the long run. Their transformation from indentured workers to smallholders afforded them not only a basis for communal life but also a possibility for economic and social mobility. Moreover, as early as the 1850s East Indians had also begun pursuing nonagricultural occupations, becoming shopkeepers, carters, goldsmiths, hucksters, domestics, and even moneylenders. Despite numerous obstacles, some East Indians were able to attain a measure of success. The vast sums of money that some immigrants returning to India took with them astounded the authorities, who wondered how they could save such sums with wages of a mere 25 cents a day. Individual success stories of East Indian business tycoons also fostered the germination of the ubiquitous stereotype of the thrifty, industrious, and persevering East Indian.

In the late nineteenth and early twentieth centuries few alternatives existed for the East Indians to improve their lot on the estates. They could rebel against the oppressive regimes, and indeed minor skirmishes, or "Coolie uprisings," took place frequently in the estates (Jha 1973). Yet after the 1884 Hosay riots,[38] when police killed several East Indians, the futility of armed revolt became apparent to East Indians and they sought to change their method of protest.

The rise of organized bodies that peacefully addressed grievances and is-

---

38. On the riots, see Singh 1988.

sues facing a majority of East Indians was possible only because some East Indians had managed to improve their station. Some of them became leaders in the self-attributed duty to act as spokesmen for their community. Not all these leaders owed their upward social mobility to landownership. Many became successful because of the partial democratization of the educational system, which became important in the 1890s.

Education and Mobility

Land was the initial basis for East Indian mobility, but a few East Indians also sought mobility through education in the late nineteenth century. Colonial authorities failed for the most part to provide adequate educational facilities for East Indians because they were perceived as transients. Although East Indians could have sent their children to the government ward schools, established in 1846, for their primary education, few took this opportunity. Fear of educating their children with those of a different faith and race discouraged enrollment. Only in 1890, when it became apparent to authorities that East Indians were to be a permanent feature of colonial society, did they look to education as a means for making the Coolies "useful settlers and good citizens" (Governor Robinson, quoted by Samaroo 1975:45).

In 1890 the government merely formalized an educational system that had been established by the Canadian Presbyterian missionary John Morton in 1871. Appalled by the total spiritual neglect of the East Indians, Morton committed himself vigorously to their improvement through education. The mission schools catered solely to East Indians, and instruction was in Hindi. In contrast to the ward schools, the mission schools were relatively successful in attracting pupils. Other than the obvious economic advantages of a Western education, mission schools opened up new avenues of achievement. In constant need of teachers, the mission schools set up teacher training centers for young East Indian converts. The establishment in 1883 of Naparima College, which prepared boys for the junior and senior Cambridge examinations, held the promise of a university education in either England or America. East Indians appeared eager for education but did not display the same enthusiasm for conversion, much to the dismay of the missionaries. Samaroo writes, "The East Indian in Trinidad, therefore, was prepared to use the mission schools as levers for upward economic mobility, but was unwilling to forsake his ancient faith" (1975:51).

To a certain degree, mission schools in the early indenture period were an important means for East Indian integration into the wider community (Samaroo 1983). Not only did they facilitate communication by teaching East Indians the English language, but the missionaries actively sought to recruit

East Indian Presbyterians to participate in public organizations. Missionaries were often members of local road boards, the Agricultural Society, and other official organizations, and they encouraged East Indian participation in such local bodies. Many of the island's first East Indian notables, such as George Fitzpatrick and Rev. C. D. Lalla, who were members of the Legislative Council, were Presbyterians who had obtained their initial training in mission schools.

Yet mission schools also encouraged East Indian exclusivism. The teaching in Hindi, which attracted the East Indians, had no appeal, of course, to non–East Indians. Hence the full potential of formal education to serve as a medium of social interaction was left unrealized. This was less the fault of the missionaries than of the colonial educational system, which was based on numerous small sectarian schools. Even in the early twentieth century, when East Indians were sufficiently versed in English to enter multiracial schools, separateness was maintained, and it lasted well into the 1950s.

The curriculum content, too, did little to bridge the racial divisions because it was primarily based on the Canadian model and was removed from the local situation (Samaroo 1983). The crucial omission of the history and development of Trinidadian society and its constituent groups limited students' understanding of the dynamics behind their own society. Consequently, even educated East Indians carried the prejudices of their parents, as they were not provided with alternatives to challenge their in-group attitudes. F. E. M. Hosein, mission-trained and later a graduate of Oxford University, told the East Indian National Congress in a speech in 1913 that East Indians had heard of the great races of the earth, "but among the great ones of the earth the sons of Africa are not mentioned and when mentioned, mentioned in a humble capacity. From him, therefore, the son of India has nothing to learn, he sees in him perhaps something to ridicule" (in Samaroo 1975:54).

Samaroo suggests that the propagation of East Indian exclusivism might have been part of a deliberate strategy to keep the two non-White races apart. The missionaries were strong supporters of the planter class, and liberal planter assistance for their work was motivated primarily by the planters' desire for a "docile and tractable labour force learning the virtues of obedience and humility" (Samaroo 1975:55). Missionary and planter complicity, especially on the question of indentureship, which both groups viewed favorably, alienated not only the missionaries but also the East Indians from the Creole population. In a certain sense the missionaries themselves were responsible. Samaroo concludes:

> The Canadian Mission to the East Indians therefore played a major role in providing this group with the qualifications for entrance into a new and often

[93]

bewildering environment. Yet the missionaries, possibly believing that the controlling hand of the British would be there for all time, seem not to have envisaged the day when the country would be under the control of Africans and East Indians. Hence they saw nothing wrong with the racial separation that existed and indeed did much to preserve this. In doing so they re-enforced the exclusiveness of the East Indian whose distinctive way of life contributed to this separation. From the mid-twentieth century this separation was destined to bedevil the fortunes of an emerging Trinidad and Tobago. (1975:55)

Even in the realm of education, then, conjoined state, planter, and missionary interests served to perpetuate East Indian exclusivism.

East Indian Style of Mobility

Although education and land constituted the primary paths for East Indian mobility and the emergence of a nascent East Indian middle class at the turn of the twentieth century, the fact remains that not all East Indians achieved such success. In the same period and even before, some Creoles, too, experienced mobility. Yet a stereotype prevails to this day that East Indians have outpaced Creoles on every measure of success, whether economic wealth, educational achievement, or since 1995, political power. Therefore, we need to ask why and how East Indian individual achievements are perceived as achievements of the East Indian community whereas a Black person's success is perceived as an individual accomplishment. This difference in perception has significantly enhanced the image of the East Indians as a rapidly prospering community, especially in contrast to Afro-Trinidadians. To be sure, East Indian leaders and others have repeatedly attempted to dispel this myth through statistical analyses of the disparities in income among Creoles, Whites, and East Indians.[39] As recently as 1990 a prominent East Indian politician devoted a weekly column in a leading island newspaper challenging the alleged economic superiority of the East Indians. Yet these same leaders easily and frequently exalt the successes of "their community" with little sense of contradiction.

Segal's earlier explanation of how racial and color categories operate in Trinidad sheds light on this question. The color spectrum ranging from Black to White enabled the Negro to replace physiognomic darkness through achievements, which were perceived as "light." For the Negro, achieved social status was inscribed in the idioms of race and color, which meant that

39. See Dookeran 1985, Harewood 1971, Camejo 1971.

achievements of a dark person had a contingent status relative to his "true" color. Since achievements were regulated by proximity to imaged whiteness, they became matters of respectability and not just economic utility. As Segal (1993:102) writes, "In short, the idiom of respectability circumscribed a drive for profit pure and simple." In addition, since achievements were annexed to whiteness, their accomplishment by relatively dark persons contested the inferiority of the Negro but precluded the affirmation of Africanness or blackness, as Segal notes: "Achievements could not be represented as the collective property of Negroes; rather, their accomplishment by non-White Creoles was an individual feat" (1993:102).

East Indians, in contrast, were designated only in terms of ancestry. Their race designation maintained a constant value and was not contingent on other modifiers. Since achievements did not alter Indian identity, it could collectively claim achievements—which shifts in color and respectability denied African identity. Accordingly, Segal argues, the public representations of achievement for the two groups are markedly different. Whereas East Indians revel in mass objectifications of ancestral identity, such as the Centenary Celebrations of 1945, Negro achievements tend to be embodied in the exemplary biographies of scholarship winners such as the late Dr. Eric Williams's (1969) *Inward Hunger: The Education of a Prime Minister* (Segal 1993:103).

To conclude, the colonial social hierarchy and its concomitant classificatory systems of race and color circumscribed not only the behaviors of non-White groups but also the interpretation of their behaviors. Structures generated by the colonial state shaped the different patterns of mobility experienced by Blacks and East Indians as well as the perceptions of this mobility. A reformulation of any nation invariably involves a reinterpretation of its constituent ethnic groups' histories. The contemporary preoccupation with elevating either Afro-Trinidadian or Indo-Trinidadian histories at the expense of the other serves to slight the critical role played by the metropolitan powers and planters in shaping these histories. If we resituate the contemporary struggle in the nexus of power relations that foreshadowed it, we see how ethnicity, in any given context, is always historical.

The historical analysis partially explains why the contemporary Indo-Trinidadian challenge to the nation and the state must revolve around reformulating the category Trinidadian so it can include East Indians. On the one hand, the Indo-Trinidadian struggle attempts to overcome historical limits by challenging the dichotomy between East Indian and Trinidadian. Yet on the other hand, the Indo-Trinidadian leaders' strategy reproduces the traditional division between East Indians and Creoles. Thus historical factors shape

Indo-Trinidadians' contemporary struggle not only by informing their particular strategy but also by imposing limits.

I now turn to Cambio, a village claimed to be exclusively East Indian, to show how the traditional dichotomy between East Indian and Creole unfolds in practice in the lay discursive arena.

[5]

To Be Ethnic in a Place in Between

The Setting

The Central Region

A few days after my husband and I arrived in Cambio in central Trinidad, we met Pundit Maraj in a nearby village. That evening the pundit performed a *graa puja* for a young Indo-Trinidadian man,[1] Rohan, who had been overcome by hard times. Everything in Rohan's life appeared to be taking a turn for the worse: he was having problems with his siblings over the inheritance of his father's home, which he and his wife and children shared with his father; he was unable to find employment; and he had had a series of minor accidents. To find relief from this bad spell, Rohan engaged Pundit Maraj to perform a *graa puja*, a ritual directed at Lords Shiva and Ganesh, who pos-

---

1. The plethora of ethnic terminologies in this and the next chapter are used very precisely. Although *Indian, East Indian*, and *Indo-Trinidadian* all refer to the same group (with the qualification that *Indian* and *East Indian* can also refer to Indo-Caribbeans in general)—except for the brief discussion of recent immigrants from India, when the term *Indian* is used by both Trinidadians and myself to designate this particular group—the first two terms are used strictly as emic terms, that is, as labels employed by the Trinidadians discussed here, and as terms used by scholars I reference. Unless noted, I reserve *Indo-Trinidadian* for the voice of the analyst. Similarly, *Negro* and *Creole* are used as emic and other scholars' terms and *Afro-Trinidadian* as my term of choice to designate those claiming African ancestry. As noted earlier, my rhetorical strategy for avoiding constant and therefore cumbersome qualification of the dichotomy between those of African and Indian descent as a claimed one is the employment of the terms *Indo-Trinidadian* and *Afro-Trinidadian*, which I understand to be a projected dichotomy, not one inscribed in nature. This way I hope to avoid the reification of native ethnic categories.

sessed the necessary powers to intervene in this particular circumstance. *Pujas* are usually expensive undertakings. The supplies for the ritual itself, gifts for the pundit's services, and the cost of the customary traditional meal—usually *bussupshut* (an elaborate type of roti [flatbread]), *bodhi* (beans), *bygan* (eggplant), *channa* (chickpea curry), and *aloo* (potato) for the main meal and *prasad* (ritual food offered to the deity and the guests, small parcels containing a sweet made of flour, *ghee* (clarified butter), and sugar, and also pieces of fruit)—can amount to a sizable sum, depending on the grandiosity of the event.

That evening's event, however, was modest. The guests were few, consisting of a couple of immediate family members who were helping with the cooking, four or five children, and my husband and myself. The *puja* was conducted in the front yard under a large tree alongside a main road. Across the main road stretched a vast expanse of cane around six feet high. Unperturbed by the noisy traffic, the pundit performed his duties diligently with the help of his young son. My husband and I were the only adults in the audience, which otherwise consisted of children. The other adults went about their business except when their attention was called on during certain steps of the ritual. The pundit seemed pleased at our presence and invited David, my husband, to take part in minor parts of the ritual along with the children, such as planting the two *jhandis*—colored flags tied to long bamboo poles that signify the occurrence of a *puja* and also the specific deity venerated—in this instance a blue and a green *jhandi* for Lord Shiva. This being our first *puja*, we were reticent to use the camera, not knowing if it would be appropriate. After sensing a relaxed atmosphere, however, we hesitantly asked the pundit permission to photograph. His response was enthusiastic to say the least. From then on as he continued the *puja* he frequently paused to inform us that the impending step would be a "good shot." At times he would even insist on repeating a particular ritual in order to make sure we had captured the right angle. After the film roll ran out and the ceremony ended, I struck up a long conversation with the pundit as we sat down for the meal, served on banana leaves. Pundit Maraj, who worked in a government ministry, "moonlighted" as a pundit. His father had also been a pundit, and he hoped someday his son would continue the family tradition. When Pundit Maraj discovered that I had chosen to study a village in central Trinidad, he commended my choice of field location on the following basis. He made a distinction between Trinidadian and Indian and from this premise went on to say that I had chosen well by focusing on Indians living in Central: Central people, he said, were advanced both as Indians and as Trinidadians, in contrast to those Indians in the south, who were "backward" by Trinidadian standards. But, he quickly added, this is not to say that in the south the Indians are more "Indian," because "the Central people have retained a lot of Indian traditions too."

This chapter is about how some Central people claiming Indian descent situate themselves in relation to "other" groups—East Indians from the south, "real Indians" from India, Creoles, Whites (both local and foreign)—and negotiate their identity between the polarity they draw between being Trinidadian on the one hand and Indian on the other. More specifically, it explores how Indo-Trinidadians in the village of Cambio maintain the colonial distinction they inherited between East Indian and Creole through mechanisms of interethnic interaction and ethnic rhetoric.

Located on the western side of the island and bordering the Gulf of Paria, the plains of Caroni and the rolling hills characterizing the county of Victoria to the south constitute what is popularly known as the sugar belt. The appellation *Central people* refers to those living in that part of the sugar belt south of the Caroni River and north of the Montserrat Hills. On a clear day if we were to look out from the second story of a typical village house and rotate 360 degrees, we would see Central in almost its entirety. This basin is framed by the Northern Range, the Gulf of Paria to the west, and rolling hills to the south and east. Looking out over the vast green sea of sugarcane, one can discern individual villages only by the linear pattern of the mango and palm trees that line these villages and rise above the cane. Characterized by gently sloping or flat lands and containing pockets of deep alluvial soils, this area is well suited to agriculture. In the second half of the nineteenth century sugar plantations were concentrated here, the principal reason for the geographical concentration of the Indo-Trinidadian population. Thus the Central region, which is mostly contained by the county of Caroni, has been an East Indian enclave since the time of indenture.

Astride the Uriah Butler Highway, which links the primary urban centers of Port-of-Spain and San Fernando, and proximate to the deep-water port at Point Lisas industrial complex, the Central region is experiencing the pangs of modernization. Since the early 1970s its rural character has been radically transformed by larger economic trends overtaking the country. Foremost among them was the burst of industrialization afforded by the oil boom (1974–83) and the concomitant decline in the agricultural sector, namely, sugar.

Since its discovery in 1857 oil had come to provide an alternative to the plantation economy. In 1910 a refinery was built at Point Fortin, and in 1919 Shell became Trinidad's first producer. By 1938 oil replaced sugar as a major source of revenue, even though oil employed only 3 percent of the labor force and sugar employed 25 percent (Vertovec 1992:131). The discovery of offshore oil reserves in 1971 and phenomenal increases in world oil prices,

[99]

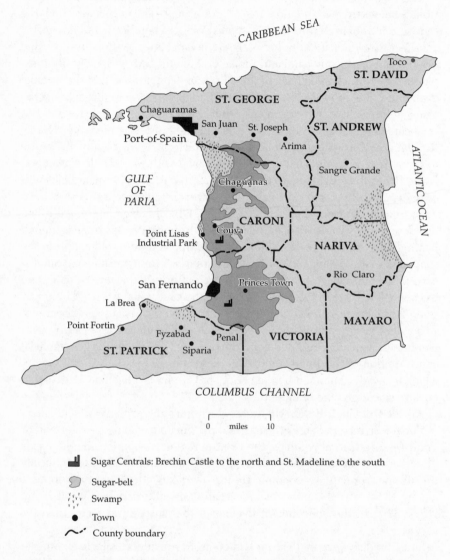

CARIBBEAN SEA

ST. DAVID

Toco

ST. GEORGE

Chaguaramas

San Juan

St. Joseph

ST. ANDREW

Port-of-Spain

Arima

ATLANTIC OCEAN

GULF
OF
PARIA

Sangre Grande

Chaguanas

CARONI

Couva

Point Lisas
Industrial Park

NARIVA

San Fernando

Princes Town

Rio Claro

La Brea

MAYARO

Point Fortin

Fyzabad

Penal

VICTORIA

ST. PATRICK

Siparia

COLUMBUS CHANNEL

0   miles   10

Sugar Centrals: Brechin Castle to the north and St. Madeline to the south

Sugar-belt

Swamp

Town

County boundary

Map 4 Trinidad's sugar belt, 1980. Source: Ministry of Finance and Planning, Government of Trinidad and Tobago, National Physical Development Plan of Trinidad and Tobago (1982), vol. 2.

engineered by OPEC in December 1973, brought an economic windfall to Trinidad. In the 1960s Trinidad obtained only TT$1.57 per barrel, but by 1975 the price increased to the astronomical figure of TT$21 and in 1980 to US$35 (Vertovec 1992:136–37). Production, too, especially from the offshore reserves, increased dramatically. Between 1971 and 1973 production rose from 129,000 barrels per day to 191,000, and by 1978 crude oil production had doubled the 1971 figures (Auty and Gelb 1986; Vertovec 1992). Because a large proportion of the oil production facilities were controlled by U.S. companies, the PNM (People's National Movement) government sought to maximize its revenues by increasing taxes and royalties. Between 1974 and 1983 oil revenues generated an estimated US$10 billion for the country (Thomas 1988 in Vertovec 1992:137).

Abandoning his previous five-year development plans,[2] Prime Minister Eric Williams used this new wealth to embark on a crash program of state-sponsored capitalism in which the government, in partnership with foreign investors, spearheaded industrial diversification. The creation of numerous industrial plants, especially in Point Lisas,[3] central Trinidad, transformed the lives of inhabitants in their vicinity significantly by opening up communities to the rhythms of modernity and industrialization. The government also used the revenues to nationalize major industrial sectors, including declining sectors such as the sugar industry, in order to maintain jobs.

To appease the populace, the government also poured petro-dollars into subsidy programs and welfare schemes. Between 1974 and 1978 TT$760 million was used to subsidize food, fuel, and utilities (Auty and Gelb 1986). The creation of a special works program in 1970, which in 1980 evolved into the Development and Environmental Works Division (DEWD), was intended to ameliorate the conditions of the poorest citizens by providing employment in community works, housing, and rehabilitation. Corroborating popular opinion, Percy Hintzen (1989) argues that DEWD catered primarily to the Afro-Trinidadian urban working class, the traditional voting bloc of the PNM. This mechanism of patronage was substantial. For example, in 1982 the government spent TT$565.1 million on the DEWD program, which at the time employed 50,000 to 124,000 workers of a total workforce of 383,000 (Hintzen 1989:73). The workload in DEWD projects was relatively light, typically commanding two hours of labor a day, and the wages were high, amounting to about TT$20 per hour (Auty and Gelb 1986:1168). Accordingly, these programs attracted workers from other sectors, particularly agriculture, where

2. See Vertovec 1992:132–33 and Ryan 1974:chap. 24 on these plans.
3. See Pantin 1988 on the Point Lisas experiment.

the pay was far less generous. Even now villagers in Cambio and the Central region who were lucky enough to have secured jobs in these projects reminisce about those golden days when people were paid to do nothing. The PNM's propagation of the welfare sector is now widely criticized for the dependency it fostered among the Afro-Trinidadian lower classes, but the extent to which such a work ethic also spread among Indo-Trinidadians must not be overlooked. The aversion among village youth to agricultural work and the constant yearning for an "easy job" with "plenty money" is largely an outcome of the "easy money, free spending" mentality that took root during the boom period.

The oil boom gave way to a consumer "revolution" in Trinidad. Between 1974 and 1982 per capita income grew from TT$3,937 to TT$19,682 (Thomas 1988 in Vertovec 1992:138). This huge increase in the spending capacity of the average consumer plunged the island society into a consuming frenzy. The number of cars increased by 65 percent between 1974 and 1980, and televisions, refrigerators, and stereos became common possessions (Vertovec 1992:138). In 1979 energy consumption per person in Trinidad was equivalent to that of France, Austria, and Romania (MacDonald 1986:193), evidence of the high-tech, modern lifestyle of the island society. The proliferation of shopping malls during this same period symbolized the spread of North American consumer culture.

The 1970s catapulted the East Indian community from its traditional economic and social enclaves into prominent mainstream sectors. Statistics for the 1975–76 period show a significant rise in the average monthly income for both ethnic groups, and for the first time the East Indian average surpassed that of Creoles by a fraction (Henry 1988:487). Examining the social mobility of different ethnic groups between 1960 and 1980, Reddock (1991) demonstrates that by the three indicators of occupation, education, and employment status, East Indians experienced the highest degree of upward mobility. Undoubtedly, Indo-Trinidadians (like the population at large) benefited greatly from the oil windfalls.

The industrial drive accelerated the deterioration of agriculture. When cocoa production had declined in the 1930s, sugar had resumed its traditional position as the mainstay of the export agriculture sector. But after the mid-1970s, sugar production increasingly fell below the 220,000-ton capacity of the industry. By 1979 production had decreased to 143,000 tons and by 1982 to a mere 80,000 tons, one-third the capacity (Pollard 1985; Auty and Gelb 1986). By 1983 the government was injecting TT$300 million per year in subsidies into this sector (Auty and Gelb 1986:1169). Yet any measure to rationalize the industry has been plagued by political controversy because most of its highly unionized and geographically concentrated workers are Indo-Trinidadians. It was estimated in 1977 that the industry directly supported 25,000 people—including the approximately 7,600 cane farmers who sell their privately grown cane to the sugar-processing factories (Pollard 1985)—and indirectly another 175,000 (Spence Report 1978).

By 1962 Caroni Limited, owned by the British firm Tate and Lyle, emerged as the dominant sugar interest on the island, producing 90 percent of the island's sugar and owning all the land under cane cultivation except for that held by cane farmers and two relatively minor estates, Forres Park Ltd. and Orange Grove (Brereton 1981:217). By the dawn of the 1970s, however, Tate and Lyle became increasingly reluctant to invest in the industry because of a decline in profitability caused by strong union demands, which extracted most of the benefits afforded by economies of scale (Auty 1976). Trade union activity in general increased in the 1970s, and when it became clear that foreign economic interests did not fully coincide with local developmental goals, Williams shifted his development strategy from "industrialization by invitation" to state-sponsored capitalism in partnership with foreign investors—a shift greatly facilitated by the oil revenues. It was such a political and economic climate that prompted the nationalization of many industries during the 1970s.

In 1970 the government purchased 51 percent of the ordinary shares of Caroni Limited. Between 1972 and 1975 it acquired another 4 percent, and in 1975 it purchased the remaining shares, thereby liquidating Caroni Limited and registering a new company, Caroni (1975) Limited. In 1976 the government also purchased Forres Park, the only other independent sugar company, and emerged as the sole owner of all the former plantations. Only the cane grown by small farmers remained outside state control. Nevertheless, even these farmers had to depend on state-owned factories for the processing of their cane. Thus by 1976 the PNM government controlled in essence the fate of all those involved in the sugar industry, most of whom were Indo-Trinidadians. State ownership of the sugar industry intensified the ethnic symbolism of the industry in the political arena (Ching 1985).

A number of factors have contributed to the rapid deterioration of the sugar industry under state control. As a nationally controlled company, Caroni has an obligation to take into account human and not just economic factors. Thus its efforts to maintain employment constrain the implementation of labor-saving technologies because of the amount of labor such technologies might displace. Escalation in production costs and problems with labor productivity are two major factors in the decline of the industry. For example, in 1979 the cost of sugar production in Trinidad stood at US$ 800 per ton compared with US$ 240 in Australia (Auty and Gelb 1986:1169). The situation grew worse in the 1980s as production dropped 65.2 percent between 1976 and 1984 and per acre tonnage declined from 29.8 to 18. In 1983 Caroni was receiving an estimated TT$300 million per year in subsidies while operating at an average cost five times greater than any other reasonably efficient producer (Auty and Gelb 1986:1169). The government treasury was able to sustain the industry during the oil boom, but the subsequent slump has forced a reevaluation.

After a series of strikes and confrontations with the government Basdeo Panday (prime minister since 1995), who had established himself as the undisputed leader (after the death of Bhadase Maraj in 1971) of the powerful sugar union—All Trinidad Sugar Estates and Factory Workers Trade Union (ATSEFWTU)—managed to secure substantial wage increases and benefits for the sugar workers. Before the strikes sugar workers were among the lowest paid in the country. In 1971 workers received an average of TT$50 per week whereas by 1982 the lowest paid manual worker in the industry received TT$51 per day. Between 1971 and 1982 most sectors enjoyed tremendous increases in wages with sugar and oil in the lead (Pollard 1985). Some sectors, such as oil, were able to absorb these wage costs through higher revenues and improved productivity, but others, such as sugar, lost competitiveness and profitability. In short, wage increases were not matched by increases in productivity. Labor productivity was limited because of strikes and other forms of noncooperation, high rates of absenteeism, and unplanned cane fires. A different set of problems arose with reference to skilled technical and managerial employees, who left the sugar industry for opportunities in the oil industry and other developing sectors promoted by the government (Pollard 1985).

Nevertheless, sugar workers themselves experienced a substantial improvement in their conditions, a result of Panday's union demands and the availability of oil revenues. Sugar workers, who are drawn almost exclusively from Central, are thus caught in an ironic position: the sugar industry has afforded them relatively high living standards, but their livelihood is threatened by the imminent demise of the industry itself, brought about partly by their increased wages.

These macroeconomic developments have altered the character of the Central region and the lives of its inhabitants. As the traditional agricultural base has eroded, urbanization and industrial and commercial activity have increased. A 1980 survey conducted by the Ministry of Finance and Planning classified the Central region as a "transitional zone" and its town centers of Chaguanas and Couva as "major developing centers," that is, having both rural and urban currents. According to the survey, the transitional zone, of which western Caroni is a part,

> displays a mixed pattern of development which is generally intermediate (in terms of level, diversity and intensity of development) between that found in the urbanized zone and that in the rural zone. The area is relatively well developed in terms of its share of population, its service hierarchy, and its communications network, with an economic base of intensive agricultural and notable secondary and tertiary activities, and a concentration of skilled manpower in the industrial towns. However, there are deficiencies in the quality of life particularly in terms of household environment. In addition the area exports large numbers of workers on a daily basis, commuting to jobs in the urbanized zone. (Ministry of Finance and Planning 1982:101)

Some of the significant secondary and tertiary activities include petroleum refining, assembly industries, construction, utilities, and services and government. The primary sector (export and domestic agriculture, forestry, and fishing) remains strong in this region, however. This relatively dynamic state of affairs is reflected in the county of Caroni's steady population growth between 1970 and 1980: from 115,254 to 142,220, or a rate of 23.39 percent, the largest increase experienced by any of the planning regions (Ministry of Finance and Planning 1982:24). In 1990 the county's ethnic composition, according to the Central Statistical Office (CSO), was the following: Indian, 113,827; African, 35,861; Mixed, 18,073; White, 260; Chinese, 245; Syrian Lebanese, 13; and "other," 129 (Central Statistical Office 1998:9). The 1990 census indicated a population of 168,831 for Caroni, the third most populated county—behind St. George (with 394,345) and Victoria (with 197,729)—of the nine counties of Trinidad and Tobago. Much of this population growth has been attributed to in-migration from less developed rural regions. This dynamic state of affairs is also reflected in the proliferation of housing starts in Caroni County between 1970 and 1980 and between 1980 and 1987. In the first period 11,895 and in the second period 13,852 dwelling units were erected, in comparison with 4,354 between 1961 and 1969 (Central Statistical Office 1989:44, 1998:58).

Pundit Maraj's assertion that Indians in Central were both Trinidadians and "real Indians" speaks to the multitude of forces that have accompanied accelerated commercial, industrial, and urban development in the region. His opinion suggests lay yardsticks for measuring the bases for identifications and highlights wider societal forces that have shaped these identities. His characterization of the Indians in the south, such as those of the villages of

Penal and Debe, resonates with a popular belief that the "real Indians," removed from cosmopolitan forces, reside in the deep country areas of southern Trinidad and work in agricultural pursuits such as cane farming and the cultivation of food crops. It needs to be emphasized, however, that this popular notion is primarily held by people outside the south. Although there may be some factual basis to such claims, it is impossible to generalize about the character of Indians in Trinidad on a regional basis because of the heterogeneity within the regions themselves. On some occasions in the Central area, for example, I was struck by the deeply rural character of the people. Moreover, variation within the south itself restricts generalization on an empirical basis. For example, an Indo-Trinidadian man I met in Tobago, who was originally from Penal in the south and had moved to Tobago around 1987, made careful distinctions in his description of the south. He said he grew up among "Negroes" because Penal, unlike Debe, which was entirely East Indian, had many "Negro" communities. He illustrated the extent of interethnic interactions by saying that his sister was married to a "Negro."

It is especially the more urbanized Indo-Trinidadians who propagate the image of Indians in the south as "real Indians." The pejorative label *country Indian* is used inside and outside the Indo-Trinidadian community to designate this "class" of Indians, whose ascribed lack of cosmopolitan sophistication is judged on the basis of style of dress, comportment, manner of speech, and most important, the degree to which Indian traditions pervade their daily lives. The sentiments of cosmopolitan, creolized East Indians toward the more traditional East Indians are nicely captured by the novelist Samuel Selvon in his keynote speech at the conference "East Indians in the Caribbean," held at the University of the West Indies in Trinidad:

> By the time I was in my teens, I was a product of my environment, as Trinidadian as anyone could claim to be, quite at ease with a cosmopolitan attitude, and I had no desire to isolate myself from the mixture of races. . . . At this time I was putting down the roots of the mixture of characteristics, attitudes and mannerisms which comprise the Trinidadian. I was one of the boys, doing my jump-up at Carnival time, giving and taking *picong*,[4] drinking coconut water around the Savannah or eating a late-night *roti* down St. James. . . . You can call this another kind of indoctrination if you like, and it was as subtle and unconscious as my childhood racial experience. I think I can say without question

4. A creolized style of speech conveying satire and irreverence, expressive of an attitude that refuses to be impressed by anything or anybody.

that this creolising process was the experience of a great many others of my generation. It was so effective that one even felt a certain embarrassment and uneasiness on visiting a friend in whose household Indian habits and customs were maintained, as if it were a social stigma not to be westernised. The *roti* and goat curry was welcome, but why did they have to play Indian music instead of putting on a calypso or one of the American tunes from the hit parade? (1987:33–34)

The easy and possibly inadvertent equation of cosmopolitan with "mixture," "Trinidadian," "creolising," "westernized," "calypso," and "American" in opposition to "Indian habits and customs" aptly illustrates the arguments presented so far and anticipates their development. Although the Indo-Trinidadian novelist Selvon[5] seems more optimistic about Indo-Trinidadian gravitation toward cosmopolitan ways than Pundit Maraj, ultimately both perceive Trinidadian and East Indian as dichotomized identities. To be Trinidadian means to be in tune with the national rhythms, that is, to incorporate wider societal norms and practices, whereas to be Indian is to retain traditional Indian culture.

The trends enveloping the Central region are particularly evident in Couva, one of the two major town centers of Caroni County.[6] Couva town bisects horizontally the ward of Couva, one of four wards in the county and located in the southwestern part. Couva town testifies to the intermediate character of the region. In 1982 the *National Physical Development Plan* (Ministry of Finance and Planning 1982) for Trinidad and Tobago classified it as a "developing" settlement (as opposed to an urban or rural one) on the basis of population size, population density, and occupational structure, then considered by the classifiers as the primary measure of urbanity. Couva overlapped with urban settlements in terms of population size and density, but its employment patterns were closer to rural trends since a high percentage of the population was engaged in agriculture.

The residents around Couva rely on the center to provide essential goods and services, and the larger social transformations overtaking Couva have a significant bearing on their lives. Some of these transformations include the creation of the industrial complex at Point Lisas, the building of housing projects, and the increasing penetration of U.S. cultural values and patterns.

5. Though Selvon is often labeled an East Indian novelist of renown, his mother was of Scottish and East Indian ancestry and his father was a Madrasee.

6. The other major town is Chaguanas. See Miller 1994:24–29 on the rapid development experienced there.

According to a medical doctor practicing in Couva, his house (which also happened to be our home), built in the 1950s, was the first modern house in the area. At that time there were three significant buildings in Couva town: his house, the Republic Bank, and the fire station. At present (1990), however, Couva is a relatively bustling town sporting two schools, churches, a mosque, two shopping centers, numerous small businesses, a major supermarket, two grocery stores, video stores, a sweet factory, a police station, a public utilities center, bakeries, music stores, a daily market selling fresh produce, a cinema, a couple of Chinese restaurants, a Kentucky Fried Chicken franchise (which is extremely popular), a nightclub, and even an athletic center that provides aerobic and karate lessons.[7]

The U.S. influence is particularly visible in the town of Couva. Most businesses experience a lull at noon when many take an informal break to watch "The Young and the Restless," a U.S. soap opera that has been elevated to a national pastime. The latest U.S. hits from the music charts blare out from the stores, competing with the indigenous calypso and the Jamaican "Dub." Except for the Wednesday matinee, which is always a movie from India, the cinema invariably shows U.S. action movies—the Schwarzenegger/Stallone movies tend to be real crowd pullers. For the outsider, however, the most visible symbol of U.S. influence is in fashion, especially among the younger generations. High-tech sneakers are considered prized possessions. Young men and women invest substantial portions of their earnings in clothing, shoes, and other cosmopolitan apparel. Women working in the service sector in particular are immaculately turned out in the latest hairstyles (with tints, highlights, and perms), clothing, and makeup.

Another significant U.S. influence in Couva, as in the Central area in general, is the presence of evangelical Christian sects. With their new buildings parading signs such as "Miracle Ministries—Air Conditioned," these institutions dotting the entire landscape of Trinidad point to a foreign spiritual encroachment. The Indian youth of all the deeply rural areas are drawn in growing numbers to these churches, which began making inroads into Trinidad in the 1960s.[8] Indo-Trinidadian political activists are particularly concerned and often irritated by the conversion of Hindu youth and explain that the success

---

7. Couva has developed even more since the time of my initial fieldwork, as confirmed during my 1998 field trip.

8. Vertovec (1992:124) claims that the fundamentalist Christian missions were able to make an incursion into the Indian community in the 1960s because Hinduism was languishing during this period. Some of my informants, however, dated the fundamentalist invasion to around 1972. Since 1972 also heralded the period of the oil boom, dating the presence of the fundamentalists to 1972 may indicate a revision of historical facts by Hindu leaders to delegitimize the fundamentalist preachers by pointing to their opportunism, that is, the fundamentalists sud-

of the missions is due to the particular vulnerability of these young people, who are said to be extremely sensitive to their apparent lack of social and cultural finesse.[9] Their inability or reluctance to relate to their ancestral traditions and the increasing economic deprivation (especially from around 1983, when the oil boom ended) have exacerbated a sense of hopelessness. They have turned to these missions primarily to gain a sense of self-worth.

Interestingly, since the evangelical crusades attract people of all ethnic groups and seek to bring them together under the paramount relationship to one God, it is possible that the ethnic antagonisms that pervade Trinidadian life become conspicuously absent or minimized in evangelical contexts of social interaction. Time and again, both followers and critics, with approval or foreboding, respectively, emphasized the role of these sects in spreading the word of harmony and unity between the "races." For those Indo-Trinidadian youths who feel stigmatized because of their cultural and rural backgrounds and who have become weary of the continuous tug-of-war between the races, the evangelical sects seem to provide a respite from the burdens of ancestral origin. Two young Indo-Trinidadian converts emphasized this theme to me. It was easy to spot them on a Sunday afternoon as they were walking to church with bibles clasped firmly in their hands. They were immaculately dressed in Western fashion—crisply ironed trousers, long-sleeved shirts buttoned up to the neck, and one was even wearing a vest. Their hair was neatly styled and kept in place with generous applications of mousse, and they were perspiring profusely in the midday heat. They explained that the message of harmony, oneness, and communal feeling propagated by the church attracted them to this faith. Here everyone, irrespective of race, they claimed, bonds, and they embrace and so forth to convey this unity. Unlike many other Indo-Trinidadians, they also seemed to approve of interethnic marriages (they were referring to unions with Afro-Trinidadians, since relations with Whites, perceived by many Indo-Trinidadians as a sign of upward mobility, rarely elicit opprobrium). Throughout my stay in Trinidad the only Indo-Trinidadians I met who held no reservations about interethnic marriage belonged to the evangelical sects.

According to Indo-Trinidadian activists and especially Hindu religious leaders, the most noxious feature of these evangelical sects is that their preachers, unlike their Catholic and Presbyterian counterparts, vehemently oppose their followers' participation in any Indian cultural or Hindu religious activities. Evangelical converts, therefore, often renounce their Indian names

---

denly became concerned with the spiritual well-being of Trinidadians when Trinidad proved to be a rich resource to tap.

9. The exact numbers of converts is unknown, but according to Vertovec 1992, it has not amounted to any drastic reduction in the Hindu community.

and refuse to partake in Indian festivals, especially those of religious significance. The encouragement of interethnic interactions by these sects too, I suspect, has exacerbated Indo-Trinidadian hostility toward them. Regarding the fundamentalist incursions made in the 1960s, Vertovec writes: "What is important is that Hindus themselves believed their community was especially singled-out and decimated by these Christian missions. The evangelists were highly spiteful toward Hindu polytheism and use of 'idols,' and they even accused Hindus of 'devil worship.' Throughout the island Hindus felt themselves to be 'on the defensive' against evangelical Christian criticism" (1992:124).

Similar apprehensions trouble the Hindu community today. But unlike the 1960s, when Hindu leaders passively accepted conversion (Haraksingh 1985:166), the newfound cultural and political confidence of Indo-Trinidadians has prompted their leaders to address aggressively the crises experienced by Hindu youth. Religious leaders seek to counter the evangelical influence by providing alternate avenues of amelioration—defined, again, in their own terms. Such attempts have taken the form of Hindu youth organizations, such as the Hindu Prachar Kendra in Longdenville near Chaguanas, that attempt to instill a sense of worth in these young people by raising their consciousness about Indian culture and their Hindu heritage. More important, they seek to combat the youths' sense of alienation by relating Hindu precepts to the Trinidadian context. Hindu youths often say they feel compelled to convert because they do not understand the *bhajans* (Hindu devotional hymns which are usually sung collectively) or what the pundit is saying during a *puja*. In short, their inability to speak and understand Hindi greatly inhibits their capacity to derive any meaning from Hindu ritual practices. The new youth organizations aim to circumvent this problem by introducing Hindi language instruction and providing English translations of hymns and prayers. In their efforts to relate Hinduism to the Trinidadian context, these organizations encourage youths to become actively involved in communities and thereby put into practice the principles of Hinduism.

Another conspicuous element in Couva town is the presence of Afro-Trinidadians, many of whom were attracted to the job opportunities at the new two-thousand-acre industrial complex at Point Lisas, about three miles to the south. Tucked between Trinidad's two major urban centers, just twenty miles south of Port-of-Spain and ten miles north of San Fernando, Point Lisas also has a port, which services the energy-based industries at the complex. The industrial projects undertaken here, often in the form of joint ventures with a foreign partner—a power plant, iron and steel plants, fertilizer factories, petrochemical plants, an aluminum smelter, and a liquid nitrogen gas plant, among others—were part of a government scheme to diversify

Trinidad's economy and to reduce dependence on petroleum by promoting energy-intensive industries based on the country's natural gas reserves.

The establishment of the industrial complex affected the people living in its vicinity even if they were not directly involved in its activities. For example, the development of transportation and communication networks and service sectors to meet the demands of the complex meant that people living nearby could also benefit from such facilities. More important, the labor needs of the complex caused a significant demographic change in the area, hence the 23.39 percent population increase in Caroni County noted earlier. Formerly a predominantly "East Indian" locality, Couva became increasingly populated by Afro-Trinidadians, primarily from urban centers that had reached the saturation point in terms of job opportunities, as well as from dilapidated rural areas. Even though Indo-Trinidadians remain dominant numerically, the presence of Afro-Trinidadians has changed the character of the Couva area. The newcomers' urban lifestyles, values, and practices contrast with the values and practices of Indo-Trinidadians here whose lives were integrally tied to a rural base in sugar cultivation. Although some neighborhoods around Couva are ethnically mixed (the majority of which have sprung up only recently), villages that evolved from former plantations continue to be overwhelmingly populated by Indo-Trinidadians. Michael Lieber's description of Trinidad's rural landscape captures the ethnic clustering of the early 1970s, before the transformations just delineated became manifest in places like Caroni:

> In rural Trinidad, districts tend to be ethnically homogeneous. One can travel through most of the villages of Caroni County and imagine himself in India. A person traveling only forty miles or so from Port-of-Spain to the northeastern corner of the island (where Herskovits studied "Africanisms") encounters a nearly exclusively Afro-Caribbean social domain.[10] A resident of Caroni may not encounter a black man or woman for weeks. A black farmer from a Northern Range village hears all sorts of things about East Indians but rarely runs across one. (1981:29)

Despite the proximity of Indo-Trinidadians and Afro-Trinidadians in Couva now, an implicit form of segregation prevails between the two groups. The Indo-Trinidadian presence in certain Afro-Trinidadian neighborhoods is

10. The axiom that East Indians are outsiders to the Caribbean is implicit even in Lieber's description, in which an exclusively East Indian area is equated with India and a Black area is equated with an Afro-Caribbean domain.

minimal and vice versa.[11] Afro-Trinidadian neighborhoods center on housing projects, which were inaugurated by the government to accommodate this new influx in population. The National Housing Authority (NHA) settlements that were funded by oil revenues are found throughout Trinidad.[12] Since these settlements primarily catered to urban working-class Afro-Trinidadians, they are perceived by many Indo-Trinidadians as evidence of the patronage system fostered by the PNM to cultivate its voting bloc. The housing projects are a focus of intense controversy. As far as many Indo-Trinidadians who have long-established roots in this region are concerned, the housing projects are a most unwelcome intrusion. Some interpret them as part of a devious scheme initiated by the PNM government to redress demographic imbalances. Unable to secure the votes of Indo-Trinidadians, the PNM is believed to have devised a master plan to populate Indo-Trinidadian enclaves with Afro-Trinidadians.

Indo-Trinidadians also point to certain disruptive elements that this migration supposedly incurred. Criminal and drug-related activities, they claim, dramatically increased with the Afro-Trinidadian presence and have transformed this once idyllic and peaceful area into a threatening and insecure environment. Ignorance and fear appear to shroud these housing projects despite their proximity to Indo-Trinidadian neighborhoods. When I asked Zeyna, an Indo-Trinidadian Muslim lawyer who lived in the more modern part of Couva two doors away from the doctor's house, how the Afro-Trinidadians in the housing projects earned a living, she immediately dismissed the question, saying, "Dey don't wok, dey live by tiefing." Harilal, an Indo-Trinidadian cane cutter living in Capildeo Block, a village close to Cambio, lamented that, of the approximately one thousand houses in the housing scheme in California—another district in the ward of Couva, immediately south of Couva town—only three or four were East Indian and that the "Negroes" spoiled the place after they arrived "with crime and drug and ting."

More recently, when the national Iron and Steel Company of Trinidad and Tobago (ISCOTT), established in 1981 at Point Lisas, was leased to a company from India (ISPAT) in 1989 for a period of ten years, another novel element was introduced to Couva: "real Indians" from India. Most of these Indians, who came in managerial, administrative, and other skilled capacities, rented houses in the higher-income neighborhoods around Couva and resided in the neighborhood of the medical doctor and the Muslim lawyer referred to earlier. The ISPAT Indians for the most part kept to themselves

11. The term *village* refers to older, rural settlements that can trace their origins to the plantation whereas *neighborhood* refers to more recent settlements that have an urban character.

12. Miller 1994:45–50 describes such a settlement in Chaguanas.

and rarely interacted with local Indo-Trinidadians. Indo-Trinidadian neighbors complained about the "unfriendliness" of ISPAT Indians. They rationalized the Indians' negative attitude by referring to the fact that in India "dey have caste and ting" and servants and that "here in Trini you don't have dat, everybody is equal." Zeyna, for example, who lived next door to some ISPAT Indians, said that they were "stuck up" and that she has never spoken to any of them.

The observation that Indo-Trinidadians are different from "real Indians" because in Trinidad social relations are constituted on a more egalitarian basis than in caste-ridden India captures the ambiguity Indo-Trinidadians sometimes display regarding their relationship to India. They draw on a mythified India to bolster their identity in Trinidad, but brushes with "real India," such as with ISPAT Indians, do not permit them the luxury of selecting which elements of India they can align with. Instead, the ISPAT Indians are an uncomfortable reminder to Indo-Trinidadians in this area of their humble Coolie origins. The presence of these Indians, whose origins cannot be traced to indenture and whose class status makes them more likely representatives of a "great tradition," delegitimizes somewhat Indo-Trinidadian claims of cultural superiority vis-à-vis Afro-Trinidadians. Indo-Trinidadians in the Couva area appear proud of the fact that caste inequalities have little significance in Trinidad in comparison with India and consider it a sign of their modernity and cosmopolitan outlook. They are aware, nevertheless, of the likelihood of their low-caste origins, as well as the likelihood that some "Indians," like the ISPAT immigrants, may judge them today on that basis.

Their "Coolie" origins and possible low-caste backgrounds are two characteristics of "Indianness" that Indo-Trinidadians would prefer to forget. Yet the submersion of that past is never complete. Asymmetrical interactions often revive Indo-Trinidadians' fear that others, whom they themselves perceive as superior, may indeed judge them on the basis of their humble origins. Mariam from Cambio told me of the time she and her family befriended a White woman during a picnic at the beach. When Mariam's family offered some food to her, Mariam became instantly embarrassed, afraid that the White woman "won't want to eat Coolie people food." When the woman accepted, Mariam was instantly relieved, and she took great pleasure in recounting to me how much the White woman relished the food.

The ISPAT Indians also remind Indo-Trinidadians that they may be poor imitators of Indian cultural practices. One evening I accompanied Harilal's wife, Meena, to a "ladies group function" in a neighboring village where Meena's family resides. Every Thursday an Indo-Guyanese woman, married to an Indo-Trinidadian pundit, conducts "get-togethers" for women in the neighboring villagers and teaches them "things Indian." The Indo-Guyanese woman had spent five years in India and was considered very knowledgeable in "things Indian." That evening's agenda consisted of meditation, prayers, a sermon on how to be a better wife, a cooking lesson, and finally a lesson on how to drape a sari properly. The instruction on draping a sari was fascinating. While the women watched and listened eagerly, the teacher throughout the demonstration kept referring to her experience in India and chided the Indo-Trinidadian women for draping their saris ungracefully. Some of the "ungraceful" techniques Indo-Trinidadian women had devised were sewing in or ironing the pleats, having too short a fall, or even wearing an elastic band in the petticoat, which sometimes had disastrous consequences when the sari dropped! Warning them against such practices, the teacher said, "Please, ladies, don't let the Indians from India laugh at us. They say how these ladies from Trinidad have such expensive saris but don't even know how to wear them."

The Village

Cambio village, like Couva, the rest of the Central area, and perhaps the Caribbean at large, is in many ways a place "in between." People here continuously vacillate, reconcile, and reconstitute their old plantation heritage and the new consequences of the increasing commercial, urban, and industrial activity. Cambio and most villages surrounding it in the ward of Couva, such as Phoenix Park, Basterhall, Waterloo, Felicity Hall, Orange Valley, Windsor Park, Dow Village, Diamond Village, and McBean, were all old plantations that the Caroni sugar company took over in its different periods of consolidation. Many of these villages' inhabitants can trace their roots, through either a consanguinal or affinal tie, to a particular plantation. All these villages, which still carry their old plantation names, are not isolated units but are integrated through their relationship to the town center, Couva, and their ties to the sugar company. The proximity of Cambio to Couva town (about a ten-minute walk) makes the village especially susceptible to the social and cultural currents characterizing the town center.

Most villages in the Couva area conform to a standard spatial arrangement. A row of houses lines either side of a secondary road, which is usually an offshoot of a main artery. Surrounding this single row of houses are cane fields belonging to that particular village's corresponding section. Sections are the administrative units of the Caroni sugar company. Toward the end of the off-season (the rainy season, between June and December), when the canes are nearly ten feet high, small villages like Cambio are lost in an ocean of green. During crop time (January to May), when the cane is burned and harvested, the scenery changes dramatically. If we were to gaze down, once again, from the second story of a village home, we would see a vast expanse of brown fields instead of the earlier smooth sheet of green, interspersed with rows of houses and clusters of trees delineating the separate villages.

Cambio village is surrounded by cane fields belonging to Cambio section, and together they constitute Cambio Estate. Cambio village, which occupies the original barrack site of the former plantation, now consists of thirty-five houses, with a population of approximately 215 people.[13] The houses are arranged in a single row alongside a secondary road, save for one house, which stands alone across this road. This lone house, adjacent to the old railroad (now dysfunctional) that bisects Cambio village, used to be the residence of the railroad guard. At present this dilapidated dwelling, constructed haphazardly with mud, particleboard, and tin, is the home of an elderly couple and their grand-children, who earn their livelihood by selling crabs at the Chaguanas market.

Cambio village is demarcated on the east by the Southern Main Road, which runs to Couva town, and proceeds south and on the west along a smaller secondary road that runs parallel to the Main Road. Across the road on the western side of the village is a small playing field with a little wooden shed, which the village youths constructed. This field, jealously guarded by the youths in Cambio, is their primary "liming" (hanging out) place. Most evenings the youths and the younger men play soccer here, and during the day a few gather now and then for a "cook," to play "c'yards," or just to hang out. It is exclusively a male recreational facility. Behind the playing field are three buildings belonging to Caroni: a small office that formerly functioned also as the company store, the modest residence of the assistant manager of Cambio Estate, and the more grandiose house and garden of the manager. The people in these dwellings do not form an integral part of Cambio village since their residence here is only temporary. Their relatively high occupational ranking as managers or staff of the sugar company also differentiates them from the vil-lagers. Accordingly, I draw the village boundary at the playing field.

The folk living on the western side, toward the playing field, are referred to as "down de road people," those on the eastern side as "up de road people," and those in between as "middle of de road people." Opposite the playing field, behind the last house "down de road," is the village's most precious pos-session, the oldest *kutiya* (Hindu temple) in Trinidad. The fate of this simple mud structure has been the center of much controversy in the village, and the various claims made on it have even led some households to sever rela-tions with the rest of the village. Whereas the playing field is a source of vil-lage solidarity, the temple is a cause of friction among the villagers.

13. One of the houses was empty when I conducted fieldwork (1990).

Around the center of this strip of houses are two adjacent snackettes, owned by siblings, that are the village bars. Apart from liquor (rum and beer), they sell a few canned goods, "sweet drinks" (sodas), chocolates, sweets, biscuits, and bread. There also exists a parlor up the road, but it is almost always empty because it does not sell liquor—hence the distinction between snackette and parlor. One member living in the household associated with one of the snackettes is also related to those running the parlor. Nearly all households in Cambio, save perhaps five, are interrelated through affinal or consanguinal ties.

Cambio is perceived by its inhabitants as an exclusively East Indian village. Thus one youth with a penchant for exaggeration, Ravi, told me I had chosen the ideal village because Cambio was the "only Indian village in Trinidad." The presence of Mr. Jones, of mixed African and Indian ancestry, and his offspring, and another Dougla boy, Tony, did not challenge the villagers' definition of their village as exclusively Indian. The villagers clearly recognized that these individuals were Dougla but included them as Indians.[14] Most of the villagers were also Hindu. Twenty-four households were Hindu, six households had both Hindu and Christian members, one was entirely Christian, and two were Muslim.

The ethnic and religious composition of Cambio has changed through the years from a highly heterogeneous enclave to the current largely homogeneous one. The older and middle-aged villagers described Cambio in the old days as a "bright place," meaning in common parlance a colorful and lively community. "Back long time," as the villagers say, Creoles, Madrasis, Punjabis, Muslims, and Hindus lived together, although they were housed in separate barracks. The fact that "back long time" Creoles too lived in their midst interrogates the ethnic exclusivity often attributed to East Indian enclaves in the past, and the older folk's positive evaluation of this period suggests that interethnic relations might even have been amicable. The Madrasi element is said to have been quite prominent then. Mr. Jones, for example, claimed that almost 50 percent of the residents in Cambio were Madrasis and that, unknown to the people in Cambio, many of their forefathers are Madrasis. The two popular explanations for the conspicuous absence of Madrasis in present-day Cambio are that "dey all die out" and that they gravitated toward Madrasi enclaves outside Cambio. Popo remembers the day some of the Madrasis returned to the village to remove their *murtis* (statues) from the

14. My observation that Indo-Trinidadians too incorporate Dougla individuals into their fold goes against the grain of both popular and academic thinking, which posits that Afro-Trinidadians are more tolerant of these people. See Miller 1994:53 and Reddock 1994:108.

temple in order to transport them to their new places of abode. With the disappearance of the Madrasis, the *murti* of the fierce south Indian goddess
Kali, which stood outside the village temple and had scared many of the village children, also disappeared.

According to various villagers' accounts, the early 1970s brought significant
changes to the village. The last remnants of the barracks were destroyed in
this period, which also coincided with the exodus of the remaining Madrasis
and possibly the few Creoles who had lingered. The "brightness" said to characterize Cambio before the 1970s was attributed to community activities
centering on the temple and an open marketplace situated in the area of the
playing field. Until 1972 workers for the company used to be paid in cash
every other Friday by the Caroni office, which was adjacent to the marketplace. After collecting their pay, the people used to go directly to the market
to buy produce and other items such as cloth and utensils. The market disappeared around 1972, when the workers began to be paid through the bank.

This change in the routine of wage payments and the concurrent disappearance of the market and the company store, although in and of themselves relatively small events, illustrate how villagers' networks have gradually moved from within the village to centers beyond its boundaries.
Dependence on banks for cash transactions; reliance on markets and grocery stores in Couva and Chaguanas for the supply of dry goods, fresh produce, and other consumption articles; and more important, the increasing
reliance on places other than their humble village temple for spiritual sustenance signify the erosion of communal centers within the village and the establishment of wider networks beyond it. The evolution of Cambio is intriguing precisely because it involves the simultaneous gravitation toward
two contrasting poles, one toward homogeneity and the other toward heterogeneity. On the one hand, Cambio developed into an exclusively "Indian" and a predominantly Hindu enclave; on the other hand, it is increasingly exposed to larger societal values and practices as villagers have been
pushed to forge links beyond the community as a result of larger societal
transformations.

Even though Cambio is often described as a "real Indian" village, the dynamics configuring this simultaneous gravitation toward contrasting poles has
generated a plethora of behaviors and practices among villagers that underscore their identity not so much as "real Indians" but as Indians who are undeniably Trinidadian. Accordingly, the village has not only a traditional
women's singing group—which provides the entertainment for farewell
nights (wedding eves), weddings, *barahis* (feasts held twelve days after the
birth of a child), and other traditional Indian ceremonial events—but also its

own calypsonian, Vickram, who when sufficiently intoxicated with rum provides ample amusement for the local patrons of the two adjacent snackettes.

Modern values also seep into traditional contexts. Formerly, Indo-Trinidadian women were strictly prohibited from dancing in public. Women were permitted to dance only on occasions that were considered female events, such as during a *barahi* or *matikor* (the ritual of digging dirt preceding the performance of the first ceremony of a Hindu marriage, usually conducted three days before the wedding itself), and even then no males were allowed to watch or participate except little boys. Though villagers adhere to these traditional rules for the most part, the spectacle of women "wining"[15] is not uncommon these days in public ceremonies such as weddings. In fact, most of the audience seems to derive immense pleasure from this spectacle, and with shrieks of laughter, invariably touched with nervousness, the audience, especially the women, urges the dancers to go on. Some Indo-Trinidadian men claim to disapprove of such "vulgar" behavior, but they nevertheless appear to enjoy the revelry.

Weddings in particular show the ingenuity with which villagers have managed to circumvent traditional rules without explicitly transgressing them. Brides, for example, always wear a customary yellow and then red sari for the ritual itself but change into a Western white bridal gown before departing for the in-laws' home. Consumption of alcohol and "fresh" (meat, usually chicken, duck, or goat) is strictly prohibited on Hindu ritual occasions such as weddings, yet this rule is often circumvented by having a neighbor supply the alcohol and the "fresh." As a result it is common to find the men congregating at the neighbors or by the road next to the cars having a lime and a "fete" while the women patiently and diligently sit through the long and elaborate services. In this way villagers maintain the sanctity of the wedding home while transforming the ritual occasion into a "fete." Similarly, in the case of dietary rules, some Hindus, who never cook beef at home, relish the hamburgers sold by the vendor at Couva. In their equation eating a hamburger has more to do with adopting a North American practice than with beef— thus for some Hindus, eating hamburgers is not seen as a contradiction.

The villagers of Cambio appear to be quite familiar with icons of U.S. popular culture. The village tends to be deserted between noon and two in the afternoon, when most villagers—men, women, and children—remain glued

15. A style of dancing that is highly sexually suggestive, involving the gyration of the hips and waist, usually associated with carnival and also with Afro-Trinidadians. See Miller 94:113–17. One has only to witness the behavior of Indo-Trinidadians at a "chutney" performance to dispel the myth that sexually suggestive dancing is associated exclusively with Creoles, however.

to their televisions watching "The Young and the Restless" and "Santa Barbara." To my surprise I also found U.S. wrestling films to be very popular, especially among some older women. Occasions such as Mother's Day, Father's Day, and Valentine's Day were celebratory events in Cambio when gifts were exchanged and elaborate meals prepared.

U.S. fashion has also penetrated Cambio. The young men and boys, who tend in general to be very fashion conscious, spend a great proportion of their incomes on clothes and shoes. One youth, Paras, who was not particularly liked by the villagers, especially by the other youths, was said to think no end of himself since he acquired a pair of TT$300.00 sneakers![16] As for women, a marked contrast exists between the older women's styles of dress and those of the younger women and girls. The older women's standard apparel consists of a simply cut modest dress with short sleeves which varies only with respect to the type of material used—a worn-out cotton or synthetic for ordinary days and usually a flamboyant self-colored polyester, often with a glossy texture, for special occasions such as a wedding. The younger women, in contrast, display a bewildering array of fashion, from shorts and mini skirts to their own variation of the most extravagant ball gowns. Catalogs from U.S. department stores are cherished. In Cambio one house possessed one of these catalogs, which all the young women in the village borrowed whenever an impending occasion called for a new dress, usually tailored by the village seamstress living "up de road."

Another relatively novel element in Cambio is evangelical religion. Evangelical sects had won converts in at least six of the houses in Cambio. The degree to which these converts embraced their new faith varied. Seventy-year-old Chandradeyo, who lives "up de road," was an ardent convert. Her life had been a difficult one. She began working when she was nine years old and continued to work until she was sixty-five, when she retired from Caroni. She came to Cambio after she married and has lived there for more than forty years. She and her husband used to load cane and drive a mule cart. At present she shares her home with a married son and his family and another son. Chandradeyo's conversion came about as a result of an illness. She had been plagued by a curious condition for almost thirty years: her nails would fall out, and the food she cooked would become infested with worms. As she recounted those times, she shuddered with horror. For years she had sought in vain for a cure and spent all her money in the process. Finally, around ten

16. The exchange rate at the time was approximately TT$4.24 = US$1. Since the average income for the young men in the village for a hard day's manual labor was approximately TT$50, this was extravagant indeed.

years ago, her daughter, who is a Christian, took her to Miracle Ministries, an evangelical church. Only then was she cured. For this result Chandradeyo is utterly grateful to God, and now, she claimed, she goes regularly to church and abstains from participating in any Hindu ritual activity. Chandradeyo, who was reputed to have a beautiful voice (hence her nickname, "hummingbird"), formerly belonged to the women's singing group in the village. Since her conversion, however, she has stopped singing (as it would breach church rules); as she put it, "I doesn't feel to sing anymore."

Lucy also takes her new faith very seriously. Originally a Presbyterian, she adopted the Pentecostal sect in 1987. Lucy was one of the few people in Cambio who claimed to take the message of racial harmony propounded by the evangelists seriously. Since going to church, she said, she has begun to consider the "Negroes" and herself one of a kind: "At church Negroes don't look at you differently, they hug you up just as one of them." Lucy's interactions with Creoles in an extra-village context, the church, had prompted her to reassess the value of traditional categories that distinguished her identity from the "Other." Lucy's remarks were especially intriguing since her father was a Dougla. The fact that she "naturally" identified herself as East Indian buttresses my earlier point that individuals who are of Dougla ancestry tend to identify themselves (and be accepted) as either Creole or East Indian, depending on which group's norms and practices they have primarily grown accustomed to. Lucy's mother was East Indian, Lucy was married to an East Indian, and she had lived all her life in Cambio. These formative factors contributed to her perception of herself as East Indian.

I have situated Cambio within larger societal trends to highlight the diverse factors that inform villagers' ethnic identity. Modern influences, U.S. cultural patterns, evangelical movements, and encounters with real Indians and Creoles all factor into how villagers negotiate their identity. Although the encroachment of such non-Indian values and practices might suggest a waning of East Indian ethnic identity, villagers nevertheless manage to perpetuate the traditional dichotomy between themselves and Creoles. Boundary maintenance is sharply conveyed in forms of interethnic interaction and ethnic rhetoric.

Interethnic Interactions

A crucial determinant of the nature of interethnic interaction is the degree of perceived ethnic homogeneity or heterogeneity configuring a particular space. Contrasting the ethnically homogeneous rural enclaves with the ethnically heterogeneous urban environment of Port-of-Spain, Lieber observed:

> In the city . . . social and cultural distances are dramatically reduced. Residential proximity . . . mean[s] that residents routinely encounter and scan . . . the behaviors and styles of members of [other] ethnic groups. . . . The ethnographer is disposed to make two contrasting guesses about what such a situation of interethnic proximity may imply. The first hypothesis proposes fear, prejudice and hostility as characteristic of a social setting where the indicted outsider is not present . . . and where, consequently, myths about the outsider may be easily sustained since they are never subject to the critique of direct evidence and disclosure. The other guess is that the tight, proximate interactive basis of urban social relations is likely to increase friction and tension. . . . In a city, lives are actually brought into proximity with each other. It is no longer merely myths that clash, but people. . . . Familiarity may lead at once to a greater ease in dealing with categorically "distant" people, while exposing and exaggerating conflicts that in more parochial, less cosmopolitan settings are more sublimated and less clarified. (1981:29, 30)

For Lieber, then, interethnic proximity, which is primarily an urban feature, does not necessarily lead to an attenuation or exaggeration of ethnic cleavages but instead carries the potential for both. With respect to the residents of Cambio the picture becomes even more complex. These people are neither wholly rural nor urban but precariously occupy the fringes of both settings.

As villagers increasingly begin to establish links outside Cambio, especially for the purposes of occupation and education, they venture into contexts that are ethnically mixed. Yet since their residential site is almost exclusively Indo-Trinidadian, conventional stereotypes prevailing in the home environment continue to shape villagers' perceptions of Afro-Trinidadians. Kamla, a young Indo-Trinidadian girl who lived in one of the "middle of de road" houses, related how during her school years she used to have "Negro" friends, but when she left school and got to know what they ("Negroes") were really like, she stopped mixing with them.[17] Thus old myths were revived in Kamla's case despite her exposure to an ethnically mixed environment during her school years.

Interethnic proximity itself is insufficient to destroy old myths once ethnic stereotypes have taken root. Indeed, as Lieber (1981) notes, as Colin Clarke

17. Kamla's rationale is worth pondering, that is, it was only when she stopped fraternizing with "Negroes" that she discovered what they were *really* like.

(1986, 1993) demonstrates in his study of San Fernando, or as Barth's (1969) model of ethnic boundary maintenance suggests, given the appropriate conditions, proximity itself can serve as the catalyst for enhancing ethnic exclusivity. Contexts of interethnic interaction, it seems, must also foster relations of familiarity before old myths can be destroyed in the face of new realities. A familiarity, defined not merely in terms of knowing the other (as Lieber's usage implies) but rather in terms of cultivating a sense of sharedness, is possible only when recognition/acknowledgment of the individual takes precedence over his/her group identity. The processes embedded in negotiating old myths with new realities implicate the complex nexus between ethnicity's rhetorical and practical dimensions. The division between East Indian and Creole had its origins in colonial history and continues to be a pivotal ideological axiom through which Trinidadians perceive and comprehend their society. In this general sense all Trinidadians—Indo-Trinidadians and Afro-Trinidadians, rural and urban, people from ethnically mixed to ethnically homogeneous areas—have access to this ideological repertoire and its related ethnic stereotypes. The articulation of ideological schemes (expressed through rhetoric) and practice (ethnic interactions) is also mediated by a crucial variable, that is, the degree of familiarity. In contexts that limit familiarity with the other, such as Cambio, ethnic stereotypes dominate interpretations of ethnic interactions even when they belie practical experience.

The interactions of the villagers with Afro-Trinidadians were predominantly limited to institutional contexts of school[18] and occupation, and they almost never fraternized with Afro-Trinidadians socially. The younger generation, including Kamla, recounted their relations with Afro-Trinidadians from school days and the older people from their experience in work situations. But the contexts of school and work did not engender sufficient familiarity to undermine ethnic stereotypes.

Boundary maintenance that limited familiar interactions was even more pronounced in Cambio because most of the younger generation left school at a relatively early stage, at the end of junior secondary school (about age fourteen) or at the end of senior comprehensive school (about age sixteen). Most men and women of the older generation were restricted to working as cane

18. In Trinidad education is compulsory at the primary school level (ages five to eleven). A common entrance examination at age eleven determines the type of secondary education a child may receive. Success at these examinations means a student receives a full five-year liberal arts education. The less successful candidates enter three-year junior secondary schools and, after taking the 14+ exams (which I am told everyone passes), advance to two-year senior comprehensive schools. Junior secondary and senior comprehensive schools emphasize vocational training in areas such as sewing, flower arranging, mechanics, office administration, and electronics.

cutters in the sugar industry, a predominantly Indo-Trinidadian enclave. Therefore, opportunities to develop enduring relations with individual Afro-Trinidadians were relatively limited. Today villagers also tend to keep within the boundaries of the village when they engage in recreational activities and rarely venture to Couva town except to watch a movie or to shop. Thus while the men and young boys lime at the snackettes, on the playing field, or at the roadside, the women and young girls usually lime in one another's houses or by the gates of their houses along the road. When villagers did leave the boundaries of the village, it was to visit family or friends in an adjacent village who happened to be, in most cases, Indo-Trinidadian. Rarely did any Afro-Trinidadians visit or lime in the vicinity of Cambio.

Villagers in Cambio make a distinction between Afro-Trinidadians in general and those individual Afro-Trinidadians with whom they share a certain degree of familiarity. They repeatedly deploy popular ethnic stereotypes to label and understand the behavior of the unfamiliar Afro-Trinidadian but tend to incorporate as "one of us" those Creoles they are accustomed to. Often a Creole who does not exhibit the character traits deemed Creole becomes "one of us" by adopting certain "Indian traits." The inclusion is never total, however: even though a particular Creole may be deemed "one of us," he/she continues to be recognized as non–East Indian. Nevertheless, as we shall see shortly, Indo-Trinidadians distinguish this familiar individualized Creole from the more distant collectivized outsider through a process of partial inclusion based on a sense of sharing—in this case "Indian traits." This capacity for a conceptual flow of personnel across boundaries not only maintains the boundary but also insulates ethnic stereotypes from contradiction. In this sense ethnic stereotypes remain privileged and may be reinforced even when they belie practice.

The villagers' pejorative rhetoric about Creoles targets not only an abstracted figure but its more visible materialization next door to their village, the Creoles in the housing projects whom they perceive as unwelcome intruders. Much of the fear regarding these Creole neighborhoods is exacerbated by ignorance and unfamiliarity because of the minimal degree of social interaction between Indo-Trinidadians who have remained in their traditional home sites and the newcomers.[19] This point became apparent to me on one particular occasion.

---

19. It is important to stress that not all Indo-Trinidadians shared these perceptions. In the mixed neighborhoods there appeared to be a high incidence of social interaction between Afro-Trinidadians and Indo-Trinidadians, which enabled these people to distinguish between "good" Creoles and "bad" Creoles and "good" Indians and "bad" Indians. Thus they, unlike those who tended to generalize about the entire community on the basis of popular stereotypes, were able

One day, within a month of our arrival in Cambio, my husband and I were exploring the southern side of the Couva main road and heard the tones of steelpan. We followed the sound until we came across a pan shed, a rough-and-tumble wooden shed with a couple of steelpans and a sign hanging above that read "Cosmic Cultural Base" and right below it, "Together we aspire, together we achieve." A Rastafarian, Selwyn, and another Afro-Trinidadian, Burt, were practicing a calypso of Lord Kitchener's for the upcoming pan competition. The pan shed was in a small playing field across from a mixed neighborhood. Selwyn, who lived in a different mixed housing settlement, visited this area regularly since it was where his father and his siblings lived and also the location of his pan shed. One of his brothers lived with an Indo-Trinidadian woman with whom he had three children. It soon became apparent that Indo-Trinidadians and Afro-Trinidadians in this neighborhood interacted amicably and freely. Indo-Trinidadian, Afro-Trinidadian, and Dougla children played together on the roadside. Indo-Trinidadian and Afro-Trinidadian women limed outside their houses, gossiping while shelling peas or engaging in other minor household activities. Men, both Indo-Trinidadian and Afro-Trinidadian but mostly Afro-Trinidadian, drifted back and forth liming or playing with the children. Toward the back of the pan shed was a Creole housing project, and Selwyn warned us that we should not venture there because it was infested with crack addicts.

Later that day Selwyn took us on a tour of Brechin Castle, the sugar factory, where he worked in the boiling room. While touring we came across Sahadeo, an Indo-Trinidadian sugar factory worker who lived in a village close to Cambio and whom we had befriended earlier. In our earlier encounters with him Sahadeo had warned us about Creoles and their "dangerous" qualities. He had previously been very forthcoming and talkative but now appeared hesitant. He looked at us suspiciously and greeted us rather reluctantly. We could only guess that seeing us in the company of Selwyn, who was not only Creole but also a Rasta, somehow prompted him to reevaluate his opinion of us. Later that evening, when we returned home, Robbie, a twenty-two-year-old Muslim youth from Cambio, the son of a cane cutter with whom we developed a close friendship, visited us. Robbie had helped us tremendously when we first established ourselves in the village, and he and his family took it on themselves to watch over us. When Robbie heard that we had spent the whole day in the pan shed neighborhood and had been in the company of Selwyn, he was alarmed. He thought we were naive to trust Selwyn

---

to distinguish the good and the bad on an individual basis, a facility that only familiarity with the "Other" permitted.

so easily. After we were finally able to reassure him, he nevertheless wanted to meet Selwyn just to make certain, and a couple of days later on the pretext of delivering a message to us, he bicycled over to the neighborhood and finally met Selwyn. Even though this neighborhood was at most a ten-minute bicycle ride from Cambio, where Robbie had lived all his life, it became clear to us that this was his first visit to this part of town.

This narrative emphasizes the distance between the two populations, a distance originating not in spatial terms but through unfamiliarity. Interestingly, even Selwyn thought it fit to warn us of the "dangerous zones" of the crack areas. Unlike most Indo-Trinidadians of this area, however, he did not equate it with Creoles but saw it in terms of illegal activity. The pertinent issue here is that the Indo-Trinidadians who engaged in minimal contact with Afro-Trinidadians were unable to differentiate among neighborhoods populated by Creoles, and thus all Creole neighborhoods were collapsed into a single entity and labeled dangerous.

In contrast, the few Afro-Trinidadians with whom villagers in Cambio have frequent interactions are perceived quite differently. On one occasion I was chatting with two Indo-Trinidadian youths from villages adjacent to Cambio who were liming at one of the snackettes. One of them had a sister living in Cambio and visited Cambio frequently. Both, Tiger and Raas, appeared different from the young men in Cambio in that their behavior and manner seemed more "creolized." They were wearing cut-away T-shirts and gold chains, had long hair, and were drinking and smoking heavily.[20] Raas was into heavy metal music and had dated several "Negro" girls. Whereas the youth in Cambio expressed a cosmopolitan air in a conservative fashion, these two young men exhibited a sense of rebelliousness. Their demeanor initially led me to assume that they might have a different perspective on the Afro-Trinidadian population. But soon it became evident that they too carried hostilities toward Afro-Trinidadians. While we were chatting, an Afro-Trinidadian man drove by the snackette, and Tiger and Raas called out to him in a very friendly manner and exchanged a few words with him. When Tiger kept on insisting that he "didn't like dem people," I reminded him of the Afro-Trinidadian man whom he obviously seemed to like. He saw no contradiction between his rhetoric and practice on the basis that "he isn't really Negro because he lives in Capildeo Block [which is predominantly populated by Indo-Trinidadians], he is married to an Indian, and he cooks and eats Indian food." Thus through his behavior this Creole had been partially

---

20. In general, the youth would rarely drink and smoke in public in Cambio, especially in front of their families, as a sign of respect or in fear of disapproval.

incorporated into the "us" category, a process possible only with interactions that engender familiarity.

Familiarity also accounts for Indo-Trinidadian inclusion of certain Dougla individuals. The fourteen-year-old Dougla boy Tony, who lived in his grand-mother's house with his mother and stepsiblings, was wholeheartedly ac-cepted by the village in general and the youths in particular. I never encoun-tered a single occasion when Tony was excluded on the basis of his mixed ancestry. On that rare occasion when Tony's mixed origins became the topic of conversation, mainly through my prodding, one youth dismissed its signif-icance, saying, "We grew up with him, he is one of us."

In *A Brighter Sun* (1971), set during the war years in Trinidad, Selvon beautifully captures the intimate relations that develop between a young East Indian couple, Tiger and Urmilla, and their Creole neighbors, Joe and Rita. When, after marriage, Tiger at the tender age of sixteen moves to Barataria with his young wife, they are catapulted into a bewildering new environment. Barataria, just four miles east of Port-of-Spain, was "cosmopolitan" with Cre-oles and East Indians in the majority. The town, with its unrelenting traffic along the eastern main road, was developing rapidly during World War II as former estates were converted into housing plots to meet the frenzied de-mand for housing by those being pushed out of the overcrowded city. All this was a far cry from the sleepy rural lifeways that both Tiger and Urmilla were accustomed to back home in Chaguanas. It is Rita and Joe who come to the aid of the young couple, and Tiger and Urmilla turn to them, not other East Indians, for advice and help. Rita not only delivers their firstborn but also as-sumes the role of surrogate mother to Urmilla, and a deep bond develops be-tween the two women. When Tiger's family come to visit after the birth of the child, prejudices are kindled by the parents, who are disturbed by this friend-ship. As soon as Rita and Joe depart,

a babble of voices broke out in the hut.

"Is only nigger friend you makeam since you come?" his *bap* [Tiger's fa-ther] asked. "Plenty Indian liveam dis side. Is true them is good neighbour, but you must look for Indian friend, like you and you wife. Indian must keep together."

"Is I who pinch him [Rita's nephew], that is why he cry," Urmilla's mother said. "Nigger boy put he black hand in my *betah* [daughter] baby face! He too fast again!"

"But, *Mai* [says Urmilla], these people good to us; we is friends. I does get little things from she, and sometimes she does borrow little things from me. They is not bad people."

Tiger said, "If it wasn't for them I—we—wouldn't know what to do."

The family continues to pester them to "keep their distance" with Creoles, and after the parents depart,

> Tiger sat on the step and watched night coming. The big thought he had postponed came back. It had happened when his parents talked about Joe and Rita. At the time rum was in his head, but now it was all clear. Why I should only look for Indian friend? What wrong with Joe and Rita? Is true I used to play with Indian friend in the estate, but that ain't no reason why I must shut my heart to other people. Ain't a man is a man, don't mind if he skin not white, or he hair curl?
>
> He thought how burned cane thrash went spinning in the wind helplessly. He and Urmilla would have been like that if Joe and Rita hadn't helped. (Selvon 1971:47–48)

Ethnic Stereotypes and Rhetoric

Members of a Creole society operate with a keen understanding of assumed fundamental differences that set apart persons in their society. Expression of this heterogeneity can assume multiple forms. All these forms, however, find root in "the notion that the social setting is populated by distinct kinds of people, who are what they are as a consequence of inborn qualities or deeply held beliefs manifest in their everyday behaviour and difficult or impossible to renounce" (Drummond 1980:354). Drummond's observations on Guyana also speak to the ethnic situation in Trinidad. The "notion that the social setting is populated by distinct kinds of people" clearly resonates with the cosmopolitan narrative of the plural society and its concomitant metaphor of the tossed salad. Such notions of difference, however, are continuously subject to transformation that depends on context. In Drummond's terms: "Classification of an actual slice of behaviour depends greatly on who is doing the classifying and where the behaviour is taking place. The very practice that is regarded as 'coolie' or 'creole' in Georgetown [in the case of Guyana] may be held up as a fine example of 'English' behaviour in the countryside or bush" (1980:357). Drummond's insightful observation on the operation of purportedly pure ethnic categories in Creole societies allows for the fluidity they reveal in practice, with specific contexts of interaction ultimately defining the semantic content of each category.[21]

---

21. Miller makes a similar observation based on informants' ethnic descriptions of persons in advertisements: "Informants performed this task with ease and alacrity but their answers were

In Trinidad, as in Guyana, a generalized system of beliefs based on the notion of fundamental difference between Creoles and East Indians prevails and is expressed mainly in the form of ethnic stereotypes. As in most Creole societies, ethnic stereotypes are ubiquitous in Trinidad.[22] Rhetoric on "race"[23] provides an appropriate lens through which to examine such stereotypes. Although an outsider may initially be shocked at the intensity of race rhetoric in Trinidad, it is important to understand that popular discourse on race is an integral and visible part of the island's cultural and social life. It constitutes a legitimate part of popular discourse, unlike, say, in the United States, where the emphasis on speech control limits race rhetoric to the "unmentionable." The dialectic between rhetoric and practice implies exactly that rhetoric does not mirror practice. Indo-Trinidadians commonly express this distinction when they say, "East Indians talk racist but it is Negroes who practice it." The truth-value of this claim notwithstanding, its premises are worth pondering.

Race rhetoric seems to assume specific meanings and roles in the Trinidadian context. Stereotypes are often the subject of humorous exchanges between the two ethnic groups. On one occasion when Indo-Trinidadians in the Couva area were celebrating Indian Arrival Day[24] in the village of Orange Valley, a truck carrying a group of Afro-Trinidadians arrived. Some Indo-Trinidadian men good-humoredly shouted to them, "This is Indian Arrival Day, we don't want no Creole here," and pretended to shove them away. The Afro-Trinidadians took it well and did not seem to mind. The Indo-Trinidadians too were laughing, and then one of the men turned to me, and patting one Afro-Trinidadian on the back exclaimed, "Dem too is Indian, dem too is Indian—it's O.K." An important aspect of the vocality of race is that although it divides groups, it also provides the medium for bridging relations through friendly exchanges. As the Indo-Trinidadian man I met in Tobago explained, "Each ethnic group has jokes about each other and it's taken in good spirits." He, for instance, often tells "Negro" jokes to his buddies, who are all "Negro," and they all have a good laugh together. The ability to laugh at what are usually contentious criteria also renders them less threatening.[25] Just as

---

remarkably inconsistent . . . individuals I took to be clear exemplifications of one ethnic category were strongly asserted to be something quite different" (1994:52).

22. See Baksh 1979.

23. Since local expressions of difference are usually phrased in the idiom of race, I retain the term *race* here to be consonant with local phrasing and not as an objective assessment of the situation.

24. May 30, Indian Arrival Day, marks the entry of the first Indians to the island in 1845. It was instituted as a national holiday in 1995.

25. Evidently, stereotypes as a source for humor can also be used pejoratively. Analyzing the image of Indians in calypso, D. V. Trotman (1989) notes that the changing behavior of Indians

the evangelical faith provides a brief respite from a racially tense environment, converting ethnic stereotypes into laughable matter can lend momentary cohesion to a potentially divisive situation.

Race rhetoric in Cambio village revolves around a number of cardinal
points. A dominant stereotype was that Creoles, unlike East Indians, had no
culture. Despite Afro-Trinidadian efforts to elevate and establish Afro-Creole culture as a legitimate and rich culture on a par with any other, Afro-
Trinidadians sometimes betray a tacit acceptance of the belief that they, in
contrast to East Indians, lack a strong culture. This belief constitutes a popular explanation, among Afro-Trinidadians, Indo-Trinidadians, and Whites
alike, for the alleged successes enjoyed by Indo-Trinidadians in contrast to
Afro-Trinidadians.[26] Mr. Merritt, an Afro-Trinidadian insurance salesman,
was a strong PNM supporter and was dismayed at the split of the African vote
between the PNM and the NAR (National Alliance for Reconstruction) during the 1986 election. The Indians, he claimed, refused to split and remained
solidary. Mr. Merritt admired the East Indians for their alleged display of
communal strength and attributed it to their culture—their language, religion, and family structure. The "Africans," according to Mr. Merritt, lacked a
communal spirit because they had lost their culture and adopted European
ways. That contemporary explanations for relative successes enjoyed by different ethnic groups should be premised on an ideological axiom of the colonial era—the notion of the culturally naked African and the culturally saturated Indian—is indeed revealing. As Pundit Maraj stated, Trinidad had no

---

was a dominant theme in Indian-related calypsos of 1946–56: "The urban-based African calypsonian, threatened by these changes, and fearing that his world was being invaded, believed that
incursion had already led to Indian economic dominance. In order to handle this uncomfortable
and threatening situation, the calypsonian employed humor, which was a standard device in an
art form that was geared to popular entertainment. It had been used in the calypso as a device
to bring to public ridicule all those who had transgressed community mores and this was valuable as a means of social control. It was also used on the 'outsider' who could be made less
threatening and more manageable by making them laughable. The attempts by Indians to break
out of traditional roles could be made less threatening·if they were depicted as laughable. The
result was a number of calypsos in which the Indian is depicted as a comic figure" (1989:179).

26. Even academic analyses reproduce this adage, particularly by linking the "tightly knit
joint family" structure of the East Indians (family, like Hinduism, being almost synecdoche for
East Indian culture) to their perceived ability to accumulate wealth. Walter Mischel, a U.S. psy-
chologist, conducted an experiment comparing East Indian and Creole capacities to defer gratification and argued that "the father-child relations inherent in the more stable Indian family
would make Indian children more prone to accept an experimental promise of a greater future
gift in place of a smaller immediate gift" (in Oxaal 1968:88). The relative absence of a male authority figure in the Creole family structure, he argued, induced Creole youths to prefer immediate gratification over the chance for a greater gift in the future. There is, however, a more pejorative Creole stereotype for East Indian success—that they are "drug dealers."

culture; only the Indians in Trinidad had one—an Indian culture. In his view, "Negroes" were looking for a culture. Steelpan, calypso, and carnival, which "Negroes" parade as culture, only provide an excuse, according to this pundit, to "drink and do all dem wicked tings." Of course, the statement that Trinidad has no culture tacitly conflates Trinidad with people of African origin, indirectly but firmly pointing to the potency of Afro-Trinidadian cultural hegemony.

East Indians are thought to be quiet and docile, going about their business growing food, building their houses, and taking care of their families in an industrious manner. "Negroes," in contrast, are said to possess none of these positive characteristics, living only day to day, as they do in Africa. A fifty-year-old cane cutter, Curlie, explained the difference between "Negroes" and Indians: "Indians, dey always progressive, dey wok for a little money, whatever dey wok for dey always put away a little, and the Negroes, whatever dey wok for dey will eat up everyting because dey want nice food, dey want woman, you understand . . . dey want to do all kind a ting with deir money." When I asked him why Indians are so different from "Negroes," he attributed it to the differences in culture:

> Indian culture is far different from Negro culture. The Negro culture, as we see it, dey like to go to party like carnival, dey like to beat pan and smoke and go to drink and ting. Indian culture don't have dat, you understand. . . . Now de Indian culture, here we have we fete too. But we Indian would take out, let we say we go to a fete. We will provide for dat fete. When I say . . . let we say I work for five hundred dollars. Say if I have to save a hundred dollars from the five hundred, I'll save my one hundred dollars. I have to buy my goods for tree hundred dollars . . . right . . . so that'll be four hundred and I might have to get one or two more tings . . . what remains from dat I will fete. And if none remain, it have no fete for me. But a Negro would prefer to do without some of these goods and go and spend all in a fete. So dat is the difference between a Indian and a Negro.

Variations on this theme abound not just in Cambio but throughout Trinidad. Another trait that is thought to perpetuate the short-term thinking of "Negroes" is their preference for handouts as opposed to fending for themselves. One schoolteacher related to me his family's "rags to riches" story and attributed the family's success, which he saw as typically East Indian, to its capacity for thrift and hard work. In contrast, the "Negroes," he claimed, were only used to handouts. Indians knew they would not get anything from anybody; thus they worked for what they needed. "It's like if you come to me and say you are hungry and I give you a fish today, and the next day, and the next, then all you know is to take. But if I give you a line and teach you to fish . . ." Ram's rephrasing of the age-old line aimed to show that "Negroes" will always remain in a state of dependence (which the PNM encouraged through its system of patronage, according to Ram), whereas East Indians have learned to fend for themselves.

The perception of the "Negro" as inefficient, "not too bright," and lazy was pervasive among the villagers at Cambio. In Joey's opinion, for example, it was the laziness of the "Negroes" that compelled their masters to beat them during slavery, "but not so with de Indians, dey used to wok!" In addition, "Negroes" were often described as a "destructive race," prone to ruin any project they undertake. According to Joey, any country populated more than 75 percent by "Negroes" is always in a mess and in a constant state of decline.

The Indo-Trinidadian belief that "Negroes" are destructive stems partly from the different statuses ascribed to Negroes and Whites in Indo-Trinidadian folk wisdom. Based on a survey conducted in 1976, Ryan concluded that Indians, more than any other group, preferred to work for a White boss (34 percent of the Indians surveyed) rather than an African or even an Indian (1988b:225). Similarly, some of the villagers in Cambio seem to operate on the assumption that Whites possess an inherent capacity and right to rule over other populations. In this sense the superiority of Whites, even vis-à-vis East Indians, is taken as a given. In contrast, villagers are often puzzled over Negro claims to superiority or even equality.

The villagers generally seem aware of Afro-Trinidadian claims to superiority on the basis of their cosmopolitan style, access to education, and since independence, their access to political power. Afro-Trinidadians, by adopting European habits, tastes, and behavioral patterns, had found a way of annexing themselves to Europeans through the avenue of achieving respectability. The contestation over status is complex because of the existence of multiple measures of superiority. Villagers denigrate Creoles for their slave origins, but these same villagers also exhibit anxiety over their own "Coolie" origins, thereby indicating an awareness of their own inferiority vis-à-vis larger societal standards. For example, one woman in Cambio explained her brother-in-law's choice to adopt a different family name on the basis that "he didn't want no coolie name." I suspect the vehemence with which most Indo-Trinidadians insist on the inferiority of the "Negro race" has much to do with their anxiety that "Negroes," according to certain measures, might be considered better than they.

The following is a snippet from my journal documenting a conversation between two elderly gentlemen in Cambio, Mr. Parasaram, who despite being a Brahmin garnered little respect from the villagers because he had a reputation for bullying his wife, and Nizaam, a gentle and reflective old man who possessed numerous talents (as village healer, fishnet mender, and gardener, to name a few) and who was greatly respected and liked: "They said how the 'nigger race' here in Trini think so high and mighty of themselves because they have education. But they are a slave race. To illustrate this point Nizaam told us of a conversation he had with a medical doctor from 'Africa.' This doctor had told Nizaam that even though the 'Trini Africans' think they are more civilized than the 'Africans' because they are Westernized and educated, he [the doctor] and the rest of the 'Africans' are not a part of the slave race." Here Nizaam attempts to delegitimize Afro-Trinidadian claims to superiority on the basis of education and Westernization by using a different yardstick, their slave origins.

The alleged inferiority of the Creole and the superiority of the White come into play particularly when villagers discuss Creole aspirations for political power and the mismanagement of the Trinidadian government. Curlie, for example, was annoyed that "Negroes now want to be on top of everything, even the Whites." Aspirations to usurp power from Whites, he felt, were preposterous because, as he explained, "for how long since we know the Whites have ruled." From Curlie's perspective, Whites were the legitimate proprietors of political power. Curlie did not think the Whites in South Africa unfair. He held the somewhat popular Indo-Trinidadian view that "Negroes," being totally inept, ruin almost anything they take charge of, "like all the 'Negro' countries, they are all in ruin." Ethiopia, Curlie explained, once was a lush resourceful country but is now reduced to a desert. He then turned to the present state of the sugar industry in Trinidad. When the industry was under the control of the British sugar company Tate and Lyle, it generated enormous profit. As soon as the government took over the sugar industry, however, it began running at a loss. This pattern was reversed in the case of the nationalized steel industry, ISCOTT. The industry was running at a loss until the government leased it to a company from India. These same examples are continuously used by many Indo-Trinidadians to justify their perceptions of Creoles as incompetent and inferior.

The villagers in Cambio, especially members of the older generation, who experienced the transition to independence, have mostly positive things to say when they reminisce about the "good old days" of the colonial order. The efficiency, competence, and "fairness" of British rule are often juxtaposed to the inefficient, incompetent, and corrupt practices of Creole-dominated post-colonial governments. In that same conversation Mr. Parasaram and Nizaam lamented Trinidad's present state: although a "paradise place" with endless resources, the country imported even basic foods. They recalled how well the country was managed under the British. Everything was nice, clean, and well maintained—they even used to catch mosquitoes on a regular basis! The two men then got on to the subject of voting. They believed that since the people are the government, they should have the right to vote government officials out of office if they do not perform up to the people's expectations. Later they commented how during British times you could vote only for a local assembly. At this point I interjected that the present system might be better than British rule since people then had no say in picking their governors. They seemed at first surprised by my comment, thought about it for a while, and then reasoned that the British governor was the queen's government and was sent here by the queen to govern. From their viewpoint the queen's endorsement was ample legitimacy for the governor to rule. Clearly, such statements of principle aimed to make my comment look redundant or even foolish. Nevertheless, I pursued my line of argument: "What if the governor was bad?" They both thought again for a while, and then Nizaam replied, "They were never bad, all the governors were good." British rule was beyond reproach.

The stereotype of "Negroes as a destructive race" is usually deployed by lay Indo-Trinidadians for two purposes: first, as illustrated above, to point to Creoles' incompetence and inherent tendency to ruin anything they touch and second to indicate their disposition toward criminal behavior. The villagers at Cambio and the Indo-Trinidadians in the Couva area often spoke of the "Negro" criminal element. As Zeyna said of the Creoles in the housing projects, "Dey don't work, dey live by tiefing." The villagers generally seem to be afraid of Creoles. Susan (a young woman from an adjacent village who now lives in Cambio), Lucy, and I were once discussing the high crime rate in Trinidad when Susan said it was the "Negro" people she was afraid of. The other day, she went on, when she was in a supermarket "a big Negro fella walked in" and she got so scared that she took off her gold bangles and put them in her purse. Only when the "fella" left did she put them back on again. Lucy, a recent convert to the Pentecostal faith, reacted by saying that though she could understand Susan because that is the way she too used to feel, now, having changed, she "don't look at tings dat way." Lucy's familiar interactions with Afro-Trinidadians at church prevented her from making such generalizations.

The fear of Creoles frequently crops up when villagers discuss the fate of the land just behind their houses. The question of land distribution, an integral part of Caroni's diversification program, has elicited much controversy both nationally and locally. When the cane fields behind the string of houses in Cambio were abandoned recently by the company, many villagers immediately appropriated plots adjacent to their houses to cultivate gardens. They now fear that this land will be given to Creoles as part of the land redistribution program; then, not only will they lose their gardens but, much worse, they will have Creoles living right next door. The villagers extol the virtues of

[133]

present-day Cambio because of its peaceful, quiet, and trusting environment, and they are convinced that all this will disappear if Creoles come to live in their neighborhood. As Keith, a village youth, said, the villagers are scared that Creoles will invade their space and that Cambio will turn into another Dow Village (an ethnically mixed village also in the Couva area) or the housing scheme. About ten years ago, according to Keith, Couva was a quiet place; but when the Creoles came, cocaine and crime increased rapidly. Keith also said that he and the "fellas" had discussed how best to deal with the situation if indeed Creoles were given the land. They decided that when the "Negroes" dump the construction materials on the site and leave them unguarded, the "fellas" will sneak in and transfer the materials to their homes. This, they agreed, would give the "Negroes" the message that they are not wanted.

A counterpart to the image of the "Negro" as criminal is the stereotype of the Indo-Trinidadian as victim. As Fena put it, "Negroes don't have anything so they rob the Indians because they know they [the Indians] have." This issue, as we shall see later, has become part of a national debate, especially in reference to Indo-Trinidadian migration to Canada, which has exacerbated the division between the two groups. Just as the villagers in Cambio employ the popular stereotype of the Negro as destructive or criminal to explain their victimized status, Indo-Trinidadian politicians and intellectuals use this image of the Negro to buttress their claims of racial discrimination, appropriating common race rhetoric in the national debate about crime and refugee status.

Ethnic interactions and rhetoric are two areas of boundary maintenance that explicitly seek to differentiate the Other. Even when ethnic rhetoric belies practical experience, villagers manage to insulate their folk categories from contradiction by individualizing familiar Creoles, thereby maintaining the integrity of the boundary itself. In these two areas villagers' folk categories conform to historically derived stereotypes and dichotomies that differentiated East Indians from Creoles. As we shall see, these same folk categories are used by Indo-Trinidadian leaders to legitimize their claims to the nation and the state on the basis of difference, as opposed to commonalities East Indians share with Creoles.

[6]

To Be Mixed Up in a Place in Between

The behaviors and value orientations of Caribbean people repeatedly defy neat analytic compartmentalization because of the systematicity and ease with which they entertain multiplicity and contradiction. Mintz (1977) and Trouillot (1992) have eloquently captured this disposition in their insightful evaluations of anthropological approaches to this region. Yet what is striking in their analyses and those of the works they examine (with the exception of Jayawardena 1963 and B. F. Williams 1991) is that Indo-Caribbeans[1] rarely enter into this provocative and, I believe, correct formulation of the ethos prevailing in societies labeled Creole. The tendency of analytic models of creolization to bypass Indo-Caribbean elements is an offshoot of a slippage between a theoretical conceptualization—creolization as process—and an empirically defined category operating in the lay and political discursive arenas—Creole as a noun denoting those primarily of African ancestry and which cannot include East Indian elements (Chapters 2 and 3). Thus although the concept Creole society nominally includes Indo-Caribbeans as a part of the heterogeneity characterizing this region, attempts to theorize the nature of Creole societies in terms of a complex dialectical movement between contradictory principles structuring the creolization process have largely focused on the African and European elements in the New World.[2]

---

1. I use *Indo-Caribbean* as an etic term to denote Caribbean people who claim Indian ancestry beyond the context of Trinidad.
2. Even Miller's (1994) provocative analysis of a central dualism resting on two opposed temporal orientations, transcendence and transience (which he anchors in the condition of

For example, even the path-breaking methodological treatise put forward by Mintz and Price (1976), which calls for a historically oriented anthropological approach to Afro-American cultures and societies in the Caribbean, limits its nuanced and rich observations to the African (slave/unfree) and European (master/free) dimensions.[3] I believe the insights provided by Mintz and Price in the mid-1970s have tremendous potential for illuminating the complexity structuring the Indo-Caribbean experience. Because their framework was a critical response to the contemporary academic obsession with tracing African survivals in the New World, as in the work of Melville Herskovits (1958, 1966), their insights assume particular significance for our understanding of the Indo-Caribbean experience, which remains mired in the debate surrounding issues of cultural retention and acculturation.

Disrupting the notion that enslaved Africans in the New World shared a homogeneous West African culture, Mintz and Price begin with the premise that "no group, no matter how well-equipped or how free to choose, can transfer its way of life and accompanying beliefs and values intact, from one locale to another" (1976:1). Instead, they argue, commonalities among the enslaved group need to be located in the less concrete realm of largely "unconscious" cognitive orientations or even "'grammatical principles,' which may underlie and shape behavioral response" (1976:5). For Mintz and Price the "baseline," which informs to this day the cultural practices and institutional forms of Afro-American experience, was first formulated during the initial period of capture, enslavement, and transport (the middle passage). For the purpose of this analysis I wish to highlight three points from Mintz and Price's historical approach: the determinative role played by the planta-

---

"modernity"), that structure Trinidadian life, tends to juxtapose the principle of transcendence with elements associated with the Indo-Trinidadians, such as their attitudes toward family, property, and material culture. In this way Indo-Trinidadians are included because they epitomize one polarity of this duality but remain excluded for the most part from embodying the dialectic itself. In fairness to Miller, however, the association of transcendence with Indo-Trinidadians is more at the symbolic level, for he is careful to draw attention to how both Indo-Trinidadians and Afro-Trinidadians transgress ethnic boundaries at the practical level. For example, in his discussion of inheritance patterns he points to Indo-Trinidadian inclinations toward transient practices, which goes against their traditional disposition toward transcendence (Miller 1994:148). But it is his suggestion that Indo-Trinidadians may find this transgression "difficult to embrace" to which I take exception, for as I argue, Indo-Trinidadians, like most members of a Creole society, appear relatively undisturbed by simultaneous entertainment of contradictory principles.

3. Trouillot's more recent attempt to chart a methodological (as opposed to an empirical) framework for creolization that emphasizes its processual nature carries the potential for encompassing East Indian elements within what he defines as the modernist context (1998:18–19).

tion/slavery complex in shaping Afro-American culture histories; Mintz and Price's insistence on connecting cultural to institutional (social) forms while maintaining a conceptual distinction between them; and their emphasis on the creative and "open" dimension of Creole cultures and social systems.

The acute asymmetrical relations between the free and the enslaved structuring the plantation/slavery complex, the crucible from which emerged Creole cultures, indelibly shaped the character of Creole societies. Given the conditions of its emergence, as Trouillot says, "manifestations of Afro-American cultures appear to us as the product of a repeated miracle.... Afro-American cultures were born against all odds" (1998:9, 10). The deep divisions "along lines of culture, perceived physical type, power and status" (Mintz and Price 1976:3) characterizing these societies called for a total separation between slave and free sectors, but such a separation was only an ideal, and in practice the interpenetration ("nodal points") of the two sectors was formative in the development of Creole societies. Thus although the power of the master defined the parameters within which slaves could create new institutions and practices, Mintz and Price are careful to remind us that the free population was considerably influenced and dependent on the enslaved as well, an insight nicely spelled out earlier by Edward Brathwaite (1971, 1974), who stressed the vitality of interculturation in the process of creolization as opposed to mere acculturation of Africans to European norms and practices. The significance for Indo-Caribbeans of the observation that the structuring principle behind creolization is interculturation (as opposed to acculturation or homogenization) will soon become evident, but for the moment let us return to the subject of "encounter." The emphasis on points of encounter between otherwise deeply divided and asymmetrically positioned elements, whether master and slave or metropole and colony, suggests that such divisions are part and parcel of the Creole complex. In his dialectical theory of creolization Nigel Bolland (1992:71) makes the excellent point that such polarities are internal to and constitutive of the system itself. Thus the essence of Creole societies seems to lie in the dialectical movement of opposites/dualities that are in turn generatedby conflict-ridden forces endemic to colonialism and its attendant plantation/slavery complex.

That Creole cultural systems must be understood within the overall institutional and social structural framework of domination/subordination is crucial for Mintz and Price and also Bolland (1992).[4] Creole cultural sys-

---

4. Mintz and Price define *culture* as "a body of beliefs and values, socially acquired and patterned, that serve an organized group ('a society') as guides of and for behavior" (1976:4), and *institution* as "any regular or orderly social interaction that acquires a normative character, and can hence be employed to meet recurrent needs" (1976:12).

tems emerged in conjunction with the establishment of new social relations, and though such cultural systems may have drawn on widely shared West African "cognitive orientations," they were inextricably linked to and therefore informed by the new social relations being forged in the New World;[5] the exact nature of Creole culture cannot be understood as separate from its particular institutional and social moorings. According to Bolland, the mistaken assumption by analysts that creolization is merely a *cultural* response "by individuals of different groups to their environment and each other" leads to a simplistic "dualistic view of society . . . [and] to the portrayal of creolization as a 'blending' process, a mixing of cultures that occurs without reference to structural contradictions and social conflicts" (1992:64). Thus the evolution of Creole cultural forms must be situated within an overall conceptual framework that takes into account "the activities of individuals located in institutions and differentiated by power" (Bolland 1992:67).

This interplay between the social and the cultural is crucial for understanding the creative impulse and the openness attributed to the emergent Creole cultural systems. Since the enslaved Africans did not have a common culture, they did not constitute communities of people at first and "could only become communities by processes of cultural change. What the slaves undeniably shared at the outset was their enslavement; all—or nearly all—else had to be *created by them*. In order for slave communities to take shape, normative patterns of behavior had to be established, and these patterns could be created only on the basis of particular forms of social interaction" (Mintz and Price 1976:10; emphasis in original). It is worth quoting at length Mintz and Price's elaboration of this important point:

> All slaves must have found themselves accepting, albeit out of necessity, countless "foreign" cultural practices, and this implied a gradual remodeling of their own traditional ways. . . . For most individuals, a commitment to, and engagement in, a new social and cultural world must have taken precedence rather quickly over what would have become before long largely a nostalgia for their homelands. We remind ourselves and our readers that people ordinarily do not long for a lost "cultural heritage" in the abstract, but for the immediately experienced personal relationships, developed in a specific cultural and institutional setting, that any trauma such as war or enslavement may destroy. A "culture," in these terms, becomes intimately linked to the social contexts within which affective ties are experienced and perceived. With the destruction of those ties, each individual's "cultural set" is transformed phenomenologically, until the

5. See also Bolland 1992:64–65.

creation of new institutional frameworks permits the refabrication of content, both based upon—and much removed—from the past. (1976:24)

Thus the institution of slavery and the initial cultural heterogeneity characterizing the slave populations produced "among [the slaves] a general openness to ideas and usages from other cultural traditions" (Mintz and Price 1976:26). The dehumanizing aspect of slavery, with its relentless assault on personal identity, also cultivated and "enhanced appreciation for exactly those most personal, most human characteristics which differentiate one individual from another" (1976:26), which put a high premium on an individual sense of style and a continuous demand for newness (Miller 1994:232). The ready acceptance of cultural differences, the openness to different influences, and a highly cultivated sense of style all operated to instill within these emerging cultural systems "a fundamental dynamism, an expectation of cultural change as an integral feature of these systems" (Mintz and Price 1976:26). Dynamism, change, elaboration, and most of all creativity were, then, the determinative features of the Creole cultural system.

I have chosen to elaborate at length this particular academic approach to Creole societies in order to differentiate the analytic uses of the concept from its political/ideological ones. The frequent tendency to collapse the analytical concept with the political one—a consequence not only of the semantic operation of race categories that equated Creole with African and European elements but also of the formulation of the Creole society thesis as a formal ideology for Afro-Caribbean nationalisms that further reified the identification of Creole with specifically African elements (Bolland 1992)—unfortunately foreclosed the possibility of applying the rich analytical insights afforded by the theory of creolization to Indo-Caribbean practices and values. Even more problematic, in the few studies that attempt to apply creolization to Indo-Caribbean people, creolization ironically transforms into a principle of assimilation rather than one of interculturation. Given the dichotomy between Creole and East Indian, the creolization of East Indians necessarily implied the abandonment of East Indian values and practices and the adoption of Afro-Creole ones.[6] Thus even academic assessments of the degree to which Indo-Caribbeans have creolized are measured on the basis of Indo-Caribbean adoption of Afro-Caribbean patterns. To this day Indo-Trinidadians equate creolization with assimilation to Afro-Caribbean patterns, hence their resistance to creolization, which some have even pejoratively labeled "Douglarization."

6. See, for example, Mohammed 1988, which makes a similar point.

Setting aside the political/ideological uses of the term *creolization*, in this chapter I argue for the very creoleness of Indo-Trinidadians in terms of the behavioral and normative dispositions associated with the analytic concept of creolization as formulated by Mintz and Price (1976). If we momentarily disassociate the concept from its embodiment in particular ancestral groups, we find that the characteristics informing creolization—cultural change, innovation, dynamism, openness to cultural differences, and creativity, annexed to the easy entertainment of contradiction—also permeate the lifeways of the villagers in Cambio.[7]

The two themes that follow—house building and styles of consumption, and family organization—constitute integral identity markers for "East Indian" ethnicity. They are often displayed as unique to East Indians. Closer examination, however, suggests that what is uniquely East Indian is the rhetoric of authenticity that claims them. In practice, house building and family and household organization are marked by an openness and intermeshing of diverse cultural strains, which attest to the creoleness of the East Indians themselves.

House Building and Styles of Consumption

A striking feature of the Indo-Trinidadian village landscape is the presence of modern concrete houses next to humble, modest dwellings constructed of wood, tin, or sometimes even mud. Within a village the mix of modern and humble (old or new) dwellings generally assumes one of three patterns: the modern house by itself in a single plot, the more humble structure by itself in a single plot, or the modern house next to the more humble dwelling within a single plot.

A family dwelling type not only is indicative of the relative prosperity of the family but also symbolizes the experience of the villagers in general. How people talked about their new houses and the way they found the means to build them seemed to embody a distinctive East Indian dimension—there was a resonance in family narratives about houses.

The modern concrete house is believed to embody features that are peculiarly East Indian: it establishes, in material terms, East Indians' alleged affinity to land. The evolution from the humble mud hut to the large concrete house attests to the upward mobility Indo-Trinidadians have generally

---

7. My intention here is not to claim that other scholars fail to see the dynamism or cultural creativity of Indo-Caribbeans but instead to appropriate and apply the analytic concept creolization to Indo-Caribbean behaviors and cultural patterns and thereby identify a common habitual disposition shared by both ethnic groups that is not premised on acculturation.

experienced in the last few decades; the new houses are symbols of success beyond mere utilitarian concerns. Values believed to be uniquely East Indian are made material by the hardship and sacrifice invested in the construction of these edifices. Interestingly, Daniel Miller observes of the four communities he studied (with varying degrees of interethnic mixture) in Chaguanas that Indo-Trinidadians tended to buy the land and construct their own houses, in contrast to Afro-Trinidadians, who bought their houses: "As Africans use wealth to demonstrate their escape from economic conditions where they were forced to build their own houses, Indians are developing a sentimental attachment to their own participation in building" (1994:144).

The first thing that strikes an observer about the modern houses in Cambio and those dotting the rural Trinidad landscape in general is the uniformity in architecture.[8] Individual houses may vary in terms of details of elaboration and ornamentation, but in general they are two-storied. The first floor invariably encompasses a sheltered front porch, a kitchen, and a couple of other rooms. The stairway leading to the second floor is almost always outside the house. Thus the two stories are not, at least structurally, an integrated whole but two potentially separate units. This structural feature fulfills certain functions. Since the predominant kinship pattern is the joint-family household (a problematic term elaborated on later), at least in this village, the separation of units allows for a degree of privacy through the allocation of units to different segments of the family. For example, in some cases parents and unmarried children would live upstairs and the first floor would be shared by their married sons and their families. As the predominant pattern of residence was virilocal, married daughters and their families were resident only under exceptional circumstances. Many of the houses possess two or more kitchens, also convenient for separating units. From an environmental standpoint the split-level structure signifies a suitable adaptation. Not only does the second floor enable the villagers to catch the breeze when the canes are tall, but it also ensures against disaster in case of flooding.[9]

Apart from its immediate functional value, the separation of units has symbolic importance. First, it indicates the social transformations affecting villagers' lives. The first floor usually is an extension of the original modest residence, built of tin, mud, or wood.[10] These materials were later replaced by

8. See also Miller 1994:144–47 on Trinidadians' relation to property (land and houses).

9. In many areas prone to flooding, most of the houses are still constructed on stilts.

10. In Miller's (1994:147) description of houses the second floor constitutes the original unit, built on stilts, and the area below later is converted to living spaces for married sons and their families. This difference could be attributed to location, since Chaguanas is more prone to

concrete, but the original organization of space remains. Thus the first floor usually is a self-contained unit with a kitchen, dining/living room, and one or two bedrooms. Interestingly, the feature most absent from the first floor, but present in the second, is the bathroom. A bathroom within the internal structure is symbolic of modernity. Being the most modern unit, the second floor invariably has a bathroom whereas the "outhouses" situated in the backyard remain as vestiges of the original structure of residence. Thus the extension of the modern—here symbolized by the second floor—to the old, first floor reflects the social and cultural vicissitudes that have transformed both the landscape and the lives of villagers in Cambio.

The houses also speak to the nature of the transformations in that they encompass both the suddenness and the gradualness of the break with the past. The sudden aspect is illustrated by the fact that the frenzy for modern concrete houses coincided with the increase in the standard of living experienced by Trinidadians in general as a result of the oil boom. This larger trend is also manifest in Cambio village. In 1990 approximately twenty of the thirty-five houses were made of concrete and ranged from modest, somewhat dilapidated abodes to large, well-maintained, elaborate residences. Construction of most of them began during the 1970s. Apart from the edifices themselves, this period also saw a phenomenal increase in villagers' acquisition of modern accoutrements: at the time of the fieldwork, every household in Cambio, save one, owned a television and a refrigerator; five houses had washing machines, nine households owned cars, and two had trucks.[11]

The injection of wealth into Cambio, most of whose residents were engaged in the sugar industry, came after 1975 when the leader of the sugar union, Panday, managed to wrest from the government not only a substantial increase in wages but other benefits as well, such as back pay and job security.[12] Extolling Panday's virtues, Curlie explained how the union leader's actions transformed Curlie's family's life. Before Panday came onto the scene in 1974, Curlie was earning approximately TT$7 per day as a cane cutter. By 1976 Panday had secured a 35 percent increase in wages for sugar workers

---

flooding. Even in Cambio, however, some houses were built on stilts and their original units were located on the second floor.

11. Vertovec (1992:153) notes similar physical manifestations of the boom period in Penal Rock Road, a predominantly Indo-Trinidadian village in a remote part of the south.

12. The popular belief is that revenues from oil facilitated successful bargaining on behalf of sugar workers, but it is possible that the dramatic rise in world sugar prices in 1974 from £150/ton to £650/ton was the primary factor in the wage increases. As Vertovec notes in the case of Penal Rock Road, although it was some years before the effect of the oil boom was felt, "the price rises of 1974 turned many village cane farmers into local *nouveaux riches*" (1992:145).

and Curlie received TT$1,000 as back pay. With this money Curlie's family purchased a refrigerator. Soon after, Panday negotiated successfully for a 100 percent wage increase. Another significant benefit was a guarantee of work throughout the year for permanent employees. Before, as Curlie explained, they used to work for six months (during crop time) and were unemployed for the rest of the year. During slack time most cane cutters were therefore forced into debt, which they had to repay during crop time.

Curlie's story parallels those of other Indo-Trinidadians with humble beginnings whom I encountered outside Cambio. Ram, the schoolteacher from Perseverance, also attributed his family's progress to Panday. His father, a sugar company employee, was dismissed because of his union activities. When Ram's father died, Ram's mother was forced to support her eight children by cutting cane. She did this until she turned fifty-five. The eldest boy could not attend school, as he had to supplement the meager family income, which amounted to TT$18.50 per fortnight in the 1960s. Despite the hardships the family endured, the rest of the children were sent to school. Ram remembered how he had only one pair of tennis shoes, the soles of which were so worn out that he had to repair them with rubber from bicycle tires to prevent his socks from fraying. Now, he told me proudly, his daughter owns two pairs of shoes just for school, and he, in turn, owns four. Using the symbol of the house, he illustrated the gradual upward mobility experienced by his family. Whereas his grandfather lived in a mud hut with a grass roof and his father in a dirt house with a tin roof, he and his siblings live in split-level concrete houses. Ram reiterated the sentiment that "you cannot blame de system for everyting and if you want to make it you can like de East Indians have done." To prove this point he drew my attention to the concrete houses along the Southern Main Road, claiming that they were "all East Indian owned." "If you go to Port-of-Spain," he continued, "you will find all de Negroes living in rented houses—all de Negro knows is to spend money while the East Indians will save it for a house and de chirrun." Toward the end of our conversation he explained his devotion to Panday. He was still a child when Panday took over the union and secured higher wages for the workers, and it meant they could have a refrigerator, a television, and other luxuries. This, he said, he will never forget.

Ram, in his own words, underscores the symbolic nature of the modern concrete house. The range of structures from mud to concrete signified the dramatic changes experienced by each generation as it climbed the social and economic ladder. In short, houses encapsulate a statement of arrival, the notion that East Indians have finally arrived after years of seclusion, alienation, and poverty. Proud parents, for instance, describe the achievements of their children on the basis that "dey got a nice big concrete house and ting." In addition, Ram's belief that ownership as opposed to renting of houses was a common East Indian trait once again expresses the desire of Indo-Trinidadians continuously to draw boundaries between themselves and Afro-Trinidadians. East Indian monopoly of landownership and houses was a consistent theme that figured prominently whenever Indo-Trinidadians talked about their desire for savings. When I asked for what purposes these savings were accrued, the invariable reply was "for chirrun and houses."[13]

Even though Indo-Trinidadians experienced a sharp jump in their standard of living in the 1970s, the length of time to complete construction, the arduous processes involved, and the varied stages of construction at which different houses stand, at least in Cambio, illustrate some of the gradual aspects within the larger, more abrupt transformation. In 1990 many of the concrete houses in Cambio were incomplete; one house, for example, had only the pillars for the second floor, another had yet to be painted, and for others further extensions had been planned but remained to be implemented. About twenty of the thirty-five houses were concrete. Three houses were entirely composed of board, and two others were composed of both mud and board. The houses constructed out of mud and board tended to be the most dilapidated structures. The rest of the houses were composed of various mixtures of concrete, board, and mud. Most of the houses had taken a number of years to evolve to the present stage. Each stage was inaugurated when the capital and labor became available.

According to villagers, in the 1950s the sugar company offered land to those workers who were already resident in Cambio for about TT$450.[14] Those who could afford it purchased their plots, but many did not have the resources because at that time they earned only TT$3.50 for six days' labor. Since then, however, all but four or five villagers have managed to purchase the land. Others continue to invest large sums in what is essentially government-owned property by constructing these modern houses. In the village of Calcutta, for example, Harilal owned a very elaborate house but did not own

13. Some even backed up their claims regarding East Indian ownership of land with alleged figures: one politician claimed that the ratio of East Indian to Black ownership of land approximates five to one, and a group of small businessmen stated that East Indians own almost 75 percent of privately owned lands. These are popular perceptions that cannot be backed up statistically because of the absence of ethnically based census data.

14. It appears that not every resident was automatically eligible for proprietorship but that other criteria such as length of service to the company were taken into account. The fact that some who were perceived as "less deserving" secured ownership seems to have created schisms within the village. For example, one fairly prosperous villager confided that many workers were displeased when he obtained his piece of land because he was very young (twenty years old at the time) and had not been working long in the company. But since the White manager liked him and he was a hard worker, the company offered it to him anyway. This incident may in part explain why he and his wife were not very popular in Cambio.

the land. It would cost him TT$27,000 and he hoped to buy it someday, but for now he pays a rent/tax for the land.

Non-ownership of land seems not to deter villagers from continuing to invest in concrete homes.[15] House building is often perceived as an ongoing process, something to be improved on and invested in as the family progressed.[16] In a discussion on the sugar union and party politics with a senior union official who had worked for Caroni for forty years in several capacities—cane cutting, salting (fertilizing), dispatching—the topic of houses once again emerged. When he began building his house in the 1970s, he first went to a contractor. As the contractor's estimate was too high, he hired two carpenters and did the labor himself. Even now, he keeps adding to his home, little by little, whenever he can afford it.

This union official's story parallels that of some villagers in Cambio. Averse to incurring debt, they seem to prefer to improve their homes gradually as resources become available rather than borrow from banks. The simplicity and uniformity in architecture can be attributed to another common theme: villagers rarely hired skilled or menial labor to build their houses but relied on the expertise and labor of the immediate family and relatives. All these factors contribute to the slow but unending evolution of these structures.

Curlie and his common-law wife, Ranee, their five children, and Curlie's mother live in a house that epitomizes the blending of the new with the old. The upstairs is completely modern with all the modern fixtures, and the downstairs contains much of the original structure, composed of wood. When Ranee first came to live in Cambio in the mid-1970s, she and Curlie lived in a tiny one-room shack adjacent to the main home, occupied by her in-laws. When Curlie's stepfather died, they moved into the main house. With Curlie's savings they renovated the house (at a cost of TT$12,000) and added a whole new section in the back (which cost TT$24,000). Curlie's mother contributed TT$2,000 to "fix the lighting"; by then they had spent all their savings.

Similarly, the Hoseins, who had one of the nicest houses in Cambio and were extremely proud of it, built it solely on savings. Although they had begun construction around 1987, the house was still incomplete in 1990—they had yet to paint and obtain fixtures, carpeting, and furnishings for the empty living room upstairs. The Hoseins purchased their land from the company in the 1950s for TT$450. Now they say this same land is worth

15. The tendency to build homes on rented property is not limited to Indo-Trinidadians. Herskovits and Herskovits (1947) observed that almost a quarter of the people who rented their land owned their homes in the Afro-Trinidadian village of Toco.

16. "A local adage states that the first thing a Trinidadian does on obtaining a house is to 'renovate' it" (Miller 1994:144).

TT$60,000. The whole family often reminisces about all the hard work and sweat that went into the building. Farid and his son provided all the labor. When they returned from work they would take a short rest and then work on the house until late evening. The intricate closets alone in the bedrooms upstairs had taken Farid two months to complete. When they needed specific expertise, such as for electrical wiring, they would call on a relative and repay him in kind by preparing a grand meal and providing a bottle of whiskey.[17]

The Hoseins use the upstairs only to sleep. Likewise, they prefer to use the outhouse instead of the modern bathroom upstairs. Even though they possess a huge and elaborate dining set, not once was the dining room upstairs used, even on the numerous celebratory occasions such as the son's *hakikah* (Muslim christening ceremony) or the grandson's birthday. Instead, the chairs remain covered in plastic and all the dining takes place in the modest kitchen and dining space downstairs.

The ways in which villagers talked about and related to their houses and fixtures made it plain that these were sources of pride, a statement of their status that went beyond mere utilitarian value. Even though they wanted all the modern utensils, such items were seldom used because the old methods were considered far superior: I often found women washing clothes by hand (using the machine only to wash sheets) while the machine remained in its plastic cover, or skillfully opening a tin with a knife while the electric can opener was displayed in a cabinet along with other gadgets, such as graters and mixers, in the living room.

The ornamental value of houses and their fixtures comes into play in conversations between villagers, particularly among women. One afternoon, during a casual conversation in Dolly's kitchen, Mariam mentioned to Dolly that Zeynab (Mariam's sister) was going to get a washing machine. Dolly then began describing her extensive plans for her new kitchen and how she was going to get these "special kind of chairs." Mariam quickly jumped in, saying, "You know the chairs *we have*, well dat's de kind," and added that she does not need any more chairs since they have fourteen of them. Refusing to drop the subject at a point when Mariam had the upper hand, Dolly switched to the topic of cupboards and explained how hers will be made of wood, unlike Mariam's, which were made of formica. Mariam conceded in the end by admitting that wood was much better since her type "puckers up."

Another such incident took place at Harilal's home. There were a number of illustrated books displayed on a table: a cookbook, one on American Indi-

---

17. During the oil boom villagers became accustomed to drinking whiskey instead of the local rum.

ans, and another on bears. Harilal proudly showed them to us, and while we were chatting and looking at the books, his young daughter, Rita, hovered around us trying to reach for the books. She tried hard not to attract Harilal's attention, but each time her hands would actually reach for a book Harilal would shout at her and ask her to put them back, as "they were not for her"— ironic, since they were mostly children's books. These books, in Harilal's view, were not meant to be read and cherished for the knowledge they offered but instead carried ornamental value and in essence were status symbols.

The nonutilitarian aspect of Indo-Trinidadian villagers' relation to material objects is common to most communities labeled nouveaux riches throughout the world. On what basis, then, can it be argued that such a trait is a marker of specifically East Indian identity? It is indeed intriguing that Indo-Trinidadians' pursuit of material objects is perceived by them positively, as hallmarks of success, whereas the same behavioral practices exhibited by Afro-Trinidadians are interpreted negatively, as an indication of their "free-spending," "self-gratifying" mentality. Once again stereotypes triumph in the face of reality. Identical behaviors refracted through disparate lenses—in this case ethnic stereotypes—lead to divergent interpretations that invariably reconfirm the stereotype.

Probably Afro-Trinidadians, like Indo-Trinidadians, also invested some of their newfound wealth in houses and other status-related material objects. In his survey of material culture in both Afro-Trinidadian and Indo-Trinidadian households in Chaguanas, Miller confirms this hypothesis: "I found that ethnic distinctions were of minimal importance to the selections of objects and their juxtaposition in home design" (1994:10). In the absence of evidence to suggest that Afro-Trinidadians did not act similarly, the question remains how Indo-Trinidadians were able to construct a discourse around their spending patterns that transformed individual feats into a statement about their group identity. After all, not all Indo-Trinidadians enjoyed the same success. Why, in other words, is the Indo-Trinidadian concrete house a visible symbol of East Indian success and the Afro-Trinidadian concrete house not a visible symbol of that group's success?

One answer may lie in the semantic operation of race categories in Trinidad outlined in Chapter 4. As we have seen, individual achievements by East Indians were imaged as the property of the collectivity. The common perception of the concrete house as a visible symbol of East Indian success— despite the fact that not all Indo-Trinidadians possess magnificent concrete houses and given the fact that Afro-Trinidadians, too, live in concrete houses—could be a precipitate of the semantic operation of traditional categories distinguishing different ancestral kinds. In short, successes enjoyed by Indo-Trinidadian individuals became transformed, through the visible symbol of the concrete house, into a characteristic of the whole community. This transformation affirms both Afro-Trinidadian stereotypes of Indo-Trinidadians—their belief that "the Indians are taking over the country"—and Indo-Trinidadians' perceptions of themselves as an industrious and success-oriented people.[18]

Another potential explanation could lie in the different historical experiences of the two groups in Trinidad. It is possible that because of the varied economic, social, and political positioning and spatial distribution of Indo-Trinidadians and Afro-Trinidadians historically, the Indo-Trinidadian rural masses emerged as the nouveaux riches par excellence in the 1970s as a result of the abrupt changes propelled by the oil boom. This is not to imply that the Afro-Trinidadians were not trapped in a cycle of poverty before the oil boom or that they did not indulge in spending sprees during the boom period. But rather, given the general urban and cosmopolitan character of the Afro-Trinidadians in contrast with the majority of Indo-Trinidadians in this period, it is possible that the symbolic values attached to identical objects might have varied for the two groups.

The boom years saw the emergence of Indo-Trinidadians from their rural enclaves and their increasing participation in mainstream sectors. According to Vertovec (1992:134–35), by most measures Indo-Trinidadians constituted the most depressed group in Trinidad during the 1960s and early 1970s.[19] In 1960 Indians had an annual per capita income of £195, Whites £1,250, and Blacks £260; nationally, East Indians represented the highest proportion of the poor (Vertovec 1992). In 1964 83 percent of Indo-Trinidadians lived in rural areas in comparison with 51 percent of Afro-Trinidadians. In 1970 Indo-Trinidadians also had the lowest level of education; only 7.5 percent had postprimary education, and 26.1 percent had no education at all (Dookeran 1985). An incipient Indo-Trinidadian middle class (primarily Christians and Muslims) had begun at the turn of the twentieth century to enter the higher echelons of society through education and business, but the majority of Indo-Trinidadians were rural, poor, and had little education before the oil

18. Such stereotypes are not limited to Trinidad but prevail in other Caribbean nations. See Lowenthal 1972:156–65. Creole fears of an imminent "Indian takeover" likewise prevail in Guyana. As one Afro-Guyanese villager confided to Despres, "De coolieman taking over de whole country. Dey band themselves together to get all we own. . . . Dey rent we land and take it away. Dey loan black people money and take all dey own. Dey smart people, you know. Cunning. Dey work cheap, eat cheap, and save and save. Black people can't punish themselves so. If we punish ourselves like coolieman, we slaves again" (1967:93). See also Maurer 1997:110–12 on the British Virgin Islands.

19. For example, Miller characterizes the Indian population after World War II as "the most deprived and least developed in the area" (1994:275). See also Dookeran 1985.

boom. The situation in the late 1980s was markedly different. In her analysis of social mobility experienced by different ethnic groups between 1960 and 1989 Reddock concludes that according to the three indicators of occupation, education, and employment, "Indians in general have been experiencing the most significant degrees of mobility overall" (1991:232).

Thus although the oil boom catapulted the entire island society into a free-spending, consumption frenzy characterized by calypsonian Sparrow as "capitalism gone mad," for the majority of Indo-Trinidadians the significance of these transformations was even more acute because they heralded an abrupt and momentous leap from Indo-Trinidadians' accustomed situation. Vertovec observes, "During the decade of the 1970s, the Indian community as a whole rapidly achieved more prosperity and social mobility than it had during its previous 130 years in the island" (1992:139). Just as the 1960s spelled the "arrival" of Afro-Trinidadians as independence delivered them from five centuries of subjugation, the economic and social transformations caused by the oil boom facilitated the partial arrival of Indo-Trinidadians from 130 years of discrimination limiting their upward mobility. It is not that Indo-Trinidadians in general did not improve their condition with independence. Rather, their starting point as the most depressed group at the time, coupled with the sentiment that independence really signaled a victory for Trinidadians of African descent (see Mohammed 1988:390–91), meant that Indo-Trinidadians and the wider society would interpret Indo-Trinidadian mobility from a different vantage point. Such a contextual framework, I suggest, allows one to entertain the possibility that luxuries, in the form of material objects afforded by the oil boom, may have carried larger (if not different) symbolic import for Indo-Trinidadians than for Afro-Trinidadians.

The explanations offered so far to account for Indo-Trinidadian patterns of conspicuous consumption suggest that this pattern, which is characteristic of both Afro-Trinidadians and Indo-Trinidadians, has been diverted into a discourse that once again seeks to separate the Creole from the East Indian. Yet these same practices, if we momentarily set aside the rhetoric that surrounds them, can also signify an instance of acculturation.

Such a perspective is offered by Joseph Nevadomsky (1980 and 1983), who has written prolifically on the changes experienced by rural Indo-Trinidadians based on his fieldwork in Amity in 1972–73. Nevadomsky's focus on the villagers of Amity was particularly appropriate for the study of change because this village had been the field site of Morton Klass's classic ethnography of 1961, which Nevadomsky used as a basis for comparison. Where Klass in 1959 found the persistence of north Indian values and institutions—"In basic structure, . . . Amity is an 'Indian' community and not a 'West Indian' [one]"

(Klass 1961:239)—Nevadomsky found in the late 1970s the opposite trend, acculturation:

> If social and economic changes are measured solely in terms of physical amenities, the results are quite remarkable. More than 3/4 of the households have radios and 1/6 have television sets. Nearly 50 percent own refrigerators, though this appliance is underutilized. The automobile, once purchased mainly by taxi drivers and a few civil servants, is now regarded by many as a necessity. Twenty years ago 70 percent of the houses were made of mud or board; today 70 percent are concrete block structures consisting of four or five rooms upstairs and a storage/kitchen area below. (1980:45)

This description contrasts markedly with the Amity of 1959, when village housing was extremely modest and amenities scarce.

According to Nevadomsky, the acquisition of consumer goods symbolizing a modern lifestyle signals a shift in villagers' evaluation of social status. Before, social status was integrally linked to landownership. The declining significance of farming, however, has resulted in a shift in criteria for status evaluation wherein wealth is "measured more in terms of income potential and occupation than in terms of actual cash or the value of land holdings" (Nevadomsky 1983:77). Concomitant with this change in criteria for establishing social status was the change in spending patterns:

> There seems to be a marked decrease in spending on religious ceremonies because the observance of religious rituals no longer enhances prestige. Villagers gain prestige by acquiring those consumer goods which contribute to a modern or western style of life. . . . As a rule, the younger generation accepts a standard of living that requires a greater cash income and a greater emphasis on enjoying the good things in life. Although older villagers chastise the younger generation for never having known "true hardships," most seem to agree with the life-style their children are aiming at. (Nevadomsky 1983:77)

Nevadomsky's zeal to emphasize change, however, leads him to simplify complex and often contradictory processes. The spending patterns of villagers in Cambio, along with evidence presented by Vertovec (1992), suggest that traditional patterns did not die out in the face of new ones but were instead rejuvenated with the influx of wealth.

Villagers in Cambio spent enormous sums on *pujas* and other traditional events such as weddings and *barahis*. The Hoseins, for example, talked repeatedly with pride about their lavish expenditure for their daughter's wedding, detailing the number of sweet drink cartons, the quantities of flour, the number of condensed milk cans for the traditional sweets, and other expenses incurred for the wedding feast. Similarly, the day after their son's *hakikah* (described to me as a Muslim christening ceremony), his mother recounted with pleasure the grandness of the whole affair: "plenty money" had been spent; seven cases of sweet drinks had been consumed, and the Nestlé cream for the white sweets alone had cost TT$6 per tin. Ordinarily, Mariam explained, people do not provide such a wide variety of sweets but Robbie had insisted on making them all. Mariam, who was normally very careful with money and who, as her husband described her, possessed the admirable capacity to "cut and fit" (that is, to juggle resources to make ends meet), had no reservations about spending for prayers. As she phrased it, "If you have to do something, you might as well do it well because prayers is not every day you have." Villagers carefully monitor one another's generosity when it comes to ceremonial occasions, and those who spend lavishly on their guests are generally well respected. Conversely, villagers who are reputed to be stingy become the object of much gossip and criticism.

In a similar vein Vertovec notes that an astounding increase in per capita income led to a rejuvenation of "Indian" cultural and religious activity and ethnic sentiment in the village of Penal Rock Road: "Much of their newfound wealth was poured into Hindu religious activity at the same time it was invested in tractors, taxis, and TVs" (1992:164). Nevadomsky's hasty conclusions may have been a consequence of the fact that in 1972 the oil boom had yet to unleash itself. Nevertheless, his prediction that changes in economic and occupational structures of rural Indo-Trinidadians were leading to the demise of traditional patterns—in this case criteria for establishing prestige through changes in spending styles—is simplistic and undermined by contemporary evidence.

A more sophisticated explanation is offered by Miller (1994), who observes remarkable similarities between Indo-Trinidadian and Afro-Trinidadian behavioral patterns in the town of Chaguanas despite informants' insistence on interpreting such behaviors through ethnic lenses. He describes these two related but paradoxical movements as "first . . . the growth of actual syncretism of the Indian and African populations; [and] second . . . the increasing tendency to define them in terms of a dualistic polarity" (1994:279). Without falling into the common trap of attributing such similarities to the "creolization" of Indo-Trinidadians (as in Indo-Trinidadians adopting Afro-Trinidadian patterns), Miller insists that we see the emergent syncretism as a two-way process, that is, the simultaneous movement toward *creolization* and *Indianization*. But even such an interpretation is unsatisfactory to Miller, who prefers to interpret such shifts as "part of a larger syncretic pattern which is reducing the significance of ethnic contrasts in relation to a wide range of social and cultural practices. Most significant here is the evidence for homogenisation of social behaviour. . . . Whether we look to age at marriage, nature of mating arrangement, size and form of family or virtually any other characterisation of social structure the evidence is increasing similarity of practice" (1994:281).

Although I agree for the most part with Miller's observation regarding the convergence of certain practices, I take exception to his implicit argument about increasing homogenization. Ironically, even he conflates creolization with the lay and political/ideological view of the term when he describes Indianization and creolization as opposite tendencies. The instances of syncretism, I believe, should not be equated with homogenization. Rather, what appear to be paradoxical behavioral patterns on the part of both Afro-Trinidadians and Indo-Trinidadians can be entertained within a single conceptual framework afforded by the theoretical concept of creolization without reducing such practices to instances of homogeneity. As Bolland puts it: "Creolization . . . is not a homogenizing process, but rather a process of *contention* between people who are members of social formations and carriers of cultures, a process in which their own ethnicity is continually re-examined and redefined in terms of the relevant oppositions between different social formations at various historical moments" (1992:73; emphasis in original). From this perspective the fact that Afro-Trinidadians and Indo-Trinidadians engage in similar practices does not mean that the two groups derive identical symbolic meanings from such practices. As I argued earlier, the meanings Indo-Trinidadians attach to the concrete house remain distinctive for their group as a symbol of their success and as an embodiment of specific values, such as thrift, perseverance, and sacrifice, again attributed to their group. Thus if we situate the materiality of the concrete house within the different social formations through which contending groups evaluate and redefine their ethnicity, as suggested by Bolland, then we cannot divorce the surface manifestation of the concrete house from its specific social and ideological moorings. The point is that house building and styles of consumption carry the potential to reinscribe "traditional" values just as they may signify instances of acculturation. Thus to relegate what may appear to be similar practices among Afro-Trinidadians and Indo-Trinidadians as instances of acculturation (as Nevadomsky does) or homogeneity (as Miller does) occludes the tensions and paradoxes structuring a wide range of behavior patterns of which instances of "syncretism" constitute just one of the many options available. A more fruitful approach would be to entertain within a single conceptual framework instances of syncretism, acculturation, and traditional practices as part and parcel of a general Creole (in the analytic sense) disposition toward multiplicity and contradiction—a disposition shared by both ethnic groups.

Cultural tension is a noted characteristic of the entire Caribbean region. The most insightful Caribbean ethnographies have all detected a curious cultural tension in these societies. Herskovits (1937) talked about socialized ambivalence; Anthony Lauria (1964) about *respeto* and *relajo*; Chandra Jayawardena (1968) about equality and stratification; and Peter Wilson (1969, 1973) about reputation and respectability (Mintz 1977). More recent studies of the Caribbean have continued this tradition with Miller's emphasis on the dual temporal orientations of transcendence and transience and Richard Burton's (1997) characterization of Afro-Creole cultures as cultures of opposition.[20] Such analytic attempts, based on contradictory polarities, seem to capture some essence of Caribbean societies; neat compartmentalization of Caribbean peoples' behaviors as cultural persistence or acculturation or even homogenization obfuscates this tension.[21] In part this tension is generated by the very heterogeneity characterizing the Caribbean, a heterogeneity that encompasses not only diverse cultural dispositions but also systemic inequalities.

All these authors attempt to capture the complex reality of the Caribbean through analytic formulations of paired polarities. For some, like Herskovits, these polarities stem from two sets of contrasting values or behavioral dispositions, the "African" and the "European." For Wilson and Jayawardena, the polarities are rooted in systemic inequalities that generate contrasting principles for measuring equality, gender differences being the crucial variable for Wilson. The illuminating feature of these studies is that they attempt to capture intangible cultural dispositions that seem to characterize all Caribbean peoples, namely, the systematicity with which Caribbean people maintain multiplicity not only in the sense of movement between roles and types but in terms of types or roles that include movement (Trouillot 1992). These authors, Mintz believes, "are reaching out for more insightful, more illuminating devices, to help us to grasp the essentiality of Caribbean societies" (1977:79). This cultural feature has been attributed to the deeply stratified nature of slave societies, in which "slave participation in public institutions and many other overt forms of cultural expression were discouraged, [and therefore] the cultural system that did emerge had a surreptitious quality that challenges our skills of social observation and analysis" (Safa 1987:117–18).

20. See Burton 1997:158–69 on the dual value system thought to characterize West Indian culture. See Freeman 2000 for a suggestive analysis of how seemingly contradictory polarities are simultaneously enacted by Barbadian women.

21. This dilemma is wonderfully illustrated in functionalist analyses of kinship patterns that emphasize acculturation—such as Smith and Jayawardena 1959—where those patterns not conforming to the ideal type are seen as deviant. Since the majority of families or households in the Caribbean do not conform to the ideal type, however, any analysis that attempts to explain the more regular patterns with reference to the ideal type is immediately suspect.

It is possible that these same surreptitious, ambiguous, and often contradictory tensions may also apply to Indo-Caribbeans. If, as Mintz and Price (1976) and Mintz (1984) suggest, we shift our focus from cultural specifics to the more fundamental level of generative rules that pattern the behavior and value orientations of Caribbean people, we may be able to locate orientations within purported East Indian cultural patterns that attest not to the uniqueness of East Indians but instead to their very "Caribbeanness." Thus acculturation studies, which aim to portray Indo-Caribbeans as fully participating members of Creole societies by claiming that they share norms and practices of the societies at large, ironically strip their subjects of those very elements that establish their truly West Indian quality by focusing solely on surface manifestations of culture. By emphasizing Indo-Caribbean elements that conform to larger societal ideals and by deemphasizing traditional elements (norms and practices believed to be of north Indian origin), acculturation studies fail to capture what is essentially a Creole habitual disposition of Indo-Caribbean people that enables them to juggle polarized practices and norms with little sense of contradiction. Such a Creole disposition is particularly evident in patterns of family and household organization.

Family and Household

In *The Middle Passage* V. S. Naipaul characterized Indo-Caribbeans in the following manner:

> Everything that made the Indian alien in the society gave him strength. He was taboo-ridden as no other person on the island; he had complicated rules about food and about what was unclean. His religion gave him values which were not the white values of the rest of the community, and preserved him from self-contempt; he never lost his pride in his origins. More important than religion was his family organization, an enclosing self-sufficient world absorbed with its quarrels and jealousies, as difficult for the outsider to penetrate as for one of its members to escape. It protected and imprisoned a static world, awaiting decay. (1962:88)

Here Naipaul depicts Indo-Caribbean family organization as a closed system, an essentialized entity that reinforces the East Indian as alien. Yet in his depiction of Hanuman House in *A House for Mr. Biswas* (1961), the rigidity imputed above is abandoned and a sense of fluidity prevails. Naipaul's ambivalence toward Indo-Caribbeans is nicely captured by Victor J. Ramraj in his analysis of the unfolding tension between Mr. Biswas and the larger Tulsi household: "The novel focuses on Mr. Biswas's attempts to achieve some measure of individuality and independence, which are denied to him as long as he remains part of the Tulsi household" (1987:93). Naipaul, however, is careful not to depict Mr. Biswas as the victim. Rather, the weak Mr. Biswas "misinterprets the Tulsis' strength, unity and resourcefulness, so lacking in himself, as oppression" (Ramraj 1987:93). At times even Mr. Biswas admits to his need of Hanuman House when he acknowledges that this symbol of the Hindu united family "possessed a life, strength and power to comfort which was quite separate from the individuals who composed it" (Naipaul 1961 in Ramraj 1987:93). Yet Hindu ideals and practices are continually transgressed by more alien and sometimes contradictory practices:

> Like true Hindus, the Tulsis perform daily puja, . . . pray to Hindu gods, yet the two sons are sent to a Catholic college and wear crucifixes around their necks: Mrs. Tulsi burns candles in the Roman Catholic church; and she marries off her favorite daughter in a registry office. The Tulsis readily sacrifice piety to whatever is advantageous and expedient: educational opportunities are open to them if they embrace Catholicism, and much expense is saved by performing a wedding ceremony at the registry. (Ramraj 1987:98)

Naipaul's two characterizations, of Indo-Caribbean family organization in general and of the Tulsi household in particular, may appear at first to be contradictory. The intriguing point, however, is that both characterizations ring true. In the case of Cambio, at least, villagers seem to simultaneously straddle elements associated with traditional forms of household organization— those norms and practices believed to be of north Indian origin, middle-class Creole (which usually translates into "respectable" Euro-Creole)[22] ideals of

---

22. Because the term *Afro-Trinidadian* does not allow me to capture the finer distinctions drawn among people labeled *Creole*, for heuristic purposes I find it helpful to use the term *Creole* in this chapter to denote those claiming primarily African ancestry (Afro-Creole), primarily European ancestry (Euro-Creole), and Colored ancestry (mixed African and European) in the West Indies at large. Even though these categories are distinctions drawn and recognized by Trinidadians (and scholars), I use them here as etic categories to reference a plethora of values and practices associated with different groups without acceding naturalized states to these categories. When necessary I also use the prefixes *Euro* and *Afro* before *Creole* to emphasize specific values and practices associated with these respective groups with the clear understanding, however, that the term *Creole*, on its own, is usually synonymous with Afro-Creole in contemporary Trinidad. In certain contexts I maintain the strictly emic use of the term when I reference the projected dichotomy between Creole and East Indian.

household organization[23] (that is, the nuclear family unit), and sometimes even lower-class Afro-Creole patterns.

A considerable amount of scholarly inquiry has been devoted to the Indo-Trinidadian family in Trinidad, and several interesting themes emerge. The literature itself is embroiled in the traditional debate between those espousing cultural retention (Klass 1961; Niehoff 1959; Lowenthal 1972; Malik 1971; Jha 1985) and those emphasizing acculturation (Schwartz 1965; Nevadomsky 1980, 1982, and 1985; Angrosino 1976). Both factions employ the north Indian cultural model of family organization, especially the joint family unit, to ascertain the degree of either persistence or acculturation. Acculturation studies emphasizing the erosion of the joint family and the adoption of the nuclear family point to the determinant role of the changing economic context. Similarly, scholars such as John MacDonald and L. Mac-Donald (1973), Michael V. Angrosino (1976), and Raymond T. Smith and Chandra Jayawardena (1959) attempt to explain the persistence of traditional, north Indian–derived marriage and household patterns as a function of adaptation to environmental and economic factors. Since variations on the joint family unit persist, especially in rural areas, scholars such as those just noted, who reject pluralist (or culturalist) explanations, are forced to give functional explanations for the persistence of traditional forms. Vertovec (1992), who has persuasively argued that contemporary Indo-Trinidadian cultural practices are a result of homogenizing processes that took place within Trinidad,[24] critiques functional explanations for the persistence of the joint family:

Too many features of Indian family persist, in ideology if not in practice, to be written off as functionally determined. . . . Such traits include: the ideal of vir-

23. I find the distinction Solien (1960) draws between household and family useful. Empirically, the two can be often identical, especially in the case of the nuclear family. Traditional anthropological concepts of family that assume a co-residential conjugal pair, and of household that assume a family unit of some type, become problematic in the Afro-Americas, however, where the family and household units may not overlap. Solien defines the family "as a group of people bound together by that complex set of relations known as kinship ties, between at least two of whom there exists a conjugal relationship" (1960:106). Household, in contrast, "implies common residence, economic co-operation, and socialization of children" (1960:106). I include visiting, common-law, and legally married unions in the category conjugal relation.

24. This remarkable insight of Vertovec's is a radical departure from conventional wisdom that continues to attribute the seemingly homogeneous character of Indo-Trinidadian cultural practices to the passive retention of north Indian traditional forms. There is an intriguing convergence here between Vertovec's thesis and the arguments put forward by Mintz and Price (1976) for the emergence of Afro-Caribbean cultural forms.

ilocality (however shortlived), authority based on sex and age, the role of a wife as obedient and serving to the husband (*pativrata*, exemplified today among women over about 40 years old, who still follow behind their husbands at some distance and avoid addressing him by his proper name), restricted interaction of a *barka* (older brother-in-law) and *chotki* (younger brother's wife), maintenance of a family shrine and ritual duties performed by women and children, restrained behaviour by sons out of respect for the father (e.g. refraining from swearing, public smoking or drinking in the father's presence), and other non-quantifiable yet distinguishable principles. (1992:105)

Confusion around the subject of East Indian family and household organization is partly the result of differences in scholarly interpretation, which are in turn deeply influenced by scholars' initial agendas. Barton Schwartz and Nevadomsky, committed to illustrating acculturation, buttress their case for the predominance of nuclear family forms by using an extremely rigid model of the extended household. For Nevadomsky, extended households "are multiple family households several of which closely approximate the traditional joint family" (1985:6). In addition, not only does he require these households to be commensal[25] (and not just co-residential), but he also interprets the building of a separate kitchen as the birth of a new household (Nevadomsky 1985:4). Given the rigidity of this extended household model, it is hardly surprising that only 10 percent of the households in Amity conformed to this type, thereby enhancing Nevadomsky's point on acculturation.

Vertovec, however, argues that although the basic nature of kinship structure has transformed radically in Trinidad as a consequence of changing socioeconomic contexts, basic ideals of kin groups—the meanings, rules, and roles ordering north Indian family structure—persist in Trinidad. To understand this process of persistence and change, it is necessary to turn to north Indian patterns of family and households. The following discussion draws substantially on Vertovec's analysis.

North Indian families are generally patrilineal (trace descent through the male line) and virilocal (after marriage the couple lives in the male's household). Households tend to be joint in form (Vertovec 1992).[26] Principles of

25. According to Vertovec, "commensal generally includes sharing a kitchen, property, pocketbook, debts, labor, and one authority figure. 'Coresidential' can include living in the same dwelling, household, house site, or compound" (1992:63).
26. According to Vertovec, *joint family* refers to "a unit of kin composed of at least two married couples, who are related lineally or collaterally, plus their respective unmarried children" (1992:23).

marriage include subcaste endogamy and village exogamy. Usually a bride is selected for the groom by the head of the family, and marriage is considered a one-time affair. A young bride is invariably subject to the dictates of her mother-in-law and assumes the lowest-ranking position in her husband's household (Davids 1964). Lineage and household members demonstrate their links to one another by recollecting lines of descent, honoring ancestry, and worshiping a lineage deity *(kuldevata)* (Vertovec 1992:22). Household members and lineages also share a variety of links with other social groups belonging to their clan or *gotra*,[27] sets of affines in nearby villages, fictive or ritual kin, marriage networks, and subcastes. Thus in north India "a villager maintains a number of familial identities within layered, encompassing fields of social relationships, each identity being called upon in a particular context" (Vertovec 1992:22).

The exigencies of indenture profoundly disrupted this complex multilay-ered network of kinship links. Since most indentured migrants came as individuals and not with their families, and initially the ratio of the sexes was dramatically disproportionate,[28] north Indian patterns could not be replicated in Trinidad. Even though lineages, status groups effecting marriage networks, and fictive kin relations became established after several generations, such links lacked the depth and ideological import of former patterns. Nevertheless, according to Vertovec, certain ideals of kin groups, exogamy, and patrilineal descent and the broad ideal of the joint family endured.

Vertovec is able to argue that variations around the joint family ideal persist in Trinidad because he, unlike Nevadomsky, employs a less stringent model of the joint family, recognizing that even in India a whole series of forms entailing commensal and co-residential kin prevail: "Within and between generations, families in India assume many forms as children marry, parents die, households fission, and other domestic processes occur" (Vertovec 1992:23). A flexible notion of the joint family—one that entertains the variabilities around the ideal pattern as well as its cyclical nature[29]—permits Vertovec to recognize vestiges of this form even in those cases that do not fol-

27. As Vertovec notes, the distinction between clan and *gotra* is not always clear. Clan, according to Mayer (1960), "generally refers to a genealogically traceable, exogamous section of a subcaste." *Gotra*, according to Madan (1962), "is not a kinship relation but a category for grouping individuals through mythic descent, often a sage, for determining marriageability" (in Vertovec 1992:63).

28. Of the 93,946 migrants who came to Trinidad between 1874 and 1917, 68 percent were male and 32 percent female (Vertovec 1992:101).

29. Morris (1968) describes how the cyclical nature of the joint family can produce variability around the ideal: "As in all lineage systems, when the family or other structured unit passes a certain size it divides and produces two or more similar entities. . . . At the same time it is as-

low the ideal pattern. For example, he notes that when sons move out of the paternal household, they usually move next door or build a house on the same property as their father's. This pattern is prominent in Cambio. Even though technically the son's house may conform to the nuclear type, the members continue to interact with their kin in the paternal household in ways that characterize a joint household, sharing child rearing, food, leisure, and ritual activities.

The scholarly controversies regarding the nature of Indo-Trinidadian family structure and household organization, especially the debate on nuclear and joint families, illustrate again the fundamental point that Caribbean peoples' behaviors continuously resist any neat analytic compartmentalization that cannot entertain a notion of duality or multiplicity. The very fact that protagonists representing either side of the debate can buttress their arguments empirically speaks to the richness and variability of cultural forms that endure in real life. In short, Indo-Trinidadian family structure and household organization constitute a melange of diverse cultural norms and practices.

Often values and practices stemming from diverse models can coexist comfortably in a single familial unit. For example, consider the phenomenon of a son building a modest home adjacent to the paternal household in order to ensure for himself and his new bride a certain degree of independence and privacy. To interpret this practice as the birth of nuclear family unit, as Nevadomsky would, is to reduce to a sterile analytical model what is essentially a complex behavioral practice that seeks to negotiate between a number of values stemming from diverse cultural models available to the lay person.[30] On the one hand, the young man in this case may seek independence from the paternal household for a number of reasons: friction between his wife and mother, suffocating interference from parents, sibling rivalries, or an attempt to strive for that "modern" ideal in which a young couple unencumbered can indulge in all the romance, independence, and modern "lifestyles" that the contemporary world can offer. This ideal is powerfully conveyed to rural Indo-Trinidadians through U.S. television programs and movies, by "agents of mediation" (Trouillot 1988) such as those who have traveled to the United States and Canada and who relish relating their encounters with

---

sumed by the people themselves and also by official Hindu law that every family, even if it happens to be in the individual family phase of the cycle, is in fact, joint" (in Vertovec 1992:24).

30. Members of Creole society possess an inherent capacity to display a range of behaviors even though these behaviors are understood to distinguish pure types because, as Drummond states, "individuals are *cognizant* of much or all the possible range of behavior and belief in the continuum, although [they] need not behave or act as the other does, just as speakers of a creole language can generally understand utterances at either extreme of the continuum but rarely control both extremes in their own speech" (1980:353; emphasis added).

modern, Western lifestyles to eager villagers, and through familiarity with modern middle-class practices in Trinidad.

This same young man, on the other hand, by moving not to a different village but merely next door to the paternal household, is conveying other important messages. He may want privacy but not too much privacy, which would remove him completely from daily interactions with his paternal household. He may feel a sense of responsibility to his parents or siblings if he believes his daily services are crucial to the maintenance of the entire "joint family." Financial restrictions could have prevented him from acquiring his own plot of land, hence the decision to build a home on the same plot as his father's. That he could indulge in such a luxury in the first place, that is, to have the prerogative of building on his father's plot, is a consequence of a variation of a traditional model in which sons are expected to continue to live in the paternal household after marriage. Thus the simultaneous establishment of independence and dependence through building a separate home next to the paternal household is an instance in which one individual negotiates his own interests with the cultural models available to him in order to create an optimal situation for himself. Any analysis that attempts to reduce this practice to the nuclear or joint family ideal, when it combines elements of both, not only simplifies this complex process of negotiation but, more important, ignores that crucial human faculty or habitual disposition, exemplified by Caribbean peoples, to straddle or vacillate between dualities.

Such complexities also challenge macrolevel monocausal theories that attempt to explain the demise or prevalence of extended family households among rural Indo-Trinidadians in purely material or economic terms. Schwartz (1965), for example, argues in the case of Boodram that because the unit for cooperation for rice cultivation is based on the nuclear family, the extended family form is rendered redundant and is on the decline. Further, disparate economic opportunities, in which incomes in modern service and industrial sectors outweigh traditional revenues from cultivation, have also pushed villagers to adopt the nuclear family pattern of residence. According to Schwartz, the few extended families in Boodram existed for two reasons, both economic: first, in those familial units possessing adequate economic success and power to counteract alternatives offered by the wider cash economy; and second, in those familial units where members were unable to take advantage of new economic alternatives. Angrosino (1976), in contrast, offers an extra-economic explanation for the extended family. This form, according to him, prevails despite economic factors favoring an emphasis on the nuclear family. Families may structurally conform to a nuclear, neolocal pattern of residence, but they are also "spiritually" extended households "insofar as they continue to celebrate family *pujas* in common, and insofar as all members feel compelled to support one another in terms of mutual provision of goods and services from time to time" (Angrosino 1976:54). Even for Angrosino, however, ultimately the spiritual dimension is based on the material reality of landownership. Given the crucial link between the extended family and land inheritance, even those who are not directly dependent on the land have stakes in its inheritance because it acts as a marker of differential status. "The family therefore remains a vehicle for the transmission of social and spiritual rank, regardless of differences in its structural arrangements" (Angrosino 1976:63).

Although such general conclusions may be effective in capturing overall trends, they tend to obfuscate individual experiences that do not strictly conform to the overall pattern. More important, even if a particular historical subject's behavior overtly reproduces the macrolevel pattern, the subject's reasons and motivations could be entirely different from the monocausal explanation itself. This is a problem endemic to macrolevel analyses. Referring to the macrolevel Merivale paradigm,[31] which has greatly influenced studies of the behavior of ex-slaves during the postemancipation period, Trouillot has urged scholars to shift their "scale of observation" in order to generate more "interesting" explanations: "The Merivale paradigm may have been inspiring in the search for broad explanations. But similarities of direction once verified, it has not been particularly effective at generating interest in micro-level problems . . . in search of the faces behind the numbers" (1996:308). According to Trouillot, a monocausal theory that neglects the actor is not necessarily right or wrong but it can generate only a certain kind of research, and monocausal explanations become less appealing the more we move to microlevel analyses (Trouillot 1996:310). In keeping with this spirit, the ensuing discussion on household organization in Cambio focuses on the micro level.

Before we proceed to household organization in Cambio, however, we must address another important theme in the literature. On the one hand, studies emphasizing acculturation and retention compare Indo-Trinidadian family systems, first, with traditional north Indian patterns to ascertain the degree of change from original patterns, and second, with middle-class Creole family organizations to ascertain the direction of change. The debate surrounding the joint family and the nuclear family is a case in point. On the other hand, when it comes to the difference between Indo-Trinidadian and lower-class Afro-Creole patterns of family organization, studies couched in both acculturationist (Roberts and Braithwaite 1962; MacDonald and Mac-

31. The theoretical framework put forward by Merivale in 1841 (Merivale 1967) posited that the realization of the ex-slaves' "natural" desire to abandon estates at emancipation depended on the availability of land (Trouillot 1996:306).

Donald 1973) and pluralist (Bell 1970) frameworks overwhelmingly concur that there exists a fundamental difference between the two groups in mating patterns and family and household organization.[32] The tendency of rural Indo-Trinidadian women to enter into formal marriage unions at a relatively young age and the low incidence of matrifocal households and of visiting and consensual unions in Indo-Trinidadian–dominated areas as opposed to lower-class Afro-Creole areas are used to illustrate significant differences between the two groups. Thus MacDonald and MacDonald, who reject a materialist, monocausal explanation for "African and Indian family traditions" in the Caribbean, that is, a direct connection between agricultural organization and family-household structure, argue that "ethnic affiliation cross-cuts the effect of slavery in the distant past, of indenture in the recent past, and of the variety of agricultural organizations in the present" (1973:180). Anticipating Vertovec's argument almost two decades later, MacDonald and MacDonald attribute the persistence of East Indian marriage and household patterns not to cultural survivals but to processes of ethnic homogenization endemic to Trinidad. With the demise of the caste system, which traditionally regulated marriage patterns; the disappearance of the *jajmani* patron-client system, which interlocked lineages of separate subcastes in reciprocal divisions of labor down the generations; and the dissipation of the *panchayat* caste councils, which presided over local affairs, Hindu family ideals lost their functional context. According to these authors, however, even though the original indentured migrants may not have practiced the high-caste ideals of formal arranged child-marriages, patriarchal joint families, and avoidance of births out of wedlock, because of the process of sanskritization "rural Trinidad's East Indians have actually approximated to these ideals, at least in theory and generally in practice" (MacDonald and MacDonald 1973:89).

For most scholars the East Indian family, then, remains a bulwark of East Indian ethnicity. Robert R. Bell's (1970) study of marriage and family differences between lower-class Afro-Creoles and Indo-Trinidadians in hamlets in the lower regions of the Montserrat Hills also supports this contention. Indo-Trinidadians were latecomers to this area, originally dominated by Afro-Cre-

32. A notable exception to this trend is Mohammed (1988), who has written on the creolization of Indian women, especially since the postindependence period. However, given her definition of creolization as "a commitment—political and social—to the new society, as well as physical engagement with the society so that the existent cultures are mixed and enriched in the process" (392), the indices of change—the shift from joint to nuclear family forms, the decrease in rates of arranged marriage, the tendency of young women to delay marriage, and the decline in fertility rates among East Indian women—constitute a mix of middle-class and lower-class Creole values. See also Abdulah 1991 on changes in mating patterns and fertility rates among ethnic groups.

oles.[33] According to Bell, there is minimal racial conflict here and a high level of mutual help and cooperation between "Negroes" and "Indians." In fact, many Negro patterns of behavior are increasingly adopted by Indians. Yet when it comes to marriage and family, clear distinctions obtain:

> Given the close relationships [between Indians and Negroes] there is very little intermarriage between the two groups and few offspring resulting from Negro-Indian parentage. In general, the daily patterns of life are the same for the two racial groups, but the values attached to marriage and the family are quite different. . . . The differences essentially reflect the patriarchal patterns of the Indians in contrast with the female-family centered patterns of the lower-class Negro women. (Bell 1970:63, 72)

Thus although scholars disagree on the actual degree of change affecting Indo-Trinidadian family organization when middle-class (Euro) Creole patterns constitute the direction of change, they all seem to agree that essential East Indian values and practices prevail to differentiate Indo-Trinidadian family organization from lower-class (Afro) Creole patterns. The tendency to deemphasize those instances in which Indo-Trinidadians have adopted lower-class Creole patterns, albeit with their own variations—such as visiting unions, the numerous "invisible" Dougla children, children out of wedlock, and the dominance of matriarchs—is indicative of the subtle mechanisms through which academic discourse reproduces folk models regarding not only the differences between the two ethnic groups but also the image of the East Indian as essentially different, hence the outsider. This image is reproduced when scholars overlook those very moments that encapsulate the intermeshing of practices common to both ethnic groups. For example, when Bell (1970:68) used the 78 percent of Indo-Trinidadian women who chastised illegitimacy (as opposed to the 21 percent of "Negro" women) in order to illustrate differences in values between the two groups, he inadvertently slighted the very significant 22 percent of Indo-Trinidadian women who claimed to have no negative feelings on this subject. Despite the fact that these women were a minority, their sentiments speak to a dynamic state of affairs that provides insight into the cultural tensions pervading Trinidad and Caribbean societies in general.

I now turn to domestic organization in Cambio, which captures the tensions between traditional and modern forms, between "Indian" and middle-

33. "Negroes" who had been previously engaged in cocoa cultivation in the hills originally settled this area. With the demise of the cocoa plantations the "Negroes" gradually descended the hills and settled the lower regions. The "Indians" began moving into this area around the 1920s (Bell 1970:62).

class Euro-Creole values and practices, and between "Indian" and lower-class Afro-Creole values and practices.

The predominant household pattern in Cambio was neither nuclear nor extended. Twenty-eight of the thirty-four households contained family members outside the nuclear family, though the households were not strictly extended. Of the six households that were strictly nuclear, two of them had sons who were relatively young. Thus it is most probable that once the sons married, they would bring their wives to reside in their parents' home, conforming to the village's general pattern of patrilocal residence. The other four nuclear households still had close family, such as a son or daughter, living next door or a few doors away. The size of households varied from thirteen persons to one, but the median numbers constituted five or six persons per household.

The term *household*, however, fails to capture the complex dynamics behind residential patterns. For example, one lot belonging to the most significant member in residence,[34] and which could be taken to represent a single household, may contain two and sometimes three structures appended to the main house. Often a son and his wife and children reside in a simple square structure hastily put together with whatever material is available—concrete, tin, mud, or particleboard. The contrast between the recently built main house and the scanty, cramped, makeshift type arrangements other members live in can be stark. Nine of the twenty-eight households that contained members beyond the nuclear family were characterized by the presence of multiple structures on a single premise. The most predominant pattern of boundary maintenance in Cambio—nineteen of the twenty-eight households—however, took place within a single structure. In these cases lines were demarcated to separate sets of nuclear families by allocating them specific spaces. Establishing separate kitchens for daughters-in-law was popular among many women, both mothers-in-law and daughters-in-law.

The diverse ways in which members struggle to maintain the integrity of their spaces point to some of the tensions inherent in such living arrangements. More important, these struggles embody processes of negotiation whereby actors juggle between alternate norms and practices. In a nominal sense the co-habitation of several conjugal units and their offspring in a single premise (whether in separate structures or not) suggests the joint family

---

34. The heads of households were not always male. In some cases ownership of the property had transferred to a female on the death of her husband. In a majority of cases the present matriarch had inherited ownership directly from the father. See Angrosino 1976 on the complex power play involved in such an inheritance pattern. Both these examples constitute offshoots of an original patriarchal situation; a third pattern involved a female initiating her own residence independent of a husband or father by purchasing her own plot.

model. Yet within this overall framework elements supposedly antithetical to the joint family are powerfully present. As Nevadomsky observed in Amity, "There is usually a clear division of resources such as rooms, furniture, utensils and rice, and even such apparently trivial items as washing detergent may be jealously guarded for the exclusive use of a particular household" (Nevadomsky 1985:4).[35]

In Cambio the tensions found in households oriented toward the joint family typically involved mother-in-law/daughter-in-law frictions and intergenerational conflicts over values. Vickram, a young man in his late twenties employed by Caroni as a temporary worker, summed up these tensions: "Whenever relatives live too closely, there is always trouble." Vickram lived with his wife, Sophie, and their three children in what looked like a typical joint family household. He and his family lived in one of the three rooms upstairs while his two unmarried brothers occupied the other two rooms. Vickram's mother and father lived downstairs, and a third brother and his family lived in a separate structure adjoining the main house. The three conjugal pairs and their respective children had separate kitchens. Both Sophie and Vickram were displeased with their circumstances and longed for a separate residence. They were in fact contemplating moving and had found a modest home for TT$250 per month in a village close to Cambio. They had not divulged this information to the rest of the family, thinking it best to wait until all plans were finalized. Although they were threatening to move almost every week, they were still in Cambio when I left, many months later.

Sophie yearned for her own place. She wanted more space and privacy for her children. Her brother-in-law's son, she complained, was a bad influence on her own son, who was picking up "all de bad ways" from his cousin. As a result she was forced to "give licks to" (spank) her son. She also resented her mother-in-law. Even though the mother-in-law possessed a washing machine, Sophie was not allowed to use it. Instead, she scrubbed all her family's clothes by hand. Sophie described her mother-in-law with a noncommittal but nevertheless loaded characterization: "You know how some people funny and ting." My initial hunch that all was not well between Sophie and her in-laws was verified when Vickram, describing hypothetical domestic troubles in extended families, pointed to some very real sources of friction: Wouldn't I feel bad, he asked me, if say he married me, brought me to his home, and then one day after I had swept the yard his mother proceeded to sweep the yard again as if to convey to me that I had done a bad job? Wouldn't I be hurt

35. Unlike Nevadomsky, I equate household not with the commensal group but rather with common residence, as suggested by Solien (1960). Therefore, the depiction of the lack of commensality does not imply for me the existence of several households, as it does for Nevadomsky.

if I were to cook and his mother was to say there was not enough salt in the food in front of the whole family? Clearly, sons too can become victims in the constant tug-of-war between their wives and mothers. Wives complain to their husbands of mistreatment by their mothers-in-law. When confronted by their sons, mothers invariably deny harassing their sons' wives and become resentful of their sons for joining the other side. Friction also obtains among brothers when they accuse one another of mistreating one another's wives.

These tensions seem typical sources of conflict in extended families. Merely to portray such instances as endemic to extended households would be a gross oversimplification, however, because frictions within these households are usually initiated or exacerbated by specific, localized values and practices. For example, Sophie's conviction that her children would need more privacy growing up was not a value typical of the joint family. The notion of privacy is clearly a sentiment informed by Western, modern influences. Similarly, the resolution Vickram and Sophie sought, to establish their own separate residence, was not an acceptable alternative in the traditional joint family model. Most significant, however, was the wholehearted support Vickram gave his wife. He seemed to treat Sophie as his equal, which signifies a fundamental change from earlier patterns of relations between spouses.

During and after the indenture period women were able to realize an unusual degree of independence in Trinidad owing to their scarcity and position as wage earners on estates (Vertovec 1992:103; Reddock 1994). Since Indian daughters were considered valuable property, the traditional institution of dowry became replaced by bridewealth (Vertovec 1992:103; Brereton 1985:26). Contrary to some, such as Reddock 1994, Angrosino has noted that the revaluing of Indian women did not necessarily translate into greater independence for women: "Prize or not, she was still 'owned' to all intents and purposes. As such, few women have good things to say about their treatment at the hands of their in-laws, although they may view the experience as having been a necessary discipline. 'They did grind me up like *massala*,' says one lady, 'but it did bring them luck. I give them ten children, and now I have sons of my own'" (1976:52). In fact, according to Angrosino, the position of the *doolahin* (daughter-in-law) deteriorated during estate days. Traditionally, families asserted their ritual purity through land, but since few Indians possessed land during the indenture period, families had to find alternate bases for ranking. Consequently, the *doolahin* constituted the sole means through which the dominance of her husband's family could be asserted.

The greater respect shown by men of Vickram's generation to their wives compared with previous generations became apparent to me on numerous occasions in Cambio. Most of the older women, seventy years and beyond, complained bitterly of mistreatment by their in-laws and abuse by their husbands, and most of the present female-headed households in Cambio were an offshoot of such abusive relations. Unable to survive in such a hostile environment, these women returned to their parental homes with their children.[36] In contrast, women approximately forty-five and younger seemed to enjoy a greater degree of independence and respect. They were usually in charge of the family's financial resources. Even though patrilocal residence continued to be the norm in Cambio, mothers-in-law, much to their chagrin, rarely commanded the same degree of power over their *doolahins* as did their own mothers-in-law. Confident of the moral support of their husbands, younger women refused to be the pawns of dominating mothers-in-law. This was especially true of those women who were also wage earners.

Boysie, a young man in his late twenties who worked as a driver, had recently married Susan, who worked in a supermarket. Boysie's family, especially the mother, Bipti, did not seem too pleased with the marriage. Not only was Susan a divorcée with three children, but she was also Christian. Susan agreed to convert to Hinduism at Boysie's family's request. However, Bipti lamented, the conversion was pointless because Susan continued to go to the Christian church. As far as Bipti was concerned, she should never have converted in the first place. The perplexing question for Bipti was, "When something goes wrong, which God is she going to pray to?" Boysie's mother disapproved of Susan for other reasons as well. Susan, she thought, did not fulfill her duties adequately. She was supposed to live with Boysie's family in the room downstairs, yet they hardly spent any time in Cambio. Instead, they preferred to live with her family in a village close to Cambio.

Susan was also accused of being lazy. Bipti awakened every day at sunrise to cook fresh food for her husband to take to work. But according to her, "Boysie wife don't do dat, she give him stale food for lunch." One evening when I was chatting with Susan and her friend, Lucy, Susan laughingly admitted that she was not a good housewife. Lucy and Susan were good friends, and one of their common bonds was their disdain for their respective mothers-in-law. Neither appeared to be harried by the situation, however. Rather,

36. Many scholars have noted the high frequency with which Indo-Trinidadian early marriages are dissolved. In Braithwaite and Roberts' sample only 60 percent of the Indo-Trinidadian women up to age forty-five remained in their original union (Roberts and Braithwaite 1962:208). Since their study was undertaken three decades ago, their sample is representative of the generation I refer to in contemporary Cambio, that is, those women who are about sixty years and older. MacDonald and MacDonald, under the category "hidden matrifocal households," also observed the tendency for Indo-Trinidadian women to return to their fathers' households when they separate from their husbands. They conclude from their sample that "an important minority of Hindu and Muslim marriages break up before the wife reaches the age of twenty-five" (1973:179).

they seemed to get immense pleasure joking about their predicament and taking repeated digs at their foes. That same evening Bipti was in the kitchen cooking the evening meal and Susan was supposed to help her grind the *dhal*. Bipti kept shouting for Susan, who refused to budge. Susan in turn began harassing her husband, Boysie, to go and grind the *dhal* for her. After some persuasion he left. Moments later a very tired and annoyed Bipti emerged from the kitchen. Before she could say anything, Susan casually remarked, "I sent Boysie over to grind de *dhal* for me!"

Bipti could convey her disapproval of Susan through harsh glares and snide remarks, but she lacked any leverage to coerce Susan into performing the duties expected of her as a wife and daughter-in-law. Susan's relative independence from her husband's household both financially and residentially and, more important, the partnership she enjoyed with Boysie rendered Bipti's potential power as mother-in-law null. Bipti, in turn, considered herself the victim because, as she put it, she could do nothing, as she was not prepared to lose her son! Recognition of such a shift in the locus of power from mother to wife in commanding the loyalties of a son/husband has also prompted a revaluation of daughters. This sentiment was expressed by another woman, Sita, who preferred "girl chirrun" to sons because daughters are always loyal to their mother. They will stick with the family and look after the mother, while sons become influenced by their wives and join the "other side."

"Companionate" relations (Nevadomsky 1980) between spouses signal a change in traditional gender roles and values. Though women continued to perform most of the household duties such as cooking, cleaning, and laundry, their husbands would often pitch in. For example, in the Hosein household Nizaam (the patriarch) would shell peas, clean chickens, and do other minor chores. Similarly, it was customary for his son, Farid, who was a masterful cook, to prepare the traditional Sunday lunch, which always consisted of fried rice, fried chicken, and "mayonnaise" (a salad dressed in mayonnaise). The women in the house would cook the regular meals. Pamela, a woman in her late thirties who had four teen-aged daughters, claimed that she does not find her household duties burdensome at all since her husband, a mechanic at Caroni, helps her a lot. He cooks regularly, and now that their washing machine is broken, he even does the laundry.[37]

Nevadomsky observed similar behavioral patterns between spouses in Amity:

37. This was the only occasion in Cambio when a man admitted to doing laundry. Despite the fairly rapid infraction of traditional gender roles, laundry seemed one task that men categorically refused to perform. Washing clothes is commonly perceived as an acutely feminine activity, and men performing this task jeopardize their masculinity.

Purdah-like practices . . . have long been discarded. When company calls, husband and wife jointly entertain their guests. Women no longer trail behind their husbands in public; indeed, some young couples walk along the road hand in hand. Some husbands take their wives to restaurants and even to nightclubs. . . . These fairly obvious manifestations of behavioral change are indicative of new patterns of marital conduct in the direction of broadly companionate spouse relations. As yet, such changes are far from universal in the community, being stressed more by the young and educated, but virtually everyone is aware of these "bright ways" and attempts to emulate them if possible. For example, a decent husband ought not to publicly treat his wife as an inferior: he ought not to "ruin her with over-childbearing"; he ought to take her to visit her kinsfolk, and so on, otherwise he runs the risk of being regarded as "coolie-ish," that is, backward. (1980:51)

In Cambio, too, the youth abhorred the thought of beating their wives and insisted that the younger men in the village never indulged in such abusive practices. Even though some of the younger women admitted to having received a few "licks" from their husbands, the practice of wife beating was generally considered unacceptable by the younger generation. Older men who were reputed to abuse their wives commanded little respect in the village. As Nevadomsky notes, much of the change in values regarding the position of women has to do with youths' aspirations to adopt forward-thinking, "bright ways," which in turn are heavily influenced by modern norms and practices.

In other aspects of household organization traditional values are perpetuated and negotiated within frameworks symbolizing modernity, such as the nuclear family. As noted earlier, the fact that sons tend to build their houses next door to or in the same village as their parents' home embodies a practice that has successfully negotiated values stemming from alternate models, the modern nuclear family and the traditional joint family. In Cambio approximately six houses were established by sons who moved away from the paternal or, in a few instances, maternal household and built independent residences within Cambio. There were also two instances in which daughters established independent residences. In two other cases of village endogamy sons moved away from the paternal household and resided with their wives' families in Cambio, thus going against the predominant patterns of patrilocal residence and initiating uxorilocal residence patterns. The picture is further complicated by ongoing segmentation that threatens to occur down the generations within the more recently established households.

Proximity to the original paternal or maternal household enables the segmented units to maintain familial links with the main household and continue practices characteristic of joint households. For example, Ravi contin-

[169]

ued to sleep in his maternal grandfather's home after his immediate family moved to a new residence a few doors up the road. It is also common practice to call on the labors of sons, daughters, and their families when extra labor is needed to fulfill certain ritual and social obligations. Conversely, members of the paternal household, the parents and unmarried siblings, lend their services whenever their married children or siblings in the village require them. Whenever a special meal is prepared, food is circulated among these contiguous households and neighbors. In short, the spirit of the extended family prevails despite the formal establishment of an independent residence by a young couple after marriage. Ironically, in some cases the extended family "presence," speaking metaphorically, magnified with the establishment of a modern practice that promised greater autonomy to the young couple. Such was the experience of Kumar Sudeen.

Kumar had fallen in love with a young girl, Indira, from a neighboring village. Indira was considered above Kumar's station: she was well educated and came from a relatively well-to-do family. She abandoned her career plans when she eloped with Kumar at the age of sixteen. After cordial relations were reestablished with her family, her father gave the couple a "nice board house" with a little land in a remote area in Central. After living there only a month, however, Kumar and Indira returned to Cambio and resumed residence with his elder brother, Mohan, and his wife, Rani. Kumar's decision to leave was primarily due to excessive interference from his father-in-law, who used to visit them daily. Even though relations between Rani and Indira were strained and all was not well in the Sudeen household, Kumar preferred the stresses of living in a joint family arrangement with his brother to living in a separate residence with his wife. The fact that he had the choice of a separate residence was much envied by other youths. Robbie, for example, referred to Kumar's situation with awe. Robbie yearned for a home of his own that he could share with the girl he hoped to marry, and asserted he would give anything to be in Kumar's shoes. Despite Kumar's claim that he did not want anything from Indira's father, it was obvious that the young couple enjoyed many privileges provided by him. For example, Kumar used to work with Robbie as a carpenter but left the job, saying the work was too hard—a privilege Kumar could exercise because he had the confidence of familial financial support. Robbie, who intensely disliked his job, related this incident with envy. Similarly, Kumar was one of the few people in the village who owned a car, another gift from his father-in-law. As Kumar's story illustrates, the establishment of a separate residence conforming to the nuclear household pattern does not automatically guarantee greater independence for the young couple. From Kumar's perspective, the traditional joint family pattern proved to be less burdensome in the last instance. By rejoining his paternal house-

hold, he managed to enjoy both a certain degree of autonomy and the benefits of marrying into a relatively well-to-do family.

The phenomenon of "pet" children is another practice in which the spirit
of the joint family continues in the face of modern exigencies. Even after a
son's family has moved out, the parents may continue to bring up their grand-
children as pet children.[38] Thus even though a particular household may su-
perficially conform to the nuclear family type, the fact that some of the children of this conjugal pair may be residing in a separate household betrays the
persistence of a hidden extended family practice. In the case of Jennifer and
Kamal, who live in a board house adjacent to Kamal's paternal house, now occupied by his brother Roshan and his wife, their two children were brought
up separately by their respective parents, who also lived in Cambio. The little
girl, Aneesa, lived with Kamal's mother, and the little boy, Charlie, lived with
Jennifer's mother. Similarly, the Hoseins' four year-old grandson Tommy
lived with them while their daughter and husband migrated to Canada soon
after Tommy was born. Mazeena, the Hoseins' younger daughter, assumed
the role of symbolic mother, devoting all her time and energy to the little boy.

Pet children are invariably showered with love and attention. They are a
source of much joy to the grandparents and are rarely looked on as a burden,
financial or otherwise. For example, Farid urged Tommy's mother, Sihaam,
not to send any money for Tommy's upkeep and to save it for herself. Subsequently, Sihaam would send Canadian $50 only when she could afford it. The
Hoseins never perceived themselves as doing a favor to their daughter by
raising Tommy despite the expenses involved. It was only customary that they
should bring up Tommy if circumstances so dictated.

From an outsider's perspective twenty-one-year-old Mazeena seemed to
have sacrificed immensely for the sake of Tommy. Tommy depended totally
on Mazeena, and she in turn doted on him. Because Tommy would "start
bawling" whenever Mazeena was not around, her movements were severely
restricted. She almost never went out for social occasions or hung out in the
street with the other young girls in the village. Even a short trip to Chaguanas
market had to be carefully planned in accordance with Tommy's needs. She
had no time to indulge in romance and had no love interest. Her whole life
was dominated by Tommy and the ultimate dream of migrating to Canada
with him when Sihaam could afford to bring them over. Sihaam, for her part,
would in the future assume similar responsibilities for the betterment of the
family. Both her siblings, Mazeena and her brother, had aspirations to mi-

---

38. This tradition has a long history in the Caribbean and is common to all ethnic groups,
even upper-class Whites. See also Ho 1991:118–20 on "child-fostering" patterns among Black
West Indians in a transnational context, in this case between the Caribbean and Los Angeles.

grate to Canada. It was understood by all members that Sihaam would provide the support necessary to establish her siblings in their new country. Just as Sihaam's impending assistance to the family was taken for granted, so were Mazeena's labors in providing for the child. It is in this sense that the spirit of the extended family operates even when individual families get separated because of the exigencies of modern life.

Such examples abound in Cambio. Devi, who was now about eighty years old (she could not recall her exact age), had returned to her own parents' home in Cambio many years ago when her husband became abusive. She worked as a cane cutter for Caroni and in time managed to secure her own plot of land near her parents' home. Devi now shared her home with her youngest son and his family and two other grandchildren. The latter were taken under Devi's wing when their mother "took off with another man." Though the mother visited occasionally, Devi assumed all responsibility for these two children. Accordingly, when Kamla, the granddaughter, got married, Devi met all the expenses; during the wedding ceremony itself the role of the mother was fulfilled by Kamla's aunt (Devi's daughter-in-law who lived in the same household) and Devi, and Kamla's biological mother was confined to the role of guest.

The marginalization of Kamla's biological mother sparked gossip in the village. Jennifer's mother (who is rearing Jennifer's son) commented that "it was not right" and that Kamla's mother should have been given a bigger part in the ceremony. I suggested that her marginality might have been a consequence of her widowhood. This was not a hindrance in Jennifer's mother's view because "plenty people whose husband dead still give away their daughters." But eventually the ladies agreed that since Kamla had been brought up in this household, the marginalization of her mother was an acceptable procedure. Following this same logic and recollecting that Jennifer's own daughter, Aneesa, was being reared by her paternal grandmother, I asked Jennifer's mother if this grandmother would give away Aneesa instead of Jennifer when Aneesa got married. Her response was firm: "Of course Jennifer because it's different when parents are alive."

Since Kamla's mother was alive, the reasoning behind Jennifer's mother's argument appears confusing at first. Why was Kamla's mother marginalized? An answer may lie in the very statement that "it's different when parents are alive," which in effect asserted that Kamla's mother was symbolically dead. Though both Aneesa and Kamla could be considered pet children, their respective statuses were quite different with regard to their relations with their biological mothers. In Aneesa's case her mother and grandmother had entered into a customary practice requiring the fulfillment of reciprocal obligations by both parties. Jennifer was never chastised for not rearing her children and was a respected member of the village. Aneesa's situation, in short, was not due to a breach of conduct on her mother's part. In contrast, Kamla's circumstance was a consequence of her mother's unacceptable behavior. Not only had her mother taken up with another man, but this man too lacked any redeeming qualities, according to Devi, who moaned, "If you see the fella she taken up with!" Devi became sad whenever she referred to Kamla's mother. She was Devi's favorite child but "she gone bad." Since other villagers who had breached acceptable codes of behavior continued to command respect in the village, however, it seems that Kamla's mother's sin was not solely due to "taking up with another man." It is possible that Kamla's mother's ostracism was in part based on her violation of the highly sophisticated and subtle principles of reciprocal obligations regulating not only the relations among kin but also those among villagers. It seems that Kamla's mother did not assume any kind of responsibility for her children, nor did she participate in maintaining familial obligations with her kin. Her abandonment of her children to her mother was a literal abandonment, unlike that of Jennifer, who was merely partaking in habitual practice. Hence the symbolic death of Kamla's mother.

I have deliberately contrasted Kamla's and Aneesa's statuses as pet children to illustrate how structurally similar patterns of family organization can be the result of quite different motivations. A microlevel analysis that explores the specific circumstances that generate certain behaviors in historical subjects emphasizes the processes through which actual subjects evaluate their options and then act on them. For Aneesa's grandmother it was the simple fact that she had no "little chirrun" that prompted her to keep Aneesa. Devi probably had little choice but to take in her grandchildren, inheriting them by default. The roles and values of the traditional joint family provided an avenue for these two women to resolve their respective difficulties. It was not a passive reproduction of an ideal pattern, however, since the very concept pet children constitutes a variation of a routine practice that characterizes the joint family, the socialization of children by members of the joint family.

The cases just presented center on the tensions relating to the dualities posed by two contrasting models of family organization, the extended and nuclear family patterns. Other tensions are created by the incursion of modern[39] attitudes on traditional values and practices, an interface that the

---

39. Although *modern* is conventionally understood to pertain to external and therefore "inauthentic" influences, like Bolland, Mintz, Trouillot, Robotham, and others I choose to locate modernity within the internal dynamics of Creole systems, given the fact that these systems emerged precisely through intense global interaction. In my use of the two concepts here I see *modern* and *traditional* not as opposites but merely as concepts that allow me to speak of no-

younger generations in particular confront daily. Modern attitudes are especially marked in courting practices in Cambio, and they have inadvertently contributed to the decline of the traditional north Indian practice of village exogamy. Within Cambio, for those of Mariam's age group (the mid-forties) and older, the predominant marriage pattern was village exogamy. As a result, most of these women's homes were located outside Cambio. In contrast, there were about nine instances of village endogamy between men and women below the age of forty, which in turn implicated affinal ties between eighteen of the thirty-four households in Cambio. This increasing tendency to marry within the village was also prevalent in Amity. According to Nevadomsky, in the late 1970s there was a strong bias toward exogamous marriage among women over thirty-five years of age and a slight bias toward endogamous marriages among women thirty-five and younger (1980:47). Formerly, the preference for exogamy was based on the prescriptive rule that one could not marry anyone to whom cognatic, affinal, or fictive kinship could be traced. This norm, however, is gradually being replaced by the "second cousin rule" as the prescriptive boundary for exogamy.

The reevaluation of the rules pertaining to marriage partners is largely a consequence of modern influences that have prompted younger generations to choose their own spouses. As early as the 1960s Leo Davids observed that even when arranged marriages prevail, young people almost always have veto power over the proceedings (1964:390). Among the younger generations a high premium is placed on "being in love" as a necessary qualification for marriage, and this notion is premised on familiarity and frequent contact between potential mates. Consequently, many of the youths in Cambio had love interests in the village itself. They spent an enormous amount of time and energy wooing their girlfriends—writing love poems, agonizing over the most appropriate gift for Valentine's Day, and, a lot of the time, daydreaming. Hardly any of these village romances were criticized for posing a potential breach of the rule of village exogamy. More to the point, young people seemed completely unaware of even the existence of such a rule.

The significance of the impact of modernity on the younger generation seems to vary with gender. Women in their mid to late forties who have benefited from some of the modern changes but remain committed to certain traditional ideals worried about the current state of young girls, who are also potential mates for their sons. Fena constantly fretted over her son, Teddy, who was engaged to Sandra. Not only did Sandra demand "dis and dat" from

---

ticeable changes in values and practices. Thus what I now label a traditional practice can be, analytically speaking, considered a thoroughly modern one in the sense suggested by Mintz and other scholars who argue that the Caribbean was modern even before Europe.

Teddy, but she did not know how to cook meat (Sandra's family was Hindu and vegetarian)[40] or even how to sew a simple dress. Worse, Sandra was reputed to have a "long eye" (that is, to be a flirt), and with Teddy's jealous temperament, Fena feared the worst.

Women of Fena's generation condemned the young girls for their demanding natures, flirtatious behavior, love of fine things, and alleged aversion to hard work, but they simultaneously insisted that it is better to have "girl chirrun" than "boy chirrun," a significant deviation indeed from traditional Indian values that placed a high premium on sons. Villagers, it seemed, differentiated between those young women and girls who maintained the virtues of their traditional roles and those who transgressed beyond the boundaries of acceptable behavior. The more modern women, such as Lucy and Susan, were perceived critically because "dey want to dress nice and ting" and spend money "too bad" and because they were reputed to be lazy. Conversely, other young women were praised constantly. Their most significant virtues included their industrious natures, their ability to manage money, and their abstinence from indulgent behaviors such as bad talking (gossiping), liming, and frivolous spending. The women distinguished among themselves on the basis of these two types. Lucy, for example, during one of her many liming sessions, pointed to her sister-in-law, Tracy, who was frantically sweeping the house in preparation for a *puja* the following day, and commented that she could never work like that. On the day of the *puja* itself, while Tracy and the few neighbors who had offered to help Mrs. Lal were laboring over the cooking, Mrs. Lal (who also had a reputation for being lazy and for exploiting her daughter's labor) and Lucy appeared to do very little. Lucy did not emerge unscathed, however. She became the butt of many caustic remarks and jokes concerning her general ineptness in cooking and other areas. Such were the not so subtle ways in which villagers condemned unacceptable types of behavior, and such was the price Lucy had to pay for being too modern.

The more industrious type of women paid a different kind of price. Although they rarely invited rebuke from other villagers, they often expressed unhappiness over their situation. Geeta, the youngest daughter of the only Brahmin family in Cambio, complained incessantly about the amount of work she had to do. Since her mother's death all the household chores, which involved the upkeep of her father, two brothers, a nephew, and another sister, had passed to her. When she finished work at the Montessori school and returned home around 2:30 in the afternoon, she spent the rest of the day

40. Interestingly, the issue of religious difference (since Teddy was Muslim) was never made an issue by Teddy's family.

cooking, cleaning, and doing laundry. None of the family members, she complained, not even her sister, would help. She constantly threatened to migrate to the United States, where many of her siblings resided. This was her only hope of relieving her currently oppressive situation. Similarly, Mazeena too dreamed of the day she would leave for Canada to join her sister. As she put it, there was no future for her in Trinidad. For these women who continued somewhat in the tradition of their mothers, the exigencies of modern life had exposed them to an alternate lifestyle, which induced in them a deep dissatisfaction with their current situation. Although they dutifully performed their expected roles, they realized that within the traditional confines of family life their dreams could never be fulfilled.

Earlier I mentioned that the impact of modernity varied with gender. We have seen how modern values and roles were incorporated in differential degrees by younger women, reflected in lay categorization of younger women into two types. In contrast, the impact of modernity appeared to be more uniform in the case of younger men. The preference of mothers for "girl chirrun" was in part based on their recognition that sons were more inclined to pick up the negative effects of modernity. Mothers constantly complained of their sons' idle ways, excessive drinking, tendency to gad about, frivolous spending habits (especially on girlfriends), aversion to hard work, and most important, their joblessness. Keith's mother, who had four daughters and four sons, extolled the virtues of her daughters. They helped her with the gardening, cooking, laundry, and cleaning, unlike the boys, who did not help at all. Even when they were building their house, it was the girls, she claimed, who did most of the work, mixing concrete and even laying the steel bars. Robbie's mother, Mariam, often contrasted Robbie with Mazeena. Mazeena, it seemed, possessed that much admired gift of being able to save something from nothing. She had no regular source of income, yet her bank account slowly but steadily increased. When she was given money to take a taxi, she would catch the bus instead and save the remaining few dollars. Her grandfather would give her TT$25 every month when he got his pension. This she tucked away safely for her impending trip to Canada. Robbie, however, who found work now and then as a carpenter and earned a modest but adequate income of TT$50 per day, ran through his money immediately. His generous nature and his desire for fine clothes, shoes, and other apparel coupled with his girlfriend's demands drained all his resources. Indeed, as Mariam laughingly said, he was often in the embarrassing position of having to beg money from Mazeena. Robbie was also chastised by his family for not contributing to the family, both economically and with the daily chores.

In short, youths such as Keith and Robbie possessed those very Creole habits that were thought to differentiate the East Indian from the Creole.

Most of the youths in Cambio were unemployed, not just because of the un-availability of opportunities but because of a lack of initiative on their part. Averse to occupations in agriculture or even construction, which required back-breaking work, they preferred to "skylark" (sit around and wait for something to turn up). Those few who had managed to secure temporary cushy jobs, such as Keith (who worked briefly for the dairy) and Raja (who found employment as a painter for Caroni also for a brief period), were highly envied by the rest. "Harassment" at home and sheer necessity would push some to take up manual labor, but they would quit as soon as they obtained some cash.

The youths' relations with their kin were complex. On the one hand, they found tremendous comfort in the extended family network. Even though they were unemployed, they were always guaranteed a place to eat and sleep. Sensitive to Robbie's dislike of vegetarian food, Mariam would always prepare some chicken or goat especially for him. Similarly, Robbie's aspirations to migrate to Canada could be fulfilled only by relying on familial ties, that is, the help of his sister, Sihaam. Robbie's value as a potential marriage partner was also significantly bolstered by the fact that he would someday inherit the family home. On the other hand, Robbie and the rest of the youths found the pressures from their families burdensome. They resented the constant interference and struggled continuously to assert some degree of autonomy. For example, when Robbie originally made plans for marriage, he insisted that he would not live with his family. Yet a couple of weeks later when he realized that he lacked the resources to establish an independent residence and that he and his bride-to-be would have to be content living in a single room in his family's household, he had a serious conversation with his family and firmly demarcated boundaries they could and could not cross. A few weeks later, however, Robbie appeared increasingly agitated and annoyed with his family. To ensure some privacy for himself and his wife, Robbie had requested the room downstairs. The family had denied his request on the basis that it would restrict their movements downstairs. Despite his parents' assertion that the house would someday belong to Robbie, it seemed he had no say when it came to his own interests. As he put it, the house is his only to maintain! Teddy too was unhappy with his family situation. He resented the excessive degree to which his mother, Fena, and sister monitored all his movements and activities. They spied on his bank book, sneaked up to his room (which he had strictly forbidden) to uncover any gifts he might have recently purchased for Sandra, and engaged in other covert operations that blatantly infringed on the rules he had laid down. Teddy reacted by being increasingly secretive, which in turn drove Fena crazy and made her even more suspicious. And so the cycle continued.

[177]

Another intriguing facet of the dualities structuring behavioral patterns in Cambio is the presence of what are commonly believed to be lower-class Afro-Creole practices. As other studies have concluded for Indo-Trinidadians in different enclaves (Roberts and Braithwaite 1962; MacDonald and Mac-Donald 1973; Bell 1970), mating patterns and family organizations associated with lower-class Afro-Creole practices, however slight, obtained in Cambio as well.

A variation of the matrifocal household, which MacDonald and MacDonald (1973) categorized as "hidden matrifocality," was quite common in Cambio. The reintegration of a married daughter and her children into the paternal household after the dissolution of her marriage was common practice in Cambio, especially among the older generation of women. Though villagers openly denigrated the "illegal" status of Creole unions, in Cambio those few unions that were "common law" went for the most part unscathed. For example, Curlie and Ranee, both respected members of the village, were not legally or ritually married. They had been in common-law union for the past fifteen years and had five children. Curlie's mother, however, who had established a common-law union with an old man and had lived with him until his death in her home (where Curlie also resides), invited some admonishment from villagers. The "ripe" age at which she initiated this relationship is what villagers objected to. As Mariam remarked, "Look how old she be when she took up with de old man." Thus villagers are quick to chastise the illegality of Creole common-law unions, but the criteria for acceptability become more complex and tolerant when such a union involves neighbors.

One villager also confessed to fathering a Dougla son, whom his sister subsequently adopted. He was very proud of this son, who currently worked as a drafter for an oil company and earned as much as TT$5,000 a month. Though the presence of Dougla children was minimal in Cambio, it became evident that a few Indo-Trinidadian men had fathered children as a consequence of their relations with Afro-Trinidadian women. Dougla children fathered by Indo-Trinidadian men tend to be incorporated into the Afro-Trinidadian mother's family, hence the relative invisibility of Dougla individuals in Cambio. Even though the residential patterns of these men and their legitimate families conformed to the formal monogamous pattern, the existence of children from visiting unions implicates indirectly practices deemed lower-class Afro-Creole within Cambio itself. Once again, a formal appearance betrays a hidden practice.

Many of the "scandals" in Cambio involved village women and their lovers. Dolly, for example, who commanded a lot of respect in the village, nevertheless had a particularly bad reputation. Twenty years ago Dolly left her first husband, the father of seven of her nine children, to live with Dave, who

lived with his family farther down the road. Dave's wife in turn had abandoned him for a Creole lover. Dolly now lived with Dave in a common-law
union. It was also rumored that a different villager living "down de road"
sired one of Dolly's daughters. Mrs. Mangur openly indulged in a visiting
union with a lover while she continued to live with her husband. In fact,
when her elder daughter got married, her lover as opposed to her husband
assumed the more prominent role. Mrs. Mangur's younger daughter was rumored to be the daughter of this lover. Similarly, Mrs. Harilal, who was considered very good-looking in her time, was known to have had several lovers,
one of whom it was rumored fathered her eldest son.

All these women (and others) formally appeared to be in monogamous relations with their husbands, but the spirit of monogamy had been consistently violated in practice and, more significant, by women in the village.
Such violations were evidenced by the presence of offspring purported to
have been fathered by lovers and not husbands. Although at the level of rhetoric villagers deployed these same characteristics to distinguish themselves
from Creoles, their nonchalant attitude toward these very practices when
they implicated their "own kind" indicates that such practices may not be that
uncommon or foreign to them at all.

It was first Leach (1954) and then Barth (1969) who made the powerful
observation that members of social groups need not share distinct cultural
traits and that subjective categorical ascriptions have no necessary relationship to observers' perception of cultural discontinuities. From this premise
Barth proceeded to illustrate that cultural diacritica in and of themselves
mattered little and gained significance only as mechanisms through which
boundaries between social units could be maintained. Specific diacritica that
have the potential to differentiate between social groups are deployed depending on the situation. In short, specific cultural traits that all members of
a particular social group do not necessarily share become deployed if those
traits are distinguishable from the traits signifying the "Other." Such diacritica then become the vehicle through which the foreignness of the Other is
established.

The evidence from Cambio presents another interesting twist to this argument. Here one finds that cultural traits commonly ascribed to the Other—
Creoles in this instance—are also evident among Indo-Trinidadians. Nevertheless, the villagers continue to distinguish Creoles on the basis of such
cultural traits at the level of rhetoric whereas in practice Indo-Trinidadians
who display those very same cultural traits are rarely depicted as being "Creole like." It seems that cultural diacritica that are used to distinguish social
groups are not in and of themselves foreign, that is, they do not necessarily
distinguish the two groups, but become foreign only when practiced by the

[179]

unfamiliar Other. In short, the foreignness of illegitimacy, common-law unions, or matrifocal residence patterns becomes apparent only when practiced by Creoles and not Indo-Trinidadians. Thus the fluidity of ethnic boundaries is evidenced not only by the crossing of boundaries by personnel (as Barth argues) but also by the violation of cultural diacritica that serve to mark the boundary in the first place. It needs to be said, however, that the degree of fluidity is invariably contingent on the degree of familiarity enjoyed between those doing the ascribing and the targets of ascription. For example, family members and neighbors of villagers rarely become "Creole" by indulging in purportedly Creole practices, and similarly, those familiar Creoles who have adopted "East Indian ways" often become included as "one of us." The significance of familiarity at the level of interaction, as opposed to rhetoric, between ethnic groups and its implications for boundary maintenance has yet to be explored.

In this discussion of family and household organization in Cambio I have not provided a formal, macrolevel analysis typical of the literature on Indo-Trinidadian kinship systems. Nor have I framed the discussion in terms of cultural retention or acculturation. Rather, I have attempted to describe family and household organization in Cambio as a patchwork[41] of institutions, practices, and values that derives its raw material from various cultural models believed to be characteristic of the discrete "pure types" making up the heterogeneous population of Trinidad: East Indian, Creole (or lower-class Afro-Creole), and Euro-Creole (which has come to signify middle-class Creole or the ideal societal norms and values). Using a microlevel perspective and drawing from the experiences of specific historical subjects and families, I have attempted to show how actors juggle, reconcile, and sometimes creatively generate novel forms from the diverse and often contradictory strains available to them.

Family and household organization in Cambio serve to distinguish Indo-Trinidadians from other groups while simultaneously attesting to the commonalities Indo-Trinidadians have with other groups. Indeed, the "East Indian family" has long been heralded by both scholars and lay people as the bulwark of Indo-Trinidadians' ethnicity. Much of their initial social mobility was and continues to be attributed to the strong support system provided by the extended family. But what makes Indo-Trinidadian family organization

41. Patchwork, in my usage, does not imply fragmentation or instability. I see creolization as a process that is driven simultaneously by contradiction and integrative impulses. As Mintz observes, "What typified creolization was not the fragmentation of culture and the destruction of the very concept, but the creation and construction of culture out of fragmented, violent and disjunct pasts" (1994:302).

distinct is not merely the persistence of north Indian patterns but the curious combinations that result from the interweaving of such patterns with modern, Afro-Creole, and Euro-Creole strains. The resulting amalgam establishes the Indo-Trinidadian as both unique and very Trinidadian.

It is important to acknowledge the creative dimension of Indo-Trinidadian cultural practices precisely because of their grossly overstated depiction (in scholarly literature and in lay Trinidadian imagination) as mere retainers of an essential culture. The creative aspect of Creole cultures continues to be widely accepted by scholars, but the genesis of a new culture in the New World seems to factor in only European and African elements. The very framework used to understand and depict the creativeness and uniqueness of Caribbean cultures often slights Indo-Caribbean elements. Thus despite the innovations and transformations implicating Indo-Trinidadians in practice, they continue to remain outside the society in terms of symbolic positioning. Indo-Trinidadians do not need to imitate Creole (meaning Afro-Creole) practices to become Creole. Instead, what is needed is recognition of the creolization of the Indo-Trinidadians that has already taken place. The very battle Indo-Trinidadian activists face in their struggle to create a "tossed salad" vision of Trinidadian society from what truly prevails in practice, a "callaloo," is in itself indicative of the creoleness of Indo-Trinidadians. It is precisely their creoleness that also makes them East Indian in an irrevocably Trinidadian fashion.

In the political arena Indo-Trinidadian leaders underplay the creoleness of Indo-Trinidadians and emphasize only those aspects of lay ethnicity that highlight difference between East Indians and Creoles. The historical chapters, by delineating structural limits imposed in part by history, explained why it is necessary for Indo-Trinidadian leaders to adopt such a strategy. The village ethnographic chapters show why it is possible for Indo-Trinidadian leaders to adopt this strategy. Since the dichotomy between East Indian and Creole is pervasive in the folk idiom, political leaders' rhetoric resonates with lay conceptions of ethnicity, thereby legitimating their challenges to the Trinidadian nation and the state.

I now turn to the development of the Trinidadian nation and the state to understand not only how the contemporary Indo-Trinidadian challenge was precipitated but also the nature of the challenge itself.

[7]

Nation Building within the State: Consolidating an Afro-Caribbean Nation

Colored and Black Agitation for Reform

Indo-Trinidadian estrangement from the state was firmly established during the colonial period. Physical isolation on remote estates, alien status, lack of education, and language difficulties—all largely engineered by the state—prevented Indo-Trinidadians from influencing state policy directly. The formation of Indo-Trinidadian organizations in the late nineteenth and early twentieth centuries signaled not only the emergence of a middle class among Indo-Trinidadians but also their initiation into politics. The Indo-Trinidadian leaders' political positioning vis-à-vis the colonial state differed from that of Colored and Black middle classes, whose agitation for reforms, however limited, was underscored by the assumption of imminent political power for their group.[1] In contrast, Indo-Trinidadian leaders assumed a conservative posture that viewed the colonial state as a necessary neutral arbiter of competing interests.

Colored and Black middle-class attempts to claim a stake in the political life of the colony must be understood against the backdrop of those ideologi-

1. Since a primary goal of this chapter is to illustrate how the significance of projected differences symbolized by categories such as *Black, Colored, Afro-Creole,* and *Creole* changed during the period under discussion, my use of these categories to denote particular ancestral groups is in accordance with these noted changes. A very general working definition of these terms is that *Creole* encompasses *Blacks* (those claiming primarily African ancestry) and *Coloreds* (those claiming African and European ancestry). *Afro-Creole* nominally includes all with some African ancestry; the prefix *Afro* functions to emphasize the African component.

cal currents shaping British colonial policy. Liberal democratic ideals that posited symmetry between people's legal and political relations with society gained ascendancy in Britain in the years leading up to emancipation. Well-ordered and self-regulating societies were built on the concept of the modern citizen, who ideally enjoyed both legal and political equality but not necessarily economic equality. Innovation, enterprise, practical education, self-reliance, and the mutuality and interdependence of social classes were themes ingrained in the liberal bourgeois ideal of progress (Holt 1992). These principles in turn shaped Britain's policy toward its colonies, if not in practice at least in theory. Thus for Lord Glenelg, the colonial secretary when apprenticeship ended, freedom for ex-slaves meant the qualitative realization of political, economic, and social freedom.

Yet as Thomas C. Holt (1992) describes for Jamaica and the West Indian colonies, colonial practice blatantly contradicted liberal democratic ideology in the ensuing years. Colonial and planter fears of impending Black power spearheaded institutional arrangements that rendered majority rule impossible. Nevertheless, stark demographic facts, if nothing else, augured the inevitability of Black and Colored political ascendancy in the West Indian colonies. Accordingly, constitutional reforms during the second half of the nineteenth century and the beginning of the twentieth, however reluctant, had to acknowledge this impending reality.

The overt contradictions between liberal democratic ideology and colonial practice were partly rationalized through racist explanations. In Jamaica in the early 1840s class was perceived to be the primary social divider whereas later it was supplanted by a discourse on race. Holt observes: "By mid-century the recognition reflected [earlier] in Governor Metcalfe's statement . . . that the Afro-Jamaican majority was also a working class majority with interests necessarily at odds with those of the largely white, planter-merchant elite was obscured. For Colonial Secretary Grey it was their blackness that was most relevant politically and most to be feared" (1992:216). The subsumption of class by race transformed Glenelg's simple doctrine of equality under the law into imperialist justifications for White power: "Potential black empowerment was to be thwarted through novel political arrangements" (Holt 1992:216). This evolving racial ideology directly influenced the distinction imperial policy makers drew between their white colonies, such as Canada and Ireland, and their black colonies in the West Indies. White colonies were to be groomed for greater independence in local affairs whereas black colonies were to be placed under "benevolent guardianship." Fitness for government was denied to the latter on the basis that these societies were fraught by racial divisions, divisions that "rent the social fabric, threatened social order, and retarded progress" (Holt 1992:237).

[183]

Indeed, the heterogeneity ascribed to Trinidadian society was a primary justification for establishing the crown colony system of government.[2] Older colonies such as Barbados and Jamaica had elected assemblies that enjoyed lawmaking powers, but in Trinidad executive powers were vested solely in the governor. Although there was a council of advisers composed of prominent local residents appointed by the governor, they lacked lawmaking power.

In 1810, backed by White planter interests, Governor Hislop and his allies in the council pushed for an elective assembly. The Free Coloreds intervened at this point, fearing that the establishment of an elected assembly could lead to a consolidation of hostile political interests that would threaten their political and legal status. Their leaders asked the Colonial Office to consider their participation in any new form of government, but from the perspective of the Colonial Office, enfranchising Coloreds was not an option. The Colonial Office also recognized that the Free Coloreds would never accept an assembly that denied them representation, so it used their objections to deny an elected assembly, which it never intended to grant in the first place. In imperialist schemes the philosophy of trusteeship was meant to act as a check on both the White oligarchy and "the incompetent rule of color" (Magid 1988:57).

Nevertheless, the British government knew some reform was necessary. The legal system in Trinidad was a confused mix of Spanish and British laws. On the recommendation of the Commission of Legal Inquiry (1827),[3] a Council of Government, presided over by the governor, was established in 1832.[4] Council members consisted of six Officials, who were leading officers of local government, and six Unofficials, propertied and wealthy local residents. Even though Unofficials were nominated (not elected), the council enjoyed lawmaking powers. Intermittent demands for elected members were assuaged by increasing the representation of Unofficials in the council, and from 1862 to 1898, when the secretary of state for the colonies, Joseph Chamberlain, restored the Official majority,[5] Trinidad had an Unofficial majority. Yet this majority proved ineffective in its opposition to the government since its interests, to a large degree, ran parallel to those of the government.

The great myth about crown colony government, as Brereton (1981:139)

2. See Millette 1985 on the crown colony system in Trinidad.
3. See Brereton 1981:72–73.
4. In 1863 the Council of Government was renamed the Legislative Council.
5. See Magid 1988:58–59 for Chamberlain's motivations.

observes, was the notion "that governors and officials were impartial administrators" and guardians of the poor against propertied interests. Governors rarely exercised their autocratic powers to override the interests of local oligarchs since both groups had stakes in preserving the status quo, even if at times for different reasons. They also shared the assumption that only men with substantial economic investments in the island, especially in sugar, had the country's best interest at heart. Accordingly, Unofficials were largely sugar planters and merchants. In 1870, for example, of the eight Unofficials, five were sugar planters, one was a doctor with sugar and cocoa properties, and two were lawyers, one of whom was the legal counsel to the Colonial Company (Brereton 1981:139). Thus the operation of the crown colony system during the nineteenth century ensured the dominance of large propertied interests at the expense of all others. It was partly in reaction to the dominance of Unofficials that reform movements subsequently emerged.[6]

One of the two significant reform movements that agitated for elected members emerged in the 1880s and was led by a French Creole, Philip Rostant, publisher of the Port-of-Spain newspaper *Public Opinion.*[7] Rostant, a member of an elite landowning family, had deep respect for propertied interests despite his populist tendencies. He sought enfranchisement only for those who understood the responsibilities of citizenship, that is, the propertied and educated men of the respectable classes. As a French Creole, however, he was also passionately anticolonial, albeit in a limited sense, and sought in vain to mobilize rural peasants and urban laborers for constitutional reform. Alarmed by such populist tendencies, the few planters and merchants who initially pledged support for the movement defected. The lack of support from propertied interests facilitated the Colonial Office's decision to deny any concessions to the reformers.

The second reform movement, which emerged in the 1890s, was led by the Black and Colored middle classes. Within this nonwhite middle class the Free Coloreds of the pre-emancipation era comprised the elite. Catholic, and French-speaking until the turn of the nineteenth century, members of this group cherished aristocratic traditions and distinguished themselves

---

6. On the early reform movements (1895–1914), see Magid 1988. See also Brereton 1979.

7. I do not include the Legislative Reform Committee, formed in 1856 by French Creole cocoa interests, British merchants, and a few Colored professionals who united in opposition to Indian immigration, because its members were exclusively elitist in their outlook and never enjoyed the support of the masses. By 1880 this committee was no longer in the vanguard for reform. See Magid 1988:45–47.

from those latecomers who had risen to the ranks of the middle class through education.[8]

Colored and Black lawyers such as Henry Alcazar, C. P. David, and Vincent Brown provided the leadership for the second reform movement. They drew their support from teachers, journalists, and artisans in towns and villages and, unlike Rostant a decade earlier, did not attempt to mobilize the working classes. Since they were an aspiring elite, perhaps they could not afford the luxury of radicalism. More important, their interests were focused on gaining privileges for the respectable classes and not the masses. They sought to curb the power of the Unofficials and sugar interests by enfranchising the divergent interests they represented. Their interests, for the most part, were antithetical to sugar, as they supported minor industries, the opening of crown lands, and the encouragement of smallholders. Some also opposed Indian immigration on the basis that it was an unjustified subsidy to the sugar industry.

Their primary target, however, was the high-handed administration. They resented expatriate officials and expatriate appointments to the civil service. A main goal of the reformers was to open the higher ranks of the civil service to Blacks and Colored Creoles. Their education and training, they felt, qualified them to take an active part in government. Moreover, their "creoleness" embodied a commitment to the country that surpassed those who had only transient stakes, such as planters and merchants.

Creoleness as a legitimating discourse for Colored and Black political power was symptomatic of the West Indian political mood in the second half of the nineteenth century. In Jamaica the unifying political theme for Colored assemblymen was their creoleness. The distinction they drew between those with "a merely temporary interest in the country" and "the men who are the bones and sinews of the country, [and who had] a permanent stake in its fortunes," constituted a crucial legitimating principle for their claims (Heuman 1981). In a similar vein Black and Colored middle-class reformers in Trinidad sought active participation in the political process under the slogan "Trinidad for the Trinidadians" (Brereton 1981:143).

Even though the reform movements in Trinidad failed in all their objec-

8. After emancipation the ranks of the middle class were augmented by Colored and Black men who had elevated their status through their own efforts (as opposed to birthright) and through education. Lacking capital, few owned plantations or businesses. These "self-made" Black and Colored men were primarily teachers, professionals, journalists, printers, clerks, and civil servants. Education was pivotal to their mobility. Indeed, by providing a public education system, British colonialism fostered the emergence of an educated middle class that in time contested the very basis of its authority (Brereton 1981:127–29).

tives, the vigorous involvement of Blacks and Colored Creoles significantly influenced the tone of subsequent colonial politics. However conservative, the movement provided Black and Colored middle classes with political training and laid the ground for more radical movements. It also signaled the imminent political ascendancy of this group when suffrage was to be granted. More important, their mobilization evoked a native element—creoleness—as a principle for defining legitimate heirs to the state. If as Magid (1988) has convincingly argued the urban-based early reform movements signal the first nationalist stirrings in the island, then the very absence of significant Indo-Trinidadian involvement in such movements underscored their non-native status in the future political development of the colony. Thus the reform movements engendered an amorphous national unit positioned outside the state. Even though these would-be inheritors of the state belonged exclusively to the middle classes, their African ancestry and "native" status became metonyms for the nation. This metonymic relation meant that Afro-Creole masses would be included in the nation and Indo-Trinidadians would not.

In contrast, the issues addressed by Indo-Trinidadian pressure groups in the late nineteenth and early twentieth centuries tended to be conservative, reinforcing their collectivity's position as one outside the nation. The Immigration Ordinance of 1897, which stipulated that all free Indians had to carry a pass, without which they were subject to arrest, mobilized the Indo-Trinidadian elites (primarily those recipients of a Presbyterian education) to form the East Indian National Association in 1897 (EINA). The EINA was the main organ for voicing Indo-Trinidadian concerns until 1909, when the East Indian National Congress (EINC) was formed. The primary function of such associations was to address the grievances of their communities, to preserve the Indian way of life, and to agitate for Indo-Trinidadian representation and participation in the political process.[9] These groups were for the most part dignified debating societies, seeking moderate constitutional changes that did not challenge British rule. Indeed, their principal basis for challenging unjust practices was that Indo-Trinidadians were loyal subjects of the British crown and therefore deserved the same rights and privileges as any British citizen. Although the involvement of these pressure groups in the political process signified Indo-Trinidadians' interest in the affairs of the colony and forced the wider society to take account of their situation, how these organizations made their claims illustrate well the difference between

9. On the genesis of these two groups, see Ali 1985, Jha 1973, and Singh 1994 and 1996.

Afro-Trinidadian and Indo-Trinidadian perceptions of their society and their respective places in it.

The issue of constitutional change, addressed by Major Wood, the parliamentary undersecretary for the colonies, when he visited Trinidad in 1921, foreshadowed future political alignments in which the major ethnic groups would feel compelled to guard their terrain jealously.[10] According to Mac-Donald, "the constitutional reform issue became a question of race relations with each community fearing each other more than the small white elite that ruled" (1986:53). The Legislative Reform Committee and other radical Afro-Creole interests advocated an elected section for the Legislative Committee, in contrast to Indo-Trinidadians, who pushed for more moderate changes. The EINA, siding with propertied interests, opposed the elective principle altogether, claiming Indo-Trinidadians were insufficiently educated to maximize the possibilities of the democratic political method (Ryan 1974:31). The younger, more progressive EINC agreed to constitutional changes, but only on the basis of communal representation, because they feared that with open electoral politics the Creoles would swamp the Indo-Trinidadians. There was also a third Indo-Trinidadian organization, the Young Indian Party, whose daring radical position opposed both communal representation and the nominated system on the grounds that Indo-Trinidadians had no unique interests to protect. But this group was an exception. The aim of the majority of Indo-Trinidadian leaders was to delay as long as possible the movement for radical constitutional change, preferring instead to maintain the crown colony system, which according to Singh meant "that they had greater confidence in the ethnic group that already dominated the Legislative Council, that is, the Whites, whose elite components constituted the ruling class, than in the Black and Coloured leaders who were seeking to share in that domination" (1994:49).

The controversy over constitutional reform highlighted the diverse ways in which groups perceived the celebrated pluralism of their society (Oxaal 1968). For those who saw in the emergent mosaic of Trinidadian life an overall pattern that all members shared, Trinidad would constitute the primary ethnic and territorial unit of loyalty—these were the later nationalists. For the opponents of self-government who stressed the plural aspects of the society, however, "continuation of rule by the trusted arbiters in London" was a necessity if they were to safeguard their privileges and interests (Oxaal 1968:52). Although this was particularly true for elite ruling classes, many Indo-Trinidadians also chose the latter option, fearing Afro-Creole domi-

10. On the varied positions taken by Indo-Trinidadian elites on the issue of constitutional change, see Singh 1994:46–59.

nance of the political process. In this way Indo-Trinidadians and Afro-Creoles came to occupy different symbolic positions in relation to the nation even though both groups were positioned against the state during the colonial period.

The Years of Transition

Political Agitation

Black and Colored middle classes won limited concessions with the introduction of the elective principle to the legislature in 1925, but it was the labor movement based in the working class that came to the forefront of the political arena in the 1930s.[11] Labor unrest in the immediate aftermath of World War I was precipitated by rampant inflation (126 percent for Port-of-Spain, 167 percent for San Fernando, and 140 percent for the country areas between 1914 and 1919; Singh 1994:15) and deteriorating economic conditions for both Afro-Trinidadians and Indo-Trinidadians.

Trinidadians returning from voluntary service in the war also fueled unrest. The discrimination Black West Indians encountered in the army politicized them and oriented them toward radical labor politics. While stationed in Taranto, Italy, some of the Black West Indian (BWI) Regiment sergeants formed a secret Caribbean League, mainly in reaction to their conditions. Black soldiers were forced to perform degrading services, such as cleaning latrines and washing linens, and were also given segregated and inferior canteens, cinemas, and hospitals. The league "advocated industrial and social reforms for the West Indies, close union among the colonies, self-government for black men, and strike action after demobilization to press for higher wages" (Brereton 1981:158). Even though the league was disbanded, its ideas influenced the reform groups and their leaders, especially Captain Arthur Cipriani. Cipriani, a White Trinidadian of Corsican descent and an officer in the BWI Regiment in Taranto, fought vigorously against the injustices Black troops endured, and he along with other ex-servicemen of the regiment took a leading part in the postwar upheavals.

A wave of strikes in the urban and industrial sectors crippled the country during 1919–20 (Singh 1994:15–40). Longshoremen, railwaymen, city council employees, and workers at the electric and telephone companies all demanded higher wages and better working conditions. A revived Trinidad Workingmen's Association, TWA (first established in 1897), sought to rescue the working class from its difficult economic conditions and agitated for so-

11. See Singh 1994 for an excellent analysis of the labor struggles of this period.

cial reform. Led by Captain Cipriani, who was heralded as the "champion of the barefoot man," the TWA believed that a "neutral ethnic type" at the helm would bridge the gap between Afro-Trinidadian and Indo-Trinidadian working classes (MacDonald 1986:51). Indeed, Cipriani provided a temporary bridge between the two ethnic groups, which forged intermittent alliances in their struggle for social and economic equity. According to Ryan, however, though Cipriani was able to champion the cause of urban Afro-Trinidadians, he was less successful in his dealings with Indo-Trinidadians, who remained isolated on and around the plantations:

> The bulk of the Indian population, working-class or otherwise, did not identify with the nationalist movement. The rural Indian in particular was not yet able, or in fact willing, to identify with abstract institutions like "council" or "party"; nor did such symbols as "national self-determination" and "socialism" mean much to him. . . . This is not to say that the Indians did not admire Cipriani for the stands he took on their behalf, and for his struggle to improve the working conditions of the masses; but they were decidedly aloof to his fight for self-government and federation. (1974:39)

Nevertheless, some Indo-Trinidadian leaders actively participated in the nationalist struggle. The Indo-Trinidadian elite that emerged at the end of indenture was divided between modernizers and traditionalists. The former, according to Singh (1996), took it on themselves not only to adapt the Indian sector to the Western/Creole social milieu but also to provide the necessary political and social leadership. The traditionalists' major concern, in contrast, was to "vindicate their religions from the slurs and denigration by Christian evangelists" (Singh 1996:230) and to maintain Indo-Trinidadian social, cultural, and religious forms. Unlike Creole elites, whose sectarian concerns translated rather easily into national ones, Indo-Trinidadian elites were often pulled in opposite directions, vacillating in their allegiance between ethnic/sectarian and cosmopolitan/national concerns (Ryan 1996: chap. 1; Singh 1996). Some modernizing Indo-Trinidadian leaders, such as Rienzi, Timothy Roodal, F. E. M. Hosein, and Mathura, however, collaborated with the TWA and actively participated in mainstream nationalist politics.

In the 1930s Indo-Trinidadian elite participation in nationalist politics waned with the arrival of emissaries from the Indian nationalist movement and Vedic missionaries, such as Mehta Jaimini, who visited Trinidad in 1929. This link with India witnessed a resurgence of ethnic pride among Indo-Trinidadians, and the glorification of ancient Indian civilization in numerous public lectures gave the traditional elite the moral authority to challenge the modernizing elite. Interestingly, as Singh (1996) observes, even modernizers such as Rienzi and Mathura were seduced by this emergent discourse of the "great tradition" of Indian civilization and became proponents of the Indian nationalist cause. When Indo-Trinidadian culture and religions were denigrated in the colonial period because they did not conform to European norms, Indo-Trinidadian elites found comfort in the belief that they came from an ancient and rich civilization. The discourse of the great tradition also allowed the elites to manipulate the existing system of social prestige by appropriating contemporary European race discourses to redeem the East Indian "race" at the expense of the Black population. Hosein, a prominent member of the modernizing elite and the leader of the EINC, expressed such ideas of racial superiority in a speech delivered to the East Indian Literary and Debating Association in 1928:

> The race to which you belong is the Indo-Aryan race. The term Indo-Aryan is used to distinguish it from other branches of the Aryan family who are settled in other parts of the world. . . . Those who went south-eastward crossed the passes of the Himalayas and found themselves in the valley of the Indus. Those who went westward found themselves in Europe . . . Aryans meant "tillers of the soil." Persons who till the soil show a marked advance beyond those who are only engaged in pastoral pursuits. The one, I may say, has a "fixed place of abode" whereas the other, is "nomadic." . . . The one lives in cities and the other in tents. You belong to a race which when it originally went to India had already attained a fairly high degree of civilization equal to those who built and established the Grecian and Roman Empires. (in *East Indian Weekly* 1928)

Hosein went on to establish linguistic connections between Hindus and the Germanic and Romance languages and claimed that Pythagoras borrowed his doctrine of the immortality of the soul from India: "In accepting the immortality of the soul Europe has but accepted half the truth from India. You ought therefore to feel proud to belong to a race to which the world is so deeply indebted" (*East Indian Weekly* 1928).

Hosein's speech illustrates two points. First, even those who like Hosein attempted to build alliances with Afro-Trinidadians and articulated "national" concerns were committed to reorienting the existing race hierarchy in a way that sought to elevate the racial/cultural status of the Indo-Trinidadians by annexing them to the European race without, however, undermining the hierarchy itself. Second, such a project necessarily entailed the derogation of the Black population. Thus as Indo-Trinidadian elites entered politics in the first half of the twentieth century, they developed a racial/cultural discourse that was aimed at repositioning Indo-Trinidadians from the bottom of the

[191]

racial hierarchy to an intermediate position. The question which of the two subordinate groups occupied the lowest rungs of this hierarchy then was hardly an unambiguous one as Afro-Trinidadians and Indo-Trinidadians jostled each other for primacy beneath the Whites. An American visitor, L. Bates, commented in 1912: "Both had a comfortable sense of superiority, the Negro because he is free to loaf while the coolie is indentured for five years, the coolie because of his traditions of ancient civilization and the pride of caste" (in Brereton 1985:30). The Indo-Trinidadian elite's appropriation of the Aryan connection to redeem its own group culturally and racially dovetailed with its acceptance of the colonial discourse around the moral degeneracy of the Black population, providing fertile ground for succeeding Indo-Trinidadian leaders to make claims on the state precisely on their group's alleged moral and cultural superiority.

The 1930s were a tumultuous period. Both the religious and the modernizing sectors of the Indo-Trinidadian elite were divided by petty struggles for leadership. Cipriani fell from his zenith to his nadir of power as he took more moderate positions against the radical factions of the labor movement. In the early 1930s Tubal Uriah Butler, a Black Grenadian, emerged as the leader of the predominantly Afro-Creole oil workers and seriously challenged Cipriani's leadership.

Despite the handsome revenues that oil was generating for British investors, the conditions for workers were dismal. Indeed, the high profits were primarily due to the workers' low wages. In 1936 the average oil worker earned less than in the 1920s, a consequence of company efforts to reduce costs by cutting work hours (Brereton 1981:178). Inflation aggravated the oil workers' plight, which was also marred by job insecurities: lack of compensation for industrial accidents, no extra pay for overtime, and the absence of a pension or retirement plan. The oil workers, concentrated in large numbers in the oilfields, comprised a modern industrial proletariat of skilled workers and were easier to organize than the disparate agricultural workers, whose conditions were even worse. The latter had begun to agitate to draw attention to their plight and in 1934 undertook hunger marches (Singh 1996; Brereton 1981:chap. 9). The following year Afro-Trinidadian oil workers in Fyzabad went on strike under Butler's leadership. The urban working class in Port-of-Spain soon followed suit with its own hunger marches, adding momentum to the movement. When mass demonstrations initiated by Butler broke out in the oilfields in 1937, the middle-class moderate champions of labor—such as the leaders of the TLP (the TWA was renamed the Trinidad Labor Party, or TLP, in 1934)—sought to distance themselves from these radical elements. Leaders such as Cipriani, who had championed the causes of a semi-industrial working class during the struggles of 1919, tempered their radicalism when it came to supporting the highly industrialized proletariat of the oil-fields fifteen years later in the trough of economic depression.

Labor unrest was not limited to Trinidad during this period but character-ized the West Indies generally. In 1938–39 the British government, alarmed at the instability overtaking its colonies, especially with the threat of war, sent a commission to the West Indies headed by Lord Moyne to investigate con-ditions in the British Caribbean. The commission's recommendations re-sulted in limited constitutional change, the encouragement of an orthodox trade union movement, and social welfare policies. After the strikes of 1937 workers had recognized the need for labor organizations to represent their interests.

According to Singh, among the Indo-Trinidadian leaders it was only Rienzi who "understood that at the root of Indian working-class distress was the structure of the colonial economy and that such a structure could not be ef-fectively challenged without active collaboration between the African and In-dian working classes" (1996:241). Rienzi was instrumental in organizing the sugar and oil workers, and in 1937 the OWTU (Oilfield Workers Trade Union) and the ATSEFWTU (All Trinidad Sugar Estates and Factory Work-ers Trade Union) were established under his leadership. Between 1936 and 1943 the two major ethnic groups worked together in the labor movement. This solidarity was short-lived, however. The issue of universal suffrage (which was introduced in 1946) and the proposed language test to determine comprehension of spoken English as a necessary qualification to vote (which clearly put Indo-Trinidadians at a disadvantage because of their relatively low literacy rate) prompted Indo-Trinidadian leaders to close ranks once again. Even though Rienzi and some other Indo-Trinidadian leaders championed universal suffrage, most opposed it as inimical to the interests of their com-munity. Rienzi too was finally forced back into the ethnic fold on the issue of the language test.

Fearful that they would be overrun by an intolerant Black majority, Indo-Trinidadian leaders aimed at delaying as long as possible the transfer of power to local politicians (Ryan 1996:9). For much of the 1940s the modern-izing elite diverted its attention to the educational and cultural development of the Indo-Trinidadian masses, and the few who were politically active, such as the Sinanan brothers, Ashford and Mitra, opted to join the Butler Party rather than build an Indo-Trinidadian political party. For Singh (1996) this decision was an astute one in terms of providing the necessary leverage to deal with the colonial establishment. This alliance too was short-lived, how-ever. The rise of the traditional elite under the leadership of Bhadase Sagan Maraj, who assumed control of the major Hindu religious organization, the Sanatan Dharma Maha Sabha; the sugar workers' union; and the primarily

[193]

Indo-Trinidadian–based political party, the People's Democratic Party, in 1953, set the stage for the political future of the nation by consolidating political parties on the basis of ethnic cleavages.

Thus despite the political alliances forged between the two major ethnic groups during the first half of the twentieth century, for the most part the major actors in the movement demanding constitutional change had been the Creole middle and industrial working classes. As Ryan states, "The radical element was very much a minority within the Indian community generally and more particularly within the Hindu community. The bulk of the Indian population, working-class or otherwise, did not identify with the nationalist movement" (1996:5). This conservative stance would later prompt nationalists to accuse Indo-Trinidadians of lacking patriotism. In short, Indo-Trinidadians' reticence in the nationalist struggle reinforced their outsider status by suggesting to the public at large that Indo-Trinidadian interests were basically antithetical to nationalist interests. It is important to understand this reticence as a defensive strategy rather than a categorical opposition to independence, however. It was implicitly understood by all—the colonial authorities,[12] Creoles, local Whites, and even Indo-Trinidadians—that Creoles, whose nationalist agitation had by then firmly established their "nativeness," would be the inheritors of state power.

Discovering Creole Culture

Political developments that augured decolonization went hand in hand with certain cultural developments. Political decolonization meant minimizing economic, political, and cultural dependence on the metropolis. The movement for self-determination involved the deployment of a particular culture history, one that would legitimate the incipient vision of the nation,[13] thereby providing the formula for homogenization programs. In Trinidad the

12. It is clear that the colonial establishment did not consider Indo-Trinidadians legitimate contenders for state power during the transition to independence. For example, one of the reasons for the postponement of the 1955 elections was that the strongest single party at the time was the PDP, led by Maraj, and "neither Britain nor local interest groups welcomed the possibility of a PDP government" (Brereton 1981:232).

13. I use *incipient nation* not to denote a teleological unfolding of a predetermined "national essence" but instead to suggest that a symbolic space for the nation—in terms of identifying "legitimate national subjects" who will assume the mantle of power with independence—can be constituted even during the period of colonial domination when the "nation" is positioned against the state (Trouillot 1990). This important point is wonderfully illustrated by Maurer (1997) for the case of the British Virgin Islands. Not only does he persuasively demonstrate the

"discovery" and deployment of Creole lower-class cultural patterns by Creole middle and upper classes took place at this historical juncture. Middle-class artists looked to lower-class Afro-Creole forms for local inspiration, and politicians found these forms to be suitable cultural raw material for their nation-building agenda.

The move toward generating truly West Indian forms of art, particularly literature, emerged in the 1930s. Notables such as C. L. R. James, Albert Gomes, Alfred Mendes, and Eric Williams were among those who supported this burgeoning of creative activity in drama, poetry, fiction, and music (Brereton 1981:223). The appearance of two politicized journals, *Trinidad* (1929–30) and *The Beacon* (1931–33), reflected the efforts of a White and Creole middle-class intelligentsia to fashion a national literature around urban lower-class Creole lifestyles that defied bourgeois colonial/Victorian moralities and values of respectability (Rosenberg 2000). Although their rhetorical strategies were not without contradiction, sometimes reproducing the very moralities they wished to undermine, the tendency of the *Beacon* writers, especially Gomes, Mendes, and James, to appropriate "the urban Afro-Caribbean woman of the yard as central figures in their fiction" (Rosenberg 2000:208), especially her sexual "transgressions" as an inversion of the English domestic ideal, meant that Indo-Trinidadian elites, who at the time were very much invested in restoring the respectability of their own women, would find little appeal in this emergent national literature. Then again, Indo-Trinidadians at the time were not perceived as an integral part of national life. As Rosenberg suggests, the *Beacon* viewed the Afro-Trinidadian working class as the core of Trinidadian identity and culture: "The focus on Afro-Caribbeans severely restricted [their] . . . ability to represent the Indo-Trinidadian population and its interaction with Afro-Trinidadians. It reflects an unwillingness or inability to represent inter-ethnic creolization or a breaking down of the barrier between Indo- and Afro-Trinidad" (Rosenberg 2000:210).

Indo-Trinidadians had a nominal presence in this national literature, but the style of inclusion reinforced their alien status. For example, the *Beacon* had an "India Section" covering Indian nationalist agitation and cultural issues (Rosenberg 2000: 245), an inclusionary move that ironically reinforced Indo-Trinidadians' ties to India, not to Trinidad. Many stories obliquely acknowledge Indo-Trinidadian connections to Trinidad through their focus on

---

presence of a national identity in a colonial situation, but more significantly he argues that the very axis around which this identity revolves, law, "fosters continued colonial rule" (1997:227).

Dougla characters.[14] Yet as Rosenberg argues, not only were they reduced to mere erotic figures but there was very little that was Indo-Trinidadian about them—meaning that they represented Afro-Creole sensibilities in all but bio-genetic composition.

This representation of the Dougla figure exemplifies the argument presented in the preceding chapter that mixture or creolization invariably translates into a principle of assimilation when it comes to Indo-Trinidadians, that is, Indo-Trinidadian instances of creolization emphasize not interculturation but "Africanization" of the Indo-Trinidadian. Even those like the *Beacon* group, who were intent on challenging conventional colonial representations of lower-class cultural forms by highlighting the creative ways in which these peoples forged their own cultural patterns under miserable conditions of existence, were somehow incapable of recognizing the same creative impulses that motivated the Indo-Trinidadian to establish local connections in ways that were indelibly Creole (in the analytic sense).

Mendes's short story "Good Friday at the Church of La Divina Pastora" (*Beacon*, June 1932) provides an apt example.[15] La Divina Pastora (the Divine Shepherdess) is a statue of an Amerindian girl, ordained the patron saint of all Capuchin missions in 1795, which was brought to Siparia by a Roman Catholic priest during the nineteenth century (Anthony 1997:190). Because of the statue's reputation as a healer, the church became a site for pilgrimage and festivities. Indo-Trinidadians have long been known to worship this saint, a consequence of mistaken identity: "East Indians in Siparia—Hindus and Moslems—claim La Divina Pastora as their own. For they point out that she is the patron saint of Indians, without bearing in mind that the 'Indian' in this case refers to the natives of the Americas, and not to people from India" (Anthony 1997:191). Mistaken identities like the appropriation of saints belonging to "other" religions were the circumstances through which new and vibrant cultures emerged in this part of the world. Sadly, Mendes is unable to recognize this vitality. Instead, his reaction to seeing Indo-Trinidadians in such a Creole milieu is one of horror, disbelief, and shock:

> And so we entered the church. There was, I felt, some mistake when we entered. What I saw I could not believe. I still do not believe in what I saw at that moment and all the succeeding moments. If you entered a lunatic asylum and heard no insane scream, no senseless speech, no battering of head against hard partition, you would stop and wonder if you really were in a lunatic asylum. If

14. The tendency to highlight Dougla characters by the *Beacon* group I take as a radical move on its part, given the nominal recognition of East Indian mixing.

15. I'm grateful to Leah Rosenberg for drawing my attention to this story.

you entered a Christian church and could hear only the hullaballoo [*sic*] of Hindustani chatter, the pattering feet of children and the shrieks of babies, you would wonder if you were in a Christian church. . . . And as for the evidence of my eyes,—it was the most incongruous, most amazing sight I had ever seen. Almost every pew in the church was filled with East Indians. The aisles were congested with little groups gesticulating and hotly engaged in choruses of conversation—on what topics I do not know. Shrewd guesses might suggest the blackeye pea crop, the village feud, or perhaps how Mulemeah was raped by Sookdeo.

Later, observing an Indo-Trinidadian family make its offerings at the altar, Mendes notices a large silver crucifix and fantasizes: "I look down upon the figure of Christ and play with the fancy of its miraculously rising up and using the cross as a weapon for striking the idolaters out of the house of God." As Mendes and his companions leave the church, they notice "a black man lying prone beside a pillar of the church with his face in the dust," which prompts one of his companions to remark: "There lies the only Christian in the place to-day." Mendes's concluding note is indeed revealing: only the Black man can be a true Christian. Creolization when it involves Indo-Trinidadians is an absurdity, an alienating and disturbing phenomenon at best.[16]

Early elite interests in indigenous cultural forms coincided with an escalation of race pride and Black nationalism among Creole masses during the 1930s, especially in the aftermath of the Italian invasion of Ethiopia in 1935. Incipient attempts at ending cultural dependency on the metropolis gained momentum in the postwar period when the middle classes sought to assert the artistic validity and prestige of folk culture.

Characterizing the cultural differences between the Creole upper and middle classes and the lower classes, Braithwaite observed in the 1950s that "the upper classes and the middle class of the island . . . have always aspired toward accepting the culture of Western Europe in general, and Great Britain in particular" (1954:85). Their attitude to popular culture was one of limited tolerance mingled with contempt. Psychological and material dependency on the metropolis posed a peculiar dilemma for the middle-class intellectuals and artists in their desire to be creative. Educated in the metropolis, they were trained to deal with thoughts and objects foreign to their experience. The world of thought and imagination became separated from the world of everyday living. For artistic legitimacy and acclamation they were forced to seek an audience and a market outside themselves, again in the metropolis. As Braithwaite explains:

16. See also Rosenberg's (2000:256–60) fine and nuanced analysis of this story.

The position of the artist reflected the position of the whole society. In so far as the original cultural heritage of their ancestors (mainly African) was lost, in so far there was an easy incorporation into and participation in the life of the metropolitan area. This rendered educational and consequently political advance easier perhaps, but it shifted as a consequence the center of gravity of the community so to speak to a position outside itself. This was the price that had to be paid. (1954:87)

In their search for roots and a source of inspiration, some middle-class artists turned to the despised folk culture, spearheading interest and recognition of the culture of the man on the street.

The establishment of the Little Carib theater by Beryl McBurnie in 1948 and the middle-class discovery of steelband in the 1950s were part of this emerging cultural trend. Carnival, steelband, and calypso, which were pivotal cultural forms of the lower-class underworld, assumed the stature of national symbols.[17] Calypsonian Sparrow, for example, celebrated the rise of Creole nationalism:

> Well the way how things shaping up
> All this nigger business go stop
> I tell you soon in the West Indies
> It's please, Mister Nigger, please. (Sparrow in Brereton 1981:225)

Middle-class acknowledgment of lower-class Creole cultural forms, however, remained ambivalent during this formative period, when the incipient nation was struggling to reduce its dependency on the metropolis. Although the lower classes seemed most energetic in contributing to a national cultural distinctiveness and unity, these were the most despised forms of lower-class behavior. The singing and dancing of the lower classes were thought to lack inhibition: the "vulgarity" of words and songs offended middle- and upper-class sensibilities, and so did the seemingly erotic nature of lower-class dance. A certain domestication and institutionalization of these Creole forms was necessary to suit middle-class sensibilities and tastes.[18]

---

17. On the emergence of steelband and other popular cultural forms, see Braithwaite 1954, Brereton 1981, and Oxaal 1982. On Creole middle-class appropriation of carnival and its elevation to national symbol, see van Koningsbruggen 1997:chap. 3. See also Green 1999. On the transformation of steelband from denigrated Afro-Trinidadian lower-class cultural form to its celebrated status as national symbol, see Stuempfle 1995.

18. For example, "Carnival did not really gain significance for larger groups of the middle-class until it had been purged of the worst excesses of aggressiveness and obscenity" (van Koningsbruggen 1997:102).

Despite this tension, political decolonization of the country was accompanied by the deployment of a specific culture history as a primary referent for the incipient nation. The "nation," as Trouillot (1990) has argued, has no fixed cultural content, yet in a fundamental way it has everything to do with culture and history because these are its sole constant referents. Accordingly, nation building in Trinidad during this early phase saw the appropriation of a specific cultural corpus—a curious combination of Afro-Trinidadian lower-class and middle-class forms—to symbolize the national culture. The display of lower-class Creole forms permitted middle-class Creoles to become the legitimate representatives of all Creoles in staking a claim on the state. In an age characterized by universal suffrage and lower-class labor unrest, middle-class politicians had no option but to acknowledge popular interests. Indeed, their very political survival depended on it. As Hintzen (1989) argues, in the years to come it was precisely the PNM's manipulation of the "subjective" tie of race through such symbolic association that enabled this regime to survive for three decades despite forwarding the "objective" interests of capital, both of local elites drawn from all ethnic groups and of multinational corporations.

The culture of Indo-Trinidadians was perceived as foreign, not indigenous; so were they. Accordingly, their behavior patterns were considered less amenable to a nationalist cultural agenda. In contrast, Afro-Caribbean lower-class cultural patterns, which combined African traditions and cultural forms indigenous to the New World, were particularly attractive to the nationalists. This mix encompassed not only the correct roots—African—but also elements considered truly Trinidadian. Such an evaluation was denied Indo-Trinidadians because they were never perceived as creators of culture, only as its bearers. Ironically, the state of cultural nakedness attributed to Africans qualified them in the end as cultural contributors par excellence for the emerging nation; it was precisely the nakedness imputed to them that permitted the creation of something truly native, that is, cultural forms of their own that did not imitate those of Africa, India, or Europe. These images of Indo-Trinidadians as bearers and Afro-Trinidadians as creators of culture respectively are vividly portrayed in a 1943 report by Mayor Achong of Port-of-Spain. The occasion that provoked his remarks was an exchange with Mr. Stannard, an emissary of the British Council, on the then controversial subject of the imposition of British culture:

The function of Mr. Stannard obviously was to push down his brand of British culture into willing or unwilling throats of the people of this land. After some preliminary parrying . . . I then braced myself for direct action. We snapped brief stories of "culture." I told him in as clear a manner as I could that his no-

[199]

tion of a cloistered British culture for the Trinidad community must be ruled out as a paradox. The component parts of the community had had cultures of their own long before William the Conqueror had landed in England in 1066. It would be unwise for the Chinese and Indian sections of the people of Trinidad, I said, to forsake the past glory of their ancestral homelands and to be unmindful of their future generations for British propagandist "culture." *As for Afro-West Indians it was their solemn mission, I emphasized, to gather as far as practicable, the learning and culture of all lands and to synthesize them into an organic whole.* This was too much for the British Council's professional propagandist. He stood up, salaamed in old-time Oriental fashion, and departed. (Achong 1942–43 in Braithwaite 1954:83–84; emphasis added)

These sentiments were echoed by the West Indian novelist Earl Lovelace almost four decades later:

It is the Africans who have laid the groundwork of a Caribbean culture—those Africans who struggled against enslavement and continued their struggle against colonialism—and the reason that they did so is that they had to. They had no choice but to become Caribbean and address the Caribbean landscape and reality. No other group had to. The Europeans didn't have to . . . they retained their culture. They couldn't change it because it was through their institutions at home that they were culturally and politically empowered. . . . The Indians also were tied to their culture because in this new land where they were strangers, it gave them a sense of being. They had their pundits and divali and hosay and their weddings and teeluck and had no reason to want to change them. (1988:340)

The notion that Indo-Trinidadians were bearers of a foreign culture was underscored in the postwar period when Indo-Trinidadian culture in Trinidad became increasingly identified with India. The independence movement in India added vigor to Indo-Trinidadian consciousness. As early as the 1930s young Indo-Trinidadian intellectuals began staging island-wide demonstrations in support of India's demand for freedom. Public meetings held in Indo-Trinidadian majority areas opened and closed with Indian patriotic songs and "Vande Matram," the Indian national anthem (Malik 1971). During the centennial celebrations of Indian Arrival Day in Trinidad in 1945, Indo-Trinidadian leaders referred to "mother India" as their source of inspiration and vowed to preserve Indian culture and their community. One of the goals of the India Club, formed in 1942, was "to promote the diffusion of knowledge of India and things Indian" (*Indian Centenary Review*, Kirpalani et al. 1945:79). The *Review* also stated the urgent need for the resuscitation of Indian culture in Trinidad through greater contact with India: "In

Trinidad, Indian music and art have suffered not so much by contact with western influences as by lack of contact with the sources of inspiration in the Mother Country. Within recent years, however, there has been a marked change for the better. Introduction of high class Indian films have been largely responsible for this. It is now left for actual tours from screen, radio and stage stars to make the revival complete" (Kirpalani et al. 1945:113). Visits by a host of Indian missionaries and cultural leaders generated new interest, especially among the Indo-Trinidadian middle class, in the language and culture of their "mother country." The first Indian movie, *Bala Joban*, was shown to enthralled audiences in Trinidad in 1935.

Thus both Afro-Trinidadians and Indo-Trinidadians experienced significant cultural developments during the postwar period, but the social and political significance of the two trajectories were to be quite different (see Oxaal 1968:152). While Creole culture gained greater legitimation through its incorporation into the nationalist agenda, Indo-Trinidadian culture, with its emphasis on Mother India, was increasingly perceived as a threat to the emerging nation.

By privileging certain "human-made relationships and features" (Trouillot 1992:24) over others as referents for the nation, groups representing contrasting culture histories become defined not only outside the nation but also as appropriate subjects for homogenization. In Trinidad, "nativeness" was defined around the category Creole, which, during the colonial period, included those of both African and European ancestry. Although this association had permitted local Whites as well as Coloreds to agitate against expatriate domination on the basis of their localness during the early reform periods, the decolonization period also witnessed the subsumption of the European element by the African, as the representation of "nativeness" par excellence. Semantically, African elements in the New World became a synecdoche for Creole.[19] Such a reconfiguration of the Creole category permitted the symbolic identification of the Creole middle classes with the Creole lower classes and the gradual usurpation of local Whites' claims on the nation and the state. It is this process that partly justified the correlation some made between the ascendancy of Creole nationalism and a system of "political negritude." Ryan comments, "The mixed and Afro-Trinidadian population were and continue to be demonstrably unwilling to share symbolic space with

19. Since independence the distinction between Coloreds and Blacks has become less significant, and in popular usage the category Creole has come to denote all those with some African ancestry. This does not imply, however, that Trinidadians are not sensitive to fine gradations in color. The official census also distinguishes between "mixed" persons and those of "African descent."

Indo-Trinidadians . . . because they deemed cultural dominance to be their legitimate and prescriptive right by reason of their earlier historical presence in the territory and the greater proximity of their culture and patterns of behaviour to the superordinate colonial culture by which public norms were referenced" (1996:xxvi).

The colonial idiom of race established the foundation for two potential nationalist narratives for Trinidad, one emphasizing mixture and the other the plurality of diverse ancestral groups, and in the decolonization period these two narratives were expressed in the realm of culture. Middle-class Creole appropriations of lower-class Afro-Creole cultural forms and the attendant emphasis on specifically the African dimension indicate a gravitation of the narrative of mixture more and more toward a discourse of cultural purity firmly anchored in African culture. Nevertheless, the emphasis on specifically "Creole" as opposed to "pure African" culture—in the form of carnival, steelband, calypso, and other lower-class urban Creole patterns—continues to reinscribe the essential quality of mixture, even if it is a mixture that is understood to be more African in composition than European. Thus like the calibration of different proportions of purities embodied by mixed individuals, the African purity that emerges in this cultural discourse is one that necessarily originates in a condition of initial mixture or syncretism.[20] With the establishment during this period of *Afro*-Creole culture as *the* culture of Trinidad, it is no coincidence that the academic model of the Creole society thesis gained ascendancy precisely around this time.

As Safa (1987:116) has pointed out, the idea that Creole symbolized the synthesis of new cultural and racial identities indigenous to the New World provided a powerful counternarrative to the depiction of Caribbean societies as "a patchwork of not-yet-sewn-together fragments." This latter view was epitomized by M. G. Smith's "plural society" model, which posited an absence of a consensus of cultural values between Europeans and Africans in Caribbean societies. Smith argued that Caribbean societies were constituted by culturally distinct social segments—"Whites," "Coloreds," and "Blacks"— who practiced different forms of the same institution and that these societies were held together by the political power exercised by a dominant demographic minority (in Bolland 1992). Thus as Bolland remarks, for Smith "the connection between culture and nationalism was highly problematic in the West Indies" (1992:51): "The common culture, without which West Indian nationalism cannot develop the dynamic to create a West Indian nation, may

20. As Alexander (1977a, 1977b) notes, although the Jamaican national myth of the middle classes foregrounds the mixture of White and Black blood, the two bloods remain distinct ("pure") to the present.

by its very nature and composition preclude the nationalism that invokes it. This is merely another way of saying that the Creole culture which West Indians share is the basis of their division" (Smith 1965 in Bolland 1992:51). This projected lack of a common, unifying culture dovetailed with the widely held image of Caribbean societies as excessively dependent on the metropolis, hence Naipaul's caricature of Caribbean peoples as "Mimic Men" (1967) and his observation that "nothing was generated locally, dependence became a habit" (in Safa 1987:116). Similarly, academics such as Michael Horowitz distinguished West Indian nationalism from other Third World nationalisms "in its general avoidance of nativism and the evocation of its own past" and observed that "the metropolitan colonial country remains the model of intellectual excellence in the Caribbean" (in Safa 1987:116).

To counter the idea that cultural identity was somehow problematic for Caribbean peoples, West Indian scholars put forward the Creole society thesis,[21] which according to Bolland enhanced the

> emerging Caribbean nationalism of the third quarter of the twentieth century. More specifically, the cultural and populist aspects of the creole society viewpoint, with its emphasis on the origins of a distinctive *common* culture as a basis for national unity, constitutes the ideology of a particular social segment, namely a middle-class intelligentsia that seeks a leading role in an integrated, newly independent society. The creole society thesis, then, is a significant ideological moment in the decolonization process of the Caribbean. (1992:53; emphasis in original)

The term *Creole*, which in common Caribbean usage "refers to a local product which is the result of a mixture or blending of various ingredients that originated in the Old World" (Bolland 1992:50), appropriately suggested a possible site of unity. Creolization was seen as a process of cultural interaction, synthesis, and change whereby diverse Old World forms were combined and mixed to create novel forms indigenous to the New World. Not only could this narrative posit a basis of common cultural identity for Caribbean people, but it was also a narrative of indigenization.[22] Creole was anything and anybody native to the New World as a consequence of mixing.

21. Brathwaite 1971 is a classic example of this thesis. On the Creole society thesis as a Caribbean cultural nationalist narrative, see Bolland 1992.

22. Robotham's observation that identities in the Caribbean "tend to formulate themselves in the guise of some form of transnationalism" (1998:308) provides yet another intriguing variation on the theme of creolization. Robotham offers the example of Rastafarianism as a form of Caribbean fundamentalism which is inherently transnational in its Ethiopianism and Pan-

Yet the particular trajectory of Indo-Trinidadian culture during this period suggests that only some cultures could be represented as indigenous. The increasing identification with India and Indian culture witnessed a further symbolic distancing of Indo-Trinidadian cultural forms from processes thought to be indigenous. But as Mendes's story of La Divina Pastora powerfully illustrates, such distancing had more to do with the inability of the wider society to recognize the creolization process enveloping Indo-Trinidadian culture than with actual practices on the ground. Of equal significance is the fact that efforts by Indo-Trinidadian elites to establish links with India should have necessarily reinforced their group's alien status. Similar efforts on the part of Creole elites to revive the African dimension of Creole culture rarely jeopardized this group's native status. This paradox is resolved once we locate the symbolic privilege accorded things African within the Creole scheme. Since African elements constituted a vital ingredient in lay and academic conceptualizations of Creole, the emphasis on them could hardly undermine Creole or native status. In contrast, since Indian elements were never considered a part of emergent Creole forms, emphasis on things Indian, semantically speaking at least, functioned to exclude Indo-Trinidadians from sharing native/Creole status.

The exclusivity attributed to Indo-Trinidadian culture during this formative period in turn forced the wider society to evaluate itself as plural. To this day the plural society model remains the dominant mental grid through which locals across class and ethnic spectrums encounter their society. The simultaneous acknowledgment of narratives of mixture and purity produces a tension endemic to Creole societies, but as I argued in Chapter 4, it is not necessarily a contradiction: the Trinidadian nationalist narrative emerges out of the dialectic interplay between these seemingly contradictory narratives. It resolves the contradiction by distinguishing between two types of purities, one constituted in instances of mixture, like those embodied by "Europeans" and "Africans," and the other constituted as wholes, like that embodied by "East Indians."

The culture history of Indo-Trinidadians was, then, defined outside the native cultural referent. Accordingly, Indo-Trinidadian cultural forms were downplayed in the construction of native definitions. Indeed, at a time when the British government had begun the process of transferring power to local authorities, the stakes riding on claims to nativeness were high. It was the re-

---

Africanism. Because the historical legacy of slavery and colonialism militates against claims to autochthonous or primordial identities, discourses of indigenization in the Caribbean ironically embrace a spirit of openness and dynamism rarely associated with indigenization in other parts of the world.

alization by some Indo-Trinidadian leaders of the structural limits inhibiting their collectivity's claims that prompted them to delay as long as possible the transfer of power. Unable to display a legitimate cultural referent for the nation and therefore unable to claim the state, Indo-Trinidadians believed they needed a neutral arbiter (such as the colonial state) to safeguard the interests of their group.

The U.S. "Occupation"

In 1940 a real estate transaction between Prime Minister Churchill and President Roosevelt resulted in the exchange of a number of military bases in the West Indies for several dozen antiquated U.S. destroyers. The United States established two bases in Trinidad, a naval station at the deep-water harbor at Chaguaramas Bay and an army base in central Trinidad at Waller Field. The island not only provided fuel for the Allied war effort but also was the assembly point for the dispatch of tankers from Caribbean oil ports and the stopping point for all ships and aircraft in transit to Europe and North America (MacDonald 1986:63). During the occupation the once-disgruntled proletariat became increasingly involved in the oilfields and the new construction sites initiated by the Americans. The rise of employment at the highest wages ever witnessed in the colony resulted in a "boom time" atmosphere.

In an almost cataclysmic fashion the U.S. "occupation" also exposed Trinidadians to cosmopolitan currents. Workers were introduced to the highly efficient personnel system of U.S. employers and to the high-spending patterns of U.S. soldiers. The colony's population was soon hoping to emulate these patterns. North American consumer ideas, values, and lifestyles proliferated among the colony's population through radio, newspapers, and cinema. Significantly, though U.S. military personnel were at times criticized for their racial attitudes, their actual presence had a profound positive influence on the island's racial ideology. As many scholars have noted (Braithwaite 1975; Oxaal 1968; MacDonald 1986; Brereton 1981), "the spectacle of foreign white men engaged *en masse* in manual labor in connection with military construction tended to break down the aura of superiority and automatic deference previously accorded persons with a white skin" (Oxaal 1968:81). The "humility of a subject people" was gradually eroded (Brereton 1981:192).

At the same time, the petroleum sector expanded rapidly. Oil accounted for only 10 percent of exports in 1919, but by 1932 it had increased to 50 percent and by 1943 it had reached 80 percent (Brereton 1981:205). Brereton notes, however, that despite this strong acceleration in the petroleum sector, traditional agriculture, namely the sugar industry, continued to employ the

[205]

great majority of Trinidadians for the first forty years of the century. Ryan (1974:387), describing the island's dependence on oil in the late 1960s, claims that even though oil was responsible for 27 percent of government revenues, 28 percent of GNP, and 81 percent of the total gross exports, it provided only 5 percent of total employment (fifteen thousand persons). In any case, the economy grew rapidly after the war. GDP between 1946 and 1956 rose 76 percent (Carrington 1967), increasing between 1951 and 1961 at an average annual rate of 8.5 percent (Brereton 1981:220).

All these factors—the U.S. occupation, cultural developments, and labor agitation—prepared Trinidadians for the age of mass political participation with the introduction of universal suffrage in 1946.

The Scramble for the State

The British government hoped to implement constitutional reform gradually as outlined by the Moyne Commission. Between 1941 and 1944 the number of electives to the council was increased and the number of Officials reduced. Yet the ultimate responsibility of government still rested on the governor. Under the recommendation of the Moyne Commission a local committee was set up consisting of thirty-three notables, including Rienzi and Albert Gomes, a prominent Portuguese Creole union leader, to decide on the question of widening the franchise. The motion recommending universal suffrage was passed in 1944 by the bare majority of one. And since neither the secretary of state nor the governor was prepared to override a majority vote, the recommendation was accepted.

Trinidadians had demonstrated a profound enthusiasm for political involvement especially since the labor struggles beginning in 1919, but when the idea of universal suffrage was introduced, a cohesive middle-class political party capable of enjoying both trade-union and working-class support across ethnic lines had yet to materialize. The elections of 1946 and 1950 witnessed a proliferation of groups and politicians manipulating voters and their diverse interests in the confused transition from one system of political authority to another (Brereton 1981). The political climate of Trinidad was marred by a factionalized left and by individual broker-politicians "maneuvering and negotiating between the established but waning political power of the old colonialists and the groups of elected politicians and special interests who were dividedly contending for a place in the sun" (Oxaal 1968:94). Again, it was the absence of a strong nationalist party that led to the survival of such mavericks. As MacDonald contends, "The lack of any strong nationalistic party, in a time of growing racial awareness and communal tensions, made it necessary to deal with individuals who could easily traverse racial barriers and create multiracial alliances" (1986:82).

The politics of individual and group alliances that characterized the 1946 and 1950 elections soon gave way to race-based political parties with the establishment of the People's Democratic Party (PDP) in 1953 under the leadership of Bhadase Sagan Maraj (Singh 1994:226). The PDP was primarily an Indo-Trinidadian, Hindu political body that drew its support from the Indo-Trinidadian rural masses led by "a conservative group of East Indian businessmen and professionals" (Hintzen 1989:44). Maraj was born in 1919 in Caroni, the heart of the sugar belt, and was the son of a village headman. During the U.S. occupation he amassed a fortune through the disposal of surplus war goods from the U.S. bases, and his activities on behalf of the Indo-Trinidadians had made him a preeminent leader of that community. Despite his dedication to the building of Indo-Trinidadian schools and Hindu temples and his "carefully cultivated generosity" (Ryan 1974:139), however, Bhadase was a controversial figure, noted for his strong-arm tactics and his intolerance for those who questioned his authority. His plantation origins, his lack of cosmopolitan savvy, and the disreputable practice of business limited his ability to win a secure place as a national leader. Yet these same qualities endeared him to the majority of Indo-Trinidadians, who were both Hindu and rural and could identify with the sectarian causes he championed. Maraj's major political base was the Sanatan Dharma Maha Sabha (SDMS), the organ of the majority Sanatanist Hindu sect (Brereton 1981:236). Established in 1952 through a merger of two Sanatanist Hindu bodies under the leadership of Maraj, the SDMS was intended to preserve Hindu culture and tradition in the face of Christian missionary activities (MacDonald 1986:107). Maraj was also the leader of the major sugar union, the ATSEFWTU. With his control over three important political and cultural bodies, Maraj was a formidable force in the upcoming 1955 elections.

By then the politically opportune moment for class-based alliances that had characterized the 1919–46 period had passed. The controversy over the literacy test for universal suffrage and federation had nudged even the more radical Indo-Trinidadian leaders back to the ethnic fold. The position that only those who understood spoken English should be allowed to vote was interpreted as a direct assault on the Indo-Trinidadian community.[23] As Rienzi contended: "To insist that a voter should understand the English language when spoken would lead to the irresistible conclusion that this qualification has been introduced to deprive a large proportion of the Indian community

23. See Kirpalani et al. 1945:109–11.

of the right to vote. . . . This is quite naturally resented as an unfair discrimination against an important section of the population which has made a valuable contribution to the prosperity of the colony" (in Ryan 1974:69). In the face of substantial Indo-Trinidadian opposition to the provision, the literacy qualification was ultimately withdrawn. The damage had been done, however. The issue of suffrage undermined the potential for interethnic alliances and reinforced once again the image of Indo-Trinidadians as antithetical to larger national interests. The position Indo-Trinidadian leaders took on the proposed Caribbean Federation further entrenched such a perception.

Prospects for a Caribbean federation had been first outlined in the Montego Bay Conference in 1946. Except for British Guiana and British Honduras, which opted for individual independence, the rest of the ten British colonies in the Caribbean were expected to achieve independence as a pan-island West Indian nation with Jamaica and Trinidad at the forefront.[24] Many Indo-Trinidadians and their leaders opposed such a federation because they feared a collective domination by Afro-Caribbeans throughout the region.[25] Since Trinidad's transition to independence was integrally tied to the federal issue, the Indo-Trinidadian position was once more seen as antinationalist and conservative. Nevertheless, by 1955, "when a new constitution for self-government was to be written, these [Indo-Trinidadian] leaders appeared poised to assume control of the state" (Hintzen 1989:44). Such a situation was not acceptable to the colonial authorities, especially in light of their strong commitment to a West Indian federation. Accordingly, Britain postponed the elections to the following year, providing Eric Williams and his supporters an opportune moment to forge a "legitimate" national party to contest and win the 1956 elections with the help of colonial authorities.[26]

24. On the federation, see Oxaal 1968, Ryan 1974, and E. Williams 1982.

25. As we shall soon see, the centrality Eric Williams attributed to slavery and colonialism in the nationalist program and his definition of native status based on West Indianness assume particular significance in the context of the federation. The features he delineated were common to all the British colonies and therefore constituted appropriate culture history referents for an imagined community composed of all the colonies of the federation.

26. In the September 1956 election the PNM won thirteen of the twenty-four elected seats and was clearly the majority party in the legislature. This result was insufficient to give the PNM a parliamentary majority when the two ex officio and five nominated members were counted in, however. To avoid parliamentary stalemate and to make a gesture of support for what he believed to be a "stable, disciplined party led by responsible and educated professional men" (Brereton 1981:237), Governor Beetham gave the PNM a clear majority by permitting it to appoint two party members to the nominated seats and by pledging that the two ex officio members would vote for the government; thus the PNM commanded seventeen of the thirty-one seats in the legislature (Brereton 1981:237; Oxaal 1968:115).

The PNM Years: Consolidation of an Afro-Caribbean Nation

Like other gifted young colonials before him, Eric Williams traveled as a "scholarship boy" to Oxford in 1932 at the age of twenty-one to study history. In England he was exposed to the intellectual and political milieu of the center of the empire. As Anderson (1991) argues, for those "colonial functionaries" who undertook "pilgrimages" to centers of empire, the education of colonial subjects in the metropolis likewise provided them with the ideological, political, and intellectual tools to struggle for freedom when they returned to the colonies, in an idiom familiar to, if not founded in, the metropole itself.[27]

In universities and other intellectual enclaves colonial subjects were exposed to individuals and groups that encouraged nationalist aspirations. Unlike his counterpart, C. L. R. James, who plunged into the radical niches of the European left of the day, Williams kept largely to the somber intellectual corridors of Oxford University, his energies devoted to the single task of graduating with a top degree from Oxford.[28] His outstanding performance at Oxford would later allow him to command respectability: he was able to demonstrate that he was at least the equal of his metropolitan masters.

Williams's doctoral dissertation, published in 1944 as *Capitalism and Slavery*, not only established his reputation as a historian of distinction but also signified his commitment to redress the colonial condition. He attacked the belief that abolition was due to the humanitarian efforts of the British abolitionists and argued instead that the economic interests of the new industrial bourgeoisie in the nineteenth century was the major determinant of emancipation.[29] His intellectual commitment to subjects such as slavery, colonialism, and capitalism, as further evidenced by *The Negro in the Caribbean* (first published in 1942), overflowed into the political arena when, on his return to Trinidad in 1948, he sought to educate the Trinidadian masses through a series of public lectures.

Williams came to Trinidad as deputy chairman of the Caribbean Commis-

27. On the inevitable irony of the colonial predicament, Braithwaite says, "Even when the British were being beaten they were beaten with a British stick" (1954:85).

28. See Oxaal 1968:chap. 4 on these two West Indian scholars' diverse trajectories during their stint in the metropolis.

29. Holt, criticizing most contemporary summaries of Williams's thesis, claims that "Williams never denied the sincerity of the so-called Saints, whom he praised, nor the genuineness and importance that humanitarian sensibility played in destroying slavery, which he readily conceded. He simply claimed that sentiment played a subordinate, auxiliary role in the process" (1992:23).

sion, a regional development agency sponsored jointly by the U.S., British, French, and Dutch governments (Segal 1989:199). In this prestigious and visible capacity, Williams disseminated his vast knowledge of West Indian history in numerous public appearances. He became especially popular among culturally and politically conscious middle-class individuals and groups, who soon recognized his extraordinary qualities. He also became a valuable member of the Teachers Educational and Cultural Association (TECA), a group of progressive teachers which later, through the People's Educational Movement (PEM), provided a platform for Williams to conduct his public lectures. Through these lectures Williams aroused tremendous pride among his Black admirers, exploiting his historical knowledge to the hilt: "He became the center of various informal study groups in which well-educated nationalists met to talk politics and listen to his discourse, such as the Bachacs, while his public speeches made him well known to the people. By 1954, in fact, Williams had developed a popular reputation, a wide circle of middle-class admirers, and a coterie of close friends and disciples, many of them members of TECA" (Brereton 1981:233). Williams also had style, a personal trait that Trinidadians highly value: "With his dignified bearing, sharp tongue, his ever-present trinity of props—hearing aid, dark glasses and cigarette drooping from his lips—'The Doc' was a sharply etched, unique public personality" (Oxaal 1968:112–13).

In 1954 Williams gained more notoriety when he challenged the noted Catholic educator and sociologist Dom Basil Matthews in a series of debates concerning state versus denominational control of education.[30] Making the most of his public acclamation, Williams and his supporters began to organize in earnest for a political party under his leadership. They started by forming a semisecret political cell, the Political Education Group (PEG), whose hand-picked members' chief purpose was to promote Williams's candidacy for political office in Trinidad (Oxaal 1968:108; Brereton 1981:233).

Meanwhile, Williams's relations with the Caribbean Commission had increasingly soured, and on June 21, 1955, from a bandstand at Woodford Square,[31] Williams announced his dismissal from the commission and proclaimed his commitment to the anticolonial struggle in Trinidad:[32] "I was

30. On this famous debate, see Oxaal 1968:104–5.

31. Woodford Square is a public square in the heart of the business district in Port-of-Spain where urban Creoles used to gather to hear Williams lecture.

32. Williams's clever rendition of his relations with the commission won him the sympathy of his colleagues and the masses. Oxaal reflects on this speech: "Eric Williams boldly presented himself to his audience in Woodford Square that evening as a martyr in the anti-imperialist struggle. . . . His dramatic narrative of his vicissitudes within a quasi-colonial establishment . . . served to project the image of one who had suffered in the anti-colonial cause. For some of his

born here, and here I stay, with the people of Trinidad and Tobago, who educated me free of charge for nine years at Queen's Royal College and for five years at Oxford, who have made me whatever I am. . . . I am going to let down my bucket where I am, now, right here with you in the British West Indies" (in Sutton 1981:280).

Defining "the Native": Creating a National Discursive Space

In his early speeches Williams defined the native as irrevocably West Indian: those born in the country, whose fates were intimately intertwined by their common colonial condition: "The man in the West Indies is more than white, more than mulatto, more than Negro, more than Indian, more than Chinese. He is West Indian, West Indian by birth, West Indian in customs, West Indian in dialect or language, West Indian, finally in aspiration" (in Sutton 1981:210). West Indianness itself was determined by the history of colonialism and slavery, encoding, at least theoretically, both fragmentary and cohesive qualities. In speeches on the "national community," such as "The Historical Background of Race Relations in the Caribbean" (1955) and "Massa Day Done" (1961), Williams emphatically blamed the colonial structures and ideologies (embodied in the concept "Massa") for creating and consolidating the fragmentary principles through "racialism," that is, placing the diverse ancestral origins of West Indians in a hierarchical order and according them differential value. The PNM, in contrast, he claimed, disavowed any form of racialism by recognizing the national subject as West Indian before anything else:

> Massa believed in the inequality of races. Today, as never before, the PNM has held out to the population of Trinidad and Tobago and the West Indies and the world the vision and the practice of interracial solidarity which . . . stands out in sharp contrast as an open challenge to Massa's barbarous ideas and practices of racial domination. . . . We of the PNM . . . have been able to incorporate into our People's National Movement people of all races and colours and from all

---

middle class supporters this cavalier treatment at the hands of an expatriate white elite must have aroused strong sympathies; for the black lower class the image of a scrappy, apparently radical underdog doing battle with the big men was, and would continue to be, a highly satisfactory portrayal of how a leader in the tradition of Cipriani and Butler ought to behave. . . . It appeared from his account of his relations with the Caribbean Commission that he had outwitted and outmaneuvered his enemies at every turn. Here was not a dry recitation of services rendered but a lively, executive-suite drama in which the hero, in announcing his decision to stay in Trinidad and continue the struggle, invited his audience to participate in writing the final scenes. It was epic theater, in the flesh" (1968:110–11).

walks of life, with the common bond of a national community dedicated to the pursuit of national ends without any special privilege being granted to race, colour, class, creed, national origin or previous condition of servitude. (in Sutton 1981:215)

Thus for Williams the culture history referent for the nation rested on the legacy of slavery and colonialism. It was clearly a rubric within which all segments of the Trinidadian population could be included. His speeches continuously referred to the Chinese, the East Indians, and the Africans as West Indian persons whose experience in the New World had been indelibly conditioned by colonial subjugation. He spoke of indenture with the same indignation as he had for slavery and other forms of colonial subjugation: "In Trinidad the Negro, the Indian, French and Spaniard, English and Portuguese, Syrian and Lebanese, Chinese and Jew, all have messed out of the same pot, all are victims of the same subordination, all have been tarred with the same brush of political inferiority" (Williams 1982:278). In this excerpt we see the tension between the two nationalist narratives unfold—the simultaneous reference to discrete ancestral diversities and the appeal to a homogeneous identity forged in the crucible of colonial subordination. This tension is particularly evident in the oft-quoted passage from Williams's *History of the People of Trinidad and Tobago* (1962), whose publication he timed to coincide with independence:

There can be no Mother India for those whose ancestors came from India. . . . There can be no Mother Africa for those of African origin, and the Trinidad and Tobago society is living a lie and heading for trouble if it seeks to create the impression or to allow others to act under the delusion that Trinidad and Tobago is an African society. There can be no Mother England and no dual loyalties; no person can be allowed to get the best of both worlds, and to enjoy the privileges of citizenship in Trinidad and Tobago whilst expecting to retain United Kingdom citizenship. There can be no Mother China, . . . no Mother Syria or no Mother Lebanon. A nation, like an individual, can have only one Mother. The only Mother we recognise is Mother Trinidad and Tobago, and Mother cannot discriminate between her children. All must be equal in her eyes. (Williams 1982 [1962]:279)

Williams is apprehensive of the threat of diversity; if he "is to legitimize a Trinidadian nation," Shalini Puri argues, "he must produce it as *both* hybrid *and* homogeneous" (1999:16; emphasis in original). But Williams did not create this rhetorical strategy; rather, as I argued earlier, narratives that could entertain both hybridity (here meaning diverse and discrete ancestral kinds) and homogeneity (resulting from the shared experience of colonial subjugation), however variously conceived, were already in place. These dual but not necessarily mutually exclusive narratives provided Williams with the ideological raw material to project his party, the PNM, as the national party (through the narrative of homogeneity) while appealing to communal sentiments (and hence the narrative of diverse ancestral kinds) to ensure regime survival. Hintzen, for example, makes the provocative observation that the Indo-Trinidadian opposition political parties never really posed a threat to the PNM but indirectly ensured the PNM's longevity because "the sustaining of the ruling party's racial appeal depended on the existence of an organized communal opposition" (1989:90).

Indeed, despite Williams's emphasis on colonial subjugation as the primary referent for envisioning a homogeneous nation, in less self-conscious moments this same rubric led Williams to identify the nation with those of African ancestry, unwittingly privileging the identification of the PNM with Afro-Trinidadians. Consider, for example, Williams's defense of Indo-Trinidadian supporters of the PNM who had been heckled by Afro-Trinidadians: "It is a crime against PNM, treason to the national community, for PNM supporters to sneer, as some did a few days ago . . . at Indians wearing PNM shirts. . . . I call upon all party members to stop once and for all this infuriating nonsense that every Indian is anti-PNM. Every Indian is not anti-PNM, nor is every white. A PNM Indian, trustworthy, loyal, devoted to the PNM is a thousand times better citizen than an anti-PNM African" (in Sutton 1981:117). For Williams, then, whereas a PNM Indo-Trinidadian merits particular admiration an anti-PNM Afro-Trinidadian is a disgrace because Williams assumes, first, that loyalty to the PNM is loyalty to the nation, and second, that Afro-Trinidadians can be presumed to possess this loyalty (Segal 1989). Thus the Afro-Trinidadian's devotion to the nation via the PNM is "natural," in contrast to that of the Indo-Trinidadian, who has to struggle against inherent tendencies to make the same commitment.

How Williams defined his public served to alienate the Indo-Trinidadians. His public was not conceived as carriers of an ancestral civilization, a pivotal criterion for the subordination of Indo-Trinidadians in the colonial era. Instead, he defined national subjects as those who were of and subordinated in the West Indies. This definition of the public and the solution Williams offered evoked the values of the creole continuum and engaged only that principle of subordination limited to the Creoles. As Segal observes, semantically, "this was fundamentally a mode of mass identification and redemption for 'non-white creoles,' and not 'East Indians'" (1989:206–7). Thus even Williams's potentially inclusive definition of West Indian served to marginalize Indo-Trinidadians by appending West Indian to the Creole experience.

In other instances, especially those that did not deal explicitly with the concerns of interethnic relations, the conflation of a particular ethnic group with the nation in Williams's discourse was markedly visible. In "We Are Independent," a 1960 speech, the "We" that Williams declared independent, in spirit overtly pointed to a particular ancestral group, Africans: "We march to show the world that if we are not yet independent in law, we today and after today are independent in fact. Our enemies said we would never be free. They said we would never be fit for freedom. They said we could never govern ourselves. They said that we are a lazy, servile race, desirous only of sitting in the sun eating yams and pumpkins, capable only of aping the graces of our European masters" (in Sutton 1981:314–15). The "We" here clearly refers to those of African descent, and the redemption the speech promises speaks to Afro-Trinidadian concerns. In short, the nation-building process as articulated and realized through Williams and the PNM effectively excluded Indo-Trinidadians.

Contemporary Indo-Trinidadian leaders accuse the PNM leadership of having slighted the Indo-Trinidadians in the period of nation building, but it is important to recognize that for Williams the priority in the nationalist struggle was the battle against imperialism and the material and psychological ramifications of slavery. Much of the mass adulation for the "philosopher-king" (Oxaal 1968:97) rested on his untiring efforts at raising the consciousness of the Creole lower classes by exposing them to West Indian history through public speeches, formal debates, and most important, his lectures at the "University of Woodford Square." As Oxaal notes, through such forums "the Doctor did not so much descend into mass partisan politics as he attempted to elevate mass politics to the status of adult education" (1968:113).

Williams had hoped to prepare Trinidadians for independence through political education. The main venue for the dissemination of his knowledge was Woodford Square. Yet the crowds who gathered here were largely urban lower-class Afro-Trinidadians. As late as 1964 83 percent of the Indo-Trinidadian population was rural, in contrast with 51 percent of Afro-Trinidadians. Thus the majority of Indo-Trinidadians remained unexposed to Williams's mass education campaigns. The labor agitation of the early decades had also thoroughly politicized the urban Afro-Trinidadian working classes, making them particularly receptive to Williams's message. As Oxaal (1968:100) observes, "For many lower class Negroes, particularly Creole women, Williams was nothing less than a messiah who came to lead the black children into the Promised Land."[33]

33. Oxaal's unwitting identification of the category Creole with Negro and Black attests to my argument that during and after independence *Creole* came to designate primarily those of African descent and not local Whites.

Williams also commanded a following within the educated and Western-ized Afro-Trinidadian middle classes. He became the center of various infor-mal study groups and through his activity in TECA managed to build a wide network of supporters among culturally and politically conscious middle-class individuals and groups. Williams was able to bridge the gap between Afro-Trinidadian middle and lower classes because his persona signified "someone metropolitan in achievement and colonial in oppression" (Segal 1989:196). With this dual status signification Williams, like so many other Third World nationalist leaders, was able to claim authority over both inter-national and local spaces. Since Williams had made his achievements in the metropolis, unlike Butler, he was able to identify with the lower classes with-out jeopardizing his own respectability.

His dual status allowed Williams to amass votes across the creole spec-trum, that is, among those respectable persons deemed light and also among those persons considered dark who lacked respectability. The public, in turn, accepted Williams's downward identification because his persona suggested the promise of their own redemption through gains in respectability (Segal 1989). The political mood of the Afro-Trinidadian working classes had changed since the 1930s. The U.S. occupation and the expansion of the pe-troleum sector had elevated their concerns from those expressed by their "barefoot" semi-industrial predecessors and had made them particularly sus-ceptible to respectable channels of upward mobility and the mass political education Williams initiated.

Williams's speeches on the legacy of colonialism and slavery had immense impact on his audience. Williams gradually lifted the veil of ignorance and shame that some Afro-Trinidadians felt about Africa and their slave ancestry and instilled in them a sense of personal dignity. At the end of a weekend of lectures on emerging African nations given by Williams and other PNM lead-ers, one woman, in an emotional pledge of gratitude to the speakers, de-clared that "before Dr. Williams had begun his lectures ten years earlier she and many others had actually believed that their African ancestors were sub-human animals living in the trees of the jungle" (Oxaal 1968:100). Another Williams supporter with "devastating simplicity" explained, "He told us how we had become what we were" (Oxaal 1968:98).

These same speeches alienated non-Creoles, however. Members of the White community who identified with the dominant institutions of colonial society felt that Williams's obsession with slavery had given him a warped sense of history and was indicative of the deep racial resentments he had har-bored as an "ambitious black boy" who had continuously to struggle to affirm his equality with dominant White men (Oxaal 1968:98).

Williams's attempts to lure Indo-Trinidadians to join the nationalist struggle were for the most part unsuccessful. Williams fervently believed that Indo-Trinidadians should join Afro-Trinidadians in the nationalist effort because of their common oppression in the sugar estates. Yet such an association between slavery and indenture has never resonated in the Indo-Trinidadian folk imagination. Instead, most Indo-Trinidadian leaders found the conflation of indenture and slavery distasteful because in their view "the voluntary indenture of the East Indian 'pioneers' who had 'rescued' the agricultural economy represented quite a distinct social species from the slave who after emancipation had turned his back on the land and cultivated his Creole passion for irresponsibility" (Oxaal 1968:99). Thus much of the public education that was allegedly for the masses spoke mostly to Afro-Trinidadians and served inadvertently to alienate the rest. These groups, unable to identify with the reasons for nationalist struggle as articulated by Williams, began increasingly to occupy a defensive posture in fear of impending Black totalitarianism.

Formalizing Ethnicity against the Nation: The Rise of Party Politics

The pattern of leadership and organization of the party also contributed to the greater identification between the PNM and Afro-Creoles. The organization of the PNM was determined by two separate but related factors. When the party was formally launched in January 1956, it claimed to be preeminently a national movement, aiming to rise above all factionalisms, namely, those between labor and capital and between East Indian and Creole. Accordingly, Williams and his supporters refused to make any deals with the labor movement or established politicians. One of the requisites for membership in the party was that candidates could not be members of existing political parties. Discipline and loyalty to the political leader, cardinal principles of the party, were thought to be necessary to combat what Williams perceived as the "incorrigible" individualism of Trinidadians, which had factionalized earlier political parties.[34] Yet by limiting party membership to the polit-

---

34. For Williams the institutional bulwarks underpinning colonialism and slavery were the primary causes for the "incorrigible individualism" characterizing the West Indies: "In this climate, political rather than physical, social climbing has become the major industry of Trinidad and Tobago—invitations to cocktail parties, and appearing in the photographs and social columns of the newspapers. Legal slavery and political slavery implicit in the nominated system have led to a capacity for individual ingratiation with the political powers or the social arbiters. . . . The pronounced materialism and disastrous individualism have spread to all parts of the fabric of the society. . . . The political parties are riddled with individualism. The trade unions are riddled with individualism. The professions are riddled with individualism. Each

ically "untainted," the PNM leadership erected a powerful institutional barrier to the creation of a truly multiracial party.

PNM leaders were also determined not to seek an alliance with contending political groups. By refusing to collaborate with Maraj, who commanded the loyalty of rural Indo-Trinidadians, or other influential Indo-Trinidadian leaders, PNM activists compromised their ideal of representing a national party. They sought to rationalize this contradiction by taking the position that "since it was a 'national' party, and because it was genuine in its espousal of racial harmony, the dominantly East Indian opposition party was a kind of mirage which did not really exist, or which would vanish if only opportunistic East Indian politicians would not exploit the ignorant country Indians by 'preaching race'" (Oxaal 1968:142).

Strict membership criteria also limited the incorporation of diverse interests at the level of leadership. The PNM's political organization and leadership patterns were based on those of the PEG/TECA cell out of which the party had emerged. Here recruitment was based on "invitation only" and required the endorsement of an already trusted member. Accordingly, membership in the movement proceeded along a highly personalized network, and prominent positions were reserved for the "old guards" of the PEG/TECA cell, which had a solid Creole middle-class base. Below the upper echelons of leadership, party activists were predominantly lower-middle-class Creoles who were influential in their respective localities. To prove its "national" spirit, however, the PNM made a special effort to recruit non-Creole individuals. Thus K. Mohammed, a Muslim Indo-Trinidadian, and W. Mahabir, a Christian Indo-Trinidadian, were given conspicuous leadership positions to convey this message. Hindu Indo-Trinidadians were noticeably missing in the choice of recruits. The Creole middle-class bias of the PNM leadership was not so much a consequence of deliberate policy but a result of the structural limitations imposed by early membership criteria and informal recruitment processes that were meant to overcome the factionalisms that had plagued earlier political organizations.

Unable to identify with the nationalist discourse generated by Williams or his "nationalist" party, many Indo-Trinidadians turned to the PDP, under the leadership of Maraj. The 1956 elections, as Vertovec (1992:85) says, "marked the beginning of a legacy of racial party politics for which Trinidad became well-known." Having targeted the PDP as its main opponent, the PNM sought to delegitimize and isolate it by driving a wedge between the orthodox

---

seeks aggrandisement at the expense of his neighbour, giving rise to attitudes that threaten democracy" (1982:281).

Hindus on the one hand and the reformist Hindus, Muslims, and Christianized Indo-Trinidadians on the other. PNM leaders portrayed the PDP as an obscurantist, reactionary communal Hindu organization (Ryan 1974:140; Brereton 1981:236). Williams's attacks on the PDP won the PNM substantial support from Muslim and Christian Indians and urbanized Hindus. In the 1956 elections the PDP, isolated in the rural Hindu districts, contested only fourteen seats and won only five. The PNM, with the help of Governor Beetham, managed to secure a parliamentary majority.

The federal elections of 1958 provided an appropriate moment for anti-PNM forces to unite. Despite its opposition to federation, the PDP prepared for the forthcoming election by uniting with other anti-PNM parties—the TLP and Party of Political Progress Groups (POPPG)—to form the Democratic Labor Party (DLP) with Maraj as party leader. Underestimating the opposition and embroiled in problems of government, the PNM launched a lackluster campaign, in contrast to the DLP, which campaigned vigorously with a formidable political slate headed by Maraj, Albert Gomes, Victor Bryan, and Roy Joseph (Brereton 1981:238). In a stunning turn of events the DLP secured six out of the ten seats, defeating the PNM. Having fought hard to realize the federation, Williams was shocked and felt betrayed. In his frustration he lashed out at the opposition, namely, the Indo-Trinidadians.

Williams's address at Woodford Square on April 1, 1958, titled "The Dangers Facing Trinidad and Tobago and the West Indian Nation," which was an attempt to account for the PNM's defeat, significantly exacerbated racial cleavages. The reason for the defeat, according to Williams, was "race, pure and unadulterated . . . by hook or by crook, they brought out the Indian vote—the young and old, the literate and illiterate, the lame, the halt and the blind" (Ryan 1974:191). He characterized Indo-Trinidadians as a "recalcitrant and hostile minority masquerading as the Indian nation, and prostituting the name of India for its selfish, reactionary political ends" (Ryan 1974:192). Williams portrayed Indo-Trinidadians as the greatest danger facing the country and as an impediment to West Indian progress. The speech suggested that "Indian illiterates from the country areas were threatening to submerge the masses whom Williams had enlightened" (Mahabir 1978 in MacDonald 1986:120). These were indeed harsh charges, especially alarming since they were made by the country's chief minister. Williams also capitalized on the Creole fear of Indo-Trinidadian political ascendancy:

We sympathize deeply with those misguided unfortunates who, having ears to hear, heard not, having eyes to see, saw not, who were complacent, for whom everything was in the bag, who had the DLP covered, who were too tired or busy to vote, who wanted a car to take them to the polling station around the corner. They will understand hereafter that he or she who stays home and does not come out to vote PNM, in effect votes DLP. They have learnt their lesson. Today they regret it bitterly, and they are *already swearing that it must never happen again.* (in Ryan 1974:193; emphasis in original)

Williams's outburst greatly embarrassed Indo-Trinidadian elites in his own party and enraged Indo-Trinidadians in general. One Indo-Trinidadian cabinet minister, Winston Mahabir, sought to rectify the antagonistic climate by appealing to tolerance and multiracialism in a warning to his own party, the PNM. Yet the damage had been done. With the ascent of the PNM in 1956 Afro-Trinidadians had increasingly begun to think in terms of their right to govern, fueling racial antagonisms. The 1958 fiasco injected further hysteria into this volatile climate, and "open or disguised appeals to race became the major strategy of party politics" (Brereton 1981:239).

The 1961 elections spurred the Hindu community into forming a more powerful collectivity under the leadership of Dr. Rudranath Capildeo (who replaced Maraj in 1960), a brilliant mathematician and lawyer from a prominent Brahmin family. The decisive victory of the PNM and Williams's success in leading the country to independence in 1962, however, spelled the decline of the opposition party, in terms of both leadership and Hindu political vivacity. Williams was to remain in power until his death in 1981, and his party continued to reign until 1986. Thus for almost three decades the PNM determined the trajectory of the nation through its policies on education and culture and its programs for industrialization and the allocation of state resources, while the Indo-Trinidadians, relegated to the opposition, remained alienated in the face of rising Creole nationalism.

The Ideal of Diversity Betrayed: Homogenization Programs in Practice

Williams's proposals for constitutional reform in 1955 clearly indicated his working assumption that Trinidad was a plural society (Ryan 1974). Once in power, however, Williams became "a strict and uncompromising majoritarian; any ethnic group which did not rally behind the PNM was either recalcitrant, treasonable, or obscurantist. Despite his genuine intellectual commitment to multiracialism, he refused to concede minority communities the right to elect their own kind, or to articulate their own version of the national community" (Ryan 1974:373).

The insensitivity of the PNM regime to the needs of other ethnic groups was in part an outcome of a deliberate strategy that gave priority to the anticolonial struggle at the expense of interethnic consensus. It was also partly

[219]

due to a misreading of the social situation by the Creole middle classes, who genuinely believed that the Indo-Trinidadians had been assimilated into the society and that the commonality they shared with Afro-Trinidadians—their colonial subjugation as West Indians—would spur them toward joining a national movement intent on overthrowing the colonial structures (Ryan 1974:376). For Williams and his party, nation building was integrally linked to an anticolonial struggle that embodied the redemption of a particular subjugated race, the African. Such a stance was symptomatic of the larger Caribbean independence experience, characterized by what some have labeled an ideology of racial paramountcy, in which people of African descent believe that political leadership is their moral right "by virtue of the numerical preponderance of their race in the Caribbean and what is held to be the greater suffering of that race compared with other races in the history of the region" (Singh 1985:59).

The thirty years of PNM rule left behind two principal legacies: the identification of the state with the culture history of Creoles, that is, with those of African ancestry; and the proclivity to mute ethnic differences for the good of the nation. The latter tendency is evidenced by the adherence of Creole middle classes, intellectuals, and (more ambiguously) politicians to the theory of "plural acculturation" (Crowley 1957), another variant of the Creole society thesis, especially during the era of Caribbean independence. This theory posits that despite the conglomeration of racial and cultural mixtures in Trinidad—and by extension other Caribbean societies—a fluid yet stable system of intergroup relations obtains because each group has internalized and learned to appreciate the different lifestyles of other groups (Oxaal 1968:23). An important agenda for Caribbean intellectuals preparing for independence was to find a common cultural basis to unite the people. Likewise, middle-class politicians steering their countries toward independence preferred acculturation theories to the pluralist models. Thus the dialogue between academic and political discourses was particularly heightened during this period. In the political sphere the tendency to downplay ethnic differences was also evident in the PNM's policies toward education and culture.

One of the primary fields on which nationalist battles are waged is the domain of education. Ernest Gellner (1991) has persuasively argued that the educational apparatus provides the crucial medium for exo-socialization, so vital for the functioning of modern industrial societies. Education is also the nexus where the state and "high" culture conjoin. Gellner maintains that the industrial age is also the age of universal high culture because a diversified, locality-tied, illiterate, folk-transmitted culture cannot fulfill the needs of industrial society: a generic cultural base for the populace to meet the demands of occupational mobility, and an explicit and precise mode of communication. In modern societies education constitutes the primary medium for the dissemination of this generic cultural base. Given, then, the indispensable role of education, state control over the educational apparatus becomes imperative.

The inculcation of a shared generic culture through education ultimately has everything to do with legitimacy. Culture is no longer the legitimation of a social order that is ultimately sustained by coercion but assumes instead the role of being the sole legitimating principle: "Culture is now the necessary shared medium, the life-blood or perhaps rather the minimal shared atmosphere, within which alone the members of the society can breathe and survive and produce. For a given society, it must be one in which they can all breathe and speak and produce so it must be the same culture" (Gellner 1991:37–38). Gellner's comment on cultural homogeneity does not refer to an empirical reality but is a purely theoretical observation. In practice, however, the principle of cultural homogeneity translates into the question, *Whose* culture becomes the formula for homogenization? It is at this juncture that state backing of a specific culture history engenders the unequal positioning of heterogeneous groups in relation to the nation and the state. PNM's policies on education and culture show how homogenizing programs (ideally intended to override diversity and inculcate a sense of sharedness) translate in practice into programs for exclusion.

The issue of educational reform illustrates well the purported nationalist concerns of the PNM and the defensive, almost sectional concerns of the PDP. Education was at the forefront of the PNM's national agenda. This emphasis on education was not purely determined by global nation-building trends but was significantly shaped by local currents. Since the culture history referent for the nation was premised on slavery and colonialism, education was identified as a primary medium for national redemption: "Massa was determined not to educate his society. Massa was quite right; to educate is to emancipate. That is why the PNM, the army of liberation of Trinidad, . . . has put education in the forefront of its programme. If Massa was entirely destitute of a liberal outlook and learned leisure, the PNM, come what may, will go down in history as the author of free secondary education and the architect of the University of Woodford Square" (Williams in Sutton 1981:215). From Williams's perspective education was tantamount to freedom. Yet state jurisdiction over the educational machinery was severely curtailed by the dual system in Trinidad in which both the state and denominational sects controlled schools. Williams and the PNM, with its base in the PEG, had from the outset opposed this dual system of education. In the PNM's view schools under state control were the primary medium through which a nationalist spirit could be cultivated among the masses. Denominational control, they feared, would exacerbate the existing cleavages of a society already fragmented, inhibiting the development of a common nationalist vision: "I see in the denominational school the breeding ground of disunity; I see in the state school the opportunity for cultivating a spirit of nationalism among West Indian people and eradicating the racial suspicions and antagonisms growing in our midst" (Williams in Oxaal 1968:105). Williams's statement encapsulates his particular vision of nationalism pursued in the nation-building era, a nationalism based on homogeneity rather than heterogeneous elements, which Williams associated with disunity.

The PDP, in contrast, fully supported the Sanatan Dharma Maha Sabha in its pioneering efforts to educate Indo-Trinidadians through its sponsorship of primarily Hindu schools, especially given the fact that nearly 50.6 percent of the Indo-Trinidadian population was illiterate in 1946 (Ryan 1974:143). These Hindu schools, catering almost exclusively to Indo-Trinidadians, emphasized Indian cultural and religious education and slighted the Hellenic-Christian–dominated West Indian culture, which the PNM favored as the appropriate national culture (a local derivative of Gellner's generic cultural base). As MacDonald comments:

> For the Hindus the school system provided employment for young Hindu teachers and functioned as a bulwark against Christian conversion. For the PNM it was a dangerous factor in continuing and exacerbating the divisions in Trinidad and Tobago's society. In a sense Afro-Trinidadian nationalism was colliding with Indo-Trinidadian nationalism, and the PNM's program for educational reforms alarmed the Hindu community as much as it did the Catholic Church and the Franco-Creole community. (1986:108)

It was not so much that Indo-Trinidadians during this period were anti-nationalist but rather that their structural positioning in society limited their ability to create a viable and legitimate cultural referent for imagining the national community. Unable to compete with the PNM, Indo-Trinidadian leaders had little choice but to insist on their ethnic exclusivity.

The PNM's apprehensions regarding the denominational challenge to its nationalist agenda is revealed by Williams, who attacked the idea of Hindi as a medium of instruction in Hindu schools:

> How can any responsible person argue that in 1955, the second, third generation offspring of people brought here 100 or even 40 years ago, who do not speak Hindi in their homes, have a right to demand their "mother tongue" in the schools? By what stretch of imagination can it be considered their "mother tongue"? . . . The education system of this community of ours is dominated by

one ponderous fact, disunity stemming from religious diversity. This diversity
has only been aggravated by the recognition of non-Christian denominations
which adds a racial difference . . . to religious difference. . . . I do not condemn
the recognition of non-Christian denominations, but it would be suicidal to ag-
gravate this religious diversity and religious difference by a linguistic differentiation. (Williams 1955 in Ryan 1974:143)

Both Williams and Maraj saw education as a primary means to achieve mobility. But just as the principles of subordination differed for Creoles and
East Indians, so too did the avenues for their redemption. Whereas Maraj
called on the state to support the preservation of Indian culture and the introduction of Hindi, Williams opposed any change he thought might frag-
ment the nation. By drawing on the history of slavery and indenture,
Williams sought to forge a common understanding among the descendants of
the victims of the two systems, but always in Creole terms. For Williams the
redemption of both "East Indians" and "Creoles" lay in gaining respectability,
not in the cultivation of specific cultural identities. Accordingly, he applauded
Indo-Trinidadian respectability: "Every step in the education of Indians is a
step in the production of that well-informed body of citizens on which British
West Indian democracy depends; every Indian admitted to the professions
and the civil service is a further victory in the cause of that full participation
of local men in the administration of the British West Indies without which
self government is a delusion" (in Segal 1989:213). The PNM's emphasis on
respectability was an avenue open, at least in principle, to all. In this way the
PNM managed to appeal to those outside its majority racial base. But the redemption the PDP offered was limited to Indo-Trinidadians, and the party
assumed the posture of a defensive, sectional, political body unable to garner
effective support outside its own communal political base.

That defensive posture was primarily a consequence of historically derived
structural limitations. Unlike the PNM, the PDP did not command the "appropriate" raw material—the appropriate culture or history—to create an
imagined national community. In contrast, the culture history of Creoles,
backed by the state, became firmly entrenched as national culture during the
PNM years. Exclusionary politics are the obverse of programs for cultural
homogenization.

This point was effectively illustrated for me by an Indo-Trinidadian minister of the PNM. He described how he had been repeatedly attacked by others in his party for his efforts at propagating Indian culture. On one occasion
a fellow minister reprimanded him by declaring that "it is inconceivable that
a minister of Government could be doing an Indian program in this country."
On another occasion, when a cabinet-appointed committee was asked to rec-

ommend appropriate programs for the celebration of independence day, it advised against the inclusion of Indian culture on the grounds that "it only parrots what is going on in India and as such goes against the grain of independence" (Sham Mohammed, interview 1990). Thus things Indian were aggressively discouraged because they were thought to be foreign and would retard the process of assimilation. Characterizing the period before the 1980s, John La Guerre writes:

> For most of the nationalists, the race relations problem was essentially one between the whites and the African-descended population. . . . The long-standing rivalry between the African-descended and East Indian population was forgotten—or ignored. To have remembered it and probed its consequences would have been in the thinking of the nationalists to divide the anti-imperialist forces and to weaken the integration movement. The nationalists and the intelligentsia alike accordingly buried their heads—ostrich like—in concepts such as class struggle, West Indianism or the people. (1985:18)

For nationalists such as Williams and members of the PNM, the primary struggle was against European domination. Accordingly, African elements embodied in the concept Creole (and West Indian) constituted for them the antithesis of things European—hence the Creole middle class's scramble to appropriate Creole lower-class cultural forms, which they believed were more African and indigenous to the New World, for national purposes beginning in the 1930s. Such deployments of culture formalized discrete cultural realms at the level of representation that did not necessarily obtain in practice. Thus steelband, carnival, and calypso became identified exclusively with Afro-Trinidadian culture in the popular imagination, and chutney, *tassa,* and roti with Indo-Trinidadians. But cultural forms such as the calypso, because they were also national, became vehicles for conveying the national message.

D. V. Trotman (1989), in a fascinating discussion of "the image of Indians in calypso," vividly portrays how the calypsos of the postindependence era exalted multiracial unity whereas shortly before that time they had chastised Indo-Trinidadians. In the 1958–61 period, when the political battleground was sharply drawn along racial lines, "Afro-Trinidadian calypsonians sang in support of a ruling party identified with progress, development, nationalism, and against an Indian community which they saw as racist, monolithic and backward" (Trotman 1989:183). Mighty Christo, for example, sang in 1961:

> Whip them PNM whip them
> You wearing the pants

If these people get on top is trouble
And we aint got a chance
Now we faring better
Since we got we premier
We living in contentment
So who we want? PNM government

Ah hear up in Couva
They attack a minister
And one Mr. Ramdeen
Try to thief a voting machine
Well that was ignorance
But he didn't have a chance
So they send him to Carrera
And when he come out is straight back to Calcutta
(in Trotman 1989:183)

The "we" here clearly refers to Afro-Trinidadians and the "they" in Couva to Indo-Trinidadians. The calypso reaffirms the alliance between Afro-Trinidadians and the PNM while distancing the Indo-Trinidadians from this alliance, which is clearly understood to compose the national unit. Conversely, Lord Baker's calypso of 1967 exalted racial unity in the new nation, but again the nation is identified with Afro-Trinidadian culture, that is, calypso and steelband:

It's fantastic yes it is the way how we live as one
In integration our nation is second to none
Here the negro, the white man, the Chinese, the Indian
Walk together hand in hand
In this wonderland of calypso in this wonderland of steelband
Where I was born—God bless our nation
(in Trotman 1989:186)

Lord Baker's calypso illustrates sharply how invisible hegemonic principles delineating national parameters continually alienated Indo-Trinidadians despite noble intentions. This predicament haunted the PNM time and again and evoked much frustration among Afro-Trinidadian nationalists, who were perplexed by vehement Indo-Trinidadian reactions to what they believed to be the most innocuous of statements. Whereas for Afro-Trinidadian nationalists the association between steelband and calypso and the nation was almost organic, for Indo-Trinidadians this association seriously jeopardized their claims to the nation and the state.

The fact that calypsonians assumed the role of popular spokesmen for the national cause attests to the success of Creole middle-class deployments of lower-class Afro-Creole cultural forms. It is important, nevertheless, to understand the ambivalence with which the nation-building process annexed lower-class Afro-Creole cultural forms within the nationalist agenda because it directly implicates the current Indo-Trinidadian struggle. Even though in contemporary times the nation tends to be equated with calypso, steelband, and carnival, their elevation as prominent national symbols has been relatively recent, approximately since the 1950s. From the perspective of the majority of Afro-Trinidadians the promotion and legitimation of their culture after centuries of subjugation and ridicule is only just, a natural sequence to their liberation from colonialism. What Indo-Trinidadians interpret as Afro-Caribbean/Trinidadian cultural hegemony is understood in less controversial terms by Afro-Trinidadians, who believe they are merely exercising their long-awaited right to a place in the sun. This right meant for them access to state prizes: sponsorship of cultural events and programs, access to the civil service and the military, and access to state housing and scholarships.

Indo-Trinidadians, in contrast, believed their interests had been compromised with the ascent of the PNM. Indo-Trinidadians felt they were disadvantaged not only culturally but also materially. In its efforts to achieve a more equitable distribution of income the PNM focused on the improvement of social infrastructure, especially the expansion of educational opportunity at the secondary level, and introduced a liberal scholarship program so that individuals of all classes had the chance to obtain a university education. They sought to improve the quality of life for lower classes through the provision of potable water, electricity, sewerage, and low-income housing (Henry 1988). Despite these measures, designed to improve the condition of the lower classes in general, Indo-Trinidadians claim that they benefited little from PNM policies (see Hintzen 1989). For example, the Special Works Program, aimed at easing unemployment, was implemented in urban areas of the East West corridor where Afro-Trinidadians predominate. Similarly, only 380 East Indians were given loans by the Industrial Development Corporation (IDC), the principal agent for promoting the small business sector, between 1970 and 1987, as opposed to the 781 granted to non–East Indians (Crichlow 1991).[35] Indo-Trinidadians, especially Hindus, also complained

35. The numbers were determined through a crude nomenclature method because of the absence of data on the ethnic composition of loan recipients. Crichlow estimates the disparity to be less since many Indo-Trinidadians have anglicized names and because IDC officials claimed a more equitable distribution (1991).

that members of their community were not being appointed to diplomatic and other important civil service positions. Sugar workers, they argued, were discriminated against in housing and agricultural projects,[36] and Indo-Trinidadians did not receive a fair share of public resources. Indo-Trinidadian cultural contributions, they also claimed, were not given equal public recognition and support in comparison with Afro-Trinidadian, and they charged the communications media with an anti-Indian bias (Ryan 1974). Thus Indo-Trinidadians essentially perceived the PNM as championing the interests of Afro-Trinidadians. As one Indo-Trinidadian elite member put it, "Negro is the ruler in this country and Indian is an underdog" (Malik 1971:58). The struggle of Indo-Trinidadians to redefine national culture must be understood as a step toward securing their own place in the sun, a journey on which Afro-Trinidadians had already embarked with the PNM at the helm.

36. Hintzen's (1989:176–77) evidence of the PNM's neglect of the agricultural sector suggests that Indo-Trinidadian perceptions of discrimination here have some empirical basis.

[8]

Breaking the Silence:
The Disintegration of Hegemonic Rule

Economic and political developments in the 1970s and especially the 1980s provided an appropriate climate for the contestation of the principal legacies of the PNM era, Afro-Trinidadian domination of the state and cultural representation of the nation. The Black Power movement, the oil boom and the subsequent slump, the decline in the national preeminence of sugar, demographic changes, and the rise and fall of the "one love" party—the National Alliance for Reconstruction (NAR)—created the context for a challenge to Afro-Trinidadian cultural and political hegemony.

The Black Power Movement's Challenge
to Afro-Saxon Rule

The Black Power demonstrations of February–April 1970 revealed some of the contradictions between the PNM's ideals and its economic and political programs in practice. The Black Power movement was primarily led by and composed of young West Indians of predominantly African descent, many of whom were students at the University of the West Indies in St. Augustine, Trinidad. Many of the groups supporting the marches were explicitly Afro-oriented, such as the Afro-Association of Trinidad and Tobago, the African Unity Brothers, the African Cultural Association, and the Universal Movement for the Reconstruction of Black Identity. The most important organization behind the movement, the National Joint Action Committee (NJAC), founded by Geddes Granger and David Darbeau in 1969, was theoretically multiracial, yet it drew nearly all its numerical support from east Port-of-Spain, where the population was almost exclusively Afro-Trinidadian.[1]

Black Power advocates posed a serious challenge to the PNM regime. Criticizing the PNM's economic and political agendas, they sought to redirect the national trajectory to a more radical anti-imperialist track. Between 1969 and 1972 oil production declined at an annual rate of 6.5 percent, causing an economic crisis (Vertovec 1992:133). Public spending was cut, GDP growth declined from almost 5.5 to 3.6 percent, and inflation soared from an average of 2.5 percent in the 1960s to over 10 percent in the early 1970s (Auty and Gelb 1986:1162).

Unemployment was a major factor contributing to the Black Power uprising. The PNM, through its program of "industrialization by invitation," had hoped to create a proliferation of jobs, but the large capital-intensive industrialization programs failed to deliver the expectations of Operation Jobs (Ryan 1974:385). Although the unemployment rate was reduced to 13.5 percent in 1969 and 12.5 percent in 1970, more than 45,000 people remained out of work (MacDonald 1986: 162). Unemployment was particularly acute among the younger generation. In the age group 15–19, 35 percent of the labor force remained unemployed in 1967, and among those between 20 and 24 the rate was 20 percent (Nicholls 1971:446). The persistence of racial discrimination in employment, especially in the private sector, exacerbated the situation. The PNM had sought to open up opportunities to the public by expanding the educational system. Yet the continued domination of high-status occupations by traditional elites—local Whites and Creole middle classes—meant that the society was unable to absorb this emergent generation of educated youth. As La Guerre reminds us, "1970, it should be recalled, was in many respects a call to 'open careers to talent'" (1988:199). Frustration among educated youth and the failure of the PNM government to deliver on its promise of redemption for the masses provided the necessary material conditions for the upsurge of Black Power ideology influenced by the political movement in North America.

The primary charge made by the protagonists was that the white power structure continued to dominate the nation's economic, social, and cultural spheres despite formal independence. The leaders distinguished between Black government and Black Power. Even though Trinidad possessed the former, from the perspective of the Black Power leaders the Black masses remained subjugated because political decisions continued to be dictated by the economic interests of traditional elites. As a result, the leaders charged,

1. On the Black Power movement, see Ryan 1989a and 1996:chap. 3, Oxaal 1971, Bennett 1989, Nicholls 1971, and Gosine 1986.

"our own government is no more than devoted puppets of the white foreign capitalist bastards and local white capitalists" (in Nicholls 1971:451). The Black Power leaders' primary targets were the Black middle classes, or "Afro-Saxons," whom they accused of adopting white values and exploiting the mass of Black people in the interest of the Whites. The various factions comprising the Black Power movement were united less on the basis of a common ideology than on their rejection of "white values" and their adherence to certain symbols, which were primarily African or American Negro traditions—the clenched fist; the cry of "power"; the *dashiki* (Afro-shirt) and the fat-head (Afro haircut); the red, black, and green flags; and the use of "brother" and "sister" (Nicholls 1971:451).

Such symbols and the emphasis on blackness greatly inhibited Indo-Trinidadians from joining the movement despite the fervent efforts of Black Power leaders to forge an alliance with Indo-Trinidadians. As early as 1969 NJAC had included Indo-Trinidadians in its definition of "black people." Yet in less self-conscious moments the definition of Black often became equated with African origins and the possibility of Indo-Trinidadian inclusion a mere afterthought. More important, regardless of the intentions of the movement's leaders, Indo-Trinidadians simply could not identify themselves as Blacks. As we have seen, East Indian identity evolved directly in opposition to that of Creole and by extension Black. An ideological framework capable of permitting the collapse of these two identities did not obtain in the Indo-Trinidadian imagination.[2] As one Indo-Trinidadian phrased it: "I am not Black—neither do I regard myself as such . . . and no Indian in this country would tell you he is Black. It is only in the Black Power Movement they tried to refer to us as Black in the non-White sense. . . . When the word 'Black' is used in Trinidad, it is used to mean only Negroes and every Indian and every Negro knows this. Although I am not white, I am still not Black" (in Gosine 1986:167).

Traditional Indo-Trinidadian leaders, such as Maraj, vigorously opposed the Black Power movement because it threatened their own power base. The movement's call to working-class Indo-Trinidadian sugar workers to join with poor urban Blacks infringed on that space, which Maraj had long come to regard as his privileged domain. In addition, the predicament of Blacks, their "identity crisis," which the movement promised to address, was one that Indo-Trinidadians were unable to identify with.

The Black Power movement, contrary to the expectations of its leaders, who had hoped to break down ethnic barriers, served unexpectedly to consolidate them. Indo-Trinidadian businessmen felt threatened by the Black

2. See Gosine 1986:157–70.

Power attack on commercial interests. Demonstrations led to the burning and destruction of businesses owned by Whites and Indo-Trinidadians. The fact that the few Black-owned businesses in Port-of-Spain were left unscathed by the unruly mob agitated the Indo-Trinidadian leaders, who interpreted this action to mean that the movement was not only anti-White but anti-Indian (Gosine 1986:98). Thus for some Indo-Trinidadians the Black Power movement carried the ominous possibility of the rise of a new type of "black totalitarianism," and they feared the long-term aims of the movement: "Let the Black Power advocates take control. . . . Then what are we going to have? . . . White capitalists kicked out, Chinese kicked out, Syrian capitalists kicked out! who is going to follow next? The Indians of course" (quoted by Nicholls 1971:456). Similarly, the university-based Society for the Propagation of Indian Culture (SPIC), in an article addressed "to the Black people of Trinidad," stated: "Don't call me Black. No Indian likes being called Black. . . . My characteristics are well known, I have always thought of myself as a human being, an Indian. You, the Black man, want us to join you. How can we be sure that you do not want the place of the White man for yourself alone? . . . Every Indian is united today because of your struggle. . . . We look at you as a threat. You are bringing out the Indian power which you did not know existed" (*Embryo*, March 21, 1970, in Gosine 1986:166). The Black Power movement, by providing a rallying point for Indo-Trinidadians, provoked an exercise in introspection in the Indo-Trinidadian community—an exercise ardently encouraged by Black Power advocates for the Black masses. Ken Parmasad, who was then an activist on the St. Augustine campus and a member of SPIC, claims that many Indo-Trinidadians welcomed the Black Power movement because it indirectly legitimated Indo-Trinidadians' own search for their roots (Ryan 1996:46). Parmasad also insists that radical Indo-Trinidadians identified with the Black Power movement in their opposition to the ruling elite. Thus attitudes did not always conform to ethnic divides. Although such sentiments were in the minority, the point remains that Indo-Trinidadians, like the Black masses, began to reevaluate their status in society. In short, Black Power critiques of the PNM Government and of racial discrimination opened a discursive space for a general reevaluation of the society.

The "blackness" of the movement's advocates afforded them greater legitimacy to criticize a government that purported to forward "black" interests. Whereas similar agitations by Indo-Trinidadians might have elicited charges of being "anti-nationalist," "sectionalist," or a "recalcitrant minority," "Black Power" advocates' critiques of the PNM in contrast were particularly potent. "Black Power" advocates challenged the PNM not only on its own terms—that is, as the champion of the Afro-Creole cause—but also in a capacity that afforded them greater advantage. Groups that remained outside the movement could then seize the opportunity to reassess their own situation. The Black Power movement's attack on the PNM's symbolic basis of legitimacy—the association the party had cultivated with Afro-Creole underclasses—in turn opened up possibilities for other groups, such as the Indo-Trinidadians, to question the integrity of a system that had up to then been revered by many Afro-Trinidadians. It was indeed ironic, as Trotman notes, "that the demands for economic redress were made under the banner of black power and African cultural revival against a government hitherto seemingly enjoying the benefit of undisputed black racial allegiance" (1989:177).

Oil and Sugar: The Ascent of Industry and the Demise of Agriculture

The trajectories of Trinidad's two major industries, oil and sugar, also contributed to the heightening of ethnic consciousness. The newfound wealth generated by the oil boom propelled the majority of Indo-Trinidadians from their rural enclaves into mainstream sectors. As Indo-Trinidadians moved from their traditional occupations into higher echelons, they made headway in areas jealously guarded by other sectors as their exclusive terrain. Occupational mobility served to heighten ethnic consciousness among both Indo-Trinidadians and Afro-Trinidadians. Qualified Indo-Trinidadians became acutely aware of the barriers against their penetration into sectors long considered Afro-Trinidadian preserves, such as the civil service, armed forces, and high offices in government. The Afro-Trinidadians, alarmed by the strides made by Indo-Trinidadian business and professional classes, increasingly panicked, believing in an imminent Indo-Trinidadian takeover. In the context of the 1976 elections the chairman of the state-owned National Broadcasting Station vented these fears:

> The East Indians have increasingly acquired education and have been increasingly invading the fields of the Civil Service, the professions and the Government. As their numbers must now reach parity with people of African descent, there is a real possibility that in the not too distant future, they will get control of the Government. Should this time come when the East Indian section owns most of the property, business and wealth of the country as well as control of the Government, an imbalance could develop in our society that would cause undesirable stresses and strains that would not be good for the nation. (J. A. Bain in La Guerre 1988:197)

[232]

The widespread belief among Indo-Trinidadians that owing to the PNM's discriminatory practices, Afro-Trinidadians were the primary recipients of petro-dollars also intensified their ethnic consciousness. The PNM deliberately geared its economic policies toward cultivating its traditional voting bloc of urban Creoles. Hintzen observes: "The entirely fortuitous circumstances of the post-1973 oil boom enabled the regime, through authoritative decision-making, to employ the state as an instrument for reallocating the phenomenally expanded oil income into politically strategic sectors of the domestic economy. . . . With the tremendously increased revenue, the regime was able to sustain and expand the system of patronage directed at the black lower-class population" (1989:143).

Although Indo-Trinidadians claim that they were not the direct beneficiaries of the petro-dollars, they explain their rapid mobility during this period on the basis of popular stereotypes. Both Afro-Trinidadians and Indo-Trinidadians believe the petro-dollars ultimately trickled down to Indian pockets, given the "natural dispositions" of the "African" to spend and the "East Indian" to save.

Yet the question of who benefited most from the PNM years and the oil bonanza is controversial, engaging popular, academic, and political discourses. Although some academics such as Hintzen (1989) argue that Afro-Trinidadians were the main beneficiaries, this feeling is not shared by the majority of Afro-Trinidadians. In a poll conducted by Ryan in 1987, only 10 percent of the Afro-Trinidadians questioned believed they had benefited more whereas 35 percent believed that Indo-Trinidadians benefited more (Ryan 1989b:167). In contrast, the majority of Indo-Trinidadians who were questioned believed that "Africans had received more by way of patronage in the allocation of houses, jobs, official loans, and utility services" (Ryan 1989b:167). Again, on the question of economic mobility, statistics became embroiled in an ideological debate concerning the traditional stereotypes of the persevering, thrifty, and hardworking East Indian and the laid-back African.

Scholars, and more specifically Indo-Trinidadians, repeatedly evoke essential "Indian" cultural characteristics to explain the apparent anomaly of Indo-Trinidadian economic success in the face of purported economic discrimination. Ryan, for example, writes:

The minority psychology of the Indians, coupled with the greater toughness of their family and cultural system, predisposed them to postpone consumption and use pooled family resources to educate their young and take investment risks in business activities of one sort or another. The dependent psychology of the blacks was countered by the aggressive self and group reliance of the Indian community. The latter saw the opportunities provided by the petro-dollar boom and grasped them purposefully. As a result, their share of national income increased decisively over that [*sic*] past two decades. (1989b:167–68)

In a similar vein lay Indo-Trinidadians insist that any progress experienced by their community is entirely due to their own efforts. They explain income parities between themselves and Afro-Trinidadians on the basis that Indo-Trinidadians "earned" whatever they got whereas the Afro-Trinidadians were "given" whatever they possess. This rationale for Indo-Trinidadian economic advancement is buttressed by the corollary argument that Afro-Trinidadians were the architects of their own economic stagnation, a view propagated not only by the majority of Indo-Trinidadians but also by those Afro-Trinidadian academics and politicians opposed to the PNM:

> It could be argued that it was the majority psychology of the blacks—the feeling that they had superior ancestral claims as successors to the colonial authority, a feeling that was fortified by the existence of the PNM as the ruling party, which predisposed many blacks to become "laid back," dependent and to take their continued social and political dominances as given. As Karl Hudson-Phillips, one of the two Deputy Political leaders of the NAR and a former Attorney-General in the PNM Government noted by way of reply to claims that the PNM was for the poor blacks while the NAR was for the rich, "if black people are poor in this country today, it is because the PNM made them poor; if black people have nothing in Trinidad and Tobago after 30 years of the PNM, whose fault is that?" (Ryan 1989b:167)

Many Afro-Trinidadians, however, seek to debunk such arguments by asserting that certain minorities were better poised to capitalize on the oil bonanza because they possessed a historical advantage with regard to ownership of capital assets.

Indo-Trinidadians' economic progress informs the present ethnic struggle significantly. Economic security has injected a new sense of confidence, prompting their leaders to take the initiative instead of acting defensively. Their rapid incorporation into mainstream society and the decline of their traditional enclaves, such as agriculture, meant that their destinies would be fundamentally determined by the trajectories of the nation and the state. Thus social and spatial seclusion and defensive posturing in the political arena are no longer attractive strategies for advancement for Indo-Trinidadians. Instead, they actively seek positions at the helm, charting the course of the nation.

The perceived economic success of Indo-Trinidadians is both a boon and a liability as they try to garner moral capital and legitimize their case for state power. On the one hand, they use their reputed economic prowess to emphasize the immense contribution they have made to the nation, in terms of both material and moral improvement. On the other hand, these same achievements weaken their case against ethnic discrimination. Success limits their capacity to present themselves as a deprived group, an essential ingredient in their aggregation of moral capital. Deploying traditional stereotypes, Indo-Trinidadians circumvent this dilemma by attributing their economic achievements to innate cultural characteristics, thereby transforming a potentially damaging feature into a positive strategy. Such a rationale also conveniently shifts the blame to Afro-Trinidadians for their own alleged economic stagnation. Afro-Trinidadians, in turn, retaliate by claiming that they were historically disadvantaged as a group. Like their Indo-Trinidadian counterparts, they seek to enhance their own moral capital—a necessary element in guarding and legitimating their proprietorship of the state—by representing themselves as doubly disadvantaged, both historically and, in the contemporary period, economically.

Despite the many ambiguities surrounding the question of who benefited from the spoils of the oil boom, and despite what the facts on the ground may suggest, in Indo-Trinidadian folk imagination the ascent of oil symbolized the ascent of Afro-Trinidadians, just as the decline of sugar symbolized the perpetual marginalization of Indo-Trinidadians. Such symbolic associations meant that the fate of the two industries would be continually interpreted through ethnic lenses. When Williams, for example, declared sugar to be "a dead horse . . . the crop of colonialism *par excellence*," and when he referred to oil and natural gas as "true national resources" (*Trinidad Guardian*, August 26, 1973, in Ching 1985), the political and ideological import of the statement overrode its economic verity.

Even though the sugar industry rapidly deteriorated during the 1970s and the 1980s, its decline ironically opened up new possibilities for Indo-Trinidadians. Foremost among them was the rise of Basdeo Panday to national stature through his struggle on behalf of the sugar workers. From his sugar base Panday ventured into the political arena, consolidating his position by 1978 (Ching 1985:322).[3] Panday sought to elevate the struggle of the sugar worker from fighting for "bread and butter" issues to cultivating a sense of dignity and self-confidence. A commitment to the total well-being of the sugar worker meant going beyond securing higher wages; it entailed a battle for better housing, education, and other resources that would put sugar

---

3. See Ryan 1996:chaps. 4 and 5 on Panday's rise to political preeminence through his trade union activity. See also Siewah and Moonilal 1991 for a collection of Panday's speeches.

workers on a par with members of more prestigious sectors. Such transformations, according to Panday, required political change since the PNM had denied sugar workers access to these resources.

Nevertheless, Panday was ambivalent about involvement in politics (Ryan 1996). The United Labor Front (ULF), a coalition of four of the major trade unions in the islands—the Oilfields Workers Trade Union, the All Trinidad Sugar Estates and Factories Workers Trade Union, the Transport and Industrial Workers Union, and the Island-wide Canefarmers Trade Union—was formed in 1975, but its political future was uncertain. An earlier attempt by trade unionists to enter the political arena as the Workers and Farmers Party in the 1966 elections had resulted in dismal failure, and trade union leaders and their followers remained skeptical about wedding trade union struggles with politics. Although Panday always had an eye on parliament, he sidestepped the issue, leaving the decision to the workers (Ryan 1996:67). When the ULF held a "religious march" in March 1975 which was harshly suppressed by the establishment, the way was paved for the transformation of the ULF into a political party in 1976:[4]

> That march brought home clearly to the consciousness of the workers and leaders that if you are struggling for industrial objectives, that can always be frustrated if political power is in the hands of opponents of that struggle. . . . What became clear in the minds of all workers was that the industrial struggle was not enough. In order to crystallize the gains of industrial struggle, in order to make them permanent and lasting, . . . it was necessary to transcend the industrial struggle into the political scene. (Panday in Ryan 1996:67)

After contesting the 1976 elections, the ULF, drawing its primary base of support from Indo-Trinidadian sugar workers, replaced the DLP as the formal opposition in parliament with Panday as its unofficial leader.

Panday's struggle on behalf of the sugar workers had two dimensions: first, for sugar workers qua sugar workers, and second, for sugar workers as members of "a particular ethnic category," one that, "like sugar, occup[ies] an inferior position in economy and society" (Ching 1985:328). Thus the sugar workers' struggle also encoded an ethnic project. As Ching observes, Panday "saw it essential to change the very image of sugar and the sugar workers, so that there would be no shame and no sense of inferiority connected with it, and by association, with East Indianness" (1985:328).

4. Panday tried hard to project the image of the ULF as a class-based worker's movement that transcended ethnic cleavages, but the reluctance of many Afro-Trinidadian oil workers to support it outright suggests that the ULF was primarily seen as an Indo-Trinidadian party with an Indo-Trinidadian leader (Ryan 1996:69–70).

In Panday's determination to change the image of sugar we see the germination of Indo-Trinidadians' present strategy of self-definition in their own terms. Clearly, the dynamics of the sugar industry have significantly shaped the current ethnic struggle. Struggles over the leadership of the sugar union generated a leader of national stature, Panday, who would soon challenge Afro-Trinidadian political privilege. In addition, even as the sugar industry declined in the 1970s and the 1980s, sugar workers gained substantial wage increases. Although those in the industry felt slighted by the PNM's attitude toward sugar, they experienced such discrimination, contradictory as it seems, from a position of relative confidence and empowerment.

Contemporary Indo-Trinidadian protests indicate not increasing levels of exploitation but the fact that a formerly disadvantaged subnational group has seized an opportunity afforded by the disintegration of legitimating principles behind hegemonic rule. It is appropriate to interpret the transformations overtaking the sugar industry and its workers from this perspective. The struggle of the sugar workers and their leaders to remake the fate of the sugar industry is indicative of this rather novel political mood among Indo-Trinidadians, who seek constantly to redefine in their own terms every issue that affects their collectivity.

Given the symbolic import of sugar for Indo-Trinidadians' ethnic identity, the government's plans for the diversification of the sugar industry have elicited much controversy and have assumed a central role in the current Indo-Trinidadian struggle to redefine the nation. All protagonists realize that change is inevitable; the industry cannot be sustained in the present condition for much longer. The battle, then, is waged over who gets to determine the exact course of change.

On February 8, 1989, the minister of planning and mobilization announced the state's plan for the diversification and rationalization of the sugar industry. The government proposed to cut sugar production to seventy-five thousand tons, the amount necessary to supply only the domestic market, and to withdraw itself completely from cane cultivation, which would be transferred entirely to cane farmers, to whom sufficient land would be allocated. The government also proposed to shut down the Brechin Castle factory in central Trinidad and to maintain only the Ste. Madeline factory in the south; in addition, it would aggressively pursue crop diversification (Caroni [1975] Limited 1989).

These plans stood to affect directly the livelihood of 7,200 workers, most of whom were Indo-Trinidadians. If Brechin Castle was closed, cane farmers in the central part of the sugar belt would be adversely effected. Transportation costs of cane to another factory would be prohibitively high unless subsidized by the government. Diversification projects, which would be capital intensive, also promised little possibility of absorbing those who would be displaced by the Brechin Castle closure. Thus an estimated 4,722 cultivators, 900 factory workers, and 325 staff workers stood to lose their jobs if the government plan was implemented.

The subject of land distribution became particularly contentious. Afro-Trinidadian leaders argued that since the sugar industry is a national industry long monopolized by Indo-Trinidadians, any land distribution program must include Afro-Trinidadians, who have been retrenched in other national industries. Indo-Trinidadians, particularly the sugar workers, feared not only a possible Afro-Trinidadian invasion of their space but also severe disadvantages in a state-controlled land distribution scheme. They had everything to lose if the state decided to redress the ethnic balance of this particular national industry. Many Indo-Trinidadians, especially politicians, saw the government's plan to restructure the industry as an attempt to destroy the political base of the opposition.

Because of the symbolic association between Indo-Trinidadians and the fate of sugar, many Indo-Trinidadians believe the eventual trajectory of the industry will profoundly affect not only those workers who directly depend on it for their livelihoods but also Indo-Trinidadians in general. For many Indo-Trinidadians the triumph of the government plan would signify their continued marginal status in the nation.

The fluctuations in the fortunes of Trinidad's two primary commodities, oil and sugar, enhanced the sense of persecution among Indo-Trinidadians even while empowering them. This new mix of indignation and empowerment fostered in turn a radical change in political mood and practice. Indo-Trinidadian aspirations to occupy top government positions or to practice coveted professions traditionally reserved for Afro-Trinidadians were increasingly fulfilled, and Indo-Trinidadian leaders saw for the first time a realistic chance for them to affect the direction of the state.

The Rise and Fall of the "One Love" Party

Indo-Trinidadians' confidence has also been bolstered by their numerical strength. In 1990 Trinidad and Tobago's population had the following ethnic composition: people of African descent, 39.6 percent; people of East Indian descent, 40.03 percent; Whites, 0.6 percent; Chinese, 0.4 percent; Mixed, 18.4 percent; and Others, 0.2 percent (Central Statistical Office 1997). Yet many lament that Indo-Trinidadians still believe and behave as though they were a minority. As one Indo-Trinidadian politician commented, "It is a cause of bewilderment that there is a tacit assumption both among Indians and non-Indians that this country is not yet ready for an Indian Prime Minister although Indians comprise close to fifty percent of the population" (*Sunday Guardian*, May 27, 1990, 7).

It was precisely such an assumption that led the National Alliance for Reconstruction (NAR), a primarily Indo-Trinidadian–supported coalition, to choose A. N. R. Robinson, a Black Tobagonian, as leader over Basdeo Panday. The NAR was an amalgam of anti-PNM forces: the primarily sugar worker–based United Labor Front, the urban middle class–based Organization for National Reconstruction (ONR), the Tobago-based Democratic Action Congress (DAC), and the left-leaning intelligentsia movement Tapia (Yelvington 1991). With Robinson as its leader, the NAR promised to forge an alliance among labor, business, and government and to promote ethnic harmony. The NAR won an overwhelming victory over the PNM in the 1986 elections, capturing 67.3 percent of the popular vote and 33 out of the 36 parliamentary seats (Ryan 1989b, 1996).

The choice of Robinson for leader was strategic. Even though Panday had risen to political eminence through his sugar union activities and his role as the leader of the opposition during the PNM's last ten years in power, "on the leadership question, Panday readily deferred to Robinson since he was clear in his own mind that the population would not accept him as Prime Minister" (Ryan 1989b:57). Once again, the conventional pattern of racial politics foreclosed possibilities of Indo-Trinidadian political leadership. Yet Ryan's polls indicate that the majority of Indo-Trinidadians preferred Panday to Robinson, in contrast to Afro-Trinidadians, who favored Robinson (Ryan 1989b:48–49).

Working on the premise that Trinidad was a plural society, the NAR coalition sought to reflect this plurality in the party system through slogans of "one love" and "unity out of diversity." For the first time Indo-Trinidadians had hope of directly participating in the state apparatus in their own right, in contrast to the system of indirect representation fostered by the earlier practice of token representation. Indo-Trinidadians pledged their support to the NAR in no uncertain manner: 82 percent of Indo-Trinidadians and 73 percent of Hindus voted for the NAR (Ryan 1989b:87). Many Indo-Trinidadians described to me the initial period of the NAR reign as a euphoric time when possibilities seemed endless.

The euphoria was short-lived, however. The economic situation confronting the NAR was dire. The fiscal savings generated by the oil bonanza were exhausted, and the country faced a major debt problem. The total debt (local and external) had jumped from TT$2.9 billion in 1981 to TT$7.4 billion in 1986 (Ryan 1989b:97). Such economic problems loomed larger in view of the NAR's inability to deliver the economic recovery it promised.

[239]

Much of the energies of the NAR's leadership had been invested in forming an effective coalition that could defeat the PNM, and thorny economic issues that threatened to divide the various interests had been strategically downplayed. As a consequence, the elections of 1986 delivered a new political party that lacked a systematic plan to confront the economic recession.

The new government introduced austerity measures that the general population found hard to swallow. The abolition of the preferential exchange rate in 1987 and the withdrawal of subsidies had the effect of raising the price of imports such as food and drugs. Basic food items, which had been subject to government price controls, soared in price in March 1987 (Yelvington 1991). Currency devaluation in August 1988 (when the Trinidad dollar went from 3.60 to 4.25 against the U.S. dollar), further escalated food prices by 25 percent and caused inflation to jump from 7.8 percent in 1988 to 12.2 percent in 1989. The rising level in unemployment from around 10 percent in 1982 to 22.4 percent in 1989 exacerbated the repercussions of such price hikes. Some unofficial estimates suggest unemployment figures as high as 25 to 30 percent (Yelvington 1991).

Unemployment particularly plagued the youth population: in 1988 the rates for the 15–19 and 20–24 age groups stood at 43.2 percent and 37.1 percent, respectively (Yelvington 1991:15). The removal of the cost-of-living allowance (COLA) for government employees, the implementation of a voluntary retirement plan aimed at trimming the civil service, and retrenchments in private and public companies contributed to a decline in real wages and swelled the ranks of the unemployed. The government's decision to borrow from the International Monetary Fund (IMF) in late 1988 augured even worse economic hardship for the population even though the business community stood to benefit. Public spending was cut and the number of government employees reduced. Import substitution was indirectly encouraged when the government was forced by the IMF to remove US$150 million in goods from the country's "negative list," which formerly protected local producers by excluding foreign manufactures (Yelvington 1991). The government was urged to stop subsidizing utilities and to pass the costs on to the consumer, and in January 1990 it imposed a 15 percent value-added tax on a number of items.

Trinidadians still enjoyed comparatively higher standards of living and per capita incomes than natives of most other Caribbean nations. World Bank estimates in 1990 projected a GNP per capita income of US$3,230 for Trinidad and Tobago, US$1,260 for Jamaica, US$1,360 for St. Vincent and the Grenadines, and US$340 for Guyana (World Bank 1990). Still, the relative economic deprivation incurred by the recession was jarring to an island society that only a decade earlier was reveling in the spoils of the oil bonanza. The recession forcefully altered lifestyles across all classes. While the more well-to-do complained that they could no longer afford their trips to the United States for vacations and shopping sprees, cane cutters in Cambio lamented that they had to settle for local rum whereas in former times imported whiskey never ran out!

In a context in which the state allocation of resources had to be carefully monitored, the tenuous coalition of the NAR began to fracture and ethnic factionalism returned with a vengeance. The triumph of the NAR had generated a wave of optimism throughout the country. At the same time, given the new economic limits to state action, every move of the new government was scrutinized by competing factions anxious to ensure that their privileges were maintained and their needs adequately met.

The appointment of the head of state, which drew much controversy, was eventually bestowed on the retired justice Noor Hassanali, a Muslim Indo-Trinidadian. Despite Robinson's claim to the contrary, it is evident that this appointment was made partly to assuage the Indo-Trinidadian community, which felt that "such an appointment would give symbolic effect to the 'arrival' of the Indian community in the corridors of power" (Ryan 1989b:108). Conversely, some Indo-Trinidadians were irritated when someone outside their ethnic group was chosen as minister of food production, marine exploitation, forestry, and the environment, a domain Indo-Trinidadians had come to perceive as their preserve. Afro-Trinidadians, however, feared that if this ministry was kept under an Indo-Trinidadian's control, Indo-Trinidadian dominance of agriculture would continue at their expense.

Structural obstacles prevented the NAR from effectively implementing its policies of reconstruction. The Westminster Model, on which the constitution was based, was unsuited to an ethnically stratified society in which component groups insist on being dynamically represented in the decision-making process.[5] Under the Westminster system, in which the victorious party collects all the spoils, there is no effective mechanism to incorporate the interests of those groups that backed the less successful candidates and parties. In societies deemed plural, politicians and parties become closely identified with specific interest groups, and the dismissal of a minister is tantamount to

---

5. Here it is important to reiterate the point made earlier that the model of an ethnically stratified plural society is largely a consequence of the objectification of Trinidadian society as "ethnically diverse." By this I mean not to deny "objective" distinctions but rather to emphasize ideological and material forces that have made these distinctions significant so that most Trinidadians genuinely believe and operate in their societies as if they were naturally "plural societies."

excluding from power the group he or she represents. Thus although the elevation of noted Indo-Trinidadian politicians to ministerial positions promised the inclusion of Indo-Trinidadian interests in the decision-making process, the possible marginalization of these leaders also threatened to exclude their collectivity from power.

The extensive powers accorded the prime minister under the Westminster Model also endangered the viability of the NAR coalition. Constitutional primacy was given to the prime minister in crucial areas: he alone was responsible for choosing his cabinet, and he was free to fire his ministers at will. Thus the structure of the Westminster Model itself functioned against the effective sharing of power through consensus and negotiation, which the NAR had pledged to support, at least in principle.

Another formidable obstacle to reconstruction was the administrative apparatus that the new government inherited from the outgoing regime. In the early transition period many ministers complained that the bureaucracy was throttling the introduction of key initiatives. Again, the problem was largely structural and endemic to the Westminster Model. In this system any new government inherits what is in theory a politically neutral civil service. Yet the thirty years of PNM rule had entrenched certain values and styles of operation in the bureaucracy. The NAR's proposals for reform that went beyond the traditional frame of reference of previous governmental activity came into conflict with a bureaucratic structure that was organized on a different set of principles and values.

Many public servants also resented the changes proposed by the NAR, which was committed to "clean out the Augean stables of the PNM bureaucracy" (Ryan 1989b:133). The public servants felt they had been unfairly characterized as PNM party hacks, lazy, incompetent, and corrupt. Whereas the NAR ministers resented the bureaucracy as an unnecessary obstacle to the rapid implementation of new policies, the public servants were alarmed at the ministers' disregard for "proper procedure" and the introduction of policies that seemed to go against the grain of conventional wisdom (Ryan 1989b). The conflict between the new government and the administration was also aggravated by the ethnic question. Most of the problems arose in ministries where the minister was Indo-Trinidadian and the key public officers Afro-Trinidadian (Ryan 1989b:132). Consider, for example, Panday's explanation why he was dismissed as minister in charge of immigration:

> If you apply for citizenship or permanent residence in T&T, it goes to a committee. The committee then makes a recommendation to the Minister responsible. The Minister responsible for Immigration may or may not accept the recommendation. When a name like James Rawlins for St. Kitts appears for

citizenship, it is approved. Mary Moore from Grenada is recommended for citizenship. Now Drupatee Singh from Guyana is not recommended. I decided I would deal with that. Every time they did that I would put a little note on the application and send it back asking, "Would you be so kind to tell me why are you treating this applicant differently from others who have the same qualifications." . . . I returned 24 files. The next week they went to the Prime Minister to report to him that I was racial. He subsequently removed the Immigration Portfolio from me. (Siewah and Moonilal 1991:304–5)

The first visible crack in the party appeared in May 1987 when the speaker of the house, a Muslim Indo-Trinidadian, criticized the minister in charge of allocating project work under DEWD for not assigning any projects in his constituency. He accused the minister of continuing the pattern initiated by the PNM, which catered primarily to the constituencies of the east-west corridor populated by working-class Afro-Trinidadians, at the expense of central and southern constituencies populated mostly by Indo-Trinidadians. The speaker was severely chastised by party members for airing his grievances publicly and not confining them to the back channels of the party. In the months to follow, many other party notables, primarily of the ULF faction, disappointed with the trajectory of the NAR, began to criticize their party openly, much to the chagrin of Robinson and his supporters.

Even though the NAR was ideologically committed to an "open government," some, like Panday, felt that this commitment was repeatedly betrayed in practice. The NAR had chastised the PNM style of government as autocratic, but Robinson, they argued, was perpetuating the same practices because of his refusal to consult his cabinet on important decisions and his heavy reliance on a small group of technocrats. Those who were excluded were especially resentful because this decision-making group had also been Williams's coterie of advisers. The spirit of open government was also compromised, critics claimed, because Robinson would not tolerate dissent. Panday repeatedly compared Robinson to Williams, who like him condemned racism as a sin but, according to Panday, went on to establish a racist society.

Of major concern to the former ULF members was the composition of the boards of state enterprises, the public utilities, and other statutory bodies. It was widely believed that these positions were filled by PNM loyalists and that few Indo-Trinidadians were represented. In January 1987 a transition team was established to recommended appointees to the boards. Only three Indo-Trinidadians were proposed for membership on boards of the seven most critical companies in the energy sector, and Indo-Trinidadians were recommended to chair only six relatively minor boards of the forty-one boards under review. The most prestigious positions continued to be held by French

[243]

Creoles, who headed seven boards, and Afro-Trinidadians, who were nominated to head the remaining twenty-eight. Thus of the 198 positions in question only 34, or 17 percent, were recommended for Indo-Trinidadians (Ryan 1989b:154).

The recommendations provoked an outcry from certain factions within the NAR that claimed that although the government had changed, the power structure of the last thirty years continued intact. Referring to the brutality of the state machinery, Panday told his constituents: "Injustice is still there. Discrimination is still there. And the unfairness is still there. And there is still the callousness that emanates from the state machinery" (Ryan 1989b:134). Open warfare had begun.

In an attempt to curb the open rebellion Robinson promised a cabinet reshuffle in November 1987, but the changes were less drastic than expected. Only one minister, John Humphrey (minister for housing and resettlement), was dismissed, rather than the four or five that many observers had predicted. Nevertheless, the reshuffle privileged Afro-Trinidadian dominance over the state machinery: "The net effect of the reshuffle was to tilt the balance of power further towards the 'Corridor' at the expense of 'Caroni.' The African element now held 10 Cabinet posts, French Creoles one, while the Indian element, with 4 posts, was considerably weakened, leading many to feel that the Cabinet did not properly reflect the support base of the NAR" (Ryan 1989b:142).

Panday and others whose ministerial authorities had been curbed smarted at their treatment at the hands of Robinson. Panday publicly condemned Robinson for not having consulted him as the deputy political leader on the ministerial changes. The war within the party worsened, culminating in the expelling of Panday, Trevor Sudama (junior minister of finance), and Kelvin Ramnath (minister of energy), all former ULF members who commanded significant support in the Indo-Trinidadian community, from the cabinet in February 1988.[6] They were also suspended from participating in party activities. The expelled members subsequently established the caucus CLUB 88 (Caucus for Love, Unity, and Brotherhood), and in October 1988 they launched yet another distinctly Indo-Trinidadian political party, the United National Congress (UNC).

With the expulsion of the most prominent Indo-Trinidadian leaders from the NAR an intense sense of disillusionment swept across the Indo-Trinidadian population. Indo-Trinidadians were once again relegated to their traditional seat in the opposition. It seemed as if they would remain second-class citizens as long as they were kept out of the decision-making process.

6. On the demise of the NAR, see Ryan 1989b.

The Indo-Trinidadian struggle for state power must be understood within this context. Similarly, their efforts to renovate a Trinidadian national identity that recognizes their ethnicity must be seen as part of this struggle for state power. As an "ethnic minority" they lack a legitimate basis from which to secure state control. Because the traditional culture history referent for the nation has functioned to exclude them as legitimate contenders for state power, Indo-Trinidadian leaders seek to redefine the nation. Such a project, in turn, involves the deployment of a different culture history as a legitimate referent for the nation, a culture history that is inclusive of Indo-Trinidadians. Thus they aggressively challenge any traditional representation of the Trinidadian nation that alienates them. This has led to the contemporary Indo-Trinidadian challenge to Afro-Trinidadian cultural hegemony.

[9]

Redefining the National Image

The question of national identity became paramount in the late 1980s and early 1990s in Trinidad, and the most vociferous participants in this debate were segments of the Indo-Trinidadian population. The principal allegation directed at the predominantly Afro-Trinidadian–dominated government, the National Alliance for Reconstruction, was the cultural and political marginalization of Indo-Trinidadians. This is not to say that material interests did not figure prominently in the crisis; nonetheless, the contestation by Indo-Trinidadians of what they perceived to be Afro-Trinidadian cultural and political hegemony heralded a significant change in tone from earlier forms of Indo-Trinidadian protest: they were challenging a domain previously considered incontestable, namely, the privilege of "nativeness" accorded Afro-Trinidadians as natural right. As we have seen, this privilege had historically legitimized Afro-Trinidadian claims on the state even before independence in 1962. Indo-Trinidadians' bids for the state, in contrast, have been impeded by their symbolic representation as outsiders in the nation of Trinidad and Tobago.[1] Indo-Trinidadian political parties from their very inception have been traditionally perceived by the wider society as representing not just communal Indo-Trinidadian interests but specifically those of Hindus. Even during the period 1989–90, when much of the research for this book was conducted, the political mood of the country dictated that an Indo-Trinida-

1. This outsider status is particularly evident in Afro-Trinidadian political rhetoric that suggests sectional interests would threaten national interests if Indo-Trinidadians assumed leadership of the country. See La Guerre 1991:106–7.

dian as prime minister of Trinidad and Tobago was "unthinkable."² Indo-Trinidadian attempts at redefining national culture and identity were integrally linked to the creation of a national image that could facilitate the previously unthinkable—acquisition of state power in a nation long perceived as Afro-Caribbean.

Indo-Trinidadian protests of discrimination and alienation intensified in the 1980s, a period marked by the consolidation of Indo-Trinidadian social mobility, increased cultural expression, and a historically unparalleled display of Indo-Trinidadian confidence in the political arena. Factors enumerated in the last chapter—the Black Power movement, the consolidation of Indo-Trinidadians' social mobility during the oil boom, the gradual erosion of their sugar base, and their brief experience of political power—provided an appropriate context for their new political outlook. The historical conjuncture that led to this burgeoning of ethnic consciousness is for the most part an enabling one. Indo-Trinidadian protest today is motivated less by discrimination and more by the realization that the legitimation of Afro-Trinidadian supremacy in government is open to challenge. The new issues were not issues before: who shall define the nation, and who shall run the state?

An October 1989 letter to the editor in one of the daily newspapers summed up the Indo-Trinidadian dilemma:

> There is, I have noticed, an attitude gaining increasing acceptance in our society, that those of African descent are somehow more Trinidadian than everyone else. As foolish as this is, it is being accepted hook, line and sinker by many. There are those also, who argue . . . that other groups must "prove" their Trinidadianness by giving up their heritage, spending all their time listening to calypsos and "carnivalising" everything they do, even religiously significant events, and even to go to the extent of wholesale intermarriage, as though this were some cure. (*Trinidad Guardian*, October 18, 1989)

Through their cultural and political activity Indo-Trinidadian leaders and practitioners of knowledge challenged the notion that their ethnic identity was necessarily antithetical to their national identity.³ They sought to change the culture history referent of the national image so that East Indian ele-

2. Accounting for the PNM's longevity, Ryan, for example, points to the inability of the opposition to produce a leader who was "sociologically acceptable" (1989b:3). The ambiguous phrasing is telling.

3. Indo-Trinidadians actively involved in the contemporary struggle seem to be of the upper and lower middle classes, their occupations ranging from lawyers, engineers, university professors, school teachers, journalists, and small businessmen to religious leaders. Activist networks also included grass-roots youth organizations in the countryside.

ments would be included along with the hegemonic Afro-Caribbean elements. They aimed to become a legitimate part of the nation not by redefining what it means to be *Indian* but by redefining what it means to be *Trinidadian*.[4] Despite this seemingly radical stance, the assumptions underlying the strategy reproduced, rather than challenged, colonial discourses about the nature of African and Indian culture. The solution adopted to resolve the Indo-Trinidadian identity problem rested on a premise that resonated with earlier colonial discourses positing an essential difference between East Indian and Creole cultures and their corollary identities. Hence the preferred solution called for equal representation of heterogeneous elements at the national level, as opposed to stressing a common core of creolized Caribbean values and orientations. By opting for a "tossed salad" as opposed to a "callaloo" image of the nation, the Indo-Trinidadian strategy sought to displace the creole nationalist narrative of mixture with the plural and cosmopolitan narrative. Such a strategy is understandable since it is precisely the creole narrative, which denies symbolic recognition of Indo-Trinidadian mixture, that has historically positioned Indo-Trinidadians outside the nation.

Specific moments and events in Trinidad encapsulate the dual processes of delegitimation (of Afro-Trinidadian hegemony) and renovation of the national image. The forums in which these national questions were debated—newspapers, journals representing diverse (ethnic and religious) constituencies, public seminars, and cultural events—point to the cultivation of what could be labeled a public sphere during this period. Yet contrary to Jürgen Habermas (1989), this public discursive realm was not determined solely on the merits of rational critical debate in which the identities of the participants/arguers were inconsequential (Calhoun 1994:2). Rather, the identities of the arguers were crucial in determining the tenor of the public debate. In addition, some of the forums/events were formally sponsored by the state (even if what was said went against the state's agenda) and clearly bore the imprint of staged events. But since a fundamental criterion for Habermas for the existence of a public sphere was also the "quantity of, or openness to, popular participation" (Calhoun 1994:4), I suggest that these events created a public space for Trinidadians to engage in open debate about the nature of their society and the symbolic relation of its citizenry to the nation-state. These occasions, which elicited much national controversy during the period of my fieldwork (1989–90), involved the intermeshing of political, academic, and lay discourses and indicated the emergence of a novel political climate in

4. In this chapter I use the term *Indian* in addition to *East Indian* as an emic category to refer to popular conceptions of Indians as a particular type both inside and outside the Caribbean context.

Trinidad. Despite the accusations hurled at the then-reigning political party, the NAR, it is important to remember that it was the very ascent of the "One Love" party with its promise of equity for all races and creeds that made it possible to challenge formerly incontestable issues. Indo-Trinidadian leaders were struggling to unearth what they perceived to be the racist underpinnings of their society, which they claimed consistently privileged Afro-Trinidadians. This struggle in turn fostered a frenzied political climate in which the race paradigm was used to interpret every facet of Trinidadian life, from the most controversial to the most prosaic.

Contesting the Nation

Bacchanal at City Hall

In October 1989 I went to hear a lecture titled "The History, Life, and Contribution to the Development of Trinidad and Tobago of East Indians," delivered by a prominent Indo-Trinidadian lawyer, Suren Capildeo (nephew of the former DLP leader Dr. Rudranath Capildeo and cousin of V. S. Naipaul). It was the fifth in a series of lectures called "Let Us Discover Ourselves," sponsored by the government to commemorate the five hundredth anniversary of Columbus's arrival in the New World. The previous four lectures, which related in turn the experiences of Amerindians, Syrian-Lebanese, Chinese, and Europeans, had been uneventful and received perfunctory write-ups in the newspapers. The events of that fifth lecture, however, took a dramatic turn. Rhetoric about Trinidad race relations exploded, both in the media and in private social circles. Papers ran headlines such as "Bacchanal at City Hall" and chided Trinidadians editorially for their unseemly behavior. When some realized that I witnessed the whole affair, they urged me to relate the story and even borrowed my tape recording to figure out "what all de fuss was about."

The "fuss" actually began with a warning:

The regulars, let me caution you, this is not the usual lecture you have heard. This is a horror story. . . . Now let us consider, you and I, the Indian. An extraordinary specimen of the species *Homo sapiens*. A remarkable survivor. You are looking at one, a real true, true Indian. Indians have been on this planet earth for a very long time. Whatever the period, my past, the Indian past, is as they say shrouded in the mists of antiquity. *We are like no other race. We are different. Indians are a world unto themselves. We regard ourselves as the eternal people. Our religion is the eternal religion. We have been witness to a continuous unbroken thread of Indian civilization which began before the*

[249]

memory of man. We have customs, we recite prayers, we do things Indian, as our ancestors have done thousands of years before, you say, Christ set foot on this earth. So when you look at an Indian, in Trinidad, or wherever, you just remember that. An Indian is no ordinary being. He belongs to a special race. Indians have to be honest with themselves to understand and admit that while the boast of continuity in civilization is permissible, what cannot also be forgotten and/or hidden is that *no other subcontinent in the world has been subjected to such continuous and victorious invasions. The history of the Indian subcontinent is the history of all conquering invaders.*[5]

Capildeo depicted the history of his people as marked by waves of conquering invaders beginning with the Greeks and culminating with the British. But despite this history of victimization, he declared:

The Indian mind does not submit to slavery. You cannot enslave the Indian mind. . . . That is our legacy. That is our heritage. Indians do not seek refuge behind the skirts of indentureship. That is history. History has its lessons. But we must learn and move on. The Indian experience is not to blame the *arkatiah* [recruiter of indentured workers] and the empire. It is to absorb, assimilate, and create.

Capildeo then declared how it was the Indian who saved Trinidad from impending ruin after emancipation when Europe, America, and Africa failed to rescue the country. He emphasized the hardship, ridicule, and discrimination the Indians suffered. Yet despite their appalling conditions of existence, within thirty years of their arrival the Indians began to show signs of consolidation, both culturally and economically. Not only were they sending money back home, but since 1869 many Indians had begun accepting grants of crown land in lieu of return passage under the new law, so that by the end of 1878 they had bought nearly one thousand acres of land. Capildeo then talked of East Indian achievements and contributions to agriculture:

The Indians then began to change the face of this land. Defying all efforts to confine them to the cane estates, Indians began in true frontier style to open up areas of Trinidad. . . . By the time immigration ended [in 1917], Indians in Trinidad owned one-fifth of the total land cultivated in Trinidad. An extraordinary feat, remarkable more so when you realize that chattel who were imported to plant cane ended up by being landowning cane farmers themselves.

5. The excerpts presented here are from my own recording; the transcript of the entire speech can be found in Siewah 1994.

At this point the speaker went into his own family history. His grandfather, like most Indians in Trinidad, had built their family home brick by brick.[6] Capildeo spoke of Brahmin traditions and showed slides of early Indian immigrants whose stature, adornments, and poise was meant to question explicitly the common image of the indentured laborer as the barefoot, meagerly clad, illiterate "coolie." The speech moved back and forth between the two themes of inherent Indian virtues and the contributions of Indians to Trinidad:

> Above all the Indians had brought with them the stabilizing factors of a strong family system, thrift, a penchant for savings, and an enthusiasm for hard work and burning zeal for education. The Indians have not only rescued Trinidad in no uncertain manner but have laid the foundation for its transition into a modern model nation-state.

Having worked his audience into a frenzy, toward the end Capildeo referred to the increasing alienation and frustration experienced by Indians in Trinidad:

> The Indian community is on the boil. . . . Throughout the tenure of his history here, the Indian has been made to feel alienated, that he does not belong. . . . That this is a Black country for the Black Caribbean man. *God knows how much longer it will take to accept us as part of this nation.* . . . By 1990 there will be an Indian majority in this nation still believing and behaving as a minority. If you want to dramatically consider the impact that the Indians have on this country, just imagine the scenario if the Indians were to cease all criminal activity, drug related and otherwise, withdraw their money from the banks, cease doing business, leave the fields, stop producing food and dairy products, withdraw from all services. . . . Imagine the country then—top heavy with Central Bank and statutory bodies; filled with form but empty of substance. Law and order will collapse. Bankruptcy will be the norm. Starvation will be your daily wage. Life here will cease.

The implicit threat was clear enough, but the orator quickly offered his alternative to this gloomy scenario:

> But really, seriously, what of the future? I, me, make bold to say that it shall be a great and glorious future. That given an equal chance the Indian community will take this country to heights unimagined.

6. Incidentally, this is the famous Lion House depicted in Naipaul's *A House for Mr. Biswas* (1961).

At the end of his oration Capildeo received thunderous applause from the predominantly Indo-Trinidadian audience, which had quickly realized that he was making a significant deviation from what the establishment had in mind when it sponsored this series of talks. The atmosphere was at once electrifying and tense, punctuated only by the comic relief supplied by Trinidadians' love for picong.[7] The "bacchanal" erupted during question time. People representing diverse ancestries of the much-celebrated Trinidadian "rainbow"—African, East Indian, Chinese, mixed—all queued up, patiently awaiting their turn, and many pointed to the bias inherent in Capildeo's talk, even Indo-Trinidadians. The turning point came when one member of the audience, an Afro-Trinidadian political scientist, broke out into a lengthy speech accusing Capildeo of racism. The challenger put forward an alternative view of Trinidad history:

> Mr. Capildeo, I am here tonight as an anti-racist. I'm afraid I must be quite blunt in telling you that you did not speak as an anti-racist. . . . Now, the main theme of your lecture is that Indian indentured labour saved Trinidad. Well, you know, I think that you said that we do not know our history. One of the things that I am currently doing in this country is to bring our people more in tune with the history. And if you knew your history, you would know that evidence before the 1897 (Royal West Indian Commission) clearly stated that what indentured labour had done was to delay the progress of Trinidad and Tobago. I will tell you why. Because by continuing a plantation system based on manual labour, we were unable to develop a mechanized system. (in Siewah 1994:266–67)

Capildeo supporters sprang to their feet and grabbed the microphone from the speaker. All hell broke loose, and the evening was brought to an abrupt end.

This event provides an appropriate point of entry to unravel the dynamics of the political and cultural struggle waged by Indo-Trinidadians to reconfigure the imagined community of the Trinidadian nation. Capildeo's rhetorical strategy was to identify Indo-Trinidadians as the propellers behind the modern nation-state by anchoring Indo-Trinidadian contributions to the nation in "Indian" culture. Such a rhetorical move sought to undermine the projected dichotomy between Indian ethnic and Trinidadian national identities by placing the very particularism attributed to East Indian culture at the core of the nation.

---

7. A Creole style of speech conveying satire and irreverence, expressive of an attitude that refuses to be impressed by anything or anybody.

Capildeo's depiction of the Indo-Trinidadian saga furnished a spectacular myth for his people. It incorporated all the essential ingredients of a nation-building charter such as the claim to belong to a pure ancestral race, the eternal people—hence his proclamation "you are looking at a true, true Indian." Capildeo's portrayal of the Indian as a unique species, the carrier of an ancient, rich, and essential culture, was an overt effort to create myths of homogeneity out of the realities of heterogeneity, that is, the class, caste, and religious cleavages differentiating the Indo-Trinidadian population. Capildeo also sought to deny the assimilability of the "Indian," thereby challenging the state and the nation to recognize the immutable fact of difference, a necessary ingredient for the realization of the Indo-Trinidadian vision of a plural nation. He exalted the great civilization of India and attempted to undermine the popular notion that only the dregs of Indian society set sail for Trinidad.

Yet if this was all his speech had said, the bacchanal would probably not have erupted. Capildeo tacitly juxtaposed the Indo-Trinidadians' story to the Afro-Trinidadians' story. The Afro-Trinidadians composed the invisible other that Capildeo implicitly engaged in dialogue. His caricatures of both groups drew substantially from the stereotypes that emerged during the early indenture period. Consider, for example, his characterization of East Indians as "pioneer" cultivators. Even though land policies that combined local government and planter interests were instrumental in the ultimate consolidation of Indo-Trinidadians in the rural sector and the Afro-Trinidadians in the urban centers, Capildeo chose to underplay this fact and instead evoked a "natural will" type of explanation to account for Indo-Trinidadian dominance of the agricultural sector. Indo-Trinidadians today highlight this contribution to Trinidad agriculture as a measure of their superior worth as citizens. Some Afro-Trinidadians resent this image of Indo-Trinidadian as cultivator because it diminishes their own contribution to Trinidadian society, both before and after indenture. After all, to assert a greater contribution to national development is also to stake a claim for the nation's patrimony (see B. F. Williams 1989; Maurer 1997:112–17). Indo-Trinidadian claims of saving the colony from ruin and of becoming the primary food producers of the nation constitute a major point of contention, as clearly shown by the outrage greeting the counterclaim that Indo-Trinidadians may have retarded the progress of the country.

Another pervasive stereotype that emerged during indenture is the image of the hard-working, thrifty, self-sacrificing East Indian. This stereotype reinforces alleged differences in "mentality" between the Africans and East Indians. Consider Brereton's characterization of the Black population's attitude toward East Indians during the colonial period:

Thrift, with them [the Indian], seemed like a vice. The first generation of Indians especially was single-minded in its determination to save its miserable wages, even if it meant inadequate food or clothing. This contrasted with the working-class African, famous for his love of spending money lavishly on drink, food, clothes or fete. The African, especially the Trinidad African, took clothes seriously. How easy, then, to laugh at the male Indian in his "loin cloth." He was too mean to dress decently, too uncivilized to dress in a Christian fashion. (1985:29)

Even today these caricatures abound. As shown in Chapter 5, however, Indo-Trinidadians easily transform these same traits into positive evaluations of themselves. Curlie, the fifty-year-old Indo-Trinidadian cane cutter, explained the difference to me: "Indians, dey always progressive, dey wok for a little money, whatever dey wok for dey always put away a little, and the Negroes, whatever dey wok for dey will eat up everyting because dey want nice food, dey want woman, you understand . . . dey want to do all kind of ting with deir money."

Although Indo-Trinidadians' capacity for hard work and thrift is thought to be an undisputed fact by the population at large, these very characteristics are available for diverse interpretations. As Brereton points out, some Afro-Trinidadians tend to perceive hard work and thrift not as virtues but as obstacles to enjoying the "good life," the fruits of civilization. Similar sentiments are increasingly expressed by Indo-Trinidadian youths who loathe the older generation's insistence on frugality and modest living. Some Indo-Trinidadian men also lamented to me that "these days Indian girls prefer the Negro fellows because they spend money on them." Yet other Afro-Trinidadians admire these perceived innate characteristics of Indo-Trinidadians and hope that their people will benefit from the Indo-Trinidadian example.[8] Mr. Merritt, the Afro-Trinidadian insurance salesman referred to in Chapter 5, related the following story. His wife goes to a class in Port-of-Spain which is attended mostly by Afro-Trinidadians. The teacher also conducts classes in Curepe, where the student body is primarily Indo-Trinidadian. When the teacher on one occasion asked the students in Port-of-Spain for their class assignments, "Everybody gave excuse—no time, had to do this, was not well etc." The teacher reprimanded the students by saying that she had just returned from Curepe, where "every one of them had done their work," the "them" here referring to Indo-Trinidadians. The message was clear: unless

8. The change in Afro-Trinidadians' perception of Indo-Trinidadians—from pariahs to saviors, from comic figures to admired group—is wonderfully documented by Trotman (1989) in his analysis of calypsos.

Afro-Trinidadians make a conscious effort to improve themselves, the Indo-Trinidadians will soon overtake them. After relating this story, Mr. Merritt stated that "feelings and convictions like this, regarding the nature of the other race, are deeply entrenched here [pointing to his heart] and there is nothing you can do about it." This image has also contributed to Afro-Trinidadians' apprehensions about an Indo-Trinidadian "takeover."[9] Underscoring this point, a young Indo-Trinidadian political activist told me that the "Indian" mentality, unlike the African, will never be satisfied with just a piece of the pie.

Capildeo drew on many of these popular stereotypes that essentialize Indian and African mentalities and behaviors to challenge Afro-Trinidadian conceptions of the legitimate social order and of "true" members of the ideologically defined nation. He trivialized the Afro-Trinidadian story and created a particular kind of moral discourse. Capildeo's strategy moved beyond the mere disclosure of difference to establish commonalities with the Afro-Trinidadian experience, though indirectly. His glorification of the Indian race was immediately followed by the disclosure of the suffering that Indians had endured under conquering invaders. Capildeo spent a considerable amount of time highlighting the plight of the Indian as victim, both in India (as a result of the invasions) and in Trinidad. He depicted poignantly the hardships the Indians suffered in developing Trinidad, claiming that "the life blood of this nation pulses through the Indian." He was thus attesting to the fact that Indians, too, have "bled for the nation." Such discursive strategies provided the necessary moral capital for claiming a stake in the nation. The need to build moral capital is all the more urgent for Indo-Trinidadians because Afro-Trinidadians have owned the title of victims par excellence for so long. The emphasis on Indian suffering sought to undermine the notion that victim status was exclusively an Afro-Trinidadian privilege.

The discourse on suffering, however, also implicated difference. Capildeo cleverly counterposed his illustrations of Indian suffering to East Indian contributions to the nation. This mix challenged or at least minimized Afro-Trinidadian suffering and contributions. For example, though he did not explicitly deny Afro-Trinidadian contributions to agriculture, he privileged Indo-Trinidadian contributions by arguing that despite structural limitations (that is, ordinances confining East Indians to plantations), Indo-Trinidadians pursued cultivation in frontier style until they had managed to transform themselves from "those who were imported to plant cane [to] . . . landowning cane farmers."

The strategic association of suffering with contribution relied on the com-

9. See, for example, La Guerre 1991.

mon belief that Afro-Trinidadians continually used the excuse of slavery (suffering) for their alleged failures. More important, it was meant to undermine the other popular belief that Afro-Trinidadians were "owed" rewards for their historical subjugation. After all, Capildeo asserted, Indo-Trinidadians had managed to secure and preserve substantial gains in the new society despite their suffering. Though Indo-Trinidadians too had suffered, they were able to make a positive contribution to the nation, without using their suffering as an excuse, because of innate Indian characteristics: "Indians do not seek refuge behind the skirts of indentureship. That is history. We must learn and move on." The moral discourse operated to forge links with Afro-Trinidadians through the trope of suffering at the same time as it established distance through the trope of material success. In this way Capildeo gained the upper hand on the issue of moral capital, that is, on which group suffered most *and* contributed most to the nation. Such an annexation was crucial since even Indo-Trinidadians would be hesitant to claim greater suffering in comparison with those enslaved.

The zeal with which Capildeo portrayed Indo-Trinidadian contributions and suffering was a direct challenge to the predominant Afro-Caribbean ideology of racial paramountcy, which dictates that those of African descent have the moral right to rule because none has suffered for or contributed as much to the nation as their race. Direct attacks on the invisible other were encoded in comments such as "the Indian mind does not submit to slavery" or "Indians do not hide behind the skirts of indenture," or in his depiction of the possible scenario in Trinidad if all the Indians were to leave. All these points gained weight from deeply entrenched negative stereotypes of the Africans as a fun-loving, free-spending, irresponsible, crime-oriented, non-productive people with an extractive mentality, who continually used the historical excuse of slavery to secure prizes they never earned. In this way Capildeo sought to assert not only that Indo-Trinidadians deserve to represent the nation but that, if given a chance, their representation would be superior.

The Indo-Trinidadian struggle to renovate their national identity reveals features of the nation-building process. But the idiosyncrasies of this case also suggest a new dimension to interethnic relations in the context of the nation-state, namely, a breakdown in hegemony that enables a subnational group to challenge the traditional position of a national group.

For Brackette F. Williams the interpenetration of race, class, and culture in nation-states constitutes the nexus in which the relation between ethnicity and nationalism is articulated: "As nation builders, myth makers become race-makers," she argues (1989:430). Moral, social, symbolic, and intellectual characteristics, ascribed to real or invented phenotypical features, are used to justify the institutional dominance of one population over others. Attributing cultural propensities to phenotypical features "makes of race an embodiment of culture" (1989:430). B. F. Williams then quotes Wyndham Lewis: "The classes that have been parasitic on other classes have always in the past been races. The class-privilege has been a race-privilege" (1989:433). Since race purity can be linked to concerns about material issues that underlie both state formation and class stratification, culture becomes a fundamental mechanism of state control whereby the privileged race and class selectively determines the ruling cultural ensemble of civil society.

This concept of the state-backed race/class/nation exemplifies the nation-building process begun by the PNM. State appropriation by middle-class Creoles was legitimated by identifying the nation of Trinidad with those of African descent and "their" Creole culture. The consolidation of this group's invisibility led to the definition of their respective members as the real producers of the nation's patrimony while marginalizing other groups under the rubric of ethnics. To be legitimate, national representations of societies deemed heterogeneous need either to be genuinely pluralistic in their expressions—and thereby accept projected difference as a cardinal principle configuring the nation—or to encode features that are purported to be shared by all heterogeneous elements. This latter strategy, a common feature of real (as opposed to ideal) situations for emerging nations, involves processes aimed at creating homogeneity out of heterogeneity. The assimilation of heterogeneous features in creating this homogeneity, however, gives rise to a selective process of appropriation that devalues or denies the link between the selected appropriations (now elevated to national symbols) and the contributions of marginalized others to the nation's patrimony (B. F. Williams 1989). In Trinidad the process of selective appropriation is illustrated by Eric Williams's definition of his public as a people subjugated in the West Indies and not as carriers of an ancient civilization, or by the elevation of carnival, steelband, and calypso to the status of national symbols. Groups lying outside the ideologically defined nation were put at a considerable pragmatic and ideological disadvantage. Even though Indo-Trinidadians were also a subjugated group in the West Indies, and despite the dissemination of Indo-Trinidadian cultural elements into "Creole" cultural forms, these selected criteria epitomized the Afro-Trinidadian condition, leaving the Indo-Trinidadians unacknowledged.

The struggle of ethnic groups, which by definition lie outside the ideologically defined nation, to situate themselves positively against the national unit vis-à-vis one another may capture the essence of interethnic group relations in most instances. The contemporary Trinidadian case, however, pushes Brackette Williams's argument further. In her analysis the state-backed race/class/nation constitutes the total system of stratification in which ethnic identity formations must be understood, that is, the construction of subnational boundaries occurs against this nationally legitimate unit. This in turn implies a tacit acceptance by the subnational groups of the dominant ideological precepts that underlie the nation as defined by those who come to metonymize the nation, the elite members of the race/class/culture/nation unit. The latter group constitutes the invisible other against whom the visibility and worth of ethnic groups are measured.

Although this system may accurately depict the "normal" state of affairs, when hegemony can be said to be functioning "smoothly," in Trinidad it was the very legitimacy of the state-backed race/class/culture/nation that was being questioned. The struggle in Trinidad involved not two subnational ethnic groups but a subnational group (Indo-Trinidadians) and an invisible ethnic group that has constituted the state-backed race/class/culture/nation segment from the time of independence in 1962 (Afro-Trinidadians). In the Trinidadian case the ethnic underpinning of a ruling group, which became ethnically invisible as a consequence of its claims to represent mainstream national culture, was gradually forced into visibility and its basis for authority undermined. Capildeo's speech was not aimed at positioning the Indo-Trinidadians positively against a legitimate national unit; rather, Indo-Trinidadian claims to the nation's patrimony were powerfully juxtaposed to rhetoric targeted at delegitimizing the ideologically defined nation, directly challenging Afro-Trinidadian control over the state. Moments such as the one described here, I suspect, were instrumental in the cultivation of an appropriate ideological and political climate for easing the transition of power to Indo-Trinidadians some years later. To what extent their political victory signals their symbolic arrival as legitimate Trinidadian nationals is yet to be determined, however.

Looking back at the dynamics that unfolded during the course of that evening, I couldn't help but notice a certain irony. Despite Capildeo's and his supporters' claims that Indians are essentially different from other races, the fiasco at City Hall, with its impassioned verbal exchanges, wit, and humor, served to underscore the extent of creolization experienced by the Indo-Trinidadian population. Bear in mind that of the approximately five hundred people in the audience, around four hundred appeared to be Indo-Trinidadian. One member of the audience later wrote perceptively: "I have always held the view that Suren Capildeo and others of his ilk were not Trinidadians. I believed that they were Indians masquerading as Trinidadians. The opposite is true. They are Trinidadians, one hundred plus one and a half percent, masquerading as Indians" (*Trinidad Guardian*, November 1, 1989).

This assessment of the Indo-Trinidadians' predicament inadvertently undermines the projected dichotomy between East Indian and Trinidadian. The point is not even that Indo-Trinidadians are Trinidadians masquerading as Indians, as the commentator claims; rather, to be Indo-Trinidadian is to be irrevocably both Indian and Trinidadian. In other words, to be Indian in Trinidad—what it means to be ethnic in practice—is also to be Indian in an unmistakably Trinidadian fashion. To claim an Indian purity or essence, as Capildeo did, or to regard Indian dispositions as falsities, as the commentator implies, denies the very existential basis for Indo-Trinidadian identity, which intertwines both facets. Yet the fact remains that Capildeo chose to downplay the creoleness of Indo-Trinidadians, emphasizing instead the difference between Indo-Trinidadians and Afro-Trinidadians. Such a stance was symptomatic of the dominant strategy employed by Indo-Trinidadian elites during this period and earlier, in the transition to independence. The significant difference of the contemporary strategy was the challenge to the mutual exclusivity implied by the dichotomy between Trinidadian and East Indian. Unlike their earlier counterparts, who hesitated to venture into the symbolic space of the nation even as they made bids for the state, contemporary Indo-Trinidadians aim at precisely such a space.

Challenges to the Afro-Caribbean Paradigm

Earlier I illustrated how the nation-building agenda begun by Eric Williams was predicated on the legacies of colonialism and slavery. Redemption for the Black masses meant confronting these two legacies directly. Through Williams's efforts, academic discourses on the colonial condition entered into popular consciousness, thereby linking the political struggle for independence with an intellectual or "scientific" evaluation of the Caribbean predicament. This paradigm, then predominant in the region, conveniently legitimated Afro-Caribbean racial paramountcy. Accordingly, challenges to Afro-Caribbean racial paramountcy necessarily called for a reinterpretation of the nature of Caribbean societies in general. This challenge was launched not only by Indo-Trinidadians but also by those Trinidadians of European ancestry who sought to capitalize on the political momentum afforded by the Indo-Trinidadian intervention.

From the Indo-Trinidadian perspective Afro-Trinidadian intellectuals' repeated insistence on the importance of the colonial legacy for understanding Trinidad's present dislocations is yet another excuse for not taking responsibility for Afro-Trinidadians' own incompetence and racist practices. Thus the majority of Indo-Trinidadians (and Whites) often assert, "Blacks blame everything on the white man, including the genesis of racism," as in this letter to the editor:

In this country the concept of colonialism is far more often used as an excuse rather than a reason, to explain the way things are as they are today. An effort [*sic*] of plantation psychology? I don't think so. While slavery existed here, it was not exclusive to the West Indies. Equally heinous forms of bondage and serfdom existed in Russia, as it did at various times among Muslims, Romans, Chinese, Japanese and Western Europeans to name a few. Or how many recalled . . . that at first it was the African who sold his brother to slavery? Why don't the "thinkers" also focus on the atrocities perpetrated by black leaders in African states, rather than only keeping telescopes and magnifying glasses trained on South Africa? (*Trinidad Guardian*, October 18, 1989)

A Trinidadian journalist claiming European ancestry took offense at the protest over the celebration of Columbus's Arrival Day (voiced mainly by Afro-Trinidadians) and expressed similar sentiments:

As a Trinidadian of European ancestry, I have had more than my fill of hearing about the cruelty and inhumanity of my forebears, and their ruthless oppression of the Noble Savage on every continent other than their own. . . . Genocide, oppression, slavery—and even a form of colonization—were no strangers to pre-Columbian America. Nor were they imported from Europe. However, no single event in history has done more to besmirch the Europeans in the New World than their enslavement of Africans. . . . Descendants of African slaves born four generations outside of slavery still cling to the feeling that they should be compensated for the suffering of their forefathers by the descendants of the European slave master. Over the past several decades in Trinidad there has been a conscious suppression of the recognition of any contribution to nation-building that could be perceived as European in origin. A corresponding move to elevate all things African in origin has resulted in the widespread Africanisation of every aspect of our nationhood-from our culture and history, to our perception of ourselves as a "Black Country."

This is seen by many as the reparation owing to the "sons and daughters of African slaves." (*Trinidad Guardian*, September 28, 1989)

Both commentators accuse Afro-Trinidadian "thinkers" of privileging one history at the expense of others. Herein lies a chief reason why Indo-Trinidadians and White Trinidadians are able to empathize with each other despite their vastly divergent histories; both perceive themselves as victims of Afro-Caribbean political hegemony. Some Indo-Trinidadian leaders, in private, even expressed sympathy for the Whites in Trinidad because the Whites, they claim, are even more marginalized than the Indo-Trinidadians. Held moral hostages, the Whites are said to be fearful of rocking the boat, especially since they have financial interests at stake.

It is plausible to suggest that the empathy Indo-Trinidadians feel toward the White population is to some degree bolstered by their partial acceptance of the notion of white superiority, which prevailed, as we have seen, among villagers in Cambio. It was for the most part Afro-Trinidadians and not Indo-Trinidadians who challenged European hegemony during both independence and the Black Power agitation. Historically, Indo-Trinidadians as a collectivity, as opposed to a few individuals who identified with the Afro-Caribbean struggles, rarely if ever overtly defied European dominance.[10] The Afro-Trinidadian has always been the traditional adversary of the Indo-Trinidadian. Thus whereas Indo-Trinidadians continuously challenge Afro-Caribbean forms of domination, European forms are rarely questioned. This is largely a consequence of the colonial hierarchy that positioned groups unequally according to their purported proximity to Whites. As we saw in Chapter 5, even radical Indo-Trinidadian leaders such as F. E. M. Hosein sought to elevate their group relative to those of African descent by annexing Indians to the European through the Aryan connection. Hosein clearly attempted to reconfigure the ideological underpinnings of Trinidad's racial hierarchy by appealing to what he believed to be the scientifically established "universal racial hierarchy." Since this ranking of races was itself a European invention, however, Hosein's attempts only perpetuate European ideologies of race. He thus goes full circle. As a result, the only avenue available for ennobling the Indian race is to annex it to Europe.

Since even now Indo-Trinidadians' sense of worth continues to be partly measured in terms of their purported proximity to Europeans, notions of White superiority sometimes extend into statements about the superior capacity of Whites to rule. Two incidents in particular come to mind, both related to the Chaguaramas Convention, where the Indo-Trinidadian–backed party, the United National Congress, was formally launched in July 1990. My husband, a White American, and I were standing outside the hall during an interval when a drunken Indo-Trinidadian youth approached us menacingly and proceeded to accuse my husband of being a CIA agent. The youth belonged, we suspect, to one of the informal rural Indo-Trinidadian youth organizations that are affiliated to radical Indo-Trinidadian activist groups. Later, when things had calmed down a little, one of his friends approached us, apologized on his behalf, and confided, "Just between you and me, we believe that a White man is more capable to rule this country than either a Black or Indian."

10. This is not to say that Indo-Trinidadians always accepted colonial domination passively. The Hosay protests of 1884 (Singh 1988) clearly indicate the contrary. Haraksingh (1981) has also pointed to patterns of resistance among Indian workers in sugar plantations. Yet these forms of resistance did not challenge the overall structure of colonial domination.

Indo-Trinidadian intellectuals who sought to explain the failure of a promi-nent White politician to be nominated as deputy leader of the party during the same convention reiterated this sentiment. In the months leading up to the convention John Humphrey, a White Trinidadian who had a long history in labor politics and who was dearly loved by many Indo-Trinidadians, shocked many Indo-Trinidadians and caused disarray in the party when he suddenly accused the UNC leadership of racism. This action immediately caused Humphrey's political downfall, as it was widely interpreted by Indo-Trinidadians as a direct breach of loyalty to the party leader, Panday. Until this moment Humphrey's nomination for deputy leader had been literally guaran-teed, and the elections during the convention were perceived as merely a for-mality. But because of his breach of political etiquette, Humphrey lost the nomination to a virtually unknown Indo-Trinidadian. According to some Indo-Trinidadian intellectuals, Humphrey made a gross miscalculation in thinking he would not be elected on the basis of his ancestry.[11] As these intel-lectuals explained it, contrary to Humphrey's anxiety, many East Indians would have voted for him precisely because he was White, since they believe that White men are the most capable rulers. Humphrey lost in the last in-stance not because of his ancestry but because of his perceived irresponsible conduct, and because, as some Indo-Trinidadians said, he had to be taught a lesson.

It is important to note, however, that there are a few Indo-Trinidadians who believe that their rightful place is alongside their Afro-Trinidadian brethren in the fight against European domination. For them indenture and slavery rep-resented the same subjugation. In an article denouncing "those local racists" who are only serving to enhance White domination, an Indo-Trinidadian wrote:

> They may not admit it but people like Suren Capildeo, Sat Mahraj [president of the Maha Sabha] . . . and the likes are playing right into the hands of those who push the European domination concept. . . . For most Europeans, Indians and Africans are in the same boat; they were both used for the same purpose. Whether it was slavery or indentureship, for the Europeans it meant the same thing. It is only small-minded idiots who would believe that there was a differ-ence in the colonization of both peoples in the West Indies. For Europe it was pure and simple an economic matter. . . . All battles being raged between local Indians and Africans are only strengthening the plans of those who seek white domination. Viewed at this macro-perspective level, the so-called "struggle" of

11. Although there was some speculation that internal party politics justified Humphrey's ac-cusations, the popular interpretation was that Humphrey panicked in the last instance, thinking he would not be elected because he was White. See also Ryan 1996:chap. 9.

local racists can only be seen as trivial bickering. (*TnT Mirror*, October 27, 1989, 37)

Thus this Indo-Trinidadian, in contrast to many others, sought not only to equate slavery with indenture but also to locate those of European ancestry as the real "other."

Prominent Indo-Trinidadians are often distinguished on the basis of whether they are "technocrats"[12] or a "person of the masses." The technocrats are those Indo-Trinidadian intellectuals who have risen to national status and who project a national/universalist perspective, as opposed to leaders such as Panday or Capildeo, who are seen exclusively as projecting an Indo-Trinidadian point of view.[13] From the perspective of lay Indo-Trinidadians technocrats are rarely seen as "their" leaders. Either they are cast as mere tokens exploited by the government to project an image of racial tolerance or, even more interestingly, they are perceived as "de-ethnicized" individuals who do not represent an Indo-Trinidadian voice. A respected Indo-Trinidadian scholar who holds such a technocratic viewpoint observed:

There is now a preoccupation with race as a topic in a manner that has not been experienced before. Thirty years ago such a topic would have been discussed in the context of the fear of one group seizing political power in preference to another. Today it is discussed in the context of pride with fair doses of arrogance injected. This can be extremely dangerous in the society of today where antagonism may be aroused. Instead of emphasizing differences, it would be much wiser to emphasize similarities. For example, African slavery and East Indian indentureship have one thing in common. They were both a crude form of eco-

12. There are technocrats in all ethnic groups in Trinidad. A Chinese-Trinidadian scholar described them as "those professional people with economic/scientific backgrounds who have national as opposed to communal interests" (Look Lai, personal communication 1989).

13. Not all leaders who espouse the popular Indo-Trinidadian perspective command the same degree of respect and legitimacy from the Indo-Trinidadian laity. For example, Panday's leadership remains undisputed especially among lower-class Indo-Trinidadians, but Capildeo is much less revered by these same people. On one occasion when Capildeo spoke in Orange Valley to commemorate Indian Arrival Day, many of the villagers present reacted with either indifference or outrage to his speech. Panday, in contrast, received a warm reception by the same audience a few hours later. It is possible that the majority of Indo-Trinidadians at this venue saw Capildeo as a newcomer with aspirations of dislodging their venerated Panday. Interestingly, many of the sentiments expressed publicly by Capildeo resonated with those espoused by these same people in private and thus their outrage might have been symptomatic of their fear that public venting of sensitive issues could lead to a racially volatile climate or outright race war. Panday remained the undisputed leader of the rural indo-Trinidadians; Capildeo was said to represent the views of conservative Indo-Trinidadian "yuppies."

nomic exploitation with the whip being operative in the former and the jail in
the latter . . . economic exploitation transcended the bounds of race. However,
ignorance has caused misunderstanding and it is that ignorance that has been
exploited by some politicians, past and present, to perpetuate divisions in the
society for their own political ends. (*Sunday Guardian*, October 29, 1989)

Among the diversity of opinions in the contemporary debate two para-
digms for interpreting the nature of Trinidadian society stand out. From the
popular Afro-Trinidadian perspective—enhanced by intellectual debates relating to colonialism and slavery—the battle against the colonial legacy continues, economically, ideologically, and culturally, despite this group's political ascendancy at independence. For Afro-Trinidadians the significant
enemies are the upholders of the residues of the old colonial order, namely
Whites. The majority of Indo-Trinidadian intellectuals and politicians, however, perceive a significant break at the time of independence, when with the
ascendancy of a system of "political negritude" they became further marginalized. For them the battle is against those who perpetuate this system. In
short, whereas Afro-Trinidadians emphasize colonial and neocolonial domination, for the Indo-Trinidadians, as Capildeo put it, "history has its lessons.
But we must learn and move on. The Indian experience is not to blame
the . . . empire."

Ironically, though Indo-Trinidadians claim that they have moved beyond
the injustices of the past, in many ways they continue to carry the ideological baggage of the colonial era. Much of the present rhetoric on race re-
volving around the stereotype of the Creole as lazy, fun-loving, "not too
bright," lacking in moral virtue, infantile, and destructive can be traced
back to the discourses created specifically by planters. Planters used such
stereotypes to create a moral discourse to forestall emancipation and later
to make their case for indentured labor. Indo-Trinidadians today find the
same ideological repertoire expedient for creating a legitimating discourse
for themselves.

"Going Refugee": The Exodus to Canada

In recent years large numbers of Indo-Trinidadians have been migrating to
Canada. Though it is clear that the lack of economic opportunity in the aftermath of the oil boom is a significant factor in this migration, some Indo-
Trinidadians attribute the exodus to the "increasing discrimination" they face
in Trinidad. Indeed, Indo-Trinidadian migration to Canada became embroiled in a debate about race and patriotism when certain Indo-Trinidadians

petitioned the Canadian government for refugee status. "Going refugee" has proved to be both a boon and a burden for Indo-Trinidadian attempts to renovate their image. On the one hand, it provides powerful testimony of their victim status to an international audience, enhancing their moral capital and buttressing their claims of suffering. On the other hand, "going refugee" tends to reinscribe the stereotype of the Indo-Trinidadian as a person disloyal to the nation of Trinidad.

According to a newspaper report more than fifteen thousand Trinidadian and Tobagonian nationals had applied for refugee status in Canada before a new system for determining such claims was put forward in January 1989 (*Trinidad Guardian*, March 5, 1990). Representatives of the government and concerned citizens were particularly outraged when in 1990 the Canadian authorities ruled that one Leela Mahabir had a "credible basis" for her claims and was granted permission to apply for permanent residence in Canada on the grounds that she was denied police protection: "Ms Mahabir testified that she had on various occasions been a victim of petty and serious crime by certain criminal elements in the society. . . . She further testified that whenever she went to the police, they ignored her, ridiculed her, and on one occasion a high-ranking officer made sexual advances towards her. On all occasions she was refused protection" (*Express*, March 7, 1990). Government officials and other opinion makers, alarmed by this ruling, feared not only that their nation's international reputation for upholding human rights would be tarnished but also that this ruling would provide an opening for other nationals to make similar claims. Even more appalling for this group were the racial overtones of the issue.

The situation was exacerbated when a prominent Indo-Trinidadian attorney and human rights activist, Ramesh Maharaj, delivered an address to the Trinidadian and Tobagonian Social and Cultural Organization in Toronto in October 1989, legitimizing the refugees' claims. According to a newspaper report Maharaj stated:

> The picture which emerges in Trinidad is a feeling of insecurity and fear. A feeling that justice would not be corrected and the perception that the state would use its machinery to take away or affect fundamental rights. This is therefore fertile ground for people having a reasonable and justifiable view that the grass would be greener elsewhere. Those who have left TT and are leaving, are all races and all walks of life. They have a credible claim for refugee status as the human rights situation in Trinidad and Tobago does not guarantee the security for the enjoyment and enforcement of rights. (quoted in *Trinidad Guardian*, October 18, 1989, 4)

Despite Maharaj's claim that all races are involved in this exodus, the popular opinion is that it is mainly Indo-Trinidadians who are seeking refugee status. The disclaimer on ethnicity could be interpreted as an instance of "double talk" because Maharaj is fully aware, as is the larger population, of the "implicational code" (Dominguez 1977) that links refugee status to Indo-Trinidadians. This comment, which sought to displace the ethnic factor and to establish legitimacy with an international audience, fell on deaf ears as far as the majority of Trinidadians were concerned. In turn, this message provided ample ammunition for Afro-Trinidadians once again to accuse Indo-Trinidadians of not having national interests at heart.

Another volatile issue in the refugee debate is the claim by some Indo-Trinidadians that they are the victims of Afro-Trinidadian criminal behavior, a contention that capitalizes on the common stereotype of the violent and destructive African. During a debate on crime held at city hall in Port-of-Spain, Dr. Eugenia Springer, a family life consultant, "sparked emotions among members of the audience by suggesting that the crime problem was linked to race, in that some 60 percent of the persons incarcerated were African" (*Trinidad Guardian*, October 18, 1989, 12). Another panelist, Dr. Geoffrey Frankson, attempted to sever the racial link to crime by suggesting that the ratio should incorporate the racial mix in urban areas where crime was more rampant. Nevertheless, what was supposed to be a discussion on crime degenerated once again to a furor over race. Describing the atmosphere in city hall, the *Mirror* reported:

> The tension continued to brew and exploded into loud mutterings and curses from the angry audience. This was further compounded with [*sic*] Rajnie Ramlachan . . . revealed that most of the crimes committed in TnT were against the Indian community. Boos greeted Rajnie's statement, and one ex-con went so far as to comment that the one thing thieves did not do was to discriminate. . . . Another East Indian also supported Rajnie's claims and emphasized that because of these crimes which were being perpetrated against East Indians, they were fleeing the country to seek refugee status elsewhere. Despite the fact that several spectators tried to make meaningful contributions . . . the entire conference seemed merely to be a parody . . . the discussion was steered to and turned into an ugly race issue. (*TnT Mirror* October 20, 1989)

This controversy highlights the pervasive tendency in Trinidad to polarize almost any issue on the basis of race. More significant, it illustrates the deployment of common stereotypes to interpret phenomena that have little to do with race. Frankson, reflecting on this debate and on Capildeo's speech, later expressed his frustration over the facile and irresponsible use of racial stereotypes and statistics, which only provide opportunities to "vent our personal prejudices":

> It is so easy to talk about race. It is easy to dig through African or Indian history and trot out a set of half-truths about the "contributions" of one "race" or the other. It is easy to do polls and find correlations between race and behavior . . . and draw specious conclusions about why people do the things they do. . . . When an individual produces figures and "facts" in order to promote a particular perception of a race, . . . he is also indulging in stereotyped thinking of the lowest order, for there is nothing that an individual's race can tell us about him or her other than the geographical location in which the majority of his or her ancestors evolved. (*Sunday Express*, October 22, 1989)

Despite the tendency for the person in the street to say that "most of the criminals in this country are African," and for the Indian businessman to feel that there is a systematic attack on Indian businesses by a criminal African element, Frankson insisted that academics must go out of their way to avoid stereotypes. The 66 percent figure quoted by Springer, for example, was meaningless, according to Frankson. It did not reflect the reality in Tobago or the sugar belt:

> All it does is imply that Africans are more criminally inclined than the other races. Consider, on the other hand, statistics that are not based on race: the percentage of the criminals, for example, born in city slums; the percentage from broken homes; the percentage that has been unemployed for over two years. Let us look at the figures for the types of crimes that are being committed in different parts of the country, and the nature of the crimes that are given high prominence in the media. *What about the figures on wife beating and price-gouging, for example? What you see depends on where you look, and that in turn is an indication of how you think.* (*Sunday Express*, October 22, 1989; emphasis added)

Despite Frankson's attempt to negate stereotypes, his references to wife beating and price gouging directly implicate Indo-Trinidadians (because these practices are popularly attributed to East Indians), suggesting a momentary lapse even on his part. Such a lapse illustrates the potency of racial and ethnic constructs and also points to the nature of interaction between lay and academic discourses.

Technocratic perspectives decry the wanton deployment of race by "irresponsible politicians." They argue that since race is a social construct, it lacks explanatory capacity and its deployment only serves to reify the category itself. Yet the fact that race is not "real" does not exclude the possibility that it has real consequences. Contemporary Trinidadian academic discourses on race, at this level, appear to display some naiveté because they tend to minimize the social reality of Trinidad and the Caribbean at large, where race constructions permeate all facets of life. To lay persons race is indeed very real because they have experienced its consequences firsthand. Thus it is not surprising that sober intellectual reflections on race, which invariably are part of every national debate, rarely have an impact on the population at large. In fact, Indo-Trinidadian leaders perceive technocrats' attempts at negating the relevance of race as both hypocritical (as these same technocrats have no trouble seeing the very real consequences of race in South Africa or in colonial Trinidad) and a convenient cover for the perpetuation of race discrimination against Indo-Trinidadians in the established system. Nevertheless, Frankson's statement that "what you see is ultimately dependent on how you think" tacitly accepts the ideological import of race and is an astute summation of the self-fulfilling prophecy of the racial and ethnic stereotypes that pervade Trinidadian social, political, and cultural life.

Redefining National Culture: Constructing a "Tossed Salad" from a "Callaloo"

I created several years ago a character called Callaloo. He was in everyman, with particular reference to these islands, in that who ever you were if you look at him it was your own self you would see. If you were black and you looked at he it was your own black self you going to see. White, brown or anything . . . it was your self you going to see in Callaloo. He was all of us in one. Callaloo had a speech and in the course of the speech he said to de people and dem, "de differences is here to delight not divide and destroy." (Peter Minshall)

The "white man's burden" was transformed into the "black man's burden" with the establishment of black state power. The black sought to "integrate" Indians into their world view, into Afro-creole culture by pursuing educational and cultural policies which ignored the Indian presence and the reality of a culturally plural society. (*Indian Review* 1990, 2)

The Indo-Trinidadian struggle to change the national image involved a two-pronged strategy: delegitimation (of Afro-Trinidadian hegemonic forms) and renovation. Earlier I argued that Indo-Trinidadians' aspirations for state power were curtailed by the predominantly Afro-Caribbean national image of Trinidad. The process of renovation was aimed at altering this image, and it profoundly implicated the realm of culture.

Criticizing the hegemonic culture history referent of the nation, Indo-

Trinidadian leaders propose instead multicentric cultures and histories. Such a vision in turn demands that the national image incorporate the principle of difference. The discourse generated around the notion of difference has led Indo-Trinidadian leaders to defend the concept of Indian cultural purity. Yet in the very discourse they generate one can detect the problems inherent in such a position since "Indian" culture in Trinidad has been inevitably subject to the process of creolization.

In part the problems generated are structural. Traditionally, the national principle was embodied by Creole forms, which signified native status. This meant that even those Indo-Trinidadian cultural forms that explicitly incorporated native or Creole elements in practice, such as the *hosay* festival, could never be recognized as local or native ideally, because the identities of Creole and East Indian had developed as structural exclusives. On the one hand, Indo-Trinidadian leaders attempt to overcome this dilemma by promoting specific "Indian" cultural forms—such as chutney dancing and singing and tassa drumming, which have developed styles unique to Trinidad—as appropriate national symbols because they explicitly encode "nativeness." Yet on the other hand, Indo-Trinidadian leaders promulgate Indian cultural purity by chastising the "vulgarization" of their cultural forms owing to their alleged creolization.

Indo-Trinidadian attempts at renovating national cultural identity are fraught with contradictions and inconsistencies. Although leaders often claim that Indo-Trinidadians have no problem with their cultural identity (since they, unlike Afro-Trinidadians, have firm roots in an ancient civilization), the process of recasting national culture has unearthed thorny issues that threaten to undermine those very claims. It has forced a reevaluation of Indo-Trinidadians' link to India and the relation between Hinduism and Indo-Trinidadian culture, and also threatened their claims to cultural purity by exposing the undeniable process of creolization that has enveloped Indo-Trinidadian culture.

In order to carve out a space for Indo-Trinidadian culture in the national arena, Indo-Trinidadian leaders must find ways of establishing their nativeness without admitting creolization, which from their perspective is tantamount to Africanization, for reasons enumerated earlier. Accordingly, Indo-Trinidadians reject the callaloo model of national culture, in which all ingredients blend into one taste, in preference to the tossed salad, in which all the ingredients maintain their distinctive flavors. Earlier I argued that the colonial idiom of race laid the ideological foundation for two potential nationalist narratives, one of a Creole society and the other of a Plural society. For the most part of Trinidad's history the two narratives have operated in a dialectical fashion, with a Trinidadian "purity" embodying native status emerging through this dialectic. Yet at particular historical moments we see the emphasis of one narrative over the other. During the transition to independence the Creole society thesis propagated by the nationalist intelligentsia clearly opted for the Creole narrative since they believed that the Plural model suggested a fundamental instability that threatened aspirations for national self-determination. In the contemporary period, however, Indo-Trinidadian leaders have opted for the Plural society model, which incorporates difference as the fundamental principle of the nationalist narrative, thereby allowing their collectivity into the symbolic nation without compromising the "purity" of their ethnicity.

The Indo-Trinidadian strategy of simultaneously projecting difference and nativeness has led to creative deployments of their link with India. One fascinating example is the claim that Indian vedic civilization had penetrated the New World centuries before Columbus's arrival in 1492: "It has to be pointed out that the 1492 European expansion into the 'New World' was really the European conquest of ancient vedic civilizations established by Indians who had travelled centuries before across the Pacific Ocean. In fact, it is appropriate to refer to the 'New World' as 'Asio-America'" (K. Persad in *Sunday Express*, May 27 1990, 5). Here one can detect the embryonic elements of a national myth. This view, which is hardly pervasive, attempts to make India a legitimate focus of national cultural identity. It not only establishes the longevity of the Indian presence but powerfully cements the Indian connection to the New World foundation by suggesting that the later coming of Indian indentured laborers only continued the link the New World already had with India and that Indo-Trinidadians need hardly become anything else to be considered native.

The renovation of national culture has also brought to the fore the "problem" of creolization.[14] There is a tendency among Indo-Trinidadian (Hindu) leaders to anchor Indo-Trinidadian culture in Hinduism. Creolization has been particularly problematic because of this popular conflation of Hinduism with Indo-Trinidadian culture. Although Creole elements enveloping Indo-Trinidadian cultural forms have the potential of establishing their "nativeness," Indo-Trinidadian and especially Hindu leaders rarely emphasize Cre-

14. Indo-Trinidadian leaders are also concerned about the impact of Westernization on their community. By differentiating between Westernization and modernization, some leaders have encouraged their people, especially the youth, to adopt the material benefits of modernity but reject the values and behaviors associated with Westernization. Sampath (1993:237) makes a similar distinction.

ole influences as a justification for national inclusion. Instead, they appeal to their community to abstain from the "wickedness" associated with carnival, bacchanal, and fete.

In 1969 one Ramdath Jagessar, a stalwart of Indo-Trinidadian concerns, distinguished between Afro-Trinidadian and Indo-Trinidadian cultural identity with confidence:

> New World Negroes can talk at length of their growing consciousness because they never had any before. They lost it in the Middle Passage. Indians have had this for thousands of years—and they accept it. They do not have to argue, to shout aloud that Indians are beautiful. They do not have to justify their existence and claim equality. To them Indians are a superior people, and no question about it. Their definitive statement is "I am an Indian, I am a Hindu." (in Ryan 1974:380)

Yet by 1985 Jagessar's faith in the integrity of Hindu culture had been rudely shaken. In an address delivered at the Longdenville *mandir* (temple) he observed with dismay the extent of non-Hindu (Afro-Trinidadian) influences on Hindu cultural forms: "I regret to say that some Hindus have forgotten to look at ourselves with our scriptures in mind. These days I am afraid to attend some Hindu functions, as I don't know what I will find. Hindus are forgetting what Hindus should do, and are being influenced by non-Hindus" (*Jagriti*, 1986, 1:20). At wakes, he lamented, one rarely hears the *Ramayana* or religious music. Instead, people indulge in gambling and drinking rum. These days people come to *pujas* only to eat, not to listen to the prayers. And characterizing contemporary Hindu weddings, he moaned:

> When the pundit is performing the ceremony . . . not too many people are witnessing it. Some are eating, others talking . . . some are listening to the music and some doing vulgar dancing. Outside on the road, the young men are standing up by their cars with the trunks open like crocodiles' mouths and pulling out drinks from styrotex boxes. A lot of them are with stereos and equalizers blasting non-Hindu music and giving the pundit competition. Is that Hinduism? A few people don't want to have meat or alcohol in the wedding house, so they have it next door and invite their friends quietly to go over. What kind of hypocrisy is this? . . . As soon as the pundit leaves you can sometimes see the place cleared and calypso starts to play, and a full fete breaks out. Sometimes they can't wait for the pundit to go and they keep nudging him to get out of the way. (*Jagriti*, 1986, 1:20–21)

[271]

The influences Jagessar laments are not confined to the private and familial Indo-Trinidadian cultural events he describes but are also apparent in Indo-Trinidadian public and communal cultural expressions. Certain Hindu festivals, such as Phagwa (an Indian spring festival), which display a greater degree of Creole influence than others, are pivotal in the current discourse on cultural purity.

Holi, or Phagwa, as it is commonly known in Trinidad, marks the beginning of the Hindu religious year in Trinidad around February–March. A celebratory occasion, it draws inspiration from a Puranic tale describing the trials and final victory of Prahalaad, a child devotee of Lord Vishnu, over the evil witch Holika. Before the institutionalization of Phagwa the festival was celebrated within Indo-Trinidadian villages. Recently, however, villagers and urban dwellers have begun to attend the massive extra-village celebrations organized by various religious groups at different venues. The day itself is marked by fun and frolics that center on people chasing and staining one another with *abir*, a red dye. The festivities also include music, dancing, and the singing of chowtals (devotional songs pertaining to spring). It is a time when few social restrictions apply, and many Indo-Trinidadians, especially the younger folk, eagerly look forward to this day. Contraptions for *abir* staining range from simple dishwashing liquid bottles to handmade "super soakers" (constructed from PVC pipes), a favorite of the young men, who derive immense pleasure from soaking the "gyals."

Although the festive mood and licentious behavior are an integral part of Phagwa, religious leaders worry that the secular aspect has completely overshadowed the spiritual dimension. Indeed, Phagwa is commonly referred to as "Indian Carnival." One notable Hindu "thinker, teacher, and activist" wrote: "The imitation [of carnival] is real: the parade of bands, headpieces, stage, DJ, alcohol and an increasing presence of 'flag-woman' culture. Phagwa symbolizes the larger Hindu predicament. The impact of the environment has been stunning. The ribald nature of Phagwa, which it has transported as part of its original package, has effectively enthroned itself as the central mood" (*Sunday Guardian*, March 11, 1990). According to this Hindu leader, it is urgent that the festival recapture the spirit of Hinduism. Similar sentiments are expressed by lay Indo-Trinidadians. Though most enjoy the revelry and wild abandon, others are dismayed by the "vulgarization" of their culture. Nizaam, an elder of Cambio village, refused to participate in the festival. Although he was a Muslim, he was well versed in and respected Hindu tradition and culture. Despite his limited ability to read Hindi, he had read somewhere the noble message behind Phagwa, that is, the triumph of righteousness over evil. Since then, he claimed, he never participated in the festival because "people had turned it into a vulgar event in Trini." He often said it was not right for a man who had a wife and daughters to have to put up with what goes on.

Conversely, for Peter Minshall, a White Trinidadian artist and renowned carnival bandleader and designer, the parallels between carnival and Phagwa were far more significant than the differences. During a panel discussion titled "What Is the Culture of Trinidad and Tobago?" he commented:

> "People get into tribal enclaves. No sooner is the carnival over and some holier-than-thou [persons] say publicly, "Ah yes, well you people have had your fun with your riotous Carnival now we are going to be holy and we are going to have Phagwa and this is very special and very spiritual." But the roots of both festivals are exactly the same. It is a spring festival and the throwing on of the *abir* is the throwing of the confetti [in the carnival]. My friend from India tells me, and he is a very middle-class friend, that it is one time of the year when his parents get piss drunk! [Great laughter and applause from the audience]

Here Minshall indirectly attacks those Hindu leaders' claims to moral and spiritual superiority by saying that revelry is the fundamental feature uniting the two festivals. Hindu attempts to restore "traditional" spiritual elements to the celebration of Phagwa, he implies, are "unauthentic" since even in India people get "piss drunk" during this festival.

The discourse around the alleged vulgarization of Phagwa is also a discourse about difference. For Indo-Trinidadian, and particularly Hindu, leaders the dissemination of non-Hindu elements jeopardizes the integrity of distinct cultural markers that differentiate the Indo-Trinidadian from the Afro-Trinidadian. In contrast, others such as Minshall attempt to extrapolate the commonalities, arguing that the superimposition of difference is both artificial and futile.

The concern over the creolization of Indian cultural forms has prompted an examination of the "essence" of Indian culture and Hinduism. For those Indo-Trinidadians primarily concerned with the preservation of their religion, creolization is fundamentally antithetical to the laws of dharma. Dharma, they claim, cannot be adapted to suit one's self-interest; adaptation is only an excuse to flout the laws of dharma (*Jagriti* 1986). Other opinion makers, however, consider adaptability a cardinal feature of Indian culture. Indo-Trinidadian historian Haraksingh observes:

> In frontiers new things are permitted, even mandatory. One of these is change, which properly understood posed less problems for the Indians than might be

imagined, for the essence of their cultural baggage was continuing change and adaptation; in common-sense terms the longevity of Indian civilization can hardly otherwise be explained. In Trinidad whole new constructs appeared, out of fragments and remnants. But these were not appreciated as a new creation; instead, conservatism and resistance to change were viewed as almost an Indian adornment, to be explained by the facile notion that they were allowed to keep their culture when of course cultural resilience has nothing to do with permission. (*Sunday Guardian*, May 27, 1990)

This explanation challenges the popular conception of Indo-Trinidadians as carriers and not creators of culture. By emphasizing the built-in capacity of Indian culture to change, Haraksingh asserts that a totally new form of "Indian culture" specific to the New World was created through the innovation and resilience of Indian migrants.

Both views, despite their seeming divergence, make a case for the recognition of difference. In the first view, adaptability is perceived as a threat to the maintenance of pure Indian cultural identity. Thus Creole elements in the guise of adaptation need to be curtailed in order to maintain Indo-Trinidadian cultural identity. In the second view, adaptation is perceived as an unavoidable and a positive feature of Indian culture which permits the incorporation of novel elements without undermining the integrity of difference. According to this view, a peculiarly Trinidadian Indian culture has emerged which is both local (and hence authentically native) and distinct from other New World cultural forms.

Despite the diversity of opinion, Indo-Trinidadian leaders remain united on their commitment to expressing difference. The task for Indo-Trinidadian leaders is to assert their collectivity's difference without eliciting the charge of being foreign or alien to the national spirit. They can resolve this dilemma by renovating the contemporary definition of national culture, which equates the national principle with the category Creole. The repeated challenges to the traditional definition of national culture by Indo-Trinidadians has prompted a reassessment of Trinidadian culture from all segments of the nation's diverse population.

Indo-Trinidadian contestation of the representation of national culture is particularly troubling to those who fear the resurrection of the old colonial view of Caribbean cultures as fragmentary patchworks of incompatible cultural institutions. Thus the task for the entire nation is to create a national cultural vision that can incorporate difference in a unified totality. The spirit of this new vision was captured adroitly by a Chinese-Trinidadian dramatist, James Lee Wah, during the panel discussion on the culture of Trinidad and Tobago when he said, "Although we are not jumping up to the same band in the carnival, it's nice to know that we are all playing 'mas' "!^{15}

Interestingly, Indo-Trinidadians' emphasis on "their" roots expose a privilege long enjoyed by Afro-Trinidadians. Afro-Trinidadians' search for roots and attempts to revive African elements of their culture rarely jeopardized their national patriotism and status. Why, Indo-Trinidadians ask, are they the exception? Thus Indo-Trinidadians are not alone in having to reconcile their ethnic with their national identities. It is only their cultural visibility as ethnics, unlike Afro-Trinidadians, that has transformed this reconciliation into a dilemma. Lee Wah, who differentiated between loyalty and identity, offered a possible solution:

> When Eric Williams said there can be no mother India, or mother Africa or mother China, only mother Trinidad and Tobago, he was stressing loyalty, I believe, rather than identity. I don't think Dr. Williams was suggesting that we should abandon the culture of our forefathers, forget our roots. We may be practicing a kind of cultural schizophrenia. But I don't think it's impossible for us to see ourselves as Africans, Indians, Chinese, English and at the same time to be true, true Trinidadians. In fact, we are not the only country with this problem of cultural diversity. I say problem, but it is only a problem if you make it one.

Lee Wah's sentiments resonate remarkably with those expressed by the Indo-Trinidadian community at large, that is, the assertion that one can be legitimately Indian and Trinidadian at the same time.^{16} Indo-Trinidadians, for their part, have devoted much energy into conveying their loyalty to Trinidad. I encountered such a statement during the Indian Arrival Day celebrations at Orange Valley, a village close to Cambio. Traditionally, the celebrations revolved around the arrival of a boat symbolizing the *Fatel Rozack,* the first ship to bring indentured laborers to Trinidad. On this occasion, however, the focus rested on the launching of an empty boat, symbolizing the *S.S. Ganges,* the last ship to bring indentured migrants to Trinidad. The launching was accompanied by an impassioned speech by Panday, who in essence said, "The boat is not coming back. We are sending it back empty. Trinidad is our home now, and here we will stay and fight for equality."

---

15. *Mas* is a local expression for the carnival procession.

16. Lee Wah's perspectives on other aspects of culture, however, such as his disclaimers regarding cultural purity and authenticity, diverged considerably from popular Indo-Trinidadian conceptions.

Circumventing and Reproducing Historical Limits: The Projection of "Indian" as a Unique Type

Ethnic politics in the national arena is significantly shaped by the ideological underpinnings of the colonial racial hierarchy in terms of both the goals to be achieved by Indo-Trinidadians and the strategies to be employed in realizing these goals. The preferred solution to Indo-Trinidadian discrimination is articulated in the form of equal representation of heterogeneous elements at the national level as opposed to stressing a common core of Caribbean creolized values and orientations that could establish a basis of shared identity for the different ancestral kinds that make up Trinidad's population. In political discourse the redefinition of the Trinidad nation is premised on unique East Indian qualities. It seems that lay and political formulations of Indo-Trinidadian ethnicity in contemporary Trinidad resonate with each other precisely because they are ultimately constrained by the structural limits imposed by history.

To account for the semantic and empirical variations of the category "creole" in Louisiana, Virginia Dominguez (1977) employs an "implicational code." This code is constituted by a set of implicational assumptions that syntagmatically relate concepts and facts through a series of linkages—for example, that a implies e, if a implies b, and b implies c, and c implies d, and d implies e. Historical subjects are rarely conscious of the exact linkages that lead to any one particular assumption. Yet implicational assumptions set the parameters for demarcating the imaginable from the unimaginable in systems of folk knowledge.

If we apply the same approach to the category Trinidadian as it has been historically constituted, we can arrive at the following set of implicational assumptions: Trinidadian, which means to be truly native, implies Creole, which admits miscibility. Creole implies things and/or persons with European and African ancestry. European and African ancestry implies all that is non-Indian. Such an implicational code therefore precluded the possibility of Indians being Trinidadian.

The current Indo-Trinidadian effort to redefine the nation of Trinidad is profoundly influenced by this implicational code. Indo-Trinidadian leaders maneuver the code to try to break different links in a chain of implications. Since their own strategy relies on some of the assumptions of this very code, however, they inevitably end up preserving certain of its linkages. Their inability to disrupt the entire series of linkages is partly a consequence of their own mindset, which cannot entertain the possibility that East Indians too might be considered Creole. In their urgency to disengage the African from the Indian, Indo-

Trinidadian leaders rarely challenge the implication that Creole implies African and European ancestry or suggest that Indians too might be Creole, an uncomfortable association for most Indo-Trinidadians. Thus they attempt to break the chain at the first link—Trinidadian implies Creole—by adding another possibility, *Trinidadian implies Creole and East Indian.*

Figures 1 and 2 illustrate, first, the implicational assumptions behind the historical constitution of the category Trinidadian, and second, the Indo-Trinidadian challenge to these assumptions.

Figure 1 Implicational code of the category Trinidadian

TRINIDADIAN → CREOLE → AFRICAN AND EUROPEAN → NON-INDIAN
    (a)   →   (b)   →   (c)   +   (d)   →   (e)

Figure 2 Indo-Trinidadian challenges to the implicational code

Indo-Trinidadians challenge
TRINIDADIAN → NON-INDIAN
    (a)   →   (e)
not by challenging implications
CREOLE → AFRICAN AND EUROPEAN → NON-INDIAN
  (b) → (c)   +   (d) →   (e)
but by redefining
TRINIDADIAN → CREOLE
    (a)   → (b)
by
TRINIDADIAN → CREOLE **AND EAST INDIAN**
    (a)   →   (b) +   **(f)**

Since Creole is the category that implies nativeness and hence designates common or shared elements among those of different ancestry, Indo-Trinidadians' reluctance to be considered Creole and their insistence on being considered Trinidadian inform their leaders' strategy in intriguing ways. In the political arena Indo-Trinidadian leaders make their case for national inclusion not on the basis of their commonalities with other Trinidadians but on the basis of unique East Indian qualities. They attempt to change the definition of Trinidadian by adding a qualification for inclusion other than being Creole, a qualification that measures a group's worth in terms of its contribution to the nation. This message was amply illustrated in Capildeo's speech and resonates with sentiments expressed by Indo-Trinidadians in general. Although, at least in theory, all groups could be considered legitimate candidates under the qualification "contribution to the nation," in practice the Indo-Trinidadian yardstick measures features that are assumed to be uniquely East Indian. As in Capildeo's speech, the "Indian" penchant for perseverance, thrift, and sacrifice is alluded to time and again, not only to demand inclusion but also to highlight exclusivity.

Even when Indo-Trinidadian leaders and knowledge practitioners are forced to recognize Afro-Trinidadian contributions in order to highlight their own group's contribution (as in the sentiment "we too have bled for the nation"), exclusivity is maintained by additional statements or sentiments that seek to differentiate. For example, to invoke the most potent symbol of their victimization, indenture, is to summon simultaneously an even greater symbol of oppression, slavery. Yet although Indo-Trinidadian leaders reluctantly grant such similarities between themselves and the Afro-Trinidadians, they immediately seek differentiation through qualifying statements such as "the Indian mind does not submit to slavery" or the more loaded phrase "Indians do not hide behind the skirts of indenture." The message is that although both Afro-Trinidadians and East Indians may qualify as victims and hence as legitimate contributors, fundamentally different dispositions prompt differential use of the past. Afro-Trinidadians tend to use their subjugation as an excuse for their alleged inadequacies whereas Indo-Trinidadians positively harness their lessons from history to evolve to a superior state.

The tendency to distinguish themselves as a unique type is poignantly illustrated in the debate regarding Indian Arrival Day. Many Afro-Trinidadians, especially intellectuals, as well as some Indo-Trinidadian intellectuals, argue that the arrival of Indians should not be celebrated because such celebration condones the historical genesis of a new system of slavery—indenture. Celebrating Indian Arrival Day would be akin to celebrating the advent of slavery in the New World. In this case Afro-Trinidadian strategy collapses the history of both groups to illustrate their common oppressed status.

Most Indo-Trinidadians, however, vehemently oppose such an interpretation of their history and often go to great lengths to distance it from slavery. Collapsing slavery with indenture and the African experience with the East Indian one, though politically expedient for knowledge practitioners committed to building a nation on the basis of commonalities, is almost unimaginable for ordinary Indo-Trinidadians because it slights what they believe to be crucial differences. Indo-Trinidadian leaders and lay persons are careful to point out that unlike "Negroes," they did not come shackled to Trinidad but arrived as free men and women. One woman in Cambio, for example, was puzzled by "Negro" claims to superiority. She could not understand why "Negroes" thought they were better than Indians because "long time they came as slaves when everything was owned by the White man." The Indians, in contrast, came as "skilled people." She concluded, "Maybe dey [Negroes] don't know dat, dat's why dey think dey are better."

In their attempts to separate themselves from Afro-Trinidadians, Indo-Trinidadians ironically rest their claims to superiority on the contention that they *chose* a status of servitude, a privilege not accorded Afro-Trinidadians. Yet it is unclear to what extent East Indians perceive indenture as a system of servitude. Though the exploitative aspects of indenture are amply highlighted in political and academic discourse, the very assertion that Indians did not come shackled to Trinidad seems to reflect ambiguity on the subject of servitude. Indeed, popular interpretations of the two labor systems are measured only rarely by the common denominator of servitude; usually, they are assessed on the basis of ingrained differences between the two races. This point is powerfully illustrated by a popular and common Indo-Trinidadian interpretation of a historical event, the arrival of the Indians in Trinidad.

This view of history claims that Indians were brought to Trinidad because the "Negroes" were incapable of sustaining the sugar industry. Soon after their arrival, through perseverance and hard work, East Indians delivered not only the sugar industry from imminent destruction but also the nation.[17] Thus according to Sahadeo, an Indo-Trinidadian working in the sugar factory at Brechin Castle and living in a village adjacent to Cambio, slaves could not work in the cane because they came from a "primitive culture." The Indians were then brought to Trinidad, and "it is dey who built de country up." On another occasion Joey, a young man who lived in Cambio and who enjoyed his work as a mechanic for Caroni, commented, "I like work too bad." He then expanded on his statement, saying he liked work not just for the sake of working but for what it enabled him to do, such as purchase food and clothes and provide for his family. While on the topic of work he offhandedly added, "Negro people are very lazy." I asked him why he thought so. "Good question," he replied and appeared perplexed but then went on to say that "Negroes" have been like that for generations. He illustrated his point by saying, "Dose days the masters had to beat de slaves to wok, dey were so lazy. But not so with de Indians, dey used to wok."

In Joey's account servitude is not factored in at all—the slaves were beaten because they were lazy. East Indians, because they worked hard, were not beaten. The element of coercion does not enter into either Joey's or Sahadeo's equation; rather, intrinsic racial or cultural traits are used to measure

17. Recall that the uproar following Capildeo's speech began precisely when an Afro-Trinidadian scholar offered an alternate interpretation of history, which posited that the arrival of indentured laborers retarded the development of Trinidad by bolstering the existing labor-intensive agricultural practices.

each group's varied experience and performance during slavery and indenture. The dissonance between Afro-Trinidadian knowledge practitioners' interpretations and common Indo-Trinidadian interpretations of slavery and
indenture originates in fundamentally different notions of the determining
features of indenture and slavery. For the knowledge practitioners the common denominator is a system of servitude, and hence they see the similarity
between the two systems. For ordinary Indo-Trinidadians, such as the villagers in Cambio, indenture and slavery are vehicles for symbolizing differences between the races: their varied contributions to the nation, their ingrained racial characteristics, and the variance in the degree of servitude.

The refusal of Indo-Trinidadian leaders to exploit a potentially empowering and convenient symbolic association—to equate slavery with indenture, if
only politically for national inclusion—is particularly intriguing. To claim a
stake in the nation by highlighting their status as victims of an externally imposed exploitative system of labor extraction would be to challenge Afro-
Trinidadian political hegemony on tenets understood and employed by Afro-
Caribbean political elites barely three decades earlier to propel the British
dependencies toward independence and nationhood. Afro-Trinidadian nationalists' justification for racial paramountcy was for the most part based on
their claim that the time had finally come for those of African descent to take
their destiny into their own hands after centuries of subjugation. Why, then,
do Indo-Trinidadian leaders refrain from exploiting this powerful association
with slavery?

The answer is complex. Indo-Trinidadian religious and political leaders
are familiar with lay Indo-Trinidadian interpretations of their ethnic situation and are acutely aware of the futility of forging an association between
indenture and slavery. Earlier I argued that political deployments of ethnic
rhetoric, to be effective, must appeal to three audiences: international spectators, for legitimacy; the state, representing (unequally) the national community, for concessions; and most important, the ethnic masses, for political
leverage. Forging a link between slavery and indenture might prove effective
for gaining legitimacy in the international arena, but it falls short with respect to the national and ethnic communities. The symbolic association between slavery and indenture simply does not obtain in the Indo-Trinidadian
lay imagination.

Even with respect to gaining concessions from the state, associating slavery
with indenture appears to be a weak strategy. To compete for the nation on
the same grounds as the Afro-Trinidadians would not give Indo-Trinidadians
the upper hand. Not only have the Afro-Trinidadians been in Trinidad substantially longer, but their suffering has been much greater. According to this
measure, Indo-Trinidadians are comparatively poor contenders. However, to

establish criteria for measuring national worth on the basis of attributes thought to be uniquely East Indian is also to eliminate other competitors from the contest. As a strategy, it affords Indo-Trinidadian leaders a significant advantage, which may compensate for the fact that their group is not "Creole"—a certification of inclusion Indo-Trinidadians do not particularly desire.

Historical experience also matters. The independence movement of the 1960s and the Black Power movement of 1970 both sought to unite the Trinidadian masses across ethnic lines against a common enemy. The first aimed at the British and Euro-Creole elite of the colonial order, the second at the "Afro-Saxon" ruling elite of the post-colonial order. Together they taught Indo-Trinidadian political leaders the futility of furthering their own interests by making common cause with Afro-Trinidadian political leaders. Structural and historical inequalities translated these strategies of unification into demands dictated primarily by Afro-Trinidadian leaders, the Afro-Creole elites in the first case and the self-anointed representatives of Creole underclasses in the second. In short, emphasis on commonalities has historically led to the eclipsing of Indo-Trinidadian voices by Afro-Trinidadian ones.

Still, Indo-Trinidadians' desire to stress their unique qualities as a separate people, although most clearly articulated in the political arena, should not be reduced to mere political strategy. It also stems from a belief firmly ingrained not only in the Indo-Trinidadian community but also in the Trinidadian population at large, hence the ubiquity and pervasiveness of ethnic stereotypes that Trinidadians continuously deploy to comprehend any context of social interaction. Indo-Trinidadian distancing from Creole status is significantly structured by the group's historically assigned status as outsiders. The opposition between Creole and East Indian may be so ingrained that even to consider Creole status would be to think the unthinkable. Though Indo-Trinidadian leaders now attempt to challenge an offshoot of this traditional dichotomy—the division between Indian and Trinidadian—even they, unwittingly, are forced to position themselves as Indians *or* Trinidadians. Capildeo himself, in a conversation with a journalist about his speech, acknowledged that he was indeed "a Trinidadian first and an Indian after," which suggests that even those challenging the traditional dichotomies are still trapped within them (*Trinidad Guardian*, October 4, 1989). Perhaps, given the ideological structural constraints, Indo-Trinidadian leaders have little alternative but to emphasize their uniqueness in staking a claim to the Trinidadian nation and the state.

In the early 1990s Indo-Trinidadian efforts to redefine the symbolics of the nation reinscribed the traditional dichotomy between the categories Creole and East Indian even as they disrupted the conventional association between Trinidadian and Creole. Such a strategy drew its ideological sustenance from the plural or cosmopolitan nationalist narrative of Trinidad as opposed to the Creole narrative denoting mixture. Yet it seems that in more recent times the category Creole is being contested and is open to redefinition in Trinidad. A category that in the past bestowed the privilege of native status is no longer seen to have the same import. Some Afro-Trinidadians now find the metonymic relation between their group and the category Creole troubling precisely because it deethnicizes their group. For example, in a symposium on Trinidadian musical forms in 1997, heated discussion took place over the title of one of the panels: "Chutney, *Pichakaree*, and Soca Chutney: Indian and Creole Perspectives." The use of the terms *Indian* and *Creole* in the subtitle clearly evidences the mutual exclusivity implied by the two categories, with Creole denoting Afro-Trinidadian. Some panelists, such as Afro-Trinidadian calypsonian Gypsy, took exception to this use:

> Why is it that the only thing that requires . . . explanations and connotations is the term African? Why? . . . You see an Indian man, he is an Indian man. Both of us born in Mayaro together, grow up together. We do the same thing. We born in Trinidad and Tobago; yet he is an Indian man; there is nothing to differentiate. There is the Chinese guy who is born next door to me . . . but if are walking down the road they will say "look the 'Chinee' boy and the creole boy going down the road." (Institute of Social and Economic Research 1997:103)

At this point other panelists attempted to clarify *Creole* by arguing that the term is ambiguous with two different connotations: the exclusive usage denoting Africans (as opposed to Indians) and the inclusive usage incorporating all those born in the islands. Yet Gypsy was not assuaged: "Let me just say this before I leave because if I did not, I would be amiss. I would like people as learned as yourself . . . to correct these mistakes, and when they writing things like these, for equity sake, refer to African people as Africans."

Ironically, it seems that in the late 1990s the tables have turned. It is precisely the unmarked status of "African" as Creole that Gypsy and his supporters are contesting in their insistence that *Creole* be replaced with *African* if the term *Indian* is to be used. Although I remain hesitant to draw a causal link between this reevaluation of the category Creole and the recent political ascendancy of Indo-Trinidadians, perhaps Indo-Trinidadian attempts to displace the Creole narrative as the privileged narrative denoting native status have provoked such a reevaluation. If indeed Indo-Trinidadians have managed to realize their vision of a plural nation composed of many ethnicities, or possibly even have begun establishing their own hegemony, then the rules of the game for claiming native status may have changed and the symbolic privilege of Creole may no longer carry the same valence. We may be witnessing a historical moment when the population labeled *Creole* is beginning to re-assert visibly its ethnic roots. The term *Creole*, then, which like any other his-torical category is vulnerable to social vicissitudes, is ultimately open to con-testation and negotiation. Only time will tell the direction of its evolution and whether the Creole nationalist narrative, so crucial for national definition during the time of independence, will wane with the ultimate ascendancy of the Plural narrative or a new narrative that has yet to unfold.

References

Abdulah, Norma
1991   Ethnicity, Mating Patterns, and Fertility. In *Social and Occupational Stratification in Contemporary Trinidad and Tobago,* S. Ryan, ed., pp. 454–472. St. Augustine, Trinidad and Tobago: Institute of Social and Economic Research, University of the West Indies.

Alexander, Jack
1977a   *Creole Genealogies.* 76th Annual Meeting, American Anthropological Association.
1977b   The Culture of Race in Middle-Class Kingston, Jamaica. *American Ethnologist* 4:413–435.

Ali, Shameen
1985   *The Formation and Development of East Indian Pressure Groups in Trinidad.* St. Augustine, Trinidad: University of the West Indies.

Anderson, Benedict
1991   *Imagined Communities: Reflections on the Origin and Spread of Nationalism.* London: Verso.

Angrosino, Michael V.
1976   Sexual Politics in the East Indian Family in Trinidad. *Caribbean Studies* 16(1):44–66.

Anthony, Michael
1997   *Historical Dictionary of Trinidad and Tobago.* Lanham, Md.: Scarecrow Press.

Appadurai, Arjun
1996   *Modernity at Large: Cultural Dimensions of Globalization.* Minneapolis: University of Minnesota Press.

Auty, Richard
1976   Caribbean Sugar Factory Size and Survival. *Annals of the Association of American Geographers* 66:76–88.

References

Auty, Richard, and Alan Gelb
1986   Oil Windfalls in a Small Parliamentary Democracy: Their Impact on Trinidad and To-
        bago. *World Development* 14(9):1161–1175.

Baksh, Ishmael
1979   Stereotypes of Negroes and East Indians in Trinidad: A Re-Examination. *Caribbean
        Quarterly* 25(1–2):52–71.

Balutanski, Kathleen, and Marie-Agnes Sourieau, eds.
1998   *Caribbean Creolization: Reflections on the Cultural Dynamics of Language, Litera-
        ture, and Identity*. Gainesville: University Presses of Florida.

Barth, Fredrik
1969   *Ethnic Groups and Boundaries: The Social Organization of Culture Difference*.
        Boston: Little, Brown.

Bastide, Roger
1978   *The African Religions of Brazil: Toward a Sociology of the Interpretation of Civiliza-
        tions*. Baltimore: Johns Hopkins University Press.

Bell, Robert R.
1970   Marriage and Family Differences among Lower-Class Negro and East Indian Women
        in Trinidad. *Race* 12:59–73.

Bennett, Herman L.
1989   The Challenge to the Post-Colonial State: A Case Study of the February Revolution in
        Trinidad. In *The Modern Caribbean*, F. W. Knight and C. A. Palmer, eds., pp.
        129–146. Chapel Hill: University of North Carolina Press.

Bentley, Carter
1987   Ethnicity and Practice. *Comparative Studies in Society and History* 29(1):24–55.

Bhahba, Homi K.
1990   DissemiNation: Time, Narrative, and the Margins of the Modern Nation. In *Nation
        and Narration*, H. K. Bhahba, ed., pp. 291–322. London: Routledge.
1994   *The Location of Culture*. London: Routledge.

Bolland, Nigel
1981   Systems of Domination after Slavery: The Control of Land and Labour in the British
        West Indies after 1838. *Comparative Studies in Society and History* 23(4):591–619.
1984   Reply to William A. Green's "The Perils of Comparative History." *Comparative Stud-
        ies in Society and History* 26(1):120–125.
1992   Creolization and Creole Societies: A Cultural Nationalist View of Caribbean Social
        History. In *Intellectuals in the Twentieth Century Caribbean*, vol. 1, *Spectre of the
        New Class: The Commonwealth Caribbean*, A. Hennessy, ed., pp. 51–79. London:
        Macmillan.

Braithwaite, Lloyd
1954   The Problem of Cultural Integration in Trinidad. *Social and Economic Studies*
        3(1):82–96.
1975   *Social Stratification in Trinidad*. 1953. Reprint. Mona, Jamaica: Institute of Social and
        Economic Research, University of the West Indies.

Brass, Paul
1976   Ethnicity and Nationality Formation. *Ethnicity* 3:225–241.

[286]

Brathwaite, Edward
1971   *The Development of Creole Society in Jamaica, 1770–1820*. Oxford: Clarendon Press.
1974   *Contradictory Omens: Cultural Diversity and Integration in the Caribbean*. Mona, Jamaica: Savacou Publications.

Brereton, Bridget
1974   The Foundations of Prejudice: Indians and Africans in Nineteenth-Century Trinidad. *Caribbean Issues* 1(5):15–28.
1979   *Race Relations in Colonial Trinidad, 1870–1900*. Cambridge: Cambridge University Press.
1981   A *History of Modern Trinidad, 1783–1962*. Kingston: Heinemann.
1985   The Experience of Indentureship, 1845–1917. In *Calcutta to Caroni: The East Indians of Trinidad*, J. La Guerre, ed., pp. 21–32. St. Augustine, Trinidad and Tobago: Extra Mural Studies Unit, University of the West Indies.
1993   Social Organisation and Class, Racial, and Cultural Conflict in Nineteenth-Century Trinidad. In *Trinidad Ethnicity*, K. Yelvington, ed., pp. 33–55. Knoxville: University of Tennessee Press.

Brubaker, Rogers
1992   *Citizenship and Nationhood in France and Germany*. Cambridge: Harvard University Press.

Burton, Richard
1997   *Afro-Creole: Power, Opposition, and Play in the Caribbean*. Ithaca: Cornell University Press.

Calhoun, Craig
1994   Introduction: Habermas and the Public Sphere. In *Habermas and the Public Sphere*, C. Calhoun, ed., pp. 1–48. Cambridge: MIT Press.

Camejo, Acton
1971   Racial Discrimination in Employment in the Private Sector in Trinidad and Tobago: A Study of the Business Elite and the Social Structure. *Social and Economic Studies* 20(3):294–318.

Campbell, Carl C.
1976   The Wealth of Mulatto Men. Unpublished manuscript.
1992   *Cedulants and Capitulants*. Port-of-Spain, Trinidad and Tobago: Paria Publishing Co.

Caroni (1975) Limited
1989   *Program for Implementing the Government's Decision for Restructuring the Sugar Industry*. Trinidad and Tobago.

Carrington, E.
1967   The Post-War Economy of Trinidad and Tobago. *New World Quarterly* 4(1):45–67.

Central Statistical Office
1989   *Annual Statistical Digest, 1988*. Trinidad and Tobago.
1997   *Statistics at a Glance, 1996*. Trinidad and Tobago.
1998   *Annual Statistical Digest, 1996*. Trinidad and Tobago.

Chatterjee, Partha
1993a *Nationalist Thought and the Colonial World: A Derivative Discourse*. Minneapolis: University of Minnesota Press.

References

1993b Whose Imagined Community? In *The Nation and Its Fragments: Colonial and Post-colonial Histories*, P. Chatterjee, ed., pp. 3–13. Princeton: Princeton University Press.

Ching, Annette
1985 Ethnicity Reconsidered with Reference to Sugar and Society in Trinidad. Ph.D. diss., University of Sussex.

Clarke, Colin
1986 *East Indians in a West Indian Town: San Fernando, Trinidad, 1930–1970*. London: Allen and Unwin.
1993 Spatial Pattern and Social Interaction among Creoles and Indians in Trinidad and Tobago. In *Trinidad Ethnicity*, K. Yelvington, ed., pp. 116–135. Knoxville: University of Tennessee Press.

Collens, J. H.
1888 *A Guide to Trinidad*. London: Elliot Stock.

Comaroff, John
1988 Of Totemism and Ethnicity: Consciousness, Practice, and the Signs of Inequality. *Ethnos* 52(3–4):301–323.

Cooper, F., and A. L. Stoler, eds.
1997 *Tensions of Empire: Colonial Cultures in a Bourgeois World*. Berkeley: University of California Press.

Coulon, Christian, and Françoise Morin
1979 Occitan Ethnicity. *Critique of Anthropology* 13–14(4):105–123.

Crichlow, Michaeline
1991 Stratification and the Small Business Sector in Trinidad and Tobago. In *Social and Occupational Stratification in Contemporary Trinidad and Tobago*, S. Ryan, ed., pp. 191–209. St. Augustine, Trinidad and Tobago: Institute of Social and Economic Research, University of the West Indies.

Cross, Malcolm
1972 *The East Indians of Guyana and Trinidad*. London: Minority Rights Group.
1996 East Indian–Creole Relations in Trinidad and Guiana in the Late Nineteenth Century. In *Across the Dark Waters: Ethnicity and Indian Identity in the Caribbean*, D. Dabydeen and B. S. Dabydeen, eds., pp. 14–38. London: Macmillan.

Crowley, Daniel J.
1957 Plural and Differential Acculturation in Trinidad. *American Anthropologist* 59(5):817–824.

Daniel, Valentine
1996 *Charred Lullabies: Chapters in an Anthropology of Violence*. Princeton: Princeton University Press.

Davids, Leo
1964 The East Indian Family Overseas. *Social and Economic Studies* 13:383–396.

Despres, Leo
1967 *Cultural Pluralism and Nationalist Politics in British Guiana*. Chicago: Rand McNally.

de Verteuil, Anthony
1989 *Eight East Indian Immigrants*. Port-of-Spain, Trinidad and Tobago: Paria Publishing Co.

Dominguez, Virginia
1977   Social Classification in Creole Louisiana. *American Ethnologist* 4:589–602.

Dookeran, Winston
1985   East Indians and the Economy of Trinidad and Tobago. In *Calcutta to Caroni: The East Indians of Trinidad*, J. La Guerre, ed., pp. 63–76. St. Augustine, Trinidad and Tobago: Extra Mural Studies Unit, University of the West Indies.

Drescher, Seymour
1977   *Econocide: British Slavery in the Era of Abolition*. Pittsburgh: University of Pittsburgh Press.

Drummond, Lee
1980   The Cultural Continuum: A Theory of Intersystems. *Man* 15:352–374.

Duara, Prasenjit
1996   *Rescuing History from the Nation*. 1995. Reprint. Chicago: University of Chicago Press.

Dunn, Richard
1972   *Sugar and Slaves*. New York: Norton.

Engerman, Stanley
1986   Slavery and Emancipation in Comparative Perspective: A Look at Some Recent Debates. *Journal of Economic History* 46:317–339.
1992   The Economic Response to Emancipation and Some Economic Aspects of the Meaning of Freedom. In *The Meaning of Freedom: Economics, Politics, and Culture after Slavery*, F. McGlynn and S. Drescher, eds., pp. 49–68. Pittsburgh: University of Pittsburgh Press.

Enloe, Cynthia
1981   The Growth of the State and Ethnic Mobilization: The American Experience. *Ethnic and Racial Studies* 4(2):123–136.

Equality Editorial Committee
1990   *Equality: The Journal of Ethnic Studies* 2(2).

Erickson, Edgar
1934   The Introduction of East Indian Coolies into the British West Indies. *Journal of Modern History* 6(2):127–146.

Foucault, Michel
1980   *The History of Sexuality*. New York: Vintage Books.

Fox, Richard G., ed.
1990   *Nationalist Ideologies and the Production of National Cultures*. Washington, D.C.: American Anthropological Association.

Fox, Richard, Charlotte Aull, and Louis Cimino
1981   Ethnic Nationalism and the Welfare State. In *Ethnic Change*, C. F. Keyes, ed., pp. 198–245. Seattle: University of Washington Press.

Freeman, Carla
2000   *High Tech and High Heels in the Global Economy: Women, Work, and Pink-Collar Identities in the Caribbean*. Durham: Duke University Press.

Geertz, Clifford
1973   The Integrative Revolution. In *The Interpretation of Cultures*, C. Geertz, ed., pp. 255–310. New York: Basic Books.

References

Gellner, Ernest
1991   *Nations and Nationalism*. Ithaca: Cornell University Press.

Gosine, Mahin
1986   *East Indians and Black Power in the Caribbean: The Case of Trinidad*. New York: Africana Research Publications.

Green, Garth
1999   Blasphemy, Sacrilege, and Moral Degradation in the Trinidad Carnival: The Hallelujah Controversy of 1995. In *Religion, Diaspora, and Cultural Identity*, J. Pulis, ed. London: Gordon and Breach.

Green, William
1976   *British Slave Emancipation: The Sugar Colonies and the Great Experiment, 1830–1865*. Oxford: Clarendon Press.
1984   The Perils of Comparative History: Belize and the British Sugar Colonies after Slavery. *Comparative Studies in Society and History* 26(1):112–119.

Gupta, Akhil, and James Ferguson, eds.
1997   *Culture, Power, Place*. Durham: Duke University Press.

Habermas, Jürgen
1989   *The Structural Transformation of the Public Sphere*. Cambridge: MIT Press.

Hall, Douglas
1978   The Flight from the Estates Reconsidered: The British West Indies. *Journal of Caribbean History* 10–11:7–24.

Handler, Richard
1985   On Dialogue and Destructive Analysis: Problems in Narrating Nationalism and Ethnicity. *Journal of Anthropological Research* 41(2):171–182.
1988   *Nationalism and the Politics of Culture in Quebec*. Madison: University of Wisconsin Press.

Hannerz, Ulf
1996   *Transnational Connections: Culture, People, Places*. London: Routledge.

Haraksingh, Kusha
1981   Control and Resistance among Overseas Indian Workers: A Study of Labour on the Sugar Plantations of Trinidad, 1875–1917. *Journal of Caribbean History* 14:1–17.
1985   Aspects of the Indian Experience in the Caribbean. In *Calcutta to Caroni: The East Indians of Trinidad*, J. La Guerre, ed., pp. 155–172. St. Augustine, Trinidad and Tobago: Extra Mural Studies Unit, University of the West Indies.
1988   Rice and Sugar Peasants (Trinidad and Guyana) and the Struggle for Citizenship. Paper presented at UNESCO Conference, "Slavery, Emancipation, and the Shaping of Caribbean Society."

Harewood, Jack
1971   Racial Discrimination in Employment in Trinidad and Tobago. *Social and Economic Studies* 20(3):267–293.

Hechter, Michael
1975   *Internal Colonialism: The Celtic Fringe in British National Development, 1536–1966*. Berkeley: University of California Press.

Henry, Ralph
1988   The State and Income Distribution in an Independent Trinidad and Tobago. In *The Independence Experience, 1962–1987*, S. Ryan, ed., pp. 471–494. St. Augustine, Trinidad and Tobago: Institute of Social and Economic Research, University of the West Indies.

Herskovits, Melville
1937   *Life in a Haitian Valley*. New York: Doubleday Anchor.
1958   *The Myth of the Negro Past*. Boston: Beacon Press.
1966   *The New World Negro*. Bloomington: Indiana University Press.

Herskovits, Melville, and Frances Herskovits
1947   *Trinidad Village*. New York: Knopf.

Heuman, Gad
1981   *Between Black and White: Race, Politics, and the Free Coloreds in Jamaica, 1792–1865*. Westport, Conn.: Greenwood Press.

Higman, Barry
1984   *Slave Populations of the British Caribbean, 1807–1834*. Baltimore: Johns Hopkins University Press.

Hindu Education Trust
1986   *Jagriti: Toward the Hindu Renaissance* 1. Trinidad and Tobago.

Hintzen, Percy
1989   *The Costs of Regime Survival: Racial Mobilization, Elite Domination, and Control of the State in Guyana and Trinidad*. Cambridge: Cambridge University Press.

Ho, Christine
1991   *Salt-Water Trinnies: Afro-Trinidadian Immigrant Networks and Non-Assimilation in Los Angeles*. New York: AMS Press.

Hobsbawm, Eric
1962   *The Age of Revolution, 1789–1848*. New York: Mentor Books.
1991   *Nations and Nationalism since 1780: Programme, Myth, Reality*. Cambridge: Cambridge University Press.

Hobsbawm, Eric, and Terence Ranger
1983   *The Invention of Tradition*. Cambridge: Cambridge University Press.

Hoetink, Harry
1967   *Two Variants in Caribbean Race Relations: A Contribution to the Sociology of Segmented Societies*. London: Oxford University Press.

Holt, Thomas C.
1992   *The Problem of Freedom: Race, Labor, and Politics in Jamaica and Britain, 1832–1938*. Baltimore: Johns Hopkins University Press.

Indian Review Committee
1990   *The Indian Review*. Trinidad and Tobago.

Institute of Social and Economic Research
1997   Special Issue on Calypso, Chutney, and Pitchakaree. *Caribbean Dialogue: A Policy Bulletin of Caribbean Affairs* 3(4). Trinidad and Tobago.

Isaacs, Harold
1974   Basic Group Identity: Idols of the Tribe. *Ethnicity* 1:15–42.

References

Jayawardena, Chandra
1963   *Conflict and Solidarity in a Guianese Plantation.* London: London School of Economics Monographs on Social Anthropology.
1968   Ideology and Conflict in Lower Class Communities. *Comparative Studies in Society and History* 10(4):413–450.
1980   Culture and Ethnicity in Guyana and Fiji. *Man* 15:430–450.

Jha, J. C.
1973   East Indian Pressure Groups in Trinidad, 1897–1921. Paper presented at History Conference, University of the West Indies.
1985   The Indian Heritage in Trinidad. In *Calcutta to Caroni: The East Indians of Trinidad,* J. La Guerre, ed., pp. 1–20. St. Augustine, Trinidad and Tobago: Extra Mural Studies Unit, University of the West Indies.

Kale, Madhavi
1998   *Fragments of Empire: Capital, Slavery, and Indian Indentured Labor in the British Caribbean.* Philadelphia: University of Pennsylvania Press.

Kamenka, Eugene
1973   Political Nationalism: The Evolution of the Idea. In *Nationalism,* E. Kamenka, ed., pp. 3–20. Canberra: Australian National University Press.

Kapferer, Bruce
1988   *Legends of People, Myths of State: Violence, Intolerance, and Political Culture in Sri Lanka and Australia.* Washington, D.C.: Smithsonian Institution Press.

Kelly, John D.
1995   Bhakti and Postcolonial Politics: Hindu Missions to Fiji. In *Nation and Migration: The Politics of Space in the South Asian Diaspora,* P. van der Veer, ed. Philadelphia: University of Pennsylvania Press.

Khan, Aisha
1993   What Is "a Spanish"?: Ambiguity and "Mixed" Ethnicity in Trinidad. In *Trinidad Ethnicity,* K. Yelvington, ed., pp. 180–207. Knoxville: University of Tennessee Press.
1995   Homeland, Motherland: Authenticity, Legitimacy, and Ideologies of Place among Muslims in Trinidad. In *Nation and Migration: The Politics of Space in the South Asian Diaspora,* P. van der Veer, ed. Philadelphia: University of Pennsylvania Press.

Kirpalani, M., Mitra Sinanan, S. M. Rameshwar, and L. F. Seukeran, eds.
1945   *Indian Centenary Review.* Port-of-Spain, Trinidad: Guardian Commercial Printery.

Klass, Morton
1961   *East Indians in Trinidad: A Study of Cultural Persistence.* New York: Columbia University Press.

Kohn, Hans
1994   Western and Eastern Nationalisms. In *Nationalism,* J. Hutchinson and A. Smith Hutchinson, eds., pp. 162–164. Oxford: Oxford University Press.

La Guerre, John
1985   Issues Facing the East Indian Community. In *Calcutta to Caroni: The East Indians of Trinidad,* J. La Guerre, ed., pp. 173–186. St. Augustine, Trinidad and Tobago: Extra Mural Studies Unit, University of the West Indies.
1988   Race Relations in Trinidad and Tobago. In *The Independence Experience, 1962–1987,*

S. Ryan, ed., pp. 193–206. St. Augustine, Trinidad and Tobago: Institute of Social and Economic Research, University of the West Indies.

1991 Leadership in a Plural Society: The Case of the Indians in Trinidad and Tobago. In *Social and Occupational Stratification in Contemporary Trinidad and Tobago*, S. Ryan, ed., pp. 83–112. St. Augustine, Trinidad and Tobago: Institute of Social and Economic Research, University of the West Indies.

Laurence, Keith
1985 Indians as Permanent Settlers in Trinidad before 1900. In *Calcutta to Caroni: The East Indians of Trinidad*, J. La Guerre, ed., pp. 95–116. St. Augustine, Trinidad and Tobago: Extra Mural Studies Unit, University of the West Indies.

Lauria, Anthony
1964 Respeto, Relajo, and Interpersonal Relations in Puerto Rico. *Anthropological Quarterly* 37(2):53–67.

Lavie, Smadar, and Ted Swedenberg, eds.
1996 *Displacement, Diaspora, and Geographies of Identity*. Durham: Duke University Press.

Leach, Edmund
1954 *Political Systems of Highland Burma: A Study of Kachin Social Structure*. Boston: Beacon Press.

Lewis, Gordon K.
1987 *Main Currents in Caribbean Thought: The Historical Evolution of Caribbean Society in Its Ideological Aspects, 1492–1900*. Baltimore: Johns Hopkins University Press.

Lieber, Michael
1981 *Street Scenes: Afro-American Culture in Urban Trinidad*. Cambridge, Mass.: Schenkman.

Look Lai, Walton
1993 *Indentured Labor, Caribbean Sugar: Chinese and Indian Migrants to the British West Indies, 1838–1918*. Baltimore: Johns Hopkins University Press.

Lovelace, Earl
1988 The On-Going Value of Our Indigenous Traditions. In *The Independence Experience, 1962–1987*, S. Ryan, ed., pp. 335–344. St. Augustine, Trinidad and Tobago: Institute of Social and Economic Research, University of the West Indies.

Lowe, Lisa
1996 *Immigrant Acts: On Asian American Cultural Politics*. Durham: Duke University Press.

Lowenthal, David
1972 *West Indian Societies*. London: Oxford University Press.

MacDonald, John, and L. MacDonald
1973 Transformation of African and Indian Family Traditions in the Southern Caribbean. *Comparative Studies in Society and History* 15:171–198.

MacDonald, Scott
1986 *Trinidad and Tobago: Democracy and Development in the Caribbean*. New York: Praeger.

[293]

References

Madan, T. N.
1962   Is the Brahmanic Gotra a Grouping of Kin? *Southwestern Journal of Anthropology* 18:59–77.

Magid, Alvin
1988   *Urban Nationalism: A Study of Political Development in Trinidad*. Gainesville: University Presses of Florida.

Malik, Yogendra
1971   *East Indians in Trinidad*. London: Oxford University Press.

Malkki, Liisa H.
1995   *Purity and Exile: Violence, Memory, and National Cosmology among Hutu Refugees in Tanzania*. Chicago: University of Chicago Press.

Mangru, Basdeo
1993   *Indenture and Abolition: Sacrifice and Survival on the Guyanese Sugar Plantations*. Toronto: TSAR.

Marshall, Woodville K.
1991   *The Post-Slavery Labour Problem Revisited: The 1990 Elsa Goveia Memorial Lecture*. Mona, Jamaica: University of the West Indies.

Maurer, Bill
1997   *Recharting the Caribbean: Land, Law, and Citizenship in the British Virgin Islands*. Ann Arbor: University of Michigan Press.

Mayer, Adrian
1960   *Caste and Kinship in Central India*. London: Routledge and Kegan Paul.

McDonald, M.
1986   Celtic Ethnic Kinship and the Problem of Being English. *Current Anthropology* 27(4):333–348.

McGlynn, F., and S. Drescher, eds.
1992   *The Meaning of Freedom: Economics, Politics, and Culture after Slavery*. Pittsburgh: University of Pittsburgh Press.

Merivale, Herman
1967   *Lectures on Colonization and Colonies*. 1841. Reprint. New York: A. M. Kelley.

Miller, Daniel
1994   *Modernity, an Ethnographic Approach: Dualism and Mass Consumption in Trinidad*. Oxford: Berg.

Millette, James
1985   *Society and Politics in Colonial Trinidad*. Trinidad: Zed Books.

Ministry of Finance and Planning, Government of Trinidad and Tobago
1982   *National Physical Development Plan, Trinidad and Tobago*. 2 vols. Trinidad and Tobago.

Mintz, Sidney
1977   North American Anthropological Contributions to Caribbean Studies. *Boletín de Estudios Latino Americanos y del Caribe* 22:68–82.
1978   Was the Plantation Slave a Proletarian? *Review* 2(1):81–98.
1979   Slavery and the Rise of the Peasantries. *Historical Reflection* 6(1):213–242.

1984 Africa of Latin America: An Unguarded Reflection. In *Africa in Latin America*, M. Fraginals, ed., pp. 286–305. New York: Holmes and Meier.

1992 Panglosses and Pollyannas. In *The Meaning of Freedom: Economics, Politics, and Culture after Slavery*, F. McGlynn and S. Drescher, eds., pp. 245–256. Pittsburgh: University of Pittsburgh Press.

1994 Enduring Substances, Trying Theories: The Caribbean Region as Oikoumene. *Journal of the Royal Anthropological Institute* 2:289–311.

Mintz, Sidney, and Richard Price

1976 *An Anthropological Approach to the Afro-American Past: A Caribbean Perspective.* Philadelphia: Institute for the Study of Human Issues.

Moerman, M.

1965 Ethnic Identification in a Complex Civilization: Who are the Lue? *American Anthropologist* 67:1215–1230.

1968 Being Lue: Uses and Abuses of Ethnic Identity. In *Essays on the Problem of Tribe*, J. Helm, ed., pp. 153–169. Seattle: University of Washington Press.

Mohammed, Patricia

1988 The "Creolization" of Indian Women in Trinidad. In *The Independence Experience, 1962–1987*, S. Ryan, ed., pp. 381–398. St. Augustine, Trinidad and Tobago: Institute of Social and Economic Research, University of the West Indies.

Munasinghe, Viranjini

1994 Callaloo or Tossed Salad? East Indians and National Identity in Trinidad. Ph.D. diss., Johns Hopkins University.

1997 Culture Creators and Culture Bearers: The Interface between Race and Ethnicity in Trinidad. *Transforming Anthropology* 6(1–2):72–86.

Myers, Helen

1998 *Music of Hindu Trinidad: Songs from the India Diaspora.* Chicago: University of Chicago Press.

Naipaul, V. S.

1961 *A House for Mr. Biswas.* London: Andre Deutsch.

1962 *The Middle Passage.* London: Andre Deutsch.

1967 *The Mimic Men.* London: Andre Deutsch.

Naroll, R.

1964 On Ethnic Unit Classification. *Current Anthropologist* 5:283–312.

1968 Who the Lue Are. In *Essays on the Problem of Tribe*, J. Helm, ed. Seattle: University of Washington Press.

Nevadomsky, Joseph

1980 Changes in Hindu Institutions in an Alien Environment. *Eastern Anthropologist* 33:39–53.

1982 Changing Conceptions of Family Regulation among the Hindu East Indians in Rural Trinidad. *Anthropological Quarterly* 55(4):189–197.

1983 Economic Organization, Social Mobility, and Changing Social Status among East Indians in Rural Trinidad. *Ethnology* 22:63–79.

1985 Developmental Sequences of Domestic Groups in an East Indian Community in Rural Trinidad. *Ethnology* 24:1–11.

References

Newson, L.
1976   *Aboriginal and Spanish Colonial Trinidad.* London: Academic Press.

Nicholls, David G.
1971   East Indians and Black Power in Trinidad. *Race* 12:443–459.

Niehoff, Arthur, and J. Niehoff
1960   *East Indians in the West Indies.* Milwaukee: Milwaukee Public Museum Publications in Anthropology.
1967   The Function of Caste among Indians of the Oropouche Lagoon. In *Caste in Overseas Indian Communities*, B. Schwartz, ed., pp. 149–163. San Francisco: Chandler.

Niranjana, Tejaswini
1997   "Left to the Imagination": Indian Nationalisms and Female Sexuality in Trinidad. *Small Axe* 2:1–18.

Norton, Robert
1984   Ethnicity and Class: A Conceptual Note in Reference to the Politics of Post-Colonial Societies. *Ethnic and Racial Studies* 7:426–434.

Okamura, Jonathan
1981   Situational Ethnicity. *Ethnic and Racial Studies* 4:452–465.

Oxaal, Ivar
1968   *Black Intellectuals Come to Power: The Rise of Creole Nationalism in Trinidad and Tobago.* Cambridge, Mass.: Schenkman.
1971   *Race and Revolutionary Consciousness: A Documentary Interpretation of the 1970 Black Power Revolt in Trinidad.* Cambridge, Mass.: Schenkman.

Pantin, Dennis A.
1988   Whither Point Lisas? Lessons for the Future. In *The Independence Experience, 1962–1987*, S. Ryan, ed., pp. 27–46. St. Augustine, Trinidad and Tobago: Institute of Social and Economic Research, University of the West Indies.

Patterson, Orlando
1975   Context and Choice in Ethnic Alliance: A Theoretical Framework and Caribbean Case Study. In *Ethnicity: Theory and Experience*, D. Glazer and P. Moynihan, eds., pp. 304–349. Cambridge: Harvard University Press.

Plamenatz, John
1973   Two Types of Nationalism. In *Nationalism*, E. Kamenka, ed., pp. 23–36. Canberra: Australian National University Press.

Platts, J. T.
1965   *A Dictionary of Urdu, Classical Hindi, and English.* 1930. Reprint. Oxford: Oxford University Press.

Pollard, H. J.
1985   The Erosion of Agriculture in an Oil Economy: The Case of Export Crop Production in Trinidad. *World Development* 13(7):819–835.

Puri, Shalini
1999   Canonized Hybridities: Chutney Soca, Carnival, and the Politics of Nationalism. In *Caribbean Romances*, B. Edmondson, ed., pp. 12–38. Charlottesville: University Press of Virginia.

[296]

Ragatz, L.
1971   *The Fall of the Planter Class in the British Caribbean, 1763–1833.* New York: Octagon Books.

Ragin, Charles
1979   Ethnic Political Mobilization: The Welsh Case. *American Sociological Review* 44:619–635.

Ramesar, Marianne
1994   *Survivors of Another Crossing: A History of East Indians in Trinidad, 1880–1946.* St. Augustine, Trinidad and Tobago: School of Continuing Studies, University of the West Indies.

Ramnarine, Tina Karina
1996   "Indian" Music in the Diaspora: Case Studies of "Chutney" in Trinidad and London. *British Journal of Ethnomusicology* 5:133–153.

Ramraj, Victor J.
1987   Trapdoors into a Bottomless Past: V. S. Naipaul's Ambivalent Visions of the Indian Experience. In *Indians in the Caribbean*, I. J. Bahadur Singh, ed., pp. 85–102. New Delhi: Sterling.

Reddock, Rhoda
1986   Indian Women and Indentureship in Trinidad and Tobago, 1845–1917: Freedom Denied. *Caribbean Quarterly* 32(3–4):27–49.
1991   Social Mobility in Trinidad and Tobago, 1960–1980. In *Social and Occupational Stratification in Contemporary Trinidad and Tobago*, S. Ryan, ed., pp. 210–233. St. Augustine, Trinidad and Tobago: Institute of Social and Economic Research, University of the West Indies.
1994   *Women, Labour, and Politics in Trinidad and Tobago: A History.* Kingston, Jamaica: Ian Randle.

Richardson, Bonham
1975   Livelihood in Rural Trinidad in 1900. *Annals of the Association of American Geographers* 65(2):240–251.

Roberts, G. W., and L. Braithwaite
1962   Mating among East Indian and Non-Indian Women in Trinidad. *Social and Economic Studies* 11:203–240.

Robotham, Don
1998   Transnationalism in the Caribbean: Formal and Informal. *American Ethnologist* 25:307–321.

Rosenberg, Leah Reade
2000   Creolizing Womanhood: Gender and Domesticity in Early Anglophone Caribbean National Literatures. Ph.D. diss., Cornell University.

Ryan, Selwyn
1974   *Race and Nationalism in Trinidad and Tobago.* Toronto: University of Toronto Press.
1988a *The Independence Experience, 1962–1987.* St. Augustine, Trinidad and Tobago: Institute of Social and Economic Research, University of the West Indies.
1988b Popular Attitudes towards Independence, Race Relations, and the People's National Movement. In *The Independence Experience 1962–1987*, S. Ryan, ed., pp. 217–228.

References

St. Augustine, Trinidad and Tobago: Institute of Social and Economic Research, University of the West Indies.

1989a *Revolution and Reaction: Parties and Politics in Trinidad and Tobago, 1970–1981*. St. Augustine, Trinidad: Multimedia Production Centre, University of the West Indies.

1989b *The Disillusioned Electorate: The Politics of Succession in Trinidad and Tobago*. Trinidad: Inprint Caribbean.

1996 *Pathways to Power: Indians and the Politics of National Unity in Trinidad and Tobago*. St. Augustine, Trinidad: Institute for Social and Economic Research, University of the West Indies.

Safa, Helen

1987 Popular Culture, National Identity, and Race in the Caribbean. *New West Indian Guide* 61(3–4):115–126.

Samaroo, Brinsley

1975 The Presbyterian Canadian Mission as an Agent of Integration in Trinidad during the Nineteenth and Early Twentieth Centuries. *Caribbean Studies* 14(4):41–55.

1983 Education as Socialization: Form and Content in the Syllabus of Canadian Presbyterian Schools in Trinidad from the Late Nineteenth Century. Paper presented at the 15th Annual Conference of Caribbean Historians, University of the West Indies, Mona, Jamaica.

1985 Politics and Afro-Indian Relations in Trinidad. In *Calcutta to Caroni: The East Indians of Trinidad*, J. La Guerre, ed., pp. 77–94. St. Augustine, Trinidad and Tobago: Extra Mural Studies Unit, University of the West Indies.

Sampath, Niels M

1993 An Evaluation of the "Creolisation" of Trinidad East Indian Adolescent Masculinity. In *Trinidad Ethnicity*, K. Yelvington, ed., pp. 235–253. Knoxville: University of Tennessee Press.

Sanjek, Roger

1994 The Enduring Inequalities of Race. In *Race*, S. Gregory and R. Sanjek, eds., pp. 1–17. New Brunswick: Rutgers University Press.

Schwartz, Barton M.

1965 Patterns of East Indian Family Organization in Trinidad. *Caribbean Studies* 5(1):23–36.

1967 *Caste in Overseas Indian Communities*. San Francisco: Chandler.

Sebastien, Raphael

1978 The Development of Capitalism in Trinidad, 1845–1917. Ph.D. diss., Howard University.

Segal, Daniel

1989 Nationalism in a Colonial State: A Study of Trinidad and Tobago. Ph.D. diss., University of Chicago.

1993 "Race" and "Color" in Pre-Independence Trinidad and Tobago. In *Trinidad Ethnicity*, K. Yelvington, ed., pp. 81–115. Knoxville: University of Tennessee Press.

1994 Living Ancestors: Nationalism and the Past in Postcolonial Trinidad and Tobago. In *Remapping Memory*, J. Boyarin, ed., pp. 221–239. Minneapolis: University of Minnesota Press.

Selvon, Samuel

1971 *A Brighter Sun. Trinidad and Jamaica*: Longman Caribbean.

1987   Three into One Can't Go—East Indian, Trinidadian, West Indian. In *Indians in the Caribbean*, I. J. Bahadur Singh, ed., pp. 31–44. New Delhi: Sterling.

Senders, Stefan
In press   Jus Sanguinis or Jus Mimesis? Rereading Repatriation Law. In *Aussiedler Integration*, Stefan Wolff, ed. Providence: Berghan Books.

Sewell, W. G.
1968   *The Ordeal of Free Labour in the British West Indies*. London: Frank Cass.

Shaw, Thomas
1985   To Be or Not to Be Chinese: Differential Expressions of Chinese Culture and Solidarity in the British West Indies. In *Caribbean Ethnicity Revisited*, S. Glazier, ed., pp. 71–101. London: Gordon and Breach.

Shils, Edward
1957   Primordial, Personal, Sacred, and Civil Ties. *British Journal of Sociology* 8:130–145.

Siewah, Samaroo
1994   *Lotus and the Dagger: The Capildeo Speeches (1957–1994)*. Tunapuna, Trinidad and Tobago: Chakra Publishing House.

Siewah, Samaroo, and R. Moonilal
1991   *Basdeo Panday: An Enigma Answered: A First Volume of Speeches*. Trinidad and Tobago: Chakra Publishing House.

Singh, Kelvin
1985   Indians and the Larger Society. In *Calcutta to Caroni: The East Indians of Trinidad*, J. La Guerre, ed., pp. 33–62. St. Augustine, Trinidad and Tobago: Extra Mural Studies Unit, University of the West Indies.
1988   *Bloodstained Tombs: The Muharram Massacre, 1884*. London: Macmillan.
1994   *Race and Class Struggles in a Colonial State: Trinidad, 1917–1945*. Calgary: University of Calgary Press; Trinidad and Tobago: The Press, University of the West Indies.
1996   Conflict and Collaboration: Tradition and Modernizing Indo-Trinidadian Elites (1917–56). *New West Indian Guide* 70(3–4):229–253.

Smith, Anthony
1986   *The Ethnic Origins of Nations*. Oxford: Blackwell.

Smith, Michael G.
1965   *The Plural Society in the British West Indies*. Berkeley: University of California Press.

Smith, Raymond T.
1995   On the Disutility of the Notion of "Ethnic Group" for Understanding Status Struggles in the Modern World. In *The Matrifocal Family*, R. Smith, ed., pp. 185–202. New York: Routledge.

Smith, Raymond T., and Chandra Jayawardena
1959   Marriage and Family Amongst East Indians in British Guiana. *Social and Economic Studies* 8:321–76.

Society for the Propagation of Indian Culture
1970   *Embryo*. Trinidad and Tobago.
1989   *Jaagaaran*. Trinidad and Tobago.

Solien, Nancy
1960   Household and Family in the Caribbean. *Social and Economic Studies* 9:101–106.

References

Spence Report
1978   *Report of the Committee Appointed to Consider the Rationalisation of the Sugar Industry*. Trinidad and Tobago.

Stoler, Ann Laura
1997   Sexual Affronts and Racial Frontiers: European Identities and the Cultural Politics of Exclusion in Colonial Southeast Asia. In *Tensions of Empire: Colonial Cultures in a Bourgeois World*, F. Cooper and A. L. Stoler, eds., pp. 198–237. Berkeley: University of California Press.

Stuempfle, Stephen
1995   *The Steelband Movement: The Forging of a National Art in Trinidad and Tobago*. Philadelphia: University of Pennsylvania Press.

Stutzman, Ronald
1981   El Mestizaje: An All-Inclusive Ideology of Exclusion. In *Cultural Transformations and Ethnicity in Modern Ecuador*, N. Whitten, ed., pp. 45–93. New York: Harper and Row.

Sutton, Paul
1981   *Forged from the Love of Liberty: Selected Speeches of Dr. Eric Williams*. Trinidad: College Press.

Tambiah, S. J.
1996   *Leveling Crowds: Ethnonationalist Conflicts and Collective Violence in South Asia*. Berkeley: University of California Press.

Thomas, Clive
1988   *The Poor and the Powerless*. London: Latin American Bureau.

Tinker, Hugh
1974   *A New System of Slavery*. Oxford: Oxford University Press.

Trollope, Anthony
1985   *The West Indies and the Spanish Main*. Gloucester: Alan Sutton.

Trotman, D. V.
1986   *Crime in Trinidad*. Knoxville: University of Tennessee Press.
1989   Image of Indians in Calypso. In *Indenture and Exile*, F. Birbalsingh, ed., pp. 176–190. Toronto: TSAR.

Trouillot, Michel-Rolph
1984   Labour and Emancipation in Dominica: Contribution to a Debate. *Caribbean Quarterly* 30:73–84.
1988   *Peasants and Capital: Dominica in the World Economy*. Baltimore: Johns Hopkins University Press.
1989   Discourses of Rule and the Acknowledgment of the Peasantry in Dominica, W.I., 1838–1928. *American Ethnologist* 16(4):704–718.
1990   *Haiti: State against Nation: The Origins and Legacy of Duvalierism*. New York: Monthly Review Press.
1992   The Caribbean Region: An Open Frontier in Anthropological Theory. *Annual Review of Anthropology* 21:19–42.
1996   Beyond and Below the Merivale Paradigm: Dominica's First One Hundred Days of Freedom. In *The Lesser Antilles in the Age of European Expansion*, R. L. Paquette and S. Engerman, eds., pp. 305–323. Gainesville: University Presses of Florida.

1998   Culture on the Edges: Creolization in the Plantation Context. *Plantation Societies in the Americas* 5(1):8–28.

Turner, Terence
n.d.   Class Projects, Social Consciousness, and the Contradictions of "Globalization."

van Koningsbruggen, Peter
1997   *Trinidad Carnival: A Quest for National Identity*. London: Macmillan Education.

Verdery, Katherine
1983   *Transylvanian Villagers: Three Centuries of Political, Economic, and Ethnic Change*. Berkeley: University of California Press.
1991   *National Ideology under Socialism: Identity and Cultural Politics in Ceausescu's Romania*. Berkeley: University of California Press.
1994   Ethnicity, Nationalism, and State-Making: Ethnic Groups and Boundaries: Past and Future. In *The Anthropology of Ethnicity: Beyond "Ethnic Groups and Boundaries,"* H. Vermeulen and C. Govers, eds., pp. 33–58. Amsterdam: Spinhuis.

Vertovec, Steven
1992   *Hindu Trinidad: Religion, Ethnicity, and Socio-Economic Change*. London: Macmillan Education.

Vincent, Joan
1974   The Structuring of Ethnicity. *Human Organization* 33:375–379.

Wallerstein, Immanuel
1991   The Construction of Peoplehood: Racism, Nationalism, Ethnicity. In *Race, Nation, Class*, E. Balibar and I. W. Balibar, eds., pp. 71–85. London: Verso.

Weber, Max
1978   *Economy and Society*. Berkeley: University of California Press.

Weller, Judith Ann
1968   *The East Indian Indenture in Trinidad*. Rio Pedras, Puerto Rico: Institute of Caribbean Studies.

Williams, Brackette F.
1989   A Class Act: Anthropology and the Race to Nation across Ethnic Terrain. *Annual Review of Anthropology* 18:401–44.
1991   *Stains on My Name, War in My Veins: Guyana and the Politics of Cultural Struggle*. Durham: Duke University Press.
1993   The Impact of the Precepts of Nationalism on the Concept of Culture: Making Grasshoppers of Naked Apes. *Cultural Critique* (Spring):143–191.

Williams, Eric
1961   *Capitalism and Slavery*. New York: Russel and Russel.
1969   *Inward Hunger*. London: Andre Deutsch.
1976   *The Negro in the Caribbean*. Westport, Conn.: Greenwood Press.
1982   *History of the People of Trinidad and Tobago*. Reprint. London: Andre Deutsch.
1984   *From Columbus to Castro: The History of the Caribbean*. New York: Vintage Books.

Wilson, Peter
1969   Reputation and Respectability: A Suggestion for Caribbean Ethnology. *Man* 4(1):70–84.
1973   *Crab Antics*. New Haven: Yale University Press.

References

Wolf, Eric
1994   Perilous Ideas: Race, Culture, People. *Current Anthropology* 35:1–12.

Wood, Donald
1968   *Trinidad in Transition*. Oxford: Oxford University Press.

World Bank
1990   *Social Indicators of Development, 1990*. Baltimore: Johns Hopkins University Press.
1992   *World Tables*, 1992. Baltimore: Johns Hopkins University Press.

Yelvington, Kevin
1991   Trinidad and Tobago, 1988–1989. In *Latin American and Caribbean Contemporary Record*, James Malloy and A. Gamarra, eds. New York: Holmes and Meier.
1995   *Producing Power: Ethnicity, Gender, and Class in a Caribbean Workplace*. Philadelphia: Temple University Press.

Young, Robert
1995   *Colonial Desire: Hybridity in Theory, Culture, and Race*. London: Routledge.

NEWSPAPERS

East Indian Weekly 1 (28), October 20, 1928; 2 (29), October 27, 1928
New York Times, January 1, 1996
Sunday Express (Trinidad), October 22, 1989; "Indian Arrival Day Supplement," May 27, 1990
Sunday Guardian (Trinidad), October 22 and 29, 1989; March 11, 1990; "Indian Arrival Day Supplement," May 27, 1990
TnT Mirror, October 20 and 27, 1989
Trinidad Express, June 13, 1985; March 7, 1990
Trinidad Guardian, August 26, 1973; September 28, 1989; October 4 and 18, 1989; November 1 and 18, 1989; March 5, 1990

GREAT BRITAIN PARLIAMENTARY PAPERS (HOUSE OF COMMONS)

Papers Relative to the West Indies; 1841–1842 (379) XXIX (the 1842 *Minutes of Evidence taken by the Sub-Committee of the Agricultural and Immigration Society* included here).
Report of the Select Committee on West India Colonies; 1842 (479) XIII.

Index

Index

DAC (Democratic Action Congress), 239
"Dangers Facing Trinidad and Tobago and the
    West Indian Nation, The" (Williams),
    218–19
Darbeau, David, 228
David, C. P., 186
Davids, Leo, 174
Democratic Action Congress (DAC), 239
Democratic Labor Party (DLP), 218–19
Demographics, xn, 114–15, 238–39
    and *cédula*, 45–46
    Central region, 105, 110, 111–12
    East Indian indentured immigrants, 67,
        69–72
    Indo-Trinidadian political activists, 247n
    map of ethnic groups, 3
Development and Environmental Works Divi-
    sion (DEWD), 101–2, 243
Discourse, 18n. *See also* Academic discourse;
    Colonial discourses; Lay discourse; Politi-
    cal discourse; Post-emancipation planter
    discourse
DLP (Democratic Labor Party), 218
Dominguez, Virginia, 276
Double talk, 23, 266
Dougla as term, xi, 85
Dougla people, 116, 120, 126, 163, 178, 196
Drummond, Lee, 127, 159n
Duara, Prasenjit, 32n, 33n
Duval, Jules, 64

East Indian as term, xi, 13, 97n
    and indenture system, 43n
    and outsider status, xi, xiin, 4n
    and redefinition of national identity, xii–xiii
    See also East Indian indentured immigrants;
        Headings beginning with Indo-Trinida-
        dian
East Indian/Creole dichotomy. *See* Indo-
    Trinidadian/Afro-Trinidadian dichotomy
East Indian indentured immigrants
    caste, 68, 70, 71–72, 113
    conditions in India, 67–68
    demographics, 67, 69–72
    heterogeneity, 69–71
    homogenization, 71–72
    legal status, 72, 73–76, 79
    living conditions, 73
    occupational segregation, 76–77, 79n
    See also Indenture system
East Indian National Association (EINA), 187,
    188
East Indian National Congress (EINC), 187,
    188

Economy
    industrialization, x, 99, 101–3, 104–5,
        110–11, 229
    interwar inflation, 189, 192
    and National Alliance for Reconstruction,
        239–41
    PNM welfare/patronage programs, 101–2,
        112, 131, 226–27, 233
    sugar industry deterioration, 102–4, 132,
        235
    unemployment, 229, 240
    See also Oil boom (1970s); Oil industry;
        Sugar industry
Education
    and Indo-Trinidadian upward mobility,
        92–94
    and interethnic interactions, 122
    and middle classes, 186n
    People's National Movement policies,
        220–23, 226, 229
Egalitarianism, 30
EINA (East Indian National Association), 187,
    188
EINC (East Indian National Congress), 187,
    188
Emancipation, 44, 50–52. *See also* Post-eman-
    cipation planter discourse
Emancipation Act (1833), 44, 50n
Enlightenment, 34, 38n
Erickson, Edgar, 74
Ethiopia, Italian invasion of, 197
Ethnic composition. *See* Demographics
Ethnic Groups and Boundaries (Barth), 9
Ethnicity
    in academic discourse, 19–21
    Barthian view, xii, 9, 11, 12
    destructive analysis of, xii, 11–12, 16
    ethnic situations, 21, 24–26
    and European models of nationalism, 29
    fluidity of, 127, 127–28n, 180
    as imagined cultural community, 24, 38
    in lay discourse, 18–19, 21n, 23
    and objectification, 26–27
    in political discourse, 21–23
    primordial view of, 11, 17, 19–20, 29–30
    vs. race, 8–9, 12–13, 14–16
    resource-competition model, 22
    situational/instrumentalist view of, 19–20,
        35–36n
    subjective nature of, ix–x, 10–14, 20, 28–29
    visibility of, 9–10, 31, 257, 258
    See also Ethnic terminologies; Indo-Trini-
        dadian/Afro-Trinidadian dichotomy
Ethnic situations, 21, 24–26

[306]